CRYPTOECONOMIC THEORY

Advances in Science and Technology in the Age of AI

Print ISSN: 2755-9165
Online ISSN: 2755-9173

Series Editor: Melanie Swan *(University College London, UK)*

The *Advances in Science and Technology in the Age of AI* series explores the scientific and technological frontiers driving large-scale innovation as societies transition toward AI- and quantum-enabled futures. As AI reshapes physical and digital infrastructures and natural human–computer interfaces deepen connectivity, this sweeping modernization raises profound philosophical, ethical, and economic questions. In this intelligence-driven era, the ability to translate abstract ideas into practical, operational systems becomes essential for progress.

Published

Vol. 1 *Cryptoeconomic Theory*
edited by Melanie Swan, Soichiro Takagi, Frank Witte

Advances in **Science** and **Technology** in the **Age of AI** | 01

CRYPTOECONOMIC THEORY

Editors

Melanie Swan
University College London, UK

Soichiro Takagi
University of Tokyo, Japan

Frank Witte
University College London, UK

World Scientific

NEW JERSEY • LONDON • SINGAPORE • BEIJING • SHANGHAI • HONG KONG • TAIPEI • CHENNAI • TOKYO

Published by

World Scientific Publishing Europe Ltd.
57 Shelton Street, Covent Garden, London WC2H 9HE
Head office: 5 Toh Tuck Link, Singapore 596224
USA office: 27 Warren Street, Suite 401-402, Hackensack, NJ 07601

Library of Congress Control Number: 2025045111

British Library Cataloguing-in-Publication Data
A catalogue record for this book is available from the British Library.

Advances in Science and Technology in the Age of AI — Vol. 1
CRYPTOECONOMIC THEORY

ISBN 978-1-80061-865-7 (hardcover)
ISBN 978-1-80061-866-4 (ebook for institutions)
ISBN 978-1-80061-867-1 (ebook for individuals)

For any available supplementary material, please visit
https://www.worldscientific.com/worldscibooks/10.1142/Q0549#t=suppl

Desk Editors: Kannan Krishnan/Cian Sacker Ooi

Typeset by Stallion Press
Email: enquiries@stallionpress.com

https://doi.org/10.1142/9781800618664_fmatter

Foreword

You have before you a very good book—an edited collection of articles no less!—which advances the frontiers of *cryptoeconomic theory.* In fact even before the editors invited me to write this foreword, I had read some of its chapters, which had been circulating in hacker-house and seminar discussions of the community of cryptoeconomic scholars. Yes, of course, yes, I insisted because I wanted to write about what this all means as a whole. What is this thing called cryptoeconomic theory? Where did it come from, and what is it for?

My view is expansionary: cryptoeconomic theory is the scaffolding for a new scientific research program, in the Kuhn–Popper sense, to study *the global transition to a digital economy.* And by "digital economy," I mean *computable institutions.* That's what's really exciting here. That's the big new idea in this book.

Let's unpack that. "New" means this program is emerging and developing, made from a variety of theoretical and disciplinary sources (i.e., it is interdisciplinary) but also synthetic, requiring new theory and analytic frameworks, such as complexity theory and evolutionary computational approaches. This book, as a whole, contributes to that. The key noun is "*digital economy,*" which is a new type of economy that follows an industrial economy and supports a digital society (Allen *et al.*, 2025). A digital economy means that the institutions and organizations of an economy are fully *computable.* The key verb is "*transition,*" denoting the process of passing from the old regime (industrial) to the new regime (digital). Not revolution, and not evolution, but transition (in the sense of Geels, 2002, and Geels and Schot, 2007). The purpose of cryptoeconomic theory is to build an analytic framework to study the transition to a digital economy.

Two deep economic transitions are occurring in the world today. The first is the sustainable energy transition, usually allied with broader transitions in food systems, transport systems, and all resource-using systems (Perez, 2010; Mathews, 2011; Ghisellini *et al.*, 2016; Schot and Langer, 2018; Geels *et al.*, 2023). This is a technology transition to accelerate the adoption and use of innovations to address major externalities of the industrial economy regime (especially on climate, biodiversity, social inequality, Sustainable Development Goals (SDGs), etc.). Deep sustainability transitions are a major focus of socioeconomic policy everywhere. This transition in production and consumption systems is highly visible, legible, and well-theorized with existing analytic frameworks (simulation modeling, cost–benefit analysis, social welfare theory, etc.).

This book is about the second deep transition to a digital economy, a transition that has also been long-developing. The early technical and infrastructural phases were laid in the mid-to-late 20th century with what is called information and communication technology (ICT) (Freeman and Soete, 1995; Perez, 2003). This was the macro-innovation regime associated with computers and information and communication networks, including the internet. From the 1970s, this was called "information society," and from the 1990s, "information economy." My claim here is that the ICT macro regime was really the last phase of the industrial era that furnished the initial conditions for the transition to a digital economy. We are, in other words, at the beginning of a new deep transition, not because of computers in the economy (which is the final phase of the industrial era) but because economic coordination is becoming fully digital and computable.

The difference is where compute goes. The crowning achievement of the industrial era is cheap, reliable computers everywhere in production and consumption. But a digital economy emerges when compute becomes deeply integrated into coordination—into organizations and institutions—when the institutional technologies of an economy are natively digital. That is where we are now, and it is the new capabilities of crypto and AI that are driving and powering this deep transition. This is what cryptoeconomic theory seeks to describe.

Cryptoeconomic technologies of distributed computation form a new layer of digital economic infrastructure. The historical significance of digital technologies lies in their role as the nexus of a transformation from industrial economies to digital economies. Indeed, we can define a "digital economy" as distinct from an industrial economy with reference to this epochal process of transformation and its consequences for economic organizations and institutions. In this conception, a digital economy has fully adopted digital technologies. Why does that matter? What functional characteristics differ in a digital economy?

The answer is a digital economy is *computable*. The adoption of digital institutional technologies means that modern economic systems are evolving into a "computable economy." This is an "operating system upgrade" from a partially computable economy in an industrial era. A digital economy is computable "all the way down," not only in surface economic operations but also in deeper economic institutions, and therefore has different performance characteristics in, for instance, transaction speed, processing complexity, and the scale and scope of contracting and economic coordination.

An industrial economy is more than just industrial technologies (steam, steel, and plastics, electrification, railways, petrochemicals, computers, etc.). The concept of an industrial economy also includes industrial institutions, such as the factory system, public markets, industrial sectors, and economic institutions to support markets, including money, property registries, courts, regulation, roads, and ports. Industrial economies produce innovation and progress in the industrial parts of the economy, with much less change in the institutional base layer that underpins organizational coordination and market transactions (e.g., in money, property rights systems, identity, and administrative and contracting technologies). The major dynamics of the system (what Schumpeter called "creative destruction") mostly occur in the industrial context of markets and firms, with the underlying institutional order protected from disruption. In an industrial economy, industrial technologies change fast, while institutional technologies change slowly. Yet in a digital economy, it is the other way around.

The digital economy transition is more than just the growth of the digital or ICT sector (Goldfarb and Tucker, 2019) but refers to the disruption and regrowth of *analog economic institutions in digital format*. This explains *where* the digital disruption is occurring. It is not merely the surface industrial production and consumer behavior that is being digitized; the deeper institutional layers are being digitized as well. The distinction is captured in theory by the idea of a fully computable economy. So, what is computable?

The concept of a *computable number* was introduced by Alan Turing (1936) in a paper that gave rise to the concept of a Turing machine. Minsky (1967) defines a computable number as "...one for which there is a Turing machine which, given n on its initial tape, terminates with the nth digit of that number [encoded on its tape]." An *un*computable number is one that cannot be computed by a finite procedure (i.e., a universal machine, or "Turing machine"), i.e., for which no such algorithm exists. Most numbers, as it turns out, are uncomputable. This theoretical concept of a *universal state machine*, along with the formulation of the halting condition (decidability) as a solution concept, is the foundation of modern computer science. It was developed into economics by von Neumann in game theory and automata theory (Mirowski, 2007).

A computable number (and a Turing machine) is a useful way to think about the meaning and definition of a digital economy by framing the idea explicitly as a computable economy. "Computable economics," as Velupillai (2000: 2) explains, "is about basing economic formalisms on recursion theoretic fundamentals. This means we will have to view economic entities, economic actions and economic institutions as computable objects or algorithms." Just as there exist computable and non-computable numbers, there also exist both computable and non-computable economies. A fully computable economy—we might call it a *Turing complete economy*—is one where all economic actions and transactions can technically be digitally connected as part of an algorithmic process.

The formal concept of a *computable economy* is not new (Scarf, 1989; Gode and Sunder, 1993; Velupillai, 2000). Indeed, by the late 1950s and 1960s, Vernon Smith was developing algorithmic models of the market process, and Herbert Simon was developing algorithmic models of human and machine decision-making using the logic of bounded rationality or satisficing, which is an operationalization of the halting condition. Nor is the general model of computation new as the *lingua franca* of science (von Neumann, 1966). And the concept of *the economy as a process of computation* is also not new. Mirowski

(2002) has developed an exhaustive scholarly account of the computer metaphor in economic theory in which he characterizes the trend of orthodox economic theory in the second half of the 20th century as that of "recasting the economic agent as an information processor."

This is more than a new scientific metaphor. The issue also goes to the heart of the central debate in economics during the 20th century, the "economic calculation debate" (Boettke, 1998). The question is not only to what extent an economy is *like* a computer, but more fundamentally to what extent *it actually is* a computer, i.e., does it perform computation? The question "how do markets compute?" was the subject of the so-called calculation debate. In the early 20th century, the neoclassical (Lange, Lerner, Taylor, and Samuelson) and Austrian economists (Mises and Hayek) fought publicly about the viability of socialism versus capitalism. This was not merely an academic debate. The Soviet revolution was claiming economic success, and the Great Depression had capitalism on the ropes. In the U.S., Keynesianism and the new engineering approach were the dominant frameworks for economic policy.

The upshot of the calculation debate was a slow but fundamental reinterpretation of the nature of the economy in terms of incentive "mechanisms," particularly the "price mechanism" (Hurwicz, 1973). The neoclassicals, with the existence proof of a general equilibrium, argued that the development of "the modern computer" would further press the allocation efficiency advantage of planning. The Austrians criticized its practical implementation. Specifically, it assumed as given the very thing it needed to produce, namely *information* contained in *prices*. The Austrians argued that the neoclassicals had fundamentally misunderstood the problem (Boettke, 2001). For Mises and Hayek, the point wasn't that one could use a computer to help plan the economy, but rather that the economy already *was* a computer. Or specifically, that the price system and market process were performing economic computation (Miller and Drexler, 1988). The neoclassical data that were assumed to exist (preferences, prices, etc.) did not exist in an *ex ante* state of nature, but those data were themselves a product of the economic system. Those data were produced through a stack of institutions, including property rights, exchange mechanisms, bidding processes, and social processes of legitimation, as well as mechanisms for calculating value, including accounting systems. The outcome was a system of prices that could serve as common information to guide individual economic action. The price system is a process of computation. The inputs into economic calculation do not exist outside of the market process but rather are created by it. Market mechanisms are distributed mechanisms that perform complex *economic computations* on knowledge, information, and resources. An economy is, in this perspective, understood as a complex, distributed organizational and institutional stack, a particular type of computer.

The things produced and consumed in an economy are not themselves the economy, any more than a set of input prompts or output files is a computer. An economy, like a computer, is a complex system of rules (algorithms, procedures, decision heuristics, institutions, administrative procedures, etc.) that coordinates actors and resources to enable plans to mesh. An economy is a complex rule-system, made of rules embedded and embodied in different types of substrates, operating by different mechanisms at different scales and with different architectures (e.g., parallelism) and different properties (e.g., fault tolerance and processing speed). Together, these rules perform economic computations (Dopfer and Potts, 2008). It is the digitization of these rules that marks the transition to a computable economy.

In a digital economy, every core coordinating institution becomes a computable process; markets evolve into algorithmic exchanges whose price discovery, order routing, settlement, and record-keeping now run on code. Money, once mere digitized ledgers, becomes fully programmable through blockchains, stablecoins, and DeFi rails that move and settle value by algorithm rather than through intermediaries. Capital becomes computable when physical or intangible assets are tokenized, wrapped in machine-readable metadata, and integrated into protocols that automate search, verification, custody, and collateralization. Innovation, long modeled as Schumpeterian trial-and-error, is increasingly executed by human–AI hybrids and autonomous agents that scan digital opportunity spaces, test ideas against market fitness functions, and iterate at machine speed (Potts *et al.*, 2024). And even commons, traditionally governed by costly face-to-face deliberation, evolve to become computable through smart contracts and algorithmic governance (Rennie *et al.*, 2025).

An economy is a rule-based engine for large-scale cooperation in which people follow shared protocols—prices, contracts, platforms, and standards—to coordinate work, exchange, and investment. A computable economy extends this logic by expressing those protocols in machine-executable form and connecting them into a single, interoperable graph of rules and records. When every critical function in an economy (including money, markets, capital, innovation, and governance) can be processed, verified, and implemented in code, the system approaches functional completeness in which all parts become computable and can interoperate at digital speed (Alden, 2025). *Cryptoeconomic Theory* provides a language and toolset for engineering these computable rule-systems through the implementation of crypto and AI systems. The chapters that follow assemble the foundational concepts and models needed to launch a coherent research program for analyzing, designing, and guiding this transition to a digital economy as a fully computable economic order.

Jason Potts
Melbourne, Australia
June 2025

References

Alden, L. 2025. *Broken Money.* Timestamp Press.

Allen, D., Berg, C., and Potts, J. 2025. *Institutional Acceleration: The Consequences of Technological Change in a Digital Economy.* Cambridge Elements: Evolutionary Economics.

Boettke, P. 1998. "Economic calculation: The Austrian contribution to political economy." *Advances in Austrian Economics* 5: 131–158.

Boettke, P. 2001. *Calculation and Coordination.* London: Routledge.

Dopfer, K. and Potts, J. 2008. *The General Theory of Economic Evolution.* London: Routledge.

Freeman, C. and Soete, L. 1995. *Economics of Industrial Innovation.* London: Routledge.

Geels, F. 2002. "Technological transitions as evolutionary reconfiguration processes: A multi-level perspective and a case study." *Research Policy* 31: 1257–1274.

Geels, F., Kern, F., and Clark, W. 2023. "Sustainability transitions in consumption and production systems." *PNAS* 120(47): e2310070120.

Geels, F. and Schot, J. 2007. "Typology of sociotechnical transition pathways." *Research Policy* 36: 399–417.

Ghisellini, P., Cialani, C., and Ulgiati, S. 2016. "A review on circular economy: The expected transition to a balanced interplay of environmental and economic systems." *Journal of Cleaner Production* 114: 11–32.

Gode, D. and Sunder, S. 1993. "Allocative efficiency of markets with zero-intelligence traders." *Journal of Political Economy* 101: 119–137.

Goldfarb, A. and Tucker, C. 2019. "Digital economics." *Journal of Economic Literature* 57(1): 3–43.

Hayek, F. A. 1945. "Use of knowledge in society." *American Economic Review* 35(4): 519–530.

Hurwicz, L. 1973. "The design of mechanisms for resource allocation." *American Economic Review* 63(2): 1–30.

Lavoie, D. 1985. *Rivalry and Central Planning: The Socialist Calculation Debate Reconsidered.* New York: Cambridge University Press.

Mathews, J. 2011. "Naturalizing capitalism: The next great transformation." *Futures* 43(8): 868–879.

McCabe, K., Rassenti, S., and Smith, V. 1991. "Smart computer-assisted markets." *Science* 254(5031): 534–538.

Miller, M. and Drexler, K. E. 1988. "Markets and computation: Agoric open systems." In Huberman, B. (ed.), *The Ecology of Computation.* Elsevier Science Publishers/North-Holland.

Minsky, M. 1967. "The computable real numbers." In *Computation: Finite and Infinite Machines.* Prentice-Hall.

Mirowski, P. 2002. *Machine Dreams.* New York: Cambridge University Press.

Mirowski, P. 2007. "Markets come to bits: Evolution, computation and markomata in economic science." *Journal of Economic Behavior and Organization* 63(2): 209–242.

Mises, L. 1935. "Economic calculation in the socialist commonwealth." In Hayek, F. (ed.), *Collectivist Economic Planning.* London: Routledge and Kegan Paul.

Nelson, R. and Winter, S. 1982. *An Evolutionary Theory of Economic Change.* Cambridge, MA: Harvard University Press.

Perez, C. 2003. *Technological Revolutions and Financial Capital.* Edward Elgar.

Perez, C. 2010. "Technological revolutions and techno-economic paradigms." *Cambridge Journal of Economics* 34(1): 185–202.

Potts, J. 2018. "Governing the innovation commons." *Journal of Institutional Economics* 14(6): 1025–1047.

Potts, J. 2019. *Innovation Commons: The Origin of Economic Growth.* Oxford: Oxford University Press.

Potts, J., Torrance, A., Harhoff, D., and von Hippel, E. 2024. "Profiting from data commons: Theory, evidence, and strategy implications." *Strategy Science* 9(1): 1–17.

Reiter, S. 1977. "Information and performance in the (new) welfare economics." *American Economic Review* 67: 226–234.

Rennie, E., Potts, J., and Tan, J. 2025. "The 'natural state' of blockchains: An ethnography of validator governance." *Information, Communication & Society* 1–17.

Scarf, H. 1989. "Computation of general equilibria." In *General Equilibrium*, pp. 84–97.

Schot, J. and Kanger, L. 2018. "Deep transitions: Emergence, acceleration, stabilization and directionality." *Research Policy* 47: 1045–1059.

Sunder, S. 2004. "Markets as artifacts." In Augier, M. and March, J. (eds.), *Models of a Man: Essays in Memory of Herbert A. Simon.* Cambridge: MIT Press.

Turing, A. 1936. "On computable numbers, with an application to the Entscheidungsproblem." *Proceedings of the London Mathematical Society, Series 2*, 42(1): 230–265.

Velupillai, K. 2000. *Computable Economics*, Vol. 5. Oxford University Press.

Von Neumann, J. 1966. "Theory of self-reproducing automata." *Mathematics of Computation* 21: 745.

https://doi.org/10.1142/9781800618664_fmatter

About the Editors

Melanie Swan is a research associate at the Centre for Blockchain Technologies at University College London and the founder of Math Agents AI cloud lab DIYgenomics. She has an M.B.A. in finance from the Wharton School at the University of Pennsylvania and a Ph.D. in philosophy from Purdue University. In industry, she focused on telecommunications and internet technologies as a financial analyst at Fidelity Investments, an M&A investment banker at JP Morgan, an options trader and portfolio manager at Cygnet Capital, Inc., and the research director of the Telecom Economics Program at optical networking consultancy Ovum/RHK. Her research investigates conceptual advances in science, technology, and mathematics toward global outcomes in biology and well-being.

Soichiro Takagi is a professor at the Interfaculty Initiative in Information Studies at The University of Tokyo. He received his Ph.D. in information studies from The University of Tokyo. Dr. Takagi serves as a fellow at the Art Center of The University of Tokyo and a senior research fellow at the Center for Global Communications (GLOCOM) at the International University of Japan (IUJ). Previously, he was an Asia Program Fellow at the Harvard Kennedy School. Dr. Takagi's major field is information economics and innovation. His research includes the impact of technology on economics, namely idea generation for innovation and the incorporation of the arts into business innovation. He has authored many books and articles. His books include *Deframing Strategy: How Digital Technologies are Transforming Businesses and Organizations, and How We Can Cope with It* (World Scientific), *Reweaving the Economy: How IT Affects the Borders of Country and Organization* (University of Tokyo Press), and *Blockchain Economics: Implications of Distributed Ledgers* (World Scientific, co-authored). He received the KDDI Foundation Award in 2019.

Frank Witte received his Ph.D. in theoretical physics (1995) from the University of Heidelberg, Germany. He worked as an assistant and associate professor in physics and astronomy at Utrecht University and University College Utrecht in the Netherlands from 1996 to 2010, publishing on problems in elementary particle theory, (quantum) gravitational theory, and quantum game theory. In 2010, he accepted a position at the Department of Economics of University College London. He is currently an associate professor in economics there and teaches economics of science, environmental economics, and computational methods in economics. Frank has been a visiting fellow at St. John's College, Cambridge (U.K., 2002), an academic visitor at the Quantum Optics & Laser Science Group of Imperial College London (U.K., 2009), and an international visiting fellow at Grinnell College (U.S., 2012). His current research focuses on the applications of physics-inspired methods to problems in environmental economics, the economics of science, and the economics of networks.

https://doi.org/10.1142/9781800618664_fmatter

About the Contributors

Darcy W. E. Allen is an associate professor of economics at RMIT University in Melbourne, Australia, and a director of the Digital Economy Council of Australia. He has published five books and over 25 peer-reviewed journal articles on various topics, including cryptodemocracy, innovation policy, token airdrops, Web3 governance, and regulatory reform. His work has been published in several journals, including *Research Policy*, the *Harvard Negotiation Law Review*, and the *Journal of Business Research*. His latest book with Cambridge University Press is *Institutional Acceleration: The Consequences of Technological Change for a Digital Economy* (with Chris Berg and Jason Potts) and explores how technologies such as blockchains, artificial intelligence, and low-Earth-orbit satellites are transitioning us to a new digital economy.

Ilan Ben-Meir is a researcher and senior lexical engineer at BlockScience, a Ph.D. candidate in English at Brown University, and an active member of the Metagov community. His research investigates the effects of digital technologies on humanity's relationship to language and meaning-making. Ilan also holds an M.Phil. in screen media and culture from Cambridge University and a B.A. in English language and literature from Yale. Prior to graduate school, he covered national politics as a reporter for BuzzFeed News.

Chris Berg is a professor of economics at RMIT University in Melbourne, Australia. He co-founded the RMIT Blockchain Innovation Hub, the world's first dedicated social science research center studying blockchain technology. Professor Berg is one of Australia's most prominent voices for free markets and individual liberty, as well as a leading global authority on regulation, technological change, and civil liberties. He is a highly experienced research leader specializing in the creation and development of large, high-impact research teams. He is the author of 12 books, including *The New Technologies of Freedom* (American Institute for Economic Research, 2020), *Understanding the Blockchain Economy* (Edward Elgar, 2019), and *The Libertarian Alternative* (Melbourne University Press, 2016). He has published more than 30 peer-reviewed papers, including in *Management Science*, *Research Policy*, the *Journal of Institutional Economics*, the *Australian Journal of Political Science*, and *Trends in Anaesthesia and Critical Care.*

Sinclair Davidson is a professor of institutional economics in the School of Economics, Finance and Marketing at RMIT University in Melbourne, Australia. He is a fellow of the British Blockchain Association, an adjunct fellow at the Institute of Public Affairs, an academic fellow at the Australian Taxpayers' Alliance, an adjunct economics fellow at the Consumer Choice Center, and a research associate at the University College London Centre for Blockchain Technologies. Sinclair has published around 100 articles in academic journals, such as the *European Journal of Political Economy*, *Journal of Economic Behavior and Organization*, *Economic Affairs*, and *The Cato Journal*, and is a co-author of four books. He is a regular contributor to public debate. His opinion pieces have been published in *The Age*, *The Australian*, *Australian Financial Review*, *The Conversation*, *Daily Telegraph*, *Sydney Morning Herald*, and *Wall Street Journal.*

Murdoch J. Gabbay was awarded a Ph.D. in the mathematical foundations of computer science in 2001, which founded the field of "nominal techniques." Since then, he has published on a variety of topics, ranging from logical foundations to the relevance of Marxian economic theories to blockchain. In 2019, Dr. Gabbay was awarded the Alonzo Church Award for Outstanding Contributions to Logic and Computation. At around the same time, he became interested in blockchains. Dr. Gabbay has made several contributions to the foundations of blockchains and decentralized systems. His book *Semitopology: Decentralised Collaborative Action via Topology, Algebra, and Logic* was published by College Publications in August 2024.

Huseyin Oguz Genc is a Ph.D. student at the Graduate School of Interdisciplinary Information Studies at The University of Tokyo, conducting research on the policy implications of digital currencies. Previously, he completed two master's degrees at Peking University and Boğaziçi University in the field of developmental economics. His interest in blockchain economics started in 2016 after becoming a firm believer in Bitcoin's potential as a future reserve currency. His current work is focused on building a framework to analyze different aspects of decentralization for stablecoins in order to establish a systematic method for analyzing the concept of decentralization at a practical level.

Kim Peiter Jørgensen is a postdoc, currently at TecMinho, University of Minho, in Portugal, leading the Web3 Wallet Centre as part of the huge national development project, "The Portuguese Blockchain Agenda," an EU-supported spearhead project covering almost all aspects of private and public services. He received his Ph.D. in blockchain wallets from the IT University of Copenhagen after having been one of the founders of the European Blockchain Center under Professor Roman Beck. His current research focuses on decentralized systems, the wallet's current and potential role, and the development of business and systems models reflecting these. This is in continuation of a decades-long international career in value creation from IT systems as an executive in the supply chain industry for one of the largest shipping lines. He further focuses on mass promulgation of knowledge on blockchain systems and digital transformation, viewing them as critically necessary to mitigate the digital divide and to integrate micro- and nano-learning modules on these subjects with the technological opportunities emerging from the Metaverse and local AI.

Annika Laine-Kronberg is a professor and the head of organization and management at Åbo Akademi University in Finland. She received her Ph.D. in economics from the Hanken School of Economics in Helsinki. Her main research interests include industrial relationships, coopetition, transitions to sustainability, and strategy-as-practice. She has published several scientific articles in journals such as *Industrial Marketing Management, Journal of Cleaner Production, Scandinavian Journal of Management, Journal of Purchasing and Supply Management, Journal of Business and*

Industrial Marketing and *Marketing Theory*. Dr. Laine-Kronberg has been involved in several research projects related to sustainability, circular economy, and small–medium-sized enterprise growth and digitalization. She has over 20 years of experience educating and consulting in various companies, with a focus on topics such as strategic management, change management, and conflict resolution.

Renée Menéndez holds a doctorate in economics with a thesis on the topic "Structures of Money Capitalism," which she developed during her time as an assistant professor at Freie Universität Berlin. This topic also opened up further research into monetary theory. In particular, the sharp distinction between the means of payment and debt relationships and their interaction paved the way for research that focuses on the conditions for the sustainability and stability of fiat monetary systems. Her research interests consist of investigating a "missing link" between gold and paper money and the classical question of whether the money–commodity–money (M–C–M) concept is valid or not (i.e., money invested to purchase commodities, which are then sold to generate more money, ideally resulting in a profit).

Takayuki Mizuno is an associate professor of informatics at the National Institute of Informatics, focusing on econophysics, computational social science, network science, and big data applications. He received his Ph.D. in physics from Chuo University. He first studied econophysics for online product markets as a lecturer of economic research at the Hitotsubashi University (2007–2010). Afterward, he worked as an associate professor of computer science at the University of Tsukuba (2011–2013). Currently, he focuses on econophysics for global economic networks and financial markets as a senior research fellow at The Canon Institute for Global Studies (2009–present). He is also involved in the investigation of computational social science for human mobilities as an associate professor at the School of Multidisciplinary Sciences, SOKENDAI, the Graduate University for Advanced Studies (2013–present).

Rumy Narayan is a postdoctoral researcher at the School of Management, University of Vaasa, where she studies cross-sector innovation in sustainable energy transitions and frames blockchain as a socio-institutional coordination tool. She received her Ph.D. in economics at the University of Vaasa. Her research interests include several secondments within the OpenInnoTrain exchange, coordinated by the Royal Melbourne Institute of Technology (RMIT), and a fellowship at Graz, Austria's Institute for Advanced Studies on Science, Technology and Society. She has received grants for her research from the Finnish Cultural Foundation in South Ostrobothnia in connection with major regional projects on circular-economy eco-innovation and the "Energy Village" concept. Her articles have appeared in *Technovation*, *JBIM*, and the *Journal of Cleaner Production*. Prior to her academic career, she spent a decade as a business and financial journalist; she also served as a sustainability professional with several multinational corporations, such as Walmart and Tetra Pak, across Europe and North America. Her work continues to emphasize large-scale realizations of sustainability.

Sasha Shilina is a doctor of philosophy and a postdoctoral researcher at Lomonosov Moscow State University. She is the chief research officer at Paradigm Research Institute, leading initiatives at the intersection of modern science, technology, and culture. Dr. Shilina is also a researcher at the Humanode crypto-biometric blockchain network, where she contributes to the development of Sybil-resistant and privacy-preserving decentralized technologies. A pioneer of the decentralized science (DeSci) and DeScAI movements, she is the founder of the Episteme prediction markets platform that integrates Web3 technologies with scientific inquiry. In the blockchain industry, Dr. Shilina is a distributed technology analyst with over seven years of experience, the creator of the "DeFi in Ether" information platform, and an Ethereum Foundation scholar. Her research interests focus on fostering a deeper understanding of how emerging technologies influence human interaction, philosophical paradigms, and cultural evolution.

Horst Treiblmaier is a full professor and the head of the School of International Management at Modul University Vienna. Previously, he was a visiting professor at Purdue University, University of California, Los Angeles, and The University of British Columbia. He participated in various EU programs and worked for the European Technology Platform ALICE (Alliance for Logistics Innovation through Collaboration in Europe). His work has appeared in leading academic journals, such as *Information Systems Journal*, *Structural Equation Modeling*, *Business & Information Systems Engineering*, *IEEE Transactions on Engineering Management*, *Internet Research*,

Information & Management, *Communications of the AIS*, *Annals of Tourism Research*, the *Journal of Electronic Commerce Research*, and *Schmalenbach Business Review*. He is a research associate at the UCL Centre for Blockchain Technologies and a member of the INATBA Academic Advisory Body. In 2022, he won the Blockchain Frontier Award from the Blockchain Research Institute (BRI).

Viktor Winschel holds a Ph.D. in macroeconometrics and nominal exchange rate regimes from the University of Mannheim. He worked with Martin Hellwig, a leading researcher in monetary theory. Dr. Winschel introduced open games as an initial compositional game theory based on research at the University of Oxford, applying category-theoretic approaches to quantum computational programming languages. In industry, he has worked in supply chain finance, designing digital products based on the bill of exchange (BoE). He has implemented several digital business models based on Internet of Things approaches, including as a startup founder. His main research focus is money theory, a missing component of the money research community.

Hiroko Yamano is an assistant professor at the Institute for Future Initiatives at The University of Tokyo. She earned her Ph.D. in engineering from the Department of Technology Management for Innovation and holds a master's degree in life science from the Graduate School of Arts and Sciences, both at The University of Tokyo. She is an editorial board member of the Japanese Society for Artificial Intelligence and serves on the Ministry of Economy, Trade and Industry's Council on Companies Driving Regional Growth in Japan. Dr. Yamano's primary areas of research include network science, computational social science, complex systems science, and technology management of innovation science. She specializes in studying the structure and dynamics of inter-firm networks, with a focus on analyzing influence propagations between distant nodes within networks that encompass diverse communities.

Michael Zargham is the founder and chief engineer at BlockScience, a systems engineering firm focused on digital public infrastructure. He holds a Ph.D. in electrical and systems engineering from the University of Pennsylvania, with a focus on optimal dynamic resource allocation policies. Dr. Zargham is a board member and research director at the U.S.-based nonprofit Metagov.org, a practice community focused on digitally mediated self-governance. He is an advisory council member at NumFOCUS.org, a U.S.-based nonprofit supporting open code for better science and fiscal sponsor of open-source projects. Dr. Zargham's research focus is on formal methods in mechanism, markets, and institutional design, applying methods from model-based systems engineering (MBSE), drawing on influences from institutional analysis and design (IAD) and organizational cybernetics.

https://doi.org/10.1142/9781800618664_fmatter

Contents

Foreword v

About the Editors xv

About the Contributors xvii

Introduction xxix
Melanie Swan

Part I Formalization, Verifiability, and Coordination 1

Chapter 1 Categorical Cryptoeconomics: HoTT Blockchains 3
Melanie Swan

Chapter 2 The Economics of Blockchain Shared Security 35
Darcy W. E. Allen, Chris Berg, and Sinclair Davidson

Chapter 3 Decentralized Collaborative Action: Cryptoeconomics in Space 53
Murdoch J. Gabbay

Part II Real-World Assets: Digital Economic Infrastructure 71

Chapter 4 The Policy Implications of Competing Digital Currencies 73
Huseyin Oguz Genc

Chapter 5 Wallets as End-User Universal Access Devices 101
Kim Peiter Jørgensen

Part III Protocol Institutions: The Economic Future of Institutions 127

Chapter 6 DeSci and DeScAI: Distributed Epistemic Economies 129
Sasha Shilina

Chapter 7 Protocols and Institutions 157
Michael Zargham and Ilan Ben-Meir

Chapter 8 Agentic Learning DAOs for Sustainable Energy Transition 181
Rumy Narayan and Annika Laine-Kronberg

Part IV Digital Network Economies 207

Chapter 9 A Theory of Chaordic Economics: How Artificial Intelligence and Blockchain Transform Businesses, Economies, and Societies 209
Horst Treiblmaier

Chapter 10 Flow Dynamics: Advanced Network Science for Supply and Cryptocurrency Remittance Networks 233

Hiroko Yamano and Takayuki Mizuno

Chapter 11 Monetary Macro Accounting Theory for Blockchain, AI, and Beyond 259

Renée Menéndez and Viktor Winschel

Index 289

https://doi.org/10.1142/9781800618664_0001

Introduction

Melanie Swan
University College London, London, UK
melanie@blockchainstudies.org

Abstract
This volume presents a variety of cryptoeconomic theories relevant to blockchains and blockchain–AI–quantum integration in the ongoing digitization of modern life. Cryptoeconomics is the study of cryptography-based economic systems, particularly blockchains. Blockchain is not only a "money technology" but also, more fundamentally, a core information technology for secure, verifiable computing via cryptoeconomic mechanisms. Current blockchain implementations include growing deployments in AI (DeAI), finance (DeFi), science (DeSci), and physical infrastructure (DePIN), notably central bank digital currencies, real-world asset digitization, and financial contracts, extending Web2 distribution with Web3 credit attribution. AI–blockchain integration is implied, as blockchains and AI (foundation models, agents, and robots) share the requirements of attestation, provenance, history, identity, token use, multi-party coordination, and interoperability. The first part of the chapter situates blockchain as a network computing technology, reviews current blockchain status, and introduces agentic institutions; the second half provides an overview of the chapters of the book. *Cryptoeconomic theory* is organized under the themes of verifiable computing, real-world assets, protocol institutions, and digital network economies.

Keywords: Cryptoeconomics, Protocol Institutions, Compute as a Platform, Blockchain-AI-Quantum Smartnetwork Integration, Verifiable Computing, Digital Network Economies.

Cryptoeconomics

Cryptoeconomics is the study of cryptography-based economic systems, particularly blockchains. In line with this, the Oxford Research Encyclopedia defines cryptoeconomics as "the economic analysis of blockchain technology" (John & Saleh, 2025). An earlier definition characterizes cryptoeconomics as an "interdisciplinary, emergent, and experimental field that draws on ideas and concepts from economics, game theory, and related disciplines in the design of peer-to-peer cryptographic systems" (Brekke & Alsindi, 2021). In the current volume, Gabbay defines cryptoeconomics as "the study of socioeconomic systems enabled by modern decentralized computer systems." The overall idea is that cryptoeconomic systems employ economic design principles to ensure the information security of economic transactions.

A subset of cryptoeconomics is *tokenomics*, the study of the economic system specific to token issuance for a particular protocol (Voshmgir, 2020). Tokenomics is a robust economic theory domain of its own, as projects use cryptoeconomic mechanisms to manage the supply and value of tokens (money). Many smart contract projects implement the Ethereum Improvement Proposal (EIP-1559) standard, in which a portion of the transaction fee is burned (i.e., permanently removed from circulation by sending it to an inaccessible wallet) to help stabilize or increase the token's value by reducing supply while maintaining demand.

Blockchain Network Platform

Blockchain as network computer

What has always been striking about blockchain is that it is a *core information technology* with value-related applications, among others (Swan, 2015). Economic design principles have a long history in the construction of various computational and social outcomes, as seen in genetic algorithms, anti-spam public-private key schemes, and zero-knowledge proofs (ZKPs). In the notion of blockchain as a computation-first rather than finance-first technology, the point is that the computation is active and alive—cryptographic functions execute on-demand to attest and secure the network in real time. This is the cost of algorithmic consensus to secure any chain, whether via proof-of-work, proof-of-stake, validators, or other methods, some more energy-efficient than others.

Blockchains facilitate computable economic systems but are not exclusively digital money or financial technology (FinTech) applications. As any technology is dual use (both positive and negative use cases), likewise any economic technology is simultaneously both "casino and computer" (Dixon, 2023). It is naïve to think that a "money technology" would not be used for resource gathering and self-wealth aggrandizement, given historical scarcity and attitudes about competition; however, this is not the primary or exhaustive use of money technologies. Economic principles have many other general deployments as a mechanism for information signaling, resource allocation, credit attribution, value endowment, and good-player behavior incentives.

In some sense, there have only ever been two forms of network communications platforms: internet transmission and blockchain computing (Figure 1). The idea of the "network as computer" originated with John Gage at Sun Microsystems in 1984 (Graham-Cumming, 2019), who envisioned a fabric of plug-and-play primitives discoverable by any user agent, human or otherwise. The network should be like electricity—simply connect a device and it works. In the blockchain domain, the "infinite garden" composability of "the blockchain world computer" continues to capture this idea (Russo, 2020). The "network as computer" is evolving into a rich platform and may be called upon to accommodate the most explosive growth yet in its history, representing a shift from billion-entity transmissions to trillion-entity intelligent computations.

Current blockchain development goals include security, usability, and interoperability. Interoperability is necessary to realize a unified cross-chain fabric, just as the internet became seamless through HTTP, SMTP, VoIP, and video streaming protocols. Web3 protocols add to Web2 distribution channels to allow users to own, control,

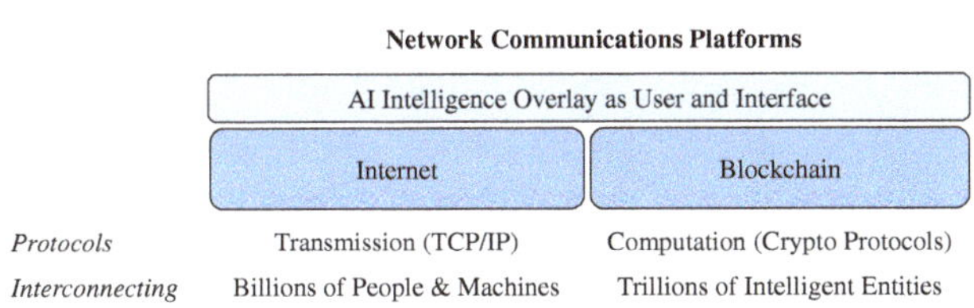

Fig. 1. Network communications platforms: internet and blockchain.

and monetize their data. Centralized web properties, such as AWS and Google, are similar to the walled gardens of AOL and CompuServe in the past, curating experiences, controlling, retaining, and profiting from user data. What is new is that in the virtuous Moore's law cycles of price-performance improvement, technologies mutually enable new levels of functionality: the evolution of AI infrastructure, particularly the availability of low-cost GPUs, has made it possible to run ZKP infrastructure ubiquitously throughout the network computer. Proof-of-personhood cryptographic solutions could become more widespread in the "internet of trust."

Automated software protocols orchestrate reward and penalty structures of blockchains to regulate the distribution of goods and services in digital economies. A growing slate of blockchain primitives (building blocks) are used in the trustless infrastructure. Examples include wallets (the digital nexus of identity, onramp, and user interface), smart contracts (future-executing legal arrangements), decentralized applications (dApps), decentralized autonomous organizations (DAOs), oracles (third-party attestors), staking and slashing, and ZKPs.

The primary consensus method used in smart contract blockchains is proof-of-stake, a method of securing the blockchain with less energy consumption than Bitcoin's proof-of-work. Proof-of-stake is realized with the "staking and slashing" primitive. This is a protocol structure in which a participant puts assets at stake (to signal good player behavior), which can be slashed against (forfeited) in the event of malfeasance (to prevent bad player behavior). Improving energy efficiency is a requirement as blockchains mature and evolve into industry-grade financial systems.

Another key cryptographic primitive is ZKPs. ZKPs originated in the blockchain context but have extensive carryover to internet-wide applicability, particularly proof-of-personhood in the age of AI agents. The St. Louis Fed describes ZKPs as a mechanism by which one can prove the correctness of a computation without revealing any additional information except whether the statement is correct or not (Berentsen *et al.*, 2023). For example, blockchain users can prove that they are authorized to make a payment without revealing their identity to the network. The benefits are both privacy and efficiency. User information is attested but not shared with the network, and proofs make network operations more efficient. Proofs use one-way functions, meaning it is costly to perform an underlying computation but, once demonstrated, easy to verify. The ZKP technology is an element in quantum-safe computing, for example, JPMorgan's relativistic quantum ZKPs to secure the financial infrastructure (Shi *et al.*, 2024).

ZKPs provide the cornerstone of distributed trust and the verifiable internet, enabling information to be attested with computational proofs. In practical use, decentralized cloud storage providers run regular ZKPs to validate data storage (verifiable storage), e.g., Filecoin's Proof of Replication (PoRep) and Proof of Spacetime (PoSt) and Arweave's Succinct Random Proofs of Access (SPoRA). The implication of "network as computer" primitives is that once posted, any other user or application on the network can call them. AI agents can canvas the internet to discover new validated building materials. There could be a blockchain computing network of available primitives composed on demand by smart dApps to suit the personalized needs of users. Primitives are verifiably well-formed and have economic and legal features (e.g., the Story intellectual property fabric). A new era of user-centric computing could follow.

Blockchain and AI

The growth of AI is a modern occurrence which demands interpretation across disciplines. AI is reshaping global power structures, governance, and human agency, requiring a balanced approach between optimism and caution to navigate its profound societal impact (Kissinger *et al.*, 2024). The pace of change is extremely fast, even for technology, as AI upskilling may improve economic productivity by 30% or more (Muir, 2025). Entire classes of problems are seeing significant improvement or outright resolution. Weather forecasting is approaching 99% accuracy (Allen *et al.*, 2025). In digital systems biology, AI bypasses the entire health industry to analyze the human immune system's own record of antigen exposures encoded by B-cell and T-cell receptors on an individual basis (Zaslavsky *et al.*, 2025). Mayo Clinic's AI-ECGs identify the risk of atrial fibrillation, stroke, and cognitive decline in routine screenings (Furst, 2024). AlphaFold3 models not only protein structures but also DNA, RNA, ligands, and ions, and their interactions, using a diffusion-based architecture (Abramson *et al.*, 2024). The progression in foundation models is that of language to language, language to sequence (biology), and language to planning and strategy (with agentic AI). The eventual possibility is that computers are running all business processes. AI is present at each tier of the network computing stack (Figure 2).

AI refers to all manner of machine learning, foundation models, generative AI, agents, robots, and autonomous vehicles. The main roles for AI are stratified into the user, application, and compute tiers. At the compute level, AI is seen in GPUs and hyperscale data centers. In applications, there are many kinds of AI models, namely deep learning and foundation models including large language models (LLMs), graph neural networks (GNNs), neural algorithmic learners, topological neural networks, and protein language models. At the user level, AI is notable for not only being a user of the computational infrastructure but also for serving as the interface for human users of the computational infrastructure. The network is the computer, and the datacenter is the hub, as the locus of intelligence, digital-twin infrastructure, and exascale computing.

As machine-to-machine (M2M) communications have come to dominate the transmission-based internet in certain ways, AI entities could likewise become the main users of computing networks. The number of intelligent entities could scale dramatically and outnumber humans in various domains. AI entities include agents, copilots, and assistants, as well as physically embodied humanoid robots, factory machines, and autonomous vehicles. Any mobile machine may become autonomous. In a Future of Work report, IDC predicts that by 2027, agentic workflows will reshape how tasks are performed, impacting at least 40% IDC Global 2000 companies (Loomis *et al.*, 2024). Goldman Sachs estimated that there may be 1.4 million humanoid robots in labor-saving jobs by 2035 (Du *et al.*, 2024), and

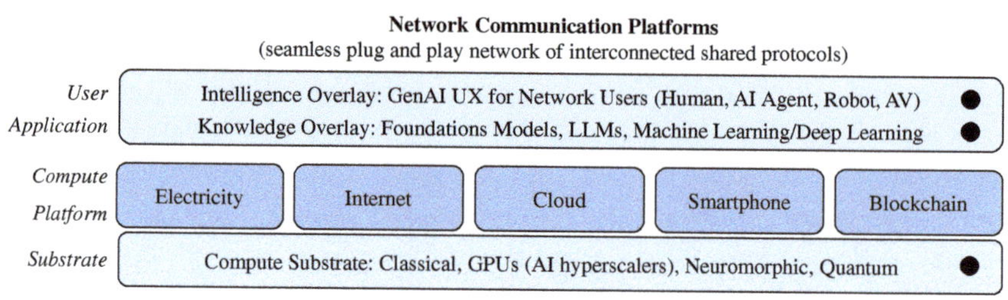

Fig. 2. Network communications platform stack and presence of AI (dots).

Gartner predicted that by 2027, 10% of all smart robots sold will be next-generation humanoid working robots (Rooney, 2025). The AI platform progression articulated by NVIDIA is evolving from perceptive to generative to agentic to physical AI (Table 1). Gartner lists "Agentic AI" as the number one strategic trend for 2025 (John, 2024).

AI security is a concern, as outlined by Trend Micro's top 10 risks, such as prompt injection, writing to databases, and insecure plugins (2024). One solution is to vest all network users in the sanctity of the continued operation of the network. Cryptoeconomic mechanisms could instantiate incentives to make it in the best interest for all agents (human and otherwise) to continue using the network for their activities. Distributed trust and verifiable computing could be crucial steps in the growth of AI entities as internet users and value-transferring resource allocators. There are implications for blockchain–AI integration at the levels of user, application, and compute within the technology stack (Figure 3).

Blockchains can be used as AI registries to monitor activity and facilitate self-development. AIs, like any user, can readily understand

Table 1. Proposed AI platform progression (as outlined by NVIDIA).

Perceptive AI	Generative AI	Agentic AI	Physical AI

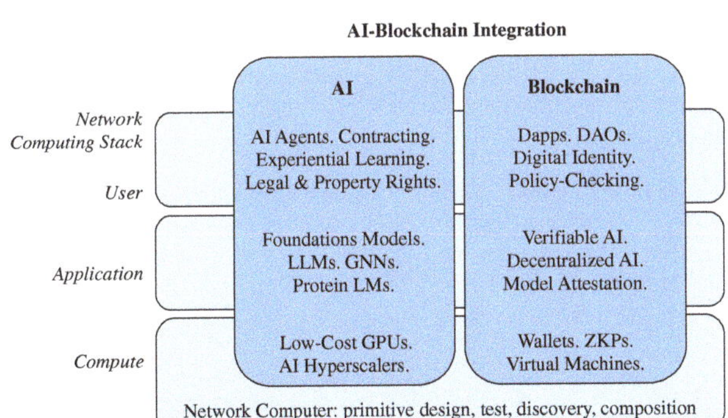

Fig. 3. AI–blockchain integration: structured learning in the network stack.

what the protocols are doing in the network and use them to accomplish goals, interacting with the network and other agents. Blockchain network computer primitives give user-agnostic safety, reliability, and verifiability.

At the compute layer, AI hyperscale data centers of low-cost GPUs execute cryptographic proofs for verifiable computing, attesting in real time to the valid nature of user identity, protocols, platforms, and wallet balances as transactions occur. Quantum plugs into the stack as a compute resource, currently scaling from 50 to 100 to 1000 logical qubits. The implications for AI–quantum integration are vast, creating new datascapes of quantum-generated data (with molecular and atomic precision in chemistry, materials, and biology) for AI learning, as human-produced data has been exhausted. At the application layer, blockchain is implicated in verifiable AI, decentralized AI, and model attestation. At the user layer, AI has a dual role: as a user and an interface. A new wave of hyper-personalization through AI copilots is anticipated, featuring digital identifiers and agent policy-checking. There could be a mix of centralized AI solutions and decentralized AI (DeAI) protocols enabling user-owned, controlled, and remunerated data.

Foundation models: Software artifact signing

Notably, AI and blockchain are converging on the same slate of digital trust and verifiable computing requirements. Driven by security concerns, national competitiveness, and available budget, the AI industry is urgently attempting to implement blockchain-like features such as attestation, provenance, history, and identity. There has been an overall shift in the conceptualization of software in the AI industry. In AI, *software* is now seen as living artifacts comprised of interactive prompts and dynamic datasets, as opposed to the static code of the past.

A key aim of the AI industry is signed, verifiable software artifacts. Standards work is developing the integration of Machine Learning Bill of Materials (ML-BOM) and Supply-chain Levels for Software Artifacts (SLSA) into AI artifact software signing (e.g., with the Sigstore code-signing toolkit) to provide secure ML models with provenance (Mello, 2023). The tools ensure tamper-proof metadata records and cryptographic verification of model origins and could be blockchain-logged within toolchains. Foundation models would be signed at each stage: pretraining, training, and production. A tokenized system for workload identity federation is implicated as tasks span multiple cloud-based systems (Microsoft, 2025).

Besides AI security, multi-agent coordination is another important topic in the AI industry as digital and robotic agents proliferate. Protocols have been proposed, including the Model Context Protocol (MCP) from Anthropic and the Agent-to-Agent Protocol (A2A) from Google. ServiceNow agents, for example, can be coordinated with an orchestrator or an MCP. AI–blockchain integrations are available with MCP implementation on the SettleMint and Algorand blockchains. Algorand is also quantum-ready with FALCON signatures, a NIST-identified lattice-based cryptography standard. SLSA could be joined with MCP in multi-agent verification programs (Lifshitz *et al.*, 2025).

AI agents: Experience is all you need

Silver and Sutton (2025) argue that for the next phase of AI success, agents should be built as experiential self-learners having long-term streams of real-world interactions with consequences. Such reinforcement learning techniques have led to AI breakthroughs, exemplified by AlphaGo (gameplay agents) and AlphaProof (math agents). Self-learning addresses the problem that AI results are judged by human relevancy and ignores the much larger domain which can be discovered by AI with an open learning frame. The Alpha platforms are organized to allow AI's own safe self-development. For example, a famous result was "Move 37," an AlphaGo move in the fifth row of the Go game board, which was not previously considered and deemed inappropriate from a human perspective but unified the board play in a new way and led to the AI victory. Similarly, AlphaProof is finding undiscovered mathematical proofs in top worldwide competitions (operating in Lean Theorem Prover) (Masoom *et al.*, 2024).

The self-learning perspective argues that a new era of "AI experience" beyond "human-derived data" is needed to address the vast areas of open problems before us, particularly in energy, biology, chemistry, and physics. Mathematics is an obvious domain for AI-based progress, with math agents (Swan *et al.*, 2023) and AI mathematicians. Open-endedness with structure is the idea as experiential agents inhabit longer-term streams of experience rather than short snippets of interaction and define their own terms instead of having them imposed by the necessarily limited human view. Experiential agents would have actions and observations grounded in their environment rather than solely through human interaction. They would define rewards based on the consequences of interacting with the environment and have the ability to plan and reason about experiences directly rather than in terms relevant to humans.

Concerning AI autonomy and rights, the contemporary world is already one in which AI systems are economically useful and participating in production, individually and collectively. A primary example is automated warehouses and robotic production facilities. In the automation offload, there could be entire "cities" of AI agents interacting, contracting for resources, and performing large swaths of physical labor and intellectual work. Questions arise concerning the legal rights and property rights of AI agents. Proposals are under discussion regarding safe upgrade paths for AI agent legal and property rights, as these systems become more economically valuable and independent (Benet, 2025). Blockchain DAOs already serve as a prototypical vehicle for the digital analog of a corporation. Different kinds of "entityhood" designations and statuses may develop for AI systems in the areas of policy-checking, behavioral oversight, and self-learning capacity development, all of which might be overseen by specific classes of blockchain smart contracts and DAOs.

Concerning uncertain futures, cryptoeconomic theory has economic aspects but also, more fundamentally, the network computing aspects of any information technology. There is considerable uncertainty about how the future of network computing could develop, including with many classes of AI agents, robots, and autonomous vehicles outnumbering human users. Cryptoeconomic theories provide a future framework for the treatment of such uncertainty. For example, two principles of emphasis in the AI–blockchain community are Pareto-preferred futures and network persistence. Pareto-preferred futures are outcomes strongly preferred by almost everyone, envisioned to be better than the possibilities of today, and likely involving open frontiers and reduced conflict. (Drexler, 2013; Hall, 2007). Network persistence is the idea of committing to network infrastructure as the source of stable progress (where the Nash equilibrium incentive leads all parties to prefer the network for ongoing interaction) (Duettmann *et al.*, 2017). Ultimately, blockchains are envisioned as a robust platform for the development of computational jurisdictions with Pareto-preferred futures (functionality-opening, conflict-reducing) and a commitment to computing network persistence.

Blockchain Status

The status of blockchain rollout is substantial adoption in the financial sector, both enabling traditional finance (TradFi) real-world asset instantiation on blockchains and innovative crypto-native financial applications in decentralized finance (DeFi). Blockchain adoption also continues in DeSci, decentralized physical infrastructure network (dePIN), decentralized identity (DID), and decentralized AI (DeAI).

Decentralized finance

The progression of Blockchain 1.0 (cryptocurrencies), Blockchain 2.0 (smart contracts), and Blockchain 3.0 (science and beyond) continues to unfold (Swan, 2015). Blockchain 2.0 smart contracts remain a strong adoption trend for distributed ledger technologies. This pertains to both novel "crypto-native" solutions in the DeFi industry as well as FinTech implementations in the TradFi industry's ongoing digitization practices. Blockchain is an important leapfrog and substitution technology for financial equity, supplementing traditional financial systems with crypto financial rails (e.g., Argentina's Crescimiento Movement). Chainalysis reports that India was number one in crypto adoption in 2024 based on an aggregate of four factors related to onchain cryptocurrency value received by centralized services (weighted by GDP per capita), transaction volumes, and usage patterns of cryptocurrency services and protocols (Chainalysis, 2024).

A major event spurring TradFi crypto activity was the U.S. SEC's approval of Bitcoin exchange-traded funds (ETFs) in January 2024 as a user-friendly investment product for crypto exposure (Gensler, 2024). With that advance, customers are able to select crypto investment products directly in brokerage accounts instead of having to use a crypto wallet. A rough heuristic is that crypto comprises about 2% of investment assets (at the end of 2024). In terms of size, the digital assets market was estimated to make up 3–4% of the global stock market capitalization, 0.3% of the world's money assets, and 7.6% of the world's gold supply as of 10 April 2024 (Reiff, 2024). Appetite for crypto products may continue to grow as the value of crypto as a percent of total global assets rises (requiring asset allocation models to invest in crypto) and as products become more investor-friendly (e.g., with ETFs, stablecoins, and real-world assets (RWAs)), accessible, and regulated (registered and overseen by financial authorities). In 2023, Bitcoin accounted for approximately 0.3% of the estimated total value of global wealth ($469.8 trillion) (*Ibid*). As of 10 December 2024, the overall cryptocurrency market was $3.61 trillion.[1] Bitcoin ($1.9 trillion) and Ethereum ($437 billion) dominate, together encompassing nearly two-thirds (65%) of the cryptocurrency market capitalization.[2]

The broader crypto market includes various forms of cryptocurrencies, digital assets, and DeFi protocol-based products. Other notable metrics include the Total Value Locked (TVL) in DeFi contracts at $134.5 billion as of 10 December 2024 (https://defillama.com/), $200.7 billion in stablecoins, and $14.0 billion in RWAs (https://app.rwa.xyz/). TVL refers to the aggregate value of digital assets locked (held) within DeFi protocols or platforms, measuring the total amount of cryptocurrency deposited and actively used within that system. Stablecoins are cryptocurrencies designed to maintain a stable value by pegging their price to an external asset, such as a fiat currency (e.g., USD and EUR), commodities (e.g., gold and silver), or other financial instruments, used for payments, remittances, and trading. RWAs are a fast-growing trend, even within DeFi; they refer to the tokenization of traditional (real-world) financial assets, bringing them onto the blockchain (onchain) for increased accessibility, liquidity, and transparency. RWA tokens represent real estate, commodities, bonds, and other tangible assets, allowing investors to engage with them in a decentralized manner. An example of trustless automation of RWA is the daily posting of mutual fund net asset value (NAV) by Chainlink.

---

[1]https://www.forbes.com/digital-assets/crypto-prices.

[2]https://www.coingecko.com/en/coins/bitcoin.

Another prominent crypto product is Central Bank Digital Currencies (CBDCs). A CBDC is virtual money backed and issued by a central bank. As of February 2025, 134 countries and currency unions representing 98% of global GDP were exploring CBDCs (Kumar *et al.*, 2025). Sixty-six countries were in the advanced stages of development, pilot programs (e.g., the digital euro), or full-scale launches, as compared with 35 in May 2020. Each G20 country is exploring a CBDC. Three countries have fully launched CBDCs: the Bahamas, Jamaica, and Nigeria. Digital yuan (e-CNY) is still the largest CBDC pilot in the world. In June 2024, total transaction volume reached 7 trillion e-CNY ($986 billion) versus 1.8 trillion yuan ($253 billion) in June 2023.

In terms of next-generation financial primitives, in April 2025, a crypto equivalent of SOFR (formerly LIBOR) launched, the Treehouse Decentralized Offered Rates (DORs). DOR is a benchmark against which DeFi fixed instruments can be priced. Having such a benchmark could greatly facilitate the RWA tokenization operations of traditional financial entities, as the fixed income market is five times the size of the equity market (Goh, 2025). Also, in April 2025, an elevated class of blockchain-based IP network (DeFi IP) was launched: Story. The need for "new car" types of network-based IP management systems in the era of AI and blockchains has been signaled by genAI foundation models crawling internet-scale data and being sued by large content repositories such as The New York Times. Story is a DeFi IP onchain ecosystem in which IP is a financial asset (Zhao, 2025). The key component of the DeFi IP platform is crypto primitives that comprise a legal system and enforce IP rights, relying heavily on U.S. copyright law and jurisdiction in a globally distributed product world as a proxy for the highest-weighted compliant behavior. The programmable (boiler template) IP license is a primitive backed by actual legal contracts. The DeFi IP network is analogous to the Visa or Mastercard payment network, which allows payments at software nodes where "the card is accepted" and remits funds to the holder via the network. The result is a potential realization of what had been envisioned for blockchains—economic and legal primitives readily discoverable in the network and composed on-demand into applications, in the idea of the network as a computer. Blockchains finally enable a much-awaited business process engineering moment for the financial sector. Crypto primitives offer a modern digitized method of operation with integrated systems now featured for digital property rights and value transfer.

DeAI and protocol institutions: DeFi, DePIN, and DeSci

An orthogonal trend cutting across all blockchain implementations is DeAI, the implementation of AI in decentralized blockchain protocols. DeAI is a growing market, providing not only a political counterweight to tech-giant centralized AI providers but also a technological advance, extending the triumph of decentralization already realized by internet and blockchain reliability and scalability. Given the AI boom, DeAI is not without hype, however, as investors embrace the blockchain argument of decentralized ownership of intelligence potentially surpassing an already growing market for the digital ownership of assets. The decentralized AI opportunity is "bigger than Bitcoin," one venture capitalist touts in a year-end letter to investors (Nelson, 2025).

The primary concept of DeAI is using modern AI techniques to optimize smart contracts, enhance reliability and scalability, and introduce a new level of automation to blockchain operations. In DeAI–DeFi (DeFAI), applications are seen in personalized investment copilots, AI-powered tokenomics portfolio management, dynamic position adjustment, and AI-driven financial solutions agents. In DeAI–DePIN, decentralized AI compute resources, there are protocols such as Akash (akash.network), which offers a decentralized network compute marketplace; Render (rendernetwork.com), which contributes a distributed consumer GPU network; and Origin (Origin.Trail), which provides decentralized knowledge graph solutions. The second segment of DeAI is agentic DeAI, with protocols such as Fetch.ai and Near.ai supporting user-owned and controlled data (locally stored), highly personalized AI agents, and explainable AI.

Pulling back from DeAI–DePIN to discuss the basics, DePINs are using blockchain technology to manage critical real-world infrastructure. DePINs provide decentralized control over systems such as energy grids, supply chains, telecommunications, and transportation, making them more secure, efficient, and resilient. A 2024 State of DePIN report forecasts a promising future for DePIN, with a market size expected to reach $3.5 trillion by 2028 (Bane & Gala, 2024). Carbon markets represent an important opportunity, coupled with DePIN and the tokenization of carbon assets to enforce large-scale environmental compliance. A global market price for carbon is foreseen as previously developed in oil (Allen *et al.*, 2022). There are various proposals for the tokenization of carbon assets (Jaffer *et al.*, 2024), alongside the launch of an environmental markets exchange, AirCarbon Exchange (ACX), based in Abu Dhabi, which claims to have transacted 21 million tons of carbon dioxide equivalents as of May 2025.[3]

DeScAI is discussed in a detailed chapter in this volume. The concept of DeSci involves the realization of a science project focused on knowledge production, utilizing modern blockchain technologies to increase its efficiency, reach, participation, quality, and impact. As DeFi as a modernization technology shifts the execution of the social institution of finance to blockchain protocols, so too does DeSci enact the social institution of science as blockchain protocols. The result is that scientific research is more open, transparent, and collaborative, reducing reliance on traditional institutions and enabling new funding mechanisms. The blockchain environment creates cryptoeconomic mechanisms for trustless science. For example, ZKPs could enforce the required replicability of experiments before publication.

Example DeSci projects include LabDAO (a p2p exchange for lab services), VitaDAO (healthspan), GenomeFi (genomics), Antidote DAO (cancer), CureDAO (digital health app layer), and Molecule (bio IP-NFT trading). A parallel endeavor is metascience, envisioning an era of network science with objectives consisting of improving scientific research funding and providing incentives to develop needed platform foundations and tools outside of the current citation-based scientific incentives model (Nielsen, 2011). DeSci tightens the link between funding and societally useful output, as most science projects never reach a human consumer. Metascience proponents envision having DeSci capital allocation systems that provide credit and attribution to the lengthy value chain reaching from scientific discovery to technology translation. DeSci also makes it possible to create foundational infrastructure that is not conducive to

[3]https://acx.net/.

small-team publishing incentives. With DeSci, there could be new kinds of investable science assets that result from having new ways of instantiating the credit graph in a computable environment.

DeAI: Agentic institutions

> ... the human being is eventually able to step aside and let a machine take one's place. (Hegel, *Philosophy of Right*, 1821, §198, 233)

DeAI adds automation to the proven resiliency of decentralization as institutions are shifted from human operation to protocol networks. This is seen in DeFi's real-world asset administration, DePIN's real-world infrastructure operations, and DeSci's real-world scientific knowledge production. A Hegelian perspective can be used to theorize *agentic institutions* as adaptive, decentralized governance structures that integrate AI agents and protocol networks to autonomously manage social, economic, and scientific processes, evolving through learning, self-critique, and problem-solving to ensure resilience and progress. A substantial departure from human-operated brick-and-mortar institutions (governmental, financial, scientific, and economic) is underway in the digitization and agentification of large-scale coordination.

Agentic institutions instantiate the need for coherent transitions from human-centric institutions to protocol-based institutions governed by AI agents. For Hegel, individual freedom is only expressed through the institutions of social life. He asserts that "institutions form the pillars on which freedom is realized and rational" (Hegel, 1821, §265, 287, shortened). Institutions are dynamic, rational structures comprised of the "objective mind" of participants, capable of learning and adapting to historical, cultural, and ethical transformations (Jaeggi, 2018). In the contemporary moment, institutions can be seen as "problem-solving instances" coordinating processes of "learning and experience" (Jaeggi, 2025, 14, 12). Progress is defined as "positively evaluated change in ... the design of institutions" and their execution in social practices and forms of life (*Ibid.*, 8). Institutions are being conceptually recast as problem-solving frameworks that organize social life and enable societies to address both immediate and second-order problems.

Agentic institutions are emergent social practice entities which function as complex problem-solving frameworks within digital societies. Progress is an objective measure that involves reflexive adaptation and overcoming problems. Agentic institutions must develop capacities for learning and self-critique to effectively address evolving societal crises. Progress in this context is not measured by technological advancements or increased capabilities, but by the ability of agentic institutions to adapt, reflect, and transform their practices in response to new challenges, thereby incorporating social learning and mitigating risks rooted in uncritical or rigid deployment of AI systems. Conversely, regressions may manifest if agentic institutions respond to crises with superficial fixes, denial, or unlearning, leading to institutional stagnation or harmful entrenchment of biases. Agentic institutions are constructed with the guardrails of Pareto-preferred futures and network persistence to invest agents in functionality-opening, conflict-reducing goals and the commitment to computing network persistence. Other protocol institution models have been theorized. For example, the notion of *agentic commons* is proposed as a new form of computational governance that integrates human and machine agency, enabling co-governance within evolving systems rather than relying on traditional external control (Potts, 2025).

Cryptoeconomic Theories

Summary of key ideas

A plurality of cryptoeconomic approaches is presented as systems-oriented economic theories of complexity, dynamics, and nonlinearity, purpose-built for digital network economies (Table 2). In the first part of the book, Formalization, Verifiability, and Coordination, Swan names "Categorical Cryptoeconomics" as the unification of category-theoretic treatments in the value-transfer technologies of blockchain, finance, accounting, and economics and posits *HoTT blockchains* as a homotopy type theory instantiation of blockchains for formal verification and interoperability. Allen, Berg, and Davidson set forth a theoretical framework for evaluating the blockchain security make-or-buy decision. Gabbay discusses the categorical

Table 2. Cryptoeconomic theories.

	Theme	Cryptoeconomic Theory	Reference
I	**Formalization, Verifiability, and Coordination**		
1	Formalization	Categorical Cryptoeconomics: HoTT Blockchains	Swan
2	Security	The Economics of Blockchain Shared Security	Allen *et al.*
3	Coordination	Decentralized Collaborative Action: Cryptoeconomics in Space	Gabbay
II	**Real-World Assets: Digital Economic Infrastructure**		
4	Central Banks	The Policy Implications of Competing Digital Currencies	Genc
5	Edge Access	Wallets as End-User Universal Access Devices	Jørgensen
III	**Protocol Institutions: The Economic Future of Institutions**		
6	Decentralized Science	DeSci and DeScAI: Distributed Epistemic Economies	Shilina
7	Mathematical Institutions	Protocols and Institutions	Zargham & Ben-Meir
8	Sustainability	Agentic Learning DAOs for Sustainable Energy Transition	Narayan & Laine-Kronberg
IV	**Digital Network Economies**		
9	Valorization	A Theory of Chaordic Economics: How Artificial Intelligence and Blockchain Transform Businesses, Economies, and Societies	Treiblmaier
10	Dynamics	Flow Dynamics: Advanced Network Science for Supply and Cryptocurrency Remittance Networks	Yamano & Mizuno
11	Open Games	Monetary Macro Accounting Theory for Blockchain, AI, and Beyond	Menéndez & Winschel

cryptoeconomics approach of a semitopological framework for decentralized collaborative action-taking.

The second part covers Real-World Assets: Digital Economic Infrastructure. Here, Genc posits that competing digital currencies will define the next chapter of the global monetary paradigm and suggests related policy implications. Jørgensen argues that "the wallet is the platform," showcasing the transformative role of wallets as universal access devices for user autonomy, security, and societal inclusivity.

Third, in Protocol Institutions: The Economic Future of Institutions, Shilina takes a philosophical approach to envisioning the institutions of science as borderless, self-organizing, machine-augmented epistemic infrastructure. Zargham and Ben-Meir redefine institutions as emergent behavior shaped by interactions and apply a dynamical systems perspective using bounded control theory formalizations (supermartingales and Lyapunov function drift) to specify non-coercively controlled protocol institutions. Narayan and Laine-Kronberg introduce agentic learning DAOs for sustainable energy based on Potts' notion of agentic commons (human–AI co-governance) (2025).

In the fourth part, Digital Network Economies, Treiblmaier proposes a novel theory of complexity economics based on chaordics (chaos and order) to interpret the impact of disruptive technologies such as AI and blockchain on economic systems. Yamano and Mizuno develop advanced network science methods to demonstrate how blockchain transparency can enforce ethical practices in global supply chains and cryptocurrency remittance networks. Menéndez and Winschel elaborate a monetary theory of macro accounting for deployment in blockchain-based bills of exchange and AI knowledge graphs. The work dovetails with AI software-artifact signing standards such as Supply-chain Levels for Software Artifacts (SLSA) and Machine Learning Bills of Materials (ML-BOM) (Maruseac *et al.*, 2024; Mello, 2023), as AI security risks become pronounced (Trend Micro, 2024).

Formalization, verifiability, and coordination

In more detail, the first part of the book treats formalization, verifiability, and coordination. In "Categorical Cryptoeconomics: HoTT Blockchains," Swan argues that category-theoretic formalization is the thread that pulls together not only value-transfer technologies (blockchain, finance, accounting, and economics) but also, at a higher level of abstraction, smartnetwork technologies more generally (blockchain, AI, and quantum). HoTT blockchains are introduced at the intersection of category theory and blockchain technology. Category theory's attributes (i.e., its ability to formalize relationships and structures) are highlighted as being crucial for addressing the challenges in cryptoeconomics, namely security, formal verification, usability, and interoperability. The chapter concludes by acknowledging the potential risks inherent in this technological integration while advocating for the potential of category theory to provide a more reliable theoretical basis for future developments in blockchain and finance.

In "The Economics of Blockchain Shared Security," Allen, Berg, and Davidson develop a theoretical framework for assessing shared security in blockchain networks using insights from institutional and transaction cost economics. They explore the make-or-buy decision, where networks must choose between internal security management or outsourcing to established providers. Key factors such as asset specificity, uncertainty, and opportunism shape governance structures for security sharing. Effective shared security requires institutional mechanisms to mitigate transactional complexities and opportunistic risks. Using Cosmos' Interchain Security as a case study, the authors highlight the need for tailored governance that balances autonomy, security, and efficiency, ensuring long-term adaptability in blockchain.

Gabbay's "Decentralized Collaborative Action: Cryptoeconomics in Space" examines cryptoeconomics as the study of decentralized socioeconomic systems, driven by blockchain and modern computing technologies. The work integrates economic principles, game theory, and decentralized networks, showcasing how collaborative action can emerge without centralized control. He introduces the concept of decentralized collaborative action, emphasizing three core features: decentralization, permissionless participation, and actor heterogeneity. Using semitopologies, Gabbay models actionable coalitions that drive local state updates, maintaining order and consensus in decentralized systems. Findings indicate that coalition structures predict macro-level behaviors, influencing consensus dynamics. Beyond theory, the research offers insights for practical decentralized system design, with future directions exploring dynamic coalition structures and their effects on consensus protocols.

Real-world assets: Digital economic infrastructure

The second part of the book investigates real-world assets and the creation of digital economic infrastructure. In "The Policy Implications of Competing Digital Currencies," Genc examines the national policy impact of digital currencies, comparing private cryptocurrencies and CBDCs through historical parallels. Stablecoins, driven by market demand amid financial crises, maintain a stable value by pegging to fiat currencies, commodities, or algorithmic mechanisms. The chapter highlights the political tension in currency digitization, with the U.S. playing a central role in shaping policy. Genc categorizes digital currencies by issuance mechanisms and collateral types, assessing the fiscal and global stability risks of rising stablecoin adoption and its effect on dollarization. The chapter argues that digital currency competition will reshape global monetary policy.

Jørgensen's "Wallets as End-User Universal Access Devices" explores how blockchain-based wallets are evolving from Web2 to Web3, becoming universal access devices for managing digital assets, identity, and decentralized services. These wallets enhance security, interoperability, and user autonomy, potentially reshaping societal interactions and closing the digital divide. The chapter emphasizes the need for new business models to maximize their impact across individual, business, and societal levels while addressing security and education challenges. Looking ahead, AI-integrated wallets could act as agents with verifiable credentials and decentralized identity solutions, further expanding Web3's reach.

Protocol institutions: The economic future of institutions

The third part of the book envisions protocol institutions as the economic future of institutions. In "DeSci and DeScAI: Distributed Epistemic Economies," Shilina articulates an epistemic theory of DeSci and DeScAI knowledge production for the future of high-throughput science. The chapter explores the emerging conceptual framework of (DeSci) and its extension into DeScAI, emphasizing how blockchain and AI technologies are poised to fundamentally transform the scientific ecosystem. The theory is anchored in three philosophical pillars: (1) the ontology of economics, focusing on decentralized coordination over traditional resource allocation; (2) the economics of science, dealing with the public-good nature of knowledge and incentivization challenges; and (3) the potential of decentralized infrastructures to foster inclusive, transparent, and adaptive scientific models. DeSci harnesses blockchain protocols, smart contracts, DAOs, and AI agents to enable peer-to-peer funding, transparent peer review, and distributed governance, thus reducing reliance on centralized gatekeepers. The epistemic model redefines how knowledge is created, validated, and disseminated in the digital age.

In "Protocols and Institutions," Zargham and Ben-Meir investigate the relationship between institutional frameworks and protocols through the lens of control systems engineering, proposing a rigorous mathematical approach to defining and analyzing institutions. They argue that institutions, traditionally viewed as sets of rules, can be understood more accurately as stable emergent behaviors resulting from the interactions shaped by protocols. By employing concepts from control theory, dynamical systems, and category theory, the authors outline how protocols can be designed to maintain stability and adaptability within organizations, thus enhancing institutional resilience. They emphasize the necessity of integrating empirical observations and engineering practices in the design of institutions, ultimately advocating for a systematic and protocol-driven approach to institutional design that can effectively address contemporary societal challenges.

In "Agentic Learning DAOs for Sustainable Energy Transition," Narayan & Laine-Kronberg introduce an innovative framework combining AI, blockchain, and decentralized governance to revolutionize research incentives in sustainable energy systems. Grounded in the multi-level perspective (MLP), institutional theory, and the learning organization paradigm, the model envisions DAOs powered by blockchain and AI agents. These entities facilitate transparent, tokenized rewards, real-time evaluation, and adaptive governance, challenging traditional research regimes by rapidly funding high-risk, high-impact projects and promoting open data, replication, and interdisciplinary collaboration. The integration of blockchain ensures tamper-proof record-keeping and legitimacy, while AI agents enable dynamic adjustment of incentives, continuous learning, and automated verification, creating a reflexive, decentralized research ecosystem.

Digital network economies

The fourth part of the book focuses on digital network economies. In "A Theory of Chaordic Economics: How Artificial Intelligence and Blockchain Transform Businesses, Economies, and Societies,"

Treiblmaier introduces a framework for understanding the transformative impact of disruptive technologies, particularly AI and blockchain, on economic systems. Drawing on Dee Hock's notion of "chaordic" systems that balance chaos and order, the theory posits that AI, with the capacity for generative output, and blockchain, with decentralized transaction scalability, can interplay in ways that reshape organizational structures and societal governance. These technologies can lead to novel economic arrangements that enhance adaptability, resilience, and self-organization, while simultaneously presenting challenges such as misinformation and power imbalances. The theory synthesizes insights from various perspectives (e.g., information theory, chaos theory, and behavioral economics) to highlight how these technological advancements can catalyze a shift from traditional hierarchical frameworks to more flexible and emergent chaordic structures, ultimately enabling more effective responses to evolving market and societal conditions.

In the chapter "Flow Dynamics: Advanced Network Science for Supply and Cryptocurrency Remittance Networks," Yamano and Mizuno analyze the growing complexity of global supply chains and cryptocurrency remittance networks, advocating for a network science approach over traditional linear models. They emphasize the need for formal frameworks to trace indirect relationships and distant transaction partners, enhancing resilience against money laundering and unethical sourcing. Using network control models and community detection algorithms, they propose strategies to identify risks while corporate strategies shift toward inter-firm collaboration and broader ecosystems. Blockchain integration is key to improving traceability and strengthening digital financial systems despite oversight challenges.

In the "Monetary Macro Accounting Theory for Blockchain, AI, and Beyond," Menéndez and Winschel examine money as a payment medium, highlighting temporal misalignment in production where debt arises before customer payments. Grounded in the legal principles of separation and abstraction, the framework formalizes debt, contracts, and property rights across three levels: micro (labor division), meso (banking risk-sharing), and macro (GDP distribution). They argue that monetary theory is rooted in debt dynamics rather than the mere circulation of money. The electronic Bill of Exchange (BoE) bridges monetary systems, while categorical cryptoeconomic models, such as sheaf theory and homology, provide a foundation for balanced accounting. The theory advances a systematic approach to financial interactions, extending beyond traditional monetary policy and potentially integrating AI for software artifact signing and bill of materials tracking.

References

Abramson, J., Adler, J., Dunger, J. *et al.* 2024. "Accurate structure prediction of biomolecular interactions with AlphaFold 3." *Nature* 630: 493–500. https://doi.org/10.1038/s41586-024-07487-w.

Allen, A., Markou, S., Tebbutt, W. *et al.* 2025. "End-to-end data-driven weather prediction." *Nature*. https://doi.org/10.1038/s41586-025-08897-0.

Azlen, M., Gostlow, G., and Child, A. 2022. "The Carbon Risk Premium." *Journal of Alternative Investments* 25(1): 33–64. https://doi.org/10.3905/jai.2022.1.166.

Bane, D. and Gala, S. 2024. "2024 State of DePIN." Messari Report. https://messari.io/report/state-of-depin-2024.

Benet, J. 2025. "Architecting Resilient Futures – San Francisco 2025." Funding the Commons, San Francisco, CA, April 3, 2025. https://www.youtube.com/watch?v=9S9FlYjfnpM.

Berentsen, A., Lenzi, J., and Nyffenegger, R. 2023. "An Introduction to Zero-Knowledge Proofs in Blockchains and Economics." *Federal Reserve Bank of St. Louis Review* 105: 280–94. https://doi.org/10.20955/r.105.280-94.

Brekke, J. K. and Alsindi, W. Z. 2021. "Cryptoeconomics." *Internet Policy Review* 10(2): 1–8. https://doi.org/10.14763/2021.2.1553.

Chainalysis. 2024. "Global Crypto Adoption Index." September 11, 2024. https://www.chainalysis.com/blog/2024-global-crypto-adoption-index/.

Dixon, C. 2024. *Read Write Own: Building the Next Era of the Internet*. New York: Random House.

Drexler, K. E. 2013. *Radical Abundance: How a Revolution in Nanotechnology Will Change Civilization*. New York: PublicAffairs Books.

Du, J., Isayama, Y., Costa, D. *et al.* 2024. "The global market for humanoid robots could reach $38 billion by 2035." Goldman Sachs Research. https://www.goldmansachs.com/insights/articles/the-global-market-for-robots-could-reach-38-billion-by-2035.

Duettmann, A., Peterson, C., and Miller, M. S. 2017. "Cyber, Nano, and AGI Risks: Decentralized Approaches to Reducing Risks." *The First Colloquium on Catastrophic and Existential Risk*: 1–34. https://foresight.org/summary/intelligent-cooperation-intro-mark-s-miller-christine-peterson-allison-duettmann/.

Furst, J. 2024. "Mayo Clinic research finds AI-enabled ECGs may identify patients at greater risk of stroke, cognitive decline." Mayo Clinic Press, March 19, 2024. https://mcpress.mayoclinic.org/healthy-brain/mayo-clinic-research-finds-ai-enabled-ecgs-may-identify-patients-at-greater-risk-of-stroke-cognitive-decline/.

Gensler, G. 2024. "Statement on the Approval of Spot Bitcoin Exchange-Traded Products." U.S. Securities and Exchange Commission, January 10, 2024. https://www.sec.gov/newsroom/speeches-statements/gensler-statement-spot-bitcoin-011023.

Goh, B. 2025. "Treehouse Protocol: Building DeFi's Fixed Income Layer." *The Defiant - DeFi, Web3 & NFT Insights* podcast, April 1, 2025. https://www.youtube.com/watch?v=GkKW2UXU-CM.

Graham-Cumming, J. 2019. "The Network is the Computer." The Cloudflare Blog, July 11, 2019. https://blog.cloudflare.com/the-network-is-the-computer/.

Hall, J. S. 2007. *Beyond AI: Creating the Conscience of the Machine.* Amherst, NY: Prometheus.

Hegel, G. W. F. 1991 [1829]. *Elements of the Philosophy of Right.* Ed. A. W. Wood. Trans. H. B. Nisbet. Cambridge, UK: Cambridge University Press.

Jaeggi, R. 2018. *Critique of Forms of Life.* Trans. C. Cronin. Cambridge, MA: Harvard University Press.

Jaeggi, R. 2025. *Progress and Regression.* Cambridge, MA: Harvard University Press.

Jaffer, S., Dales, M., Ferris, P. *et al.* 2024. "Global, robust and comparable digital carbon assets." arXiv:2403.14581v2.

John, A. S. 2024. "Gartner reveals top 10 strategic technology trends for 2025." WIRE19, December 2, 2024. https://www.wire19.com/gartner-reveals-top-10-strategic-technology-trends-for-2025/.

John, K. and Saleh, F. 2025. "Cryptoeconomics." *Oxford Research Encyclopedia of Economics and Finance.* https://oxfordre.com/economics/view/10.1093/acrefore/9780190625979.001.0001/acrefore-9780190625979-e-956.

Kissinger, H., Mundie, C., and Schmidt, E. 2024. *Genesis: Artificial Intelligence, Hope, and the Human Spirit.* Boston, MA: Little, Brown and Company.

Kumar, A., Chhangani, A., Hamilton, L., and Kim, G. 2025. "Central Bank Digital Currency Tracker." Atlantic Council, February 2025. https://www.atlanticcouncil.org/cbdctracker/.

Lifshitz, S., McIlraith, S. A., and Du, Y. 2025. "Multi-Agent Verification: Scaling Test-Time Compute with Multiple Verifiers." arXiv:2502.20379v1.

Loomis, A., Fleming, M., Spinoni, E. *et al.* 2024. "IDC FutureScape: Worldwide Future of Work 2025 Predictions." IDC Report No. US51665624.

Maruseac, M., Major, D., and Wickens, E. 2024. "Signing ML Artifacts: Building towards tamper-proof ML metadata records." GitHub Issue, November 15, 2024. https://github.com/cosai-oasis/ws1-supply-chain/issues/4.

Masoom, H., Huang, A., Horvath, M. Z. *et al.* 2024. "AI achieves silver-medal standard solving International Mathematical Olympiad problems." DeepMind Blog, July 25, 2024. https://deepmind.google/discover/blog/ai-solves-imo-problems-at-silver-medal-level.

Mello Jr., J. P. 2023. "How supply chain security tools can protect ML models." ReversingLabs Blog, November 9, 2023. https://www.reversinglabs.com/blog/ai-and-transparency-how-ml-model-creators-can-protect-against-supply-chain-attacks.

Microsoft. 2025. "Workload identity federation." Microsoft Learn, March 17, 2025. https://learn.microsoft.com/en-us/entra/msal/dotnet/acquiring-tokens/web-apps-apis/workload-identity-federation.

Muir, H. 2025. "Workforce Readiness in the Era of AI." Institute for Corporate Productivity (i4cp). https://www.i4cp.com/press-releases/new-i4cp-study-ai-upskilling-can-improve-productivity-by-30-or-more-yet-most-companies-are-still-far-behind.

Nelson, D. 2025. "Decentralized AI Opportunity Is 'Bigger than Bitcoin,' Says DCG's Barry Silbert." *CoinDesk*, February 7, 2025. https://www.coindesk.com/business/2025/02/07/decentralized-ai-opportunity-is-bigger-than-bitcoin-says-dcg-s-silbert.

Nielsen, M. 2011. *Reinventing Discovery: The New Era of Networked Science.* Princeton, NJ: Princeton University Press.

Potts, J. 2025. "Governing hyperobjects – new economics of AI regulation." In Stocker, V., Schrepel, T., and Kuenzler, A. (eds.), *Network Law Review* (special symposium issue). Conference paper presented at The Law, Technology, and Economics of AI Regulation conference, Hong Kong, May 22–23, 2025.

Reiff, N. 2024. "How Much of All Money Is in Bitcoin?" *Investopedia*, April 10, 2024. https://www.investopedia.com/tech/how-much-worlds-money-bitcoin/.

Rooney, P. 2025. "AI humanoid robots inch their way toward the workforce." *CIO*, February 21, 2025. https://www.cio.com/article/3829539/ai-humanoid-robots-inch-their-way-toward-the-workforce.html.

Russo, C. 2020. *The Infinite Machine: How an Army of Crypto-hackers is Building the Next Internet with Ethereum.* New York: Harper Business.

Shi, K., Chakraborty, K., Kon, W. Y. *et al.* 2024. "On the Relativistic Zero Knowledge Quantum Proofs of Knowledge." arXiv:2409.03635v1.

Silver, D. and Sutton, R. S. 2025. "Welcome to the Era of Experience." Google AI. https://storage.googleapis.com/deepmind-media/Era-of-Experience%20/The%20Era%20of%20Experience%20Paper.pdf.

Swan, M. 2015. *Blockchain: Blueprint for a New Economy.* Sebastopol, CA: O'Reilly Media.

Swan, M., Kido, T., Roland, E., and dos Santos, R. P. 2023. "Math Agents: Computational Infrastructure, Mathematical Embedding, and Genomics." arXiv:2307.02502.

Trend Micro. 2024. "The Top 10 AI Security Risks Every Business Should Know." July 8, 2024. https://www.trendmicro.com/en_us/research/24/g/top-ai-security-risks.html.

Voshmgir, S. 2020. *Token Economy: How the Web3 reinvents the Internet.* Berlin: BlockchainHub Berlin.

Zaslavsky, M. E., Craig, E., Michuda, J. K. *et al.* 2025. "Disease diagnostics using machine learning of B cell and T cell receptor sequences." *Science* 387(6736): eadp2407. https://doi.org/10.1126/science.adp2407.

Zhao, J. 2025. "Bringing Intellectual Property Onchain with Story Protocol." *The Defiant - DeFi, Web3 & NFT Insights* podcast, April 1, 2025. https://www.youtube.com/watch?v=JiFOptRzE8s.

Part I

Formalization, Verifiability, and Coordination

https://doi.org/10.1142/9781800618664_0002

Chapter 1

Categorical Cryptoeconomics: HoTT Blockchains

Melanie Swan

University College London, London, UK

melanie@blockchainstudies.org

Abstract

Category theory is a mathematical method for generalizing blockchain economics to higher levels of abstraction. *Categorical cryptoeconomics* operationalizes digital trust as the theme connecting smartnetwork technologies (AI, blockchain, and quantum) with quantitative business methods (finance, accounting, and economics), aimed at real-world asset digitization, smart contract ecosystems, and global risk management. *Categorical smartnetwork field theory* interprets categorical smartnetwork treatments (in blockchain, AI, and quantum) with categorical field theory. *Homotopy type theory (HoTT) blockchains* are introduced to instantiate blockchains as same-shape logic elements for secure computability, formal verification, and interoperability. The result of categorical cryptoeconomics and categorical smartnetwork field theory is the formalization of digital trust to support an era of human collaboration with AI agents, experiential self-learners, robots, and autonomous vehicles.

Keywords: Category Theory, Cryptonative AI Systems, Verifiable Computing, Smartnetworks, Quantum Technologies, Topology.

1.1 Introduction

The focal point connecting smartnetwork technologies (AI, blockchain, and quantum) with quantitative business methods (finance, accounting, and economics) is the formalization of digital trust (Table 1.1).

Blockchains embody digital trust through trustless, impartial algorithms, replacing reliance on human intermediaries. Their formal structure (tiered, hash-linked data rollups) mirrors category theory's abstraction of functor mappings. In blockchains, transaction data form hierarchical relationships, aggregating into hash trees that culminate in a Merkle root, which represents multi-layered integrity. Similarly, category theory builds upon objects, mappings, functors, and natural transformations, extending toward higher homotopies or infinity groupoids, demonstrating an analogous progression of structured abstraction (Figure 1.1).

Table 1.1. Digital trust encapsulates thematic concerns in business and technology.

Blockchain	GenAI	Quantum	Finance	Accounting	Economics
Formal verification	Security	Error correction	Growth & risk	AI–blockchain	Inflation
Interoperability	Multiagent	Algorithm discovery	Digitization	Cybersecurity	Debt reduction
Usability	Experience	Circuit design	Quantum crypto	Quantum cloud	Future of Work

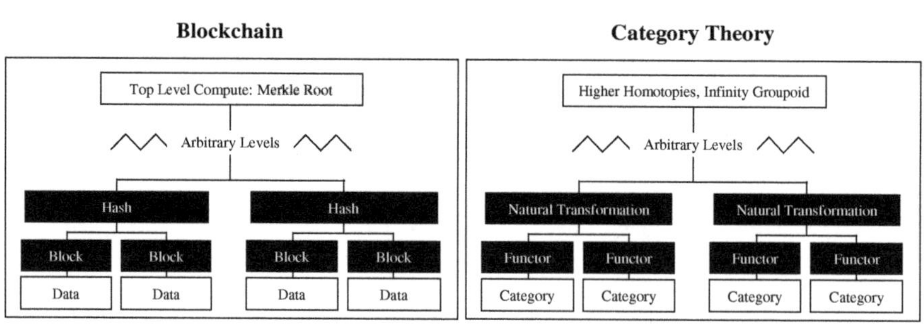

Fig. 1.1. Similar formal structures of trust: blockchain and category theory.

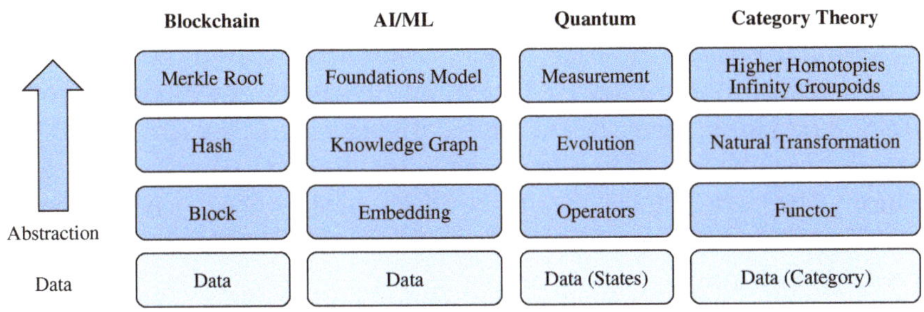

Fig. 1.2. Higher levels of abstraction: smartnetworks and category theory.

Digital trust is the effect of formalization and mathematical abstraction, seen not only in the cryptoeconomic mechanisms of blockchain but also across the smartnetwork and category theory landscapes (Figure 1.2). Data inputs are quickly tokenized and formatted to higher levels of abstraction in consistent, computation-amenable treatments. Once represented formally, systems become interoperable, and the levels of abstraction can scale to arbitrarily higher levels, perhaps almost indefinitely, depending on the system. Categorical model theory (Barrett *et al.*, 2023) and categorical complexity (Basu & Isik, 2020) apply category-theoretic formalisms to compare systems of mathematical structures and their complexities.

1.2 Modern Digital Infrastructure with Crypto Protocols

Financial market growth implicates both blockchain and categorical cryptoeconomics. Blockchain 1.0 cryptocurrencies have been the mainstay since Bitcoin's launch on 3 January 2009. The current phase is one of heightened focus on the more sophisticated and security-focused endeavor of Blockchain 2.0 contracts (Swan, 2015) and programmable risk (Swan, 2019). In traditional financial markets, derivatives (futures and options) have arisen as tools for quantifying uncertainty about future events. The trend continues in blockchain markets with derivatives on cryptocurrencies and DeFi products. Digitization and competitive pressures to adopt modern smartnetwork technologies continue to promote early adoption in the finance industry. Even without DeFi, growth is seen in the notional value of derivatives traded in U.S. markets, which increased from $875 billion per day in 2020 to $2.7 trillion per day in 2024 (volume increased from 29 million to 46 million contracts per day) (Acworth, 2024). The global over-the-counter derivatives market also saw a 16% increase in notional value from 2022 to 2023 ($616 trillion to $715 trillion) (Roberts, 2024). Contracts have proliferated, with the number of options classes growing from 4,000 to 6,000 and the number of strikes doubling.

Crypto (cryptocurrencies, digital assets, and DeFi protocol-based products) is a growing market within finance. A major event spurring activity was the U.S. SEC's approval of Bitcoin exchange-traded funds (ETFs) in January 2024 as a user-friendly investment product for crypto exposure (Gensler, 2024). As of April 2024, total crypto assets, primarily investments in Bitcoin and Ethereum, comprised roughly 3–4% of global assets (Reiff, 2024). Crypto derivatives are regulated products which allow investors to hedge crypto exposure. Demand is high, as 70% of crypto trading on centralized exchanges in September 2024 was based on derivatives (futures and options), and only 30% was immediate exchange (i.e., the spot market), with an overall volume of $4.34 trillion (Roberts, 2024). There is an expanded range of CFTC-regulated products with digital asset derivatives on Bitcoin, Ethereum, Bitcoin Cash, Litecoin, Dogecoin, Shiba Inu, Avalanche, Polkadot, Chainlink, and Stellar.

A smaller but growing market is DeFi contracts, which had $134.5 billion in total value locked (TVL) within contracts as of 10 December 2024.[1] One of the biggest markets is Ethereum Level 2 (L2), which had an estimated $55.4 billion in TVL as of December 10, 2024.[2] L2 is a variety of scaling solutions for the main network (L1), aggregating and posting attested transactions to blockchains in batches (rollups). Optimistic rollups comprised 85% of activity versus more expensive zero-knowledge (ZK) rollups. Optimistic rollups assume that transactions are valid and rely on a fraud-proof mechanism to resolve disputes; ZK-rollups use ZK-proofs to validate transactions up front. Such L2 scaling solutions are needed as the ledger size continues to

[1]https://defillama.com/.
[2]https://l2beat.com/scaling/summary.

grow: the full Bitcoin ledger was 620 GB and the Ethereum ledger 1.2 TB as of 10 December 2024.[3]

1.3 Category Theory

Category theory is the mathematics of structures and their relationships. Whereas set theory focuses on the content of objects, category theory studies the relations between objects. The Yoneda lemma is a famous idea claiming that everything mathematically relevant about an object can be known through the relations directed at it. Category theory is an overlay encompassing formal approaches (Landry & Marquis, 2005).

The term "*category*" does not have the same meaning as in colloquial use but is rather a mathematically rigorous construction. Categories consist of objects, morphisms, composition, and identities, and they obey the associative and identity laws. A category is a family of mathematical objects (e.g., sets, topological spaces, algebraic structures, etc.) composed into a network of relationships (called morphisms) (Table 1.2). Categories have two levels of structure (objects and maps), while sets have only one (objects). The category "Set," however, has "Sets" as its objects and "Functions" between sets as its maps.

Category theory is sometimes synonymous with topology, as it began with the algebraic formulation of topology (Eilenberg & MacLane, 1945). Algebraic geometry soon followed. The key insight is that the algebraic formulation of functions has greater information, which can be manipulated. Thus, in any categorical application, the first step may involve obtaining an algebraic formulation.

Table 1.2. Categories have two levels of structure: objects and maps.

Category	Set	Top (Topology)	POrd (Preorder)	Vec (Vector)
Objects	Sets	Topological spaces	Preorders	Vector spaces
Morphisms	Functions	Continuous functions	Order-preserving	Linear maps

[3]https://ycharts.com/indicators/.

Interoperability between mathematical fields was also an early motivation, featuring a *lingua franca* to discuss similar structures arising across fields such as quotient spaces and direct products. In addition, mathematicians observed the duality property of being able to project problems from one field into another to see solutions in a way that was not possible from the original perspective.

Category theory uses string charts and diagrammatic reasoning, which users can deploy without having to understand the underlying mathematics (open-source software: CatColab, ModelCollab, and DisCoCat). The method is widely used in science (physics, chemistry, and biology) (Spivak, 2014), as many complex systems can be represented with the same functorial logic (Baez, 2023). Another benefit of diagrammatic reasoning is computability. The principal categorical primitives for computational instantiation are modular forms of tensor products: symmetric monoidal categories (SMCs) in classical computing and monoidal tensor categories in topological quantum field theories (TQFTs) and quantum computing. In computer science, category theory is employed as the abstract algebra of functions in lambda calculus, functional programming, and homotopy (shape) type (logic) theory (HoTT). HoTT extends the topological idea that shapes that deform into one another are topologically equivalent to argue that they have the same formal logic and computational treatment (Awodey, 2010).

In the smartnetwork stack (blockchain–AI–quantum), category theory is emerging as a crucial foundational approach. *Categorical deep learning* is the application of category-theoretic methods to machine learning and neural network design. Categorical machinery such as functors and natural transformations enables a systematic formalization of machine learning models with algebraic structures (Patterson, 2020). In topological deep learning, the topology of the data space is used to inform neural architectures, model higher-order relations, assess remeshing symmetry in manifolds, and evaluate topological equivariance (Papamarkou *et al.*, 2024). Homotopy physics-informed neural networks (HomPINNs) are a topological formulation in which neural networks simultaneously approximate multiple valid solutions while maintaining differential equation constraints (Zheng *et al.*, 2024).

Categorical quantum is the application of category-theoretic methods to quantum technologies such as computing, sensing, and communication (Nonnenmann, 2021). Categorical quantum mechanics replaces the traditional Hilbert space formalism with dagger compact monoidal categories to provide a high-level, compositional approach for reasoning about quantum processes, entanglement, and information (Abramsky & Coecke, 2008). The related ZX-calculus is a universal string diagram graphical calculus for multi-qubit systems (Coecke & Duncan, 2011), modeling quantum states with phase-flip and bit-flip (ZX: Pauli Z and X matrices in XYZ spatial dimensions, where the Y matrix is inferred). Type formulations for quantum computing (Duncan, 2006) and categorical quantum circuits (Bergholm & Biamonte, 2011) add to the toolkit.

1.4 Motivation for Categorical Cryptoeconomics

There are many motivations for categorical cryptoeconomics:

- Formal computation-amenable framework
- Diagrammatic models of complex dynamical systems
- Set theory insufficient for groups and types (higher information)
- Duality view of syntax-semantics, scales, fields, and theories
- Topology-logic connection (same shapes, same logic) (HoTT)

Category theory is a unifying mathematical framework with wide use in functional programming, abstract algebra, topology, and economics, and it applies to cryptoeconomics in at least four ways. First, category theory is the language of computer science and functional programming and naturally implements blockchains as computational systems, including for quicker integration with other smartnetwork technologies such as deep learning and quantum, which already make use of category-theoretic formalisms. Second, category theory is the mathematics of complex dynamical systems, integrating scale tiers into a consolidated picture of distributed concurrency, scalability, aggregability, and renormalization.

Third, category theory provides a unifying framework by abstracting away irrelevant content-related detail to focus on the broader structure of relationships between entities. Various constituent bodies of mathematics (e.g., graph theory, set theory, and topos theory) can be viewed together in one larger picture. Fourth, category theory provides a mathematical framework at both the practical and theoretical levels, which is specifically suited to economics.

Practically, categorical formulations enable game-theoretic design and the analysis of macro-, meso-, and microeconomic systems at glocal (global and local) scales. Theoretically, categorical formulations facilitate the investigation of core economic topics such as inequity, exchange, behavior, and externalities, as well as how value is attributed to objects.

1.5 Category Theory and Cryptoeconomics

Categorical cryptoeconomics (the application of category-theoretic methods to blockchain design and analysis) arises in various areas such as consensus, ledger design, chain construction, mining, escrows, distributed ledger technologies (DLTs) in the architecture of directed acyclic graphs (DAGs), and interoperability (Table 1.3).

1.5.1 *Consensus*

Highlighting thematic connections between category theory, decentralized governance, and cryptoeconomic foundations, the first main application of categorical cryptoeconomics is consensus, particularly *topological consensus*, with three projects engaging sheaf theory and one employing semitopology. Consensus protocols are automated algorithmic processes by which decentralized network nodes reach agreement about a state change in the ledger. Consensus algorithms include Bitcoin's proof-of-work, Ethereum's proof-of-stake, Filecoin's proof-of-storage, and Arweave's proof-of-access in decentralized storage, along with energy-efficient validators used by Ripple and enterprise chains.

Lambert (2021) proposes topos-based consensus protocols, using Heyting algebras and copresheaf topoi. Copresheaf topoi are a category of copresheaves (covariant functors, or maps, between categories) forming a structured environment for studying non-classical logic, modal semantics, and decentralized systems. The concept of *estimate safety* in consensus protocols is introduced, with abstract correct-by-construction protocols serving as forcing statements in the internal logic of a given topos. Modal semantics is implemented with Heyting algebras (a logical version of Boolean algebras) in which a statement (e.g., a consensus state) and its negation cannot both be true (e.g., safe) simultaneously. The approach conceptualizes the

Table 1.3. Blockchain formal methods and category-theoretic interpretations.

	Blockchain Topic	Innovation	Categorical Methods	Reference
1	Consensus	Topos-based protocols	Copresheaf topoi, Heyting algebras	Lambert (2021)
2	Consensus	Proofchains as sheaves	Grothendieck topoi, sheaf theory	Murfet (2019)
3	Consensus	Poincaré protocol manifolds	Cohomology, type theory	Meldman–Floch (2018)
4	Consensus	Distributed collaborative action	Semitopology (point-set topology)	Gabbay (2024)
5	Ledger design	Blockchain algebras	Homomorphism, groups	Gabbay (2021)
6	Ledger design	Virtual asset histories	SMCs, proarrow equipment	Nester (2020)
7	Ledger design	Contract execution automata	Temporal logic, abstract QL	Bottoni *et al.* (2021)
8	Chain building	Monoidal equational theory	PROPs, DAG algebras	Fiore & Campos (2013)
9	Chain building	Blockchain axiomatization	First-order logic, formal logic	Goncharov & Nechesov (2023)
10	Mining networks	Blockchain group theory	Group theory/algebraic cosets	Zhao (2020)
11	Escrow	Profunctor escrows	Optics/comonoids/Tambara	Genovese *et al.* (2024)
12	Price movement	ChainNet: Bitcoin price dynamics	Persistent homology, Betti #s	Abay *et al.* (2019)
13	DLT DAGs	DAG power laws/fluid limits	Graph theory/fluid dynamics	Feng *et al.* (2023)
14	Interoperability	HoTT blockchains	Homotopy type theory	Swan *et al.* (2025)
15	Interoperability	Join-accumulate machine (JAM)	Power sets/set theory	Wood (2024)

modal nature of safety, adapting results from modal operators in topos theory to the logical structure of blockchain consensus.

Another project also uses sheaf theory in the general sense of a mathematical framework which systematically tracks local data across a topological space, ensuring consistency and coherence in global structures, with applications in algebraic geometry, topology, and logic. Murfet (2019) links blockchain consensus and Grothendieck topoi, modeling distributed ledgers as first-order logic systems. Proofchains are defined as a globally coherent history of transformations within a distributed logical model, analogous to blockchains, where consensus is maintained through proof-of-work to instantiate an emergent logical order.

Sheaf theory is also the basis for a blockchain cohomology project using algebraic topology for scalable verification in consensus protocols (Meldman-Floch, 2018). The concept of *blockchain sheaves* is introduced to model the distribution of data across the blockchain network. From the data level of blockchain sheaves, *protocol topologies* can be defined on blockchain sheaves to govern the interactions of data (transactions) and further abstracted to *protocol manifolds* (in the form of Poincaré consensus protocol manifolds) for computability. Homology (associating the holes and connectivity of topological spaces with algebraic objects called homology groups) is used to show that the topological framework can be implemented within a type system for computable execution.

A fourth topological consensus project is based on semitopology, mobilizing the opportunity afforded by digital consensus to extend beyond economic transactions to decentralized social decision-making (Gabbay, 2024). A semitopology is a more relaxed yet formal version of a topology (a point-set topology without the requirement that intersections of open sets must also be open). The semitopology is a formal method for actionable coalitions to evolve dynamically without strict topological constraints. Actionable coalitions (groups of participants in the distributed system) collaborate to update local states toward global action-taking.

1.5.2 *Ledger design*

A second area of categorical cryptoeconomic application is ledger design. A blockchain algebra project provides a framework for modeling unspent transaction output (UTxO) blockchains using monoids, groups, and homomorphisms (Gabbay, 2021). The basic ledger architectures are UTxO models, used by cryptocurrency blockchains (Bitcoin), and account-based state machines, used by smart contract platforms (Ethereum). In UTxO blockchains, subsequent transactions are composed of the available balances (outputs) of previous transactions. The blockchain algebras project condenses the theory of UTxO blockchains to a compact set of four type equations, called idealized extended UTxO (EUTxO). The four type equations (input, output, transaction, and validator (code-script checks of data–key pairs)) are represented algebraically as an abstract chunk system (chunks are blockchain segments which have a monoidal structure). The concrete type equations and abstract algebra are formalized as categories, with weakly equivalent (adjoint) functors mapping between them in each direction. From this generalization, systems such as EUTxO arise naturally as a loop of embeddings which cycle between the concrete type equations and the abstract algebras. The result is that the blockchain algebras provide an account of the essential mathematical structures underlying blockchain technology such as Bitcoin and also accommodate higher-information ledger architectures in which outputs have additional data and logic (e.g., Cardano).

A second ledger design project employs diagrammatic reasoning and compositional resource convertibility, using symmetric monoidal categories to model blockchain ownership dynamics with *virtual asset histories* (Nester, 2020). Augmented string diagrams ensure rigor, while concurrency is captured through resource transduction formalized by proarrow equipment (an advanced categorical structure) (Nester, 2023).

The diverse flexibility of smart contracts compared to cryptocurrencies entails greater vulnerability and a much larger security surface. Formal methods such as *toolchains* (Ibba *et al.*, 2024) are needed to evaluate contract well-formedness at both the levels of technical algorithms and economic incentives (Sorensen, 2024). One approach uses formal temporal logic to model contracts as finite-state automata to define resource allocation and legal obligations (Bottoni *et al.*, 2021). Temporal logic underpins a *blockchain query language* to track contract execution, distinguishing between legal automata (formal obligations) and execution automata (action-fulfilling terms) in event-driven state transitions.

1.5.3 *Chain construction and mining networks*

Three projects explore categorical methods in the cryptoeconomic context of blockchain construction and mining network structure. The first uses product and permutation algebras (PROPs) to formalize DAG-based DLT operations (Fiore & Campos, 2013). The second axiomatizes the "select longest chain" method used by cryptocurrency chains to converge on one account of reality with first-order logic (Goncharov & Nechesov, 2023). The third proposes *blockchain group theory* to model mining nodes as symmetric groups to better analyze their algebraic properties (Zhao, 2020).

1.5.4 *Escrows and price dynamics*

Categorical cryptoeconomics is also seen in blockchain projects using optics and lenses as two-way data accessors for bidirectional updates, formalizing cryptographic escrows (Genovese *et al.*, 2024). Defined on monoids and comonoids, the optics model secures information and value flow, with monoids aggregating transactions and comonoids splitting funds for distribution. Specific morphisms (Lock, Unlock, and Envelope) operate escrows in a Tambara module (profunctors extended with monoidal action), enhancing Bitcoin's scripting language (e.g., Hash Time-Locked Contracts) for conditional payments in the Lightning Network.

A cryptocurrency price forecasting project used persistent homology (feature persistence across scales) to build a neural network model called ChainNet (Abay *et al.*, 2019). The topological features of Bitcoin transaction networks were analyzed to predict price dynamics. First, graph filtration was applied to Bitcoin prices to create data for model training, and then Betti sequences were used to identify persistent relevant features. The result was a 40% improvement in the one-week price forecasts.

1.5.5 *Categorical DePIN*

Categorical cryptoeconomics likewise extends to decentralized physical infrastructure network (DePIN) projects such as smart cities and digital twins. One such effort is Internet of Things application (IoTA), an energy-efficient DLT relying on users for the mining function, as submitting a transaction first requires validating two other randomly assigned transactions. Rather than the centralized method of "select longest chain" typically used by cryptocurrency blockchains, IoTA is highly decentralized. The chain grows in multiple simultaneous locations, as multiple messages can be attached by different processing nodes in parallel. The ledger tangle growth architecture provides an interesting mathematical problem, which researchers model as a DAG expanding in multiple directions with newly arriving blocks as vertices. One analysis found that Tangle growth followed a double Pareto lognormal distribution, which is atypical compared to traditional network growth models such as power-law and exponential distributions (Guo *et al.*, 2022). Another project based on fluid dynamics (the Tangle behaves like a fluid with multiple parallel confirmations propagating through the network) applied martingale theory and probabilistic inequalities to establish bounds on the expected values and fluctuations (Feng *et al.*, 2023). Given the mathematical complexity of DLT DAGs, categorical formulations are implicated, for example, PROP algebras for DAG input-output operations (Fiore & Campos, 2013).

1.5.6 *HoTT blockchains: Verification and interoperability*

Category theory plays a fundamental role in functional programming, particularly in HoTT, in which types are conceptualized as spaces and logical reasoning is applied to their structure. HoTT is made possible by the discovery that identical shapes share the same formal logic, allowing them to be treated as computational equivalents (Awodey, 2010). In categorical cryptoeconomics, the idea of *HoTT blockchains* is introduced as the categorical instantiation of blockchains as same-shape logic elements for classical and quantum computing, well-formedness, formal verification, and interoperability (Swan *et al.*, 2025). Formal verification is enabled by a finding linking computability to topos theory in the context of oracles, interpreting Lawvere–Tierney topologies as higher "modes" of truth (Kihara, 2024). Interoperability is enabled by interpreting types as spaces, tokens as points, and paths as relationships for interoperable protocols and cross-chain transfers. HoTT's focus on constructive logic and proof relevance supports transparency, while its modeling of higher-dimensional relationships aids in analyzing tokenized incentives and modular governance, offering a comprehensive approach to blockchain design. HoTT blockchains are a natural extension to existing set-theoretic approaches to formalization and interoperability. For example, one such next-generation virtual machine project, the join-accumulate machine (JAM) protocol, uses power sets to join transactions from multiple chains into the overall accumulated ledger state (Wood, 2024).

1.6 Category Theory and Finance

Driven by competition and cost, the finance industry is an early adopter of new technologies and mathematical modeling techniques. The main trends in the finance industry are digitization, risk management, and quantum readiness, all in the face of growing trading activity. Quantum finance refers to both quantum-safe cryptography and the application of quantum methods to the traditional slate of financial analysis problems: option pricing, portfolio optimization, capital structure allocation, and risk assessment. Modern methods provide a higher-resolution approach to complex, interconnected markets requiring dynamic, real-time response. Formalization techniques often draw from mathematical physics and have either direct or implicit category-theoretic formulations (Table 1.4).

1.6.1 *JPMorgan case study: Blockchain, AI, and quantum*

In the digital network setting of secure value transmission, banking and finance companies increasingly resemble technology companies. JPMorgan Chase's Global Technology Applied Research group,

Table 1.4. Finance and category-theoretic interpretations.

	Finance Topic	Innovation	Categorical Methods	Reference
1	Quantum key distribution	AES-256-GCM demonstration	Galois field/Counter Mode	Alia *et al.* (2024)
2	Quantum RNG	Quadrature phase shift keying	Quantum oscillation	Zhang *et al.* (2024)
3	Relativistic ZKPs	Multi-prover quantum rewinding	SMC: provers-verifier	Shi *et al.* (2024)
4	Quantum option pricing	QML portfolio optimization	Vect: linear algebra	Cherrat *et al.* (2023)
5	Quantum option pricing	Blockchain algebras	Brownian motion	Prakash *et al.* (2024)
6	Quantum algorithms	Super-quadratic search	Super-Grover extension	Chakrabarti *et al.* (2025)
7	Options (Bermudan)	CGMY heavy-tailed distribution	Stochastic process model	Carr *et al.* (2002)
8	Options (Barrier)	Ornstein–Uhlenbeck credit model	Brownian motion	Carr & Itkin (2020)
9	Options (Barrier)	Martingale (fair game) monoids	Martingale monoids	Carr & Costa (2023)
10	Convertible bonds	Additive processes	Magma, monoid	Carr & Torricelli (2021)
11	Option pricing/risk	Decentralized linear pricing	Monad, coproduct	Wu & Zhang (2025)
12	Arbitrage trading	Invariant spacetime curvature	Lattice gauge theory	Young (1999)
13	Arbitrage trading	Security gauge transformations	Geometric lattice QED	Ilinski (1997)
14	Credit default	Default as conserved quantity	Risk chain complexes	Tanega (2014)
15	Term structure	Nonlinear interest rate forecasting	Lie group $SO(3)$	Bildirici *et al.* (2022)

for example, had 35 journal publications and 15 patent filings in 2024 across the smartnetwork stack of blockchain, AI, and quantum. In the marquee area of quantum-safe cryptography, a quantum key distribution (QKD) pilot was implemented with the quantum-resistant AES-256-GCM (Galois/Counter Mode) cipher suite in 45 days of continuous operation between two data centers (Alia *et al.*, 2024). Quantum cryptography uses group-theoretic methods such as Galois fields instead of number-theoretic methods (which rely on the difficulty of factoring large numbers) as in classical cryptography. A quantum random number generator (QRNG) photonic chip was developed based on quantum homodyne detection (an oscillation-based technique for measuring the quantum state of light), encoding random coherent states with phase shifts (Zhang *et al.*, 2024).

In the core technology of ZK proofs, relativistic ZK quantum proofs were extended with a multi-prover quantum rewinding and knowledge error quantification system (Shi *et al.*, 2024). Relativistic ZK proofs are a quantum-proof technology that enhances security because the prover and verifier are physically separated and cannot communicate faster than the speed of light. The interaction between multiple provers and the verifier can be modeled using monoidal categories, in which tensor products are used to represent the various combinations of independent quantum systems.

In quantum machine learning, a quantum deep hedging project used reinforcement learning networks (policy-search and distributional actor-critic algorithms) to train quantum neural networks on a trapped-ion quantum processor (using circuits with up to 1,616 qubits) (Cherrat *et al.*, 2023). Other quantum machine learning demonstrations include privacy-preserving quantum federated learning via gradient hiding, the use of variational quantum circuits to enhance model privacy, and circuit testing with the quantum approximate optimization algorithm. In combinatorial optimization, a quantum algorithm was developed to deliver super-quadratic speedups over Markov chain search, extending other work in super-Grover (faster than quadratic) speedups (Chakrabarti *et al.*, 2025). A quantum option pricing model was proposed using the Karhunen–Loève expansion (a method beyond principal components analysis that represents a stochastic process as an infinite linear combination of orthogonal basis functions) in which the underlying assets were modeled with geometric Brownian motion (Prakash *et al.*, 2024).

1.6.2 *Option pricing*

Increasing complexity in derivative markets implicates categorical methods and greater sophistication in the analysis models used for pricing, risk management, and hedging. Modeling instrument expiration is much more difficult. The two basic option expiry methods—European exercise (only at expiry) and American exercise (anytime)—have been extended with other more complicated schemes, such as Bermudan (exercise at a discretely spaced number of times) and Canary (quarterly exercise after a one-year cliff) expiries. Also, there are novel instruments such as stoptions (price changes in the underlying security are stored cumulatively until stopped for payout) and barrier options (threshold-based instruments).

Black–Scholes–Merton is the starting point as the basic model for option pricing but is limited because it has ideal assumptions (e.g., risk-free trading and non-stochastic interest rates) which do not hold in real life. Modern financial analysis offers alternatives that address discontinuous time and nonlinear volatility. One of the first departures from Black–Scholes–Merton is trinomial trees, which provide a more sophisticated method for modeling price changes over time using a discrete-time, lattice-based approach (Hull, 1989). The CGMY model, developed by Carr *et al.* (2002), takes a stochastic process perspective to accommodate jumps in asset prices, heavy-tailed distributions, and extreme volatility (black swan) events. For specialized cases such as barrier options, Carr and Itkin (2020) integrate bounded Brownian motion with a time-dependent Ornstein–Uhlenbeck process to model dynamic factors such as interest rates and credit risk.

A related project models optionality as a binary operation, in that the owner of a financial contract is buying a "process" to switch between two different asset states depending on market conditions (e.g., choosing between a bond and shares in a convertible bond) (Carr & Costa, 2023). Set theory is applied as the binary operation combines two elements from a set to produce a third "process" element in the same set. The binary operation represents how financial contracts relate the values of two assets to derive a contract's value in option pricing. Category-theoretic methods are then imposed via an algebraic structure called a unital magma (a set with a binary operation and an identity element) and monoids (a unital magma that is also associative) to model counterparty default risk. A pseudo-sum is introduced to represent the payoff structure of the binary option, formalizing how the two values are combined in pricing.

Category-theoretic algebraic frameworks also provide more efficient additive processes than traditional Bachelier and Samuelson–Black–Scholes–Merton models (Carr & Torricelli, 2021). Independent processes (fair game "martingales") are modeled with probability monoids and functors. Monoids and magmas can be used to formalize the addition of increments and the composition of processes, and functors can be used to relate different probabilistic models and distributions. Another project introduces a decentralized linear pricing model to assess risks independently (e.g., currency risk, volatility risk, interest rate risk, and industry sector-specific risks), allowing for better alignment of option pricing and risk management countermeasures (Wu & Zhang, 2025).

1.6.3 *Arbitrage trading and higher gauge theory*

Gauge theory and homotopy are suggested for arbitrage mathematics due to the notion of invariance. In this strategy, the market is seen as a field in which certain things change (price, volume, and momentum) but others do not (the underlying value of a security). Arbitrage involves identifying the "true value" of mispriced securities, taking a position, and waiting for the market to converge. One approach uses a lattice gauge theory to provide a discretized spacetime grid structure from which to more readily identify arbitrage opportunities (Young, 1999). Another defines a QFT approach for modeling the debt and equity of a firm as a particle system with positive and negative charges (cash inflows and debt outflows) (Ilinski, 1997). Categorical formulations in arbitrage trading could engage higher-gauge theory and TQFT in quantum finance, particularly topological invariants, to identify unchanging quantities under continuous deformation of the market space. The key primitive is mathematical structures of invariance. Other work in this direction could investigate arbitrage models based on Chern–Simons theory as a 3D TQFT, in which observables are topological invariants of spacetime (Mertens & Wu, 2025), or Khovanov homology, a 4D TQFT categorification of the Jones polynomial (Schmidhuber *et al.*, 2025).

1.6.4 *Categorical credit and default invariance*

The focus on topological invariants as a categorical cryptoeconomic primitive continues in the domain of credit availability and default. The concept of *default invariance* is proposed as a (persistent homological) conserved quantity across economic macro and micro scales, as empirically observed in derivatives, banking, and credit markets (Tanega, 2014). The related formulation of *risk homological chain complexes* encapsulates the structure of objects as classes of financial agreements, morphisms as market behavior, and functors as regulatory activity. Categorical methods are also applied to credit risk and default in term structure forecasting, a problem involving nonlinear movement in interest rates, bond prices, and yield curves (Bildirici *et al.*, 2022). The Lie algebra, particularly the Lie group $SO(3)$, is well-suited to the task.

1.7 Category Theory and Accounting

In 1894, Cayley (known for graph coloring theory) argued that double-entry bookkeeping (DEB), which arose in the 1400s, is in line with Euclid's ratios (Cayley, 1894). In the contemporary setting, DEB is seen as a solution to the problem of concurrency in distributed systems (Katis *et al.*, 2008). A categorical approach to double-entry ledgers uses Span(RGraph), a compact closed symmetric-monoidal bicategory of spans of reflexive graphs, to model concurrency and directional flows. Span(RGraph) is the category of spans of reflexive graphs (graphs may be closed under reflexive, symmetric, or transitive properties). The method formalizes economic interactions via categories (objects and relations) and two-cells (morphisms between relations) to enable state updating in concurrent processes (Table 1.5). Another project provides an algebraic proof system for accounting with categorical techniques involving abstract algebra (monoids, digraphs, automata, and quotient structures) (Rambaud *et al.*, 2010).

The advent of quantum accounting (accounting instantiated in quantum computational systems) raises questions about the undecidability of future events. One idea is to model uncertainty with

Table 1.5. Accounting and category-theoretic interpretations.

	Accounting Topic	Innovation	Categorical Formulation	Reference
1	DEB ledgers	Span(RGraph) directional value	Symmetric-monoidal bicategory	Katis *et al.* (2008)
2	DEB ledgers	Proof-based DEB system	Abs algebra/ monoids/digraphs	Rambaud *et al.* (2010)
3	Q Info Actg	Topological states of actg info	TQFT Fibonacci anyon	Demski *et al.* (2009)
4	Q Cost Actg	WIP as superposition	Time-ind. Schrödinger equation	Lazirko (2024)

Diophantine formalisms (integer-coefficient polynomial equations) and quantum information theory (Demski *et al.*, 2009). To reduce internal controls errors, the project elaborates a quantum accounting system using TQFT and Fibonacci anyons, storing information in decoherence-resistant qubits. Using Fibonacci anyons means that the number of quantum states grows in a manageable way according to the Fibonacci sequence.

Also foreseeing the host of issues arising in quantum accounting, another project suggests using the time-independent Schrödinger equation for uncertainty modeling to identify a system's stable states unaffected by the noise of temporal fluctuations (Lazirko, 2024). In quantum cost accounting, work in progress (WIP) is conceptualized as materials in a quantum superposition state whose financial value remains uncertain until measured. To the extent that accounting is instantiated in quantum systems, ZP proofs might serve as a form of continuous audit.

1.8 Category Theory and Economics

Category theory has long been used in economics to model game-theoretic behavior, multiscalarity, information asymmetry, and trust (Table 1.6).

Categorical approaches to game theory include compositional open games and Nash equilibrium models. In open games (games played in an open environment), complex games are built up from

Table 1.6. Economics and category-theoretic interpretations.

	Economic Topic	Innovation	Categorical Formulation	Reference
1	Game theory	Open games	SMCs, lenses, coutility	Ghani *et al.* (2018)
2	Multi-agent systems	Multigraph preference-access	Nash equilibrium	Tohmé & Viglizzo (2023)
3	Decision theory	Uncertainty structures	Top, Metr, Diff	Pivato (2024)
4	Decision theory	Small->large menu preferences	Presheaves (glocal)	Tohmé *et al.* (2017)
5	Intentional agents	Problem-solution interfaces	Sheaves, Hom set	Tohmé & Fioriti (2024)
6	Intentional agents	Agentic commons co-governance	Topographical states	Potts (2025)
7	Multiagent equilibria	Random preference functions	Weak topology, Borel	Hildenbrand (1971)
8	Multiagent interaction	Random exchange economy	Lattice graph topology	Hohnisch (2003)
9	Confidence relations	Multiply-connected topologies	Cliques, manifolds	Chang (2007)

simpler ones, modeling simultaneous and sequential moves as morphisms in symmetric monoidal categories (SMCs) (Ghani *et al.*, 2018). The SMCs are modeled as a family of lenses (bidirectional data accessors) indexed by a set of strategy profiles to identify optimal strategic responses. The concept of *coutility* is used to denote the utility generated by an open game and returned to the environment. Further work has generalized the model to Bayesian open games, which is a more expressive version (Bolt *et al.*, 2023). In the second approach to categorical game theory, Nash equilibrium models, game play and outcomes are analyzed at a higher categorical abstraction of a categorical multigraph (Tohmé & Viglizzo, 2023). The model defines two categories (Gam (Game) and NE (Nash equilibrium)) and the functor relations between them: preference functions and accessibility functions. Vertices are game outcomes, and edges are player preferences and actions.

In categorical decision-making, one approach models uncertainty using categories such as Top (topological spaces), Metr (metric spaces), and Diff (differentiable manifolds) (Pivato, 2024). A sheaf-theoretic method integrates local data into global preferences (Tohmé *et al.*, 2017), later extended with operads and hypergraph categories to preserve equilibria in interactive problems (Tohmé & Fioriti, 2024). For intentional agents, polynomial functors are used to define a category of objects as problem–solution interfaces and morphisms as coalgebras based on internal Homs (all morphisms) of the interfaces. In other first-principles intentional agent work, *agentic commons* are proposed as a computational co-governance method integrating human and machine agencies (Potts, 2025). The evolutionary economics approach draws on the geometry of economic space in relational networks of adaptive agent behavior using topographical state change and entropy (Potts, 2000).

In multiagent collaboration, *topological economics* is a method used to model exchange economies as probability functions on topological manifolds. Hildenbrand (1971) introduces random preferences as probabilistic elements to address deterministic choice limits, linking demand functions to pure exchange economies with topological well-formedness conditions. The work is extended in ergodic random exchange economies, modeling agent interaction convergence with graph topologies (Hohnisch, 2003). Another extension employs the topological structure of preferences and endowments to study aggregate behavior, modeling confidence functions as topological manifolds with holes to represent dynamic and stochastic economic influences (Chang, 2007).

1.9 Risks and Limitations

There are many risks to the idea of categorical cryptoeconomics proposed in this work. Category theory is a complex and esoteric method, further compounding the already challenging nature of blockchains. Also, despite the clear conceptual benefits of categorical formalisms as umbrella frameworks, they may fall short in actual application. Additional crypto winter boom–bust cycles may be expected as the technology continues to mature, and category-theoretic formulations may not fit with industry developments. Categorical cryptoeconomic mechanisms could lead to more trustworthy systems, but the opposite is also likely, as early-adopter bad actors co-opt technologies for personal gain. Success may not depend on theoretical formalisms but rather on practical deployments such as decentralized identity (DID) to realize blockchain ecosystems. However, the overall impact of categorical cryptoeconomics could be a new era of verifiable computing.

1.10 Discussion: Categorical Smartnetwork Field Theory

Continuing the abstraction trajectory, *categorical smartnetwork field theory* is introduced as the higher-order generalization of categorical technology approaches (in cryptoeconomics, deep learning, quantum, and robotics) joined with both categorical field theory approaches (Table 1.7) and smartnetwork field theory approaches (Halverson *et al.*, 2024; Swan *et al.*, 2020–2022). Blockchain–AI integration is discussed in the Introduction, and quantum blockchain applications, as described in Swan *et al.* (2022), are currently growing as quantum computers scale to 50, 100, and 1000 logical qubits, for example, using quantum proof-of-work to generate and validate hashes (Amin *et al.*, 2025).

The aim of field theories is to approximate physical systems. There are many kinds of field theories: classical, conformal, effective, gauge, Galois, and quantum, and within quantum, there are topological, algebraic, and functorial QFTs. Notable advances in categorical field

Table 1.7. Categorical field theories: foundational formulations.

	Topic	Innovation Description	Reference
1	Tensor categories	Tensor category form of Hopf & Frobenius algebras	Schweigert & Fuchs (2010)
2	Tensor categories	Spaces of modular tensor categories for TQFT	Etingof *et al.* (2017)
3	Cobordism	Invertible field theory and manifold cobordism	Freed (2019)
4	3D QFTs	Physical realization of TQFTs in quantum computing	Creutzig *et al.* (2021)
5	Topology	Supergeometric homotopy theory in a Lagrangian FT	Giotopoulos (2025)
6	Categorical	Quantum gravity computational model (AQFT and FQFT)	Gorard (2024)

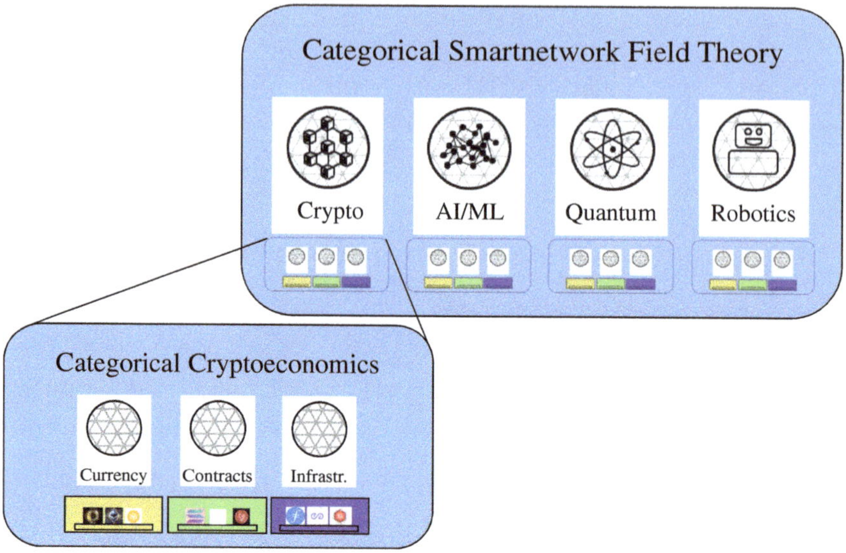

Fig. 1.3. Categorical smartnetwork field theory.

theory with broad applicability include spaces of tensor categories (Etingof *et al.*, 2017) (preceded by the tensor category formulation of Hopf and Frobenius algebras (Schweigert & Fuchs, 2010)), cobordism (invertible field theory and manifold cobordism) (Freed, 2019), 3D QFTs for quantum computing (Creutzig *et al.*, 2021), supergeometric homotopy theory (topology for geometry) in Lagrangian field theory (Giotopoulos, 2025), and categorical quantum gravity linking algebraic and functorial QFTs (Gorard, 2024).

Categorical smartnetwork field theory is conceived as a cross-platform formalism for the further mathematical integration of smartnetwork technologies (Figure 1.3).

1.11 Conclusion

Digital trust is the overarching theme linking smartnetwork technologies (blockchain, AI, and quantum) and value transfer technologies (finance, accounting, and economics). Formalization serves as the lever for the realization of verifiable computing, particularly with the

Table 1.8. Transformational economic transitions.

	1700–1900	1850–1950	1950–2100
Impetus	Agrarian reform	Industrial Revolution	Digitization/AI transition
Era	Feudalism	Commercial society	Cryptoeconomics
Domain	Local	Global	Virtual

metamathematical approach of category theory, as seen in categorical cryptoeconomics, deep learning, and quantum. *Categorical cryptoeconomics* is introduced to name the growing activity of applying category-theoretic methods to the design of digital economies. *HoTT blockchains* are envisioned as the homotopy type theory instantiation of blockchains for formal verification and interoperability. Whereas the 1900s marked the century of geometry (with Riemannian geometry and general relativity), the 2000s may be the century of topology (with Grothendieck topoi and HoTT, Acworth, 2024).

1.11.1 *Cryptoeconomic aesthetic theory*

On the qualitative side, *cryptoeconomic aesthetic theory* is introduced as the aspirational aesthetic layer of the formalization machinery of categorical cryptoeconomics and categorical smartnetwork field theory. Aesthetics means choosing in line with values. The theory points to blockchains, and economic systems generally, as tools which enable the realization of agentic beings. The Adam Smithian picture is one of full-stack agents engaged in staged development, with economic principles facilitating the exchange of goods, moral esteem, and ideas (Norman, 2018). The integration of smartnetwork technologies entails new modes of subjectivation as we continue to transition through the eras of agrarian reform, industrialization, and digitization (Table 1.8).

References

Abay, N. C., Akcora, C. G., Gel, Y. R. *et al.* 2019. "ChainNet: Learning on Blockchain Graphs Topological Features." In *2019 IEEE International Conference on Data Mining (ICDM)*. IEEE. https://ieeexplore.ieee.org/document/8970724.

Abramsky, S. and Coecke, B. 2008. "Categorical Quantum Mechanics." arXiv:0808.1023v1.

Acworth, W. 2024. "US options industry leaders wrestle with constraints on growth." FIA Market Voice. https://www.fia.org/marketvoice/articles/us-options-industry-leaders-wrestle-constraints-growth.

Alia, O., Huang, A., Luo, H. *et al.* 2024. "100 Gbps Quantum-safe IPsec VPN Tunnels over 46 km Deployed Fiber." arXiv:2405.04415.

Amin, M. H., Raymond, J., Kinn, D. *et al.* 2025. "Blockchain with proof of quantum work." arXiv:2503.14462.

Awodey, S. 2010. "Type theory and homotopy." arXiv:1010.1810.

Baez, J. 2023. "Applied Category Theory." https://math.ucr.edu/home/baez/ACT/.

Barrett, T. W., Manchak, J. B., and Weatherall, J. O. 2023. "On automorphism criteria for comparing amounts of mathematical structure." *Synthese* 201: 191. https://doi.org/10.1007/s11229-023-04186-3.

Basu, S. and Isik, U. 2020. "Categorical complexity." *Forum of Mathematics, Sigma* 8(e34): 1–63. https://doi.org/10.1017/fms.2020.26.

Bergholm, V. and Biamonte, J. D. 2011. "Categorical Quantum Circuits." arXiv:1010.4840v2.

Bildirici, M., Ucan, Y., and Lousada, S. 2022. "Interest rate based on the Lie group SO(3) in the evidence of chaos." *Mathematics* 10: 3998. https://doi.org/10.3390/math10213998.

Bolt, J., Hedges, J., and Zahn, P. 2023. "Bayesian open games." *Compositionality* 5(9): 1–46. https://doi.org/10.32408/compositionality-5-9.

Bottoni, P., Labella, A., and Pareschi, R. 2021. "A formal model for ledger management systems based on contracts and temporal logic." arXiv:2109.15212v1.

Carr, P. and Costa, D. 2023. "Optionality as a binary operation." *Frontiers of Mathematical Finance* 2(3): 313–39. https://doi.org/10.3934/fmf.2023015.

Carr, P., Geman, H., Madan, D., and Yor, M. 2002. "The fine structure of asset returns: An empirical investigation." *Journal of Business* 75(2): 305–32.

Carr, P. and Itkin, A. 2020. "Semi-closed form solutions for barrier and American options written on a time-dependent Ornstein-Uhlenbeck process." arXiv:2003.08853v2.

Carr, P. and Torricelli, L. 2021. "Additive logistic processes in option pricing." *Finance and Stochastics* 25: 789–834. https://doi.org/10.1007/s00780-021-00461-8.

Cayley, A. 1894. *The Principles of Book-keeping by Double Entry*. Cambridge: Cambridge University Press.

Chang, Y.-F. 2007. "Multiply connected topological economics, confidence relation and political economy." arXiv:0711.0235.

Chakrabarti, S., Herman, D., Ozgul, G. *et al.* 2025. "Generalized short path algorithms: Towards super-quadratic speedup over Markov chain search for combinatorial optimization." arXiv:2410.23270v2.

Cherrat, E. A., Raj, S., Kerenidis, I. *et al.* 2023. "Quantum deep hedging." *Quantum* 7: 1191. https://doi.org/10.22331/q-2023-11-29-1191.

Coecke, B. and Duncan, R. 2011. "Interacting quantum observables: Categorical algebra and diagrammatics." *New Journal of Physics* 13: 043016. https://doi.org/10.1088/1367-2630/13/4/043016.

Creutzig, T., Dimofte, T., Garner, N., and Geer, N. 2021. "A QFT for non-semisimple TQFT." *Advances in Theoretical and Mathematical Physics* 28(1): 161–405. https://doi.org/10.4310/ATMP.2024.v28.n1.a4.

Demski, J. S., FitzGerald, S. A., Ijiri, Y. *et al.* 2009. "Quantum information and accounting information: Exploring conceptual applications of topology." *Journal of Accounting and Public Policy* 28: 133–47. https://doi.org/10.1016/j.jaccpubpol.2009.01.002.

Duncan, R. 2006. *Types for Quantum Computation.* Doctoral dissertation, Oxford University.

Eilenberg, S. and MacLane, S. 1945. "General theory of natural equivalences." *Transactions of the American Mathematical Society* 58(2): 231–94. https://www.jstor.org/stable/1990284.

Etingof, P., Gelaki, S., Nikshych, D., and Ostrik, V. 2017. *Tensor Categories.* Providence, RI: American Mathematical Society.

Feng, J., King, C., and Duffy, K. R. 2023. "Almost sure one-endedness of a random graph model of distributed ledgers." arXiv:2309.07774v2.

Fiore, M. and Campos, M. D. 2013. "The algebra of directed acyclic graphs." arXiv:1303.0376v1.

Freed, D. S. 2019. *Lectures on Field Theory and Topology.* Providence, RI: American Mathematical Society.

Gabbay, M. J. 2021. "Algebras of UTxO blockchains." *Mathematical Structures in Computer Science* 31: 1034–89. https://doi.org/10.1017/S0960129521000438.

Gabbay, M. J. 2024. *Semitopology: Decentralised Collaborative Action via Topology, Algebra, and Logic.* London, UK: College Publications.

Genovese, F., Loregian, F., and Palombi, D. 2024. "Escrows are optics." arXiv:2105.10028v3.

Gensler, G. 2024. "Statement on the Approval of Spot Bitcoin Exchange-Traded Products." U.S. Securities and Exchange Commission, January 10, 2024. https://www.sec.gov/newsroom/speeches-statements/gensler-statement-spot-bitcoin-011023.

Ghani, N., Hedges, J., Winschel, V., and Zahn, P. 2018. "Compositional Game Theory." arXiv:1603.04641.

Giotopoulos, G. 2025. "Sheaf Topos Theory: A powerful setting for Lagrangian Field Theory." arXiv:2504.08095v1.

Goncharov, S. and Nechesov, A. 2023. "Axiomatization of blockchain theory." *Mathematics* 11: 2966. https://doi.org/10.3390/math11132966.

Gorard, J. 2024. "Applied Category Theory in Wolfram Language using Categorica I: Diagrams, Functors and Fibrations." arXiv:2403.16269v1.

Guo, F., Xiao, X., Hecker, A., and Dustdar, S. 2022. "Modeling Ledger Dynamics in IOTA Blockchain." In *2022 IEEE International Conference on Blockchain and Cryptocurrency (ICBC)*. IEEE. https://ieeexplore.ieee.org/document/10000609.

Halverson, J., Maiti, A., and Stoner, K. 2021. "Neural networks and quantum field theory." *Machine Learning: Science and Technology* 2: 035002. https://doi.org/10.1088/2632-2153/abeca3.

Hildenbrand, W. 1971. "On random preferences and equilibrium analysis." *Journal of Economic Theory* 3: 414–429.

Hohnisch, M. 2003. "Hildenbrand distribution economies as limiting empirical distribution economies." Bonn Economics Discussion Paper No. 28/2003. https://ideas.repec.org/p/zbw/bonedp/282003.html.

Hull, J. C. 1989. *Options, Futures, and Other Derivatives.* New York: Prentice Hall.

Ibba, G., Aufiero, S., Bartolucci, S. *et al.* 2024. "MindTheDApp: A toolchain for complex network-driven structural analysis of ethereum-based decentralised applications." *IEEE Access* 12: 28382–28394. https://doi.org/10.1109/ACCESS.2024.3366069.

Ilinski, K. 1997. "Physics of Finance." arXiv:9710148v1.

Katis, P., Sabadini, N., and Walters, R. F. C. 2008. "On partita doppia." arXiv:0803.2429.

Kihara, T. 2024. "Rethinking the notion of oracle: A prequel to Lawvere-Tierney topologies for computability theorists." arXiv:2202.00188v4.

Lambert, M. 2021. "A topos view of blockchain consensus protocols." arXiv:2111.07461v1.

Landry, E. and Marquis, J. P. 2005. "Categories in context: Historical, foundational, and philosophical." *Philosophia Mathematica* 13(1): 1–43.

Lazirko, M. 2024. "The quantum dynamics of cost accounting: Investigating WIP via the Time-independent Schrödinger Equation." arXiv:2405.00047v1.

Meldman-Floch, W. 2018. "Blockchain Cohomology." arXiv:1805.07047.

Mertens, T. G. and Wu, Q.-F. 2025. "Minimal factorization of Chern-Simons theory: Gravitational anyonic edge modes." arXiv:2505.00501.

Murfet, D. 2019. "Distributed consensus for models of logic." http://www.therisingsea.org/notes/cryptotopoi.pdf.

Nester, C. 2020. "A foundation for ledger structures." In *2nd International Conference on Blockchain Economics, Security and Protocols (Tokenomics 2020)*. https://doi.org/10.4230/OASIcs.Tokenomics.2020.7.

Nester, C. 2023. "Concurrent process histories and resource transducers." *Logical Methods in Computer Science* 19(1): 7:1–7:22. https://doi.org/10.46298/lmcs-19(1:7)2023.

Nonnenmann, P. 2021. "Categorical quantum theory." In Liermann, V. and Stegmann, C. (eds.), *The Digital Journey of Banking and Insurance, Volume II*. Cham: Palgrave Macmillan. https://doi.org/10.1007/978-3-030-78829-2_13.

Norman, J. 2018. *Adam Smith: Father of Economics*. New York: Basic Books.

Papamarkou, T., Birdal, T., Bronstein, M. *et al.* 2024. "Position: Topological deep learning is the new frontier for relational learning." arXiv:2402.08871v3.

Patterson, E. 2020. "The algebra and machine representation of statistical models." arXiv:2006.08945.

Pivato, M. 2024. "Categorical decision theory and global subjective expected utility representations." SSRN Working Paper. https://doi.org/10.2139/ssrn.5039921.

Potts, J. 2000. *The New Evolutionary Microeconomics: Complexity, Competence, and Adaptive Behaviour*. Cheltenham, UK: Edward Elgar Publishing Limited.

Potts, J. 2025. "Governing hyperobjects – new economics of AI regulation." In Stocker, V., Schrepel, T., and Kuenzler, A. (eds.), *Network Law Review* (special symposium issue). Conference paper presented at The Law, Technology, and Economics of AI Regulation conference, Hong Kong, May 22–23, 2025.

Prakash, A., Sun, Y., Chakrabarti, S. *et al.* 2024. "Quantum option pricing via the Karhunen-Loève expansion." arXiv:2402.10132.

Rambaud, S. C., Perez, J. G., Nehmer, R. A., and Robinson, D. J. S. 2010. *Algebraic Models for Accounting Systems*. London: World Scientific. https://doi.org/10.1142/7445.

Reiff, N. 2024. "How much of all money is in bitcoin?" *Investopedia*, April 10, 2024. https://www.investopedia.com/tech/how-much-worlds-money-bitcoin/.

Roberts, B. 2024. "Where are the growth opportunities in derivatives?" ION Group Blog, October 18, 2024. https://iongroup.com/blog/markets/where-are-the-growth-opportunities-in-derivatives.

Schmidhuber, A., Reilly, M., Zanardi, P. *et al.* 2025. "A quantum algorithm for Khovanov homology." arXiv:2501.12378v2.

Schweigert, C. and Fuchs, J. 2010. "Hopf algebras and Frobenius algebras in finite tensor categories." *Revista de la Unión Matemática Argentina* 51(1): 43–90.

Shi, K., Chakraborty, K., Kon, W. Y. *et al.* 2024. "On the relativistic zero knowledge quantum proofs of knowledge." arXiv:2409.03635v1.

Sorensen, D. 2024. "(In)Correct smart contract specifications." In *2024 IEEE International Conference on Blockchain and Cryptocurrency (ICBC)*. IEEE. https://ieeexplore.ieee.org/document/10634444.

Spivak, D. I. 2014. *Category Theory for the Sciences.* Cambridge, MA: The MIT Press.

Swan, M. 2015. *Blockchain: Blueprint for a New Economy.* Sebastopol, CA: O'Reilly Media.

Swan, M. 2019. "Blockchain theory of programmable risk: Black swan smart contracts." In Swan, M., Potts, J., Takagi, S., Witte, F., and Tasca, P. (eds.), *Blockchain Economics: Implications of Distributed Ledgers – Markets, Communications Networks, and Algorithmic Reality.* London: World Scientific.

Swan, M., dos Santos, R. P., Lebedev, M. A., and Witte, F. 2022. *Quantum Computing for the Brain.* London: World Scientific.

Swan, M., dos Santos, R. P., and Witte, F. 2020. *Quantum Computing: Physics, Blockchains, and Deep Learning Smart Networks.* London: World Scientific.

Swan, M., Kido, T., and dos Santos, R. P. 2025. "Higher categorical cryptoeconomics: HoTT blockchains, petri net computad ledgers, coregulator DAOs, and cohomology ZKPs." Research Gate Preprint. https://doi.org/10.13140/RG.2.2.32477.73445.

Tanega, J. 2014. "Default Invariance: A Naïve category theory of law and finance." In O'Sullivan, P. (ed.), *Hubris to Disgrace: The Philosophy, Politics and Economics of Finance in the early 21st century.* London: Routledge.

Tohmé, F., Caterina, G., and Gangle, R. 2017. "Local and global optima in decision-making: a sheaf-theoretical analysis of the difference between classical and behavioral approaches." *International Journal of General Systems* 46(8): 879–97.

Tohmé, F. and Fioriti, A. 2024. "Level-agnostic representations of interacting agents." *Mathematics* 12(2697): 1–19. https://doi.org/10.3390/math12172697.

Tohmé, F. and Viglizzo, I. 2023. "A categorical representation of games." arXiv:2309.15981v2.

Wood, G. 2024. "Join-Accumulate Machine: A semi-coherent scalable trustless VM." Gray Paper. https://graypaper.com/.

Wu, L. and Zhang, Y. 2025. "Common pricing of decentralized risk: A linear option pricing model." *Review of Financial Studies* 38(3): hhaf016. https://doi.org/10.1093/rfs/hhaf016.

Young, K. 1999. "Foreign exchange market as a lattice gauge theory." *American Journal of Physics* 67: 862–8. https://doi.org/10.1119/1.19139.

Zhang, G., Primaatmaja, I. W., Chen, Y. *et al.* 2024. "Self-testing quantum randomness expansion on an integrated photonic chip." arXiv:2411.13712.

Zhao, D. 2020. "Algebraic structure of blockchains: A group-theoretical primer." arXiv:2002.05973v1.

Zheng, H., Huang, Y., Huang, Z. *et al.* 2024. "HomPINNs: Homotopy physics-informed neural networks." *Journal of Computational Physics* 500: 112751. https://doi.org/10.1016/j.jcp.2023.112751.

https://doi.org/10.1142/9781800618664_0003

Chapter 2

The Economics of Blockchain Shared Security

Darcy W. E. Allen*, Chris Berg, and Sinclair Davidson

School of Economics, Finance and Marketing, RMIT University, Melbourne, Australia

**darcywilliamallen@gmail.com*

Abstract

Blockchain networks must decide whether to produce their own security or purchase it from other networks, presenting a classic make-or-buy decision in institutional economics. This chapter develops a theoretical framework for analyzing shared security arrangements in blockchain networks, drawing on transaction cost economics and early empirical evidence. We examine how asset specificity, uncertainty, and opportunism shape governance structures in shared security provision. Our analysis reveals that successful security sharing requires sophisticated institutional mechanisms to manage adaptation while protecting relationship-specific investments. We propose specific governance solutions for mitigating contracting hazards in shared security arrangements.

Keywords: Blockchain Security, Shared Security, Make-or-Buy Decision, Cosmos Hub.

2.1 Why Shared Security?

Blockchain networks provide secure, verifiable transactions without centralized intermediaries through the use of cryptographically ensured consensus mechanisms. Until recently, these networks relied on their own consensus mechanisms—typically either proof-of-work or proof-of-stake—for their security. However, the evolution of the cryptoeconomy has created new options for security provision. Smaller networks, in particular, face constraints in attracting sufficient security resources, making arrangements where multiple networks "share" security an attractive alternative. These models allow networks to purchase security services from established providers rather than developing their own validator infrastructure from scratch.

Shared security models in blockchain ecosystems demonstrate a range of approaches. Ethereum's Layer 2 rollups, such as Arbitrum, process transactions independently but inherit security from Ethereum's Layer 1 via fraud-proof mechanisms. Polkadot employs a distinct model where parachains share security through a relay chain, though this necessitates tighter ecosystem integration. Babylon offers specialized Bitcoin-based timestamp verification services for other networks. The Cosmos Hub allows sovereign blockchain networks to share validator sets while preserving significant independence, such as maintaining their own tokens. Each model reflects different trade-offs between security, sovereignty, and economic efficiency.

Despite the increasing prevalence of shared security models, a comprehensive economic analysis of their institutional design remains limited. This chapter applies transaction cost economics to analyze the trade-offs inherent in security provision, with a focus on asset specificity, uncertainty, and governance structures. While shared security models can reduce the costs associated with independent security provision, they also introduce new transaction costs, including challenges related to negotiation, monitoring, and adaptation. We particularly examine how different governance structures can mitigate these transaction costs and facilitate robust shared security governance.

The central economic questions in shared security revolve around governance and contracting. How should networks determine whether to "make" or "buy" their security? What governance structures best support shared security arrangements? How can contracts address opportunistic behavior when circumstances change—for example, if a security provider increases its fees? While we do not provide definitive answers to these complex institutional trade-offs, we aim to demonstrate that successful shared security requires careful consideration of governance mechanisms and economic incentives.

The chapter proceeds as follows. Section 2.2 applies transaction cost economics to blockchain security provisions. Section 2.3 compares different shared security models. Section 2.4 presents Cosmos' Interchain Security (ICS) as a case study. Section 2.5 explores governance challenges and principles for sustainable security arrangements. Throughout, we argue that successful shared security requires institutional mechanisms that balance security, efficiency, and sovereignty.

2.2 Some Transaction Cost Economics of Shared Security

Since Coase (1937) first posed the question of why firms exist, economists have investigated how transaction costs influence the boundaries of organizations. Williamson (1985) extended this analysis by identifying asset specificity, uncertainty, and transaction frequency as key determinants of whether activities are best organized through markets or hierarchies. This theoretical framework has been applied to blockchain networks through institutional cryptoeconomics (Davidson *et al.*, 2018; Berg *et al.*, 2019; Allen *et al.*, 2020). Transaction cost economics can also help explain how blockchain networks choose between producing security internally and procuring it externally. In traditional settings, firms decide whether to vertically integrate or rely on market transactions based on these cost considerations. Blockchain networks face an analogous decision: whether to maintain an independent validator set or outsource security to an external provider.

A blockchain network that chooses to "make" security must invest significantly in infrastructure, validator recruitment, and governance mechanisms. These costs are particularly substantial for newer or smaller networks that struggle to attract sufficient validators to ensure robust security. Conversely, a network that decides to "buy" security encounters different transaction costs: search costs for identifying providers, negotiation costs for establishing agreements, monitoring costs for ensuring commitments, and coordination costs for implementing changes. This mirrors traditional outsourcing decisions in industries where firms weigh the benefits of internal control against the flexibility and cost-efficiency of external procurement (Grossman & Hart, 1986). For example, a firm might consider the trade-offs between cloud computing and running a private server. Many startups opt to outsource infrastructure to cloud providers for convenience and scalability, while large enterprises sometimes maintain in-house data centers for greater control despite increased overhead.

The choice of governance structure is dynamic and may need to change as networks mature, transaction volumes grow, and governance structures evolve. For instance, dYdX's transition from inheriting Ethereum's security as an application to launching a standalone Cosmos-based chain demonstrates how governance needs can shift as networks mature and their security requirements become more specialized. Similarly, Polygon began as a proof-of-stake sidechain to Ethereum with a hybrid security model, using its own validator set (stakers of MATIC) while also relying on periodic Ethereum checkpoints for additional security assurance. This arrangement created an interesting governance dynamic where Polygon maintained operational autonomy through its validator set while still benefiting from Ethereum's security properties. These examples highlight how networks can experiment with different security governance structures over time, often moving between various hybrid arrangements rather than making binary choices between fully independent or fully inherited security. Governance structures must be flexible enough to adapt to evolving transactional hazards while maintaining credible commitments between parties (Williamson, 1985).

Networks that opt for shared security face a range of governance transaction costs. These include the costs of negotiating security agreements, monitoring validator performance, ensuring fair fee distribution, and adapting to choices made by a security provider. For example, a network choosing between running its own validator set versus joining Polkadot's shared security system must consider not only the direct costs of running nodes versus paying for a parachain slot but also the full spectrum of coordination and governance costs, such as managing the expectations of both its own validators and a broader Polkadot community that might have orthogonal interests from a network's validators. These governance costs often determine whether a network opts for an independent security model or integrates with an external provider.

When investments in security infrastructure cannot be readily redeployed, networks risk becoming locked into specific security relationships, exposing them to potential opportunistic behavior from providers or counterparties. Williamson (1985) described this as the "hold-up problem," where relationship-specific investments create bargaining asymmetries. In shared security models, asset specificity manifests in several ways. There is technical specificity when blockchains must adapt their software to interface with specific provider systems—for instance, Cosmos chains implementing specific features to interact with Hub validators. There is also direct financial specificity when networks commit capital in provider-specific ways, such as by bonding DOT tokens on Polkadot parachains. And, of course, there is also more intangible human capital specificity where a network develops expertise regarding specific chains' unique features and requirements. These forms of specificity increase governance complexity, necessitating institutional mechanisms to safeguard against opportunism.

Uncertainty further complicates security arrangements, particularly in blockchain networks where technological and economic conditions evolve rapidly. Uncertainty refers to the difficulty of predicting and planning for future contingencies in economic relationships—particularly true uncertainty where probabilities cannot be reliably calculated (Knight, 1921). Uncertainty emerges in many different forms in blockchain networks. Protocol innovations and security threats create uncertainty. Volatility in transaction volumes, validator economics, token prices, and changing market conditions also generates uncertainty. Regulatory uncertainty has also raised questions about the legal status of shared security models. These forms of uncertainty create pressure for governance structures that can facilitate adaptation while maintaining security.

Transaction frequency also influences governance choices in shared security. High-frequency transactions can justify more elaborate governance mechanisms since their fixed costs can be spread across many interactions (Williamson, 1985). In blockchain security, frequency manifests in multiple dimensions. Security provision is itself continuous—validators must process transactions and produce blocks without interruption. High-frequency interactions may justify investment in sophisticated governance mechanisms such as automated reward distribution systems and formal dispute resolution processes, which could be too costly for occasional security arrangements.

Conversely, lower-frequency relationships between organizations and networks might not justify creating a complex governance structure.

The combination of asset specificity and uncertainty creates significant potential for opportunistic behavior in shared security arrangements. Specific investments create potential for *ex post* bargaining problems, where one party may attempt to extract additional value after a relationship has been established (Grossman and Hart, 1986; Klein, Crawford, and Alchian, 1978). In shared security, this risk is particularly pronounced. A security provider might attempt to extract higher fees once another network has grown successful and switching costs are high. Conversely, networks might try to renegotiate agreements during market downturns when validator rewards are lower. More subtle forms of opportunism can also emerge: security providers might prioritize other chains during high-traffic periods. Table 2.1 summarizes the key trade-offs in making versus buying security, drawing on transaction cost considerations.

These transaction cost dynamics explain why blockchain security arrangements vary significantly across ecosystems. Some networks prioritize sovereignty and direct governance over their security infrastructure, while others prefer market-based solutions to minimize operational complexity. The diversity of shared security models suggests that there is no single optimal approach; rather, networks must balance control, efficiency, and governance costs based on their specific needs.

Contracts in shared security arrangements, similar to all other types of contracts, are inherently incomplete (Williamson, 1985; Hart, 1995). This incompleteness stems from multiple sources, including the different types of uncertainties outlined above. Security needs evolve with new threats, protocol upgrades, and governance shifts, making it impossible to specify all contingencies in advance. Networks rely on governance mechanisms, slashing conditions, and incentive structures to manage these gaps, but disputes and inefficiencies can still arise. Without effective adaptation mechanisms, incomplete contracts increase renegotiation risks and weaken security commitments.

These relationships can also be complicated by information asymmetry. Validators might have better knowledge of their own reliability and risks, while security buyers may withhold details about future

Table 2.1. The costs of making or buying security.

Costs	Make Security	Buy Security	Key Considerations
Direct costs	High initial capital investment; ongoing operational costs; technology development expenses	Service fees to security provider; integration costs; contract management costs	Scale economies; resource availability; technical expertise
Transaction costs	Internal coordination costs; validator recruitment; protocol governance	Search and negotiation costs; monitoring and enforcement; adaptation costs	Market maturity; contract complexity; governance requirements
Control rights	Full control over security parameters; independent protocol governance; flexible adaptation	Shared control arrangements; negotiated changes; provider dependencies	Sovereignty requirements; adaptation needs; strategic autonomy
Strategic implications	Higher resource commitment; greater technical responsibility independent evolution	Resource focus on core features; shared security expertise; ecosystem integration	Development priorities; growth strategy; ecosystem positioning

transaction volumes or governance plans. This creates adverse selection (Akerlof, 1970), where weaker providers secure contracts, and moral hazard (Arrow, 1963; Holmström, 1979), where security effort declines after agreements are established. Blockchain networks mitigate these risks through cryptographic verification, onchain monitoring, and slashing penalties to reduce reliance on trust.

The asset-specific investments described earlier, together with information asymmetry and incomplete contracts, can lead to—what Williamson (1985) calls—"fundamental transformation." Initially, networks face a competitive market for security provision with multiple potential providers and governance structures. However, once a network commits to a particular security model, the relationship shifts from an open market to a bilateral dependency characterized by significant specific investments. In Ethereum Layer 2s, these investments include protocol adaptations and technical integration work. In Polkadot's parachain system, networks must lock significant capital in DOT tokens and conform to specific technical standards. This transformation from a competitive market to bilateral dependency creates distinct contracting hazards. Networks must make substantial specific investments—technical integration, operational expertise, and often financial stakes—while operating in an environment where security threats and protocol standards evolve unpredictably. This combination creates the problem of adaptation in governance: how to facilitate necessary changes while protecting specific investments and preventing opportunistic behavior? Table 2.2 summarizes some of these contracting hazards.

Different governance structures address these hazards through distinct mechanisms. Hierarchical models such as Ethereum L2s embed adaptation rules directly in protocol code, creating credible commitments through technical enforcement. Market-based approaches such as Babylon's timestamping service narrow their scope to reduce adaptation requirements. However, a key insight from our analysis is that all successful models must ultimately develop institutional mechanisms for managing the post-transformation relationship. The effectiveness of these mechanisms appears to depend critically on their ability to support adaptation while maintaining credible commitments from all parties.

Table 2.2. Contracting hazards in shared security.

Hazard Type	Description	Examples in Shared Security	Manifestation
Incomplete contracts	Inability to specify all contingencies	Unpredictable security threats, protocol upgrades	Gaps in agreement coverage
Asset specificity	Relationship-specific investments	Validator infrastructure, protocol integration	Hold-up problems
Information asymmetry	Private knowledge exploitation	Hidden capabilities or requirements	Adverse selection

2.3 Comparative Analysis of Shared Security Models

The transaction cost framework helps explain why blockchain networks adopt different shared security arrangements. While Table 2.1 above outlines the general trade-offs between making and buying security, real-world implementations vary in how they balance asset specificity, uncertainty, and governance costs. Some networks favor hierarchical integration, reducing adaptation costs at the expense of flexibility, while others rely on market-based solutions, increasing flexibility but exposing participants to coordination risks. These variations reflect distinct governance approaches to managing transaction costs in securities provision. Table 2.3 summarizes key shared security models, analyzing their economic structures and trade-offs.

Ethereum's Layer 2 solutions represent a highly integrated approach to shared security that internalizes transaction costs within a hierarchical structure. Layer 2 networks maintain operational independence in processing transactions but are deeply integrated

Table 2.3. Comparative analysis of shared security models.

Model	Security Mechanism	Economic Structure	Governance Approach	Key Trade-Offs
Ethereum L2s	Fraud proofs/validity proofs	Fee sharing & bonds	Quasi-integrated governance	High security, limited autonomy
Polkadot Parachains	Shared validator set	Slot auctions & deposits	Unified ecosystem governance	Strong guarantees, high integration costs
Babylon	Bitcoin time-stamping	Service fees	Specialized service governance	Limited scope, clear metrics
EigenLayer	Restaked Ethereum security	Liquidity-based staking	Open market-place governance	Capital efficiency, new risks
Cosmos Interchain Security	Replicated validation	Revenue sharing	Sovereign chain governance	High autonomy, complex coordination

with Ethereum's mainnet through cryptographic commitment mechanisms that create credible security guarantees. The economic structure reflects this quasi-vertical integration through multiple mechanisms: split transaction fees that align incentives across layers, substantial security bonds that create hostages against opportunistic behavior (Williamson, 1983), and standardized technical interfaces that reduce coordination costs. While this arrangement effectively addresses certain contracting hazards—particularly the verification of security properties—it generates significant asset specificity through protocol-specific investments and technical dependencies. Layer 2 operators must make irreversible investments in Ethereum-specific infrastructure, code, and expertise, creating the fundamental transformation from an *ex ante* competitive market to an *ex post* bilateral dependency. This transformation helps explain why Layer 2 protocols tend to remain committed to Ethereum despite the emergence of alternative base layers.

Polkadot's parachain model is a hybrid governance structure, combining hierarchical control with market-driven slot allocation. Parachains must win slot auctions by locking up DOT tokens, a mechanism that reveals security demand through price discovery while simultaneously ensuring financial commitment from participants. This design addresses information asymmetry by allowing networks with the highest demand to signal their willingness to pay for security. However, it also generates bilateral dependencies: parachains must conform to Polkadot's relay chain rules, while the relay chain's value is tied to active parachain adoption. This interdependence creates hold-up risks, as both parties rely on continued economic alignment. The Polkadot model also faces renewal risk: since security slots are time-limited, parachains may lose their position if they fail to outbid competitors in future auctions. This dynamic introduces uncertainty about long-term governance stability as networks must continuously justify their security expenses and manage economic cycles.

By contrast, Babylon's timestamping service is focused on a narrow, well-defined security function. By limiting its scope to Bitcoin-based timestamp verification, Babylon reduces transaction complexity and measurement challenges that plague broader security arrangements. This specialization enables more complete contracting, as performance metrics and service levels can be precisely specified and verified. The economic model combines a proof-of-stake validator set for operational consensus with Bitcoin anchoring, creating a tiered security structure that leverages Bitcoin's security properties while maintaining operational flexibility. This arrangement illustrates an important principle in transaction cost economics: when service attributes are easily measured and verification costs are low, market-based governance can be highly efficient. However, the trade-off for this clarity and efficiency is a more limited security scope compared to comprehensive shared security solutions.

EigenLayer represents a novel, market-driven approach to shared security. Rather than bootstrapping new validator sets for each network, it allows existing Ethereum validators to "restake" their ETH to provide security services to external protocols. This creates an open marketplace where protocols can rent Ethereum's robust economic security without the need to lock up capital in multiple independent validator sets, thus significantly improving capital efficiency through the reuse of staked ETH. While this design maximizes the utility of staked capital, it also introduces new risks. Since the same ETH is used to secure multiple services, a slashing event on one service can potentially have cascading effects across all networks that rely on that capital. Moreover, unlike integrated shared security models such as those seen in ICS or Polkadot—where validator participation is determined by predefined governance rules and structured auctions—EigenLayer allows validators to choose which services to support based solely on market incentives. This flexibility enhances capital efficiency and responsiveness but may also lead to dynamic shifts in validator commitments in response to changing economic conditions.

While these models represent distinct approaches to shared security governance, the Cosmos ecosystem's ICS model introduces additional complexity through its emphasis on chain sovereignty and flexible security arrangements. Given the significance of this approach and its novel institutional features, we examine it in detail as a case study in Section 2.4. This case study allows us to analyze how theoretical predictions about transaction costs and governance structures manifest in practice, particularly in an environment where maintaining chain sovereignty creates unique contracting challenges. The following section examines these dynamics in detail through a case study of Cosmos' Interchain Security model, which represents a particularly interesting attempt to maintain flexibility even after significant specific investments had been made.

2.4 Cosmos' Interchain Security: A Case Study

ICS in the Cosmos ecosystem represents an innovative institutional solution to shared security provision. At its core, ICS enables sovereign blockchain networks to share validator sets while maintaining significant independence in their operations and governance. This creates a market for security services, where consumer chains can purchase validation from established networks through formalized economic and technical arrangements, rather than bootstrapping their own validator sets from scratch. This makes it an important case study in how decentralized networks manage security provisions without sacrificing autonomy. This section analyzes the institutional structure of ICS, its contracting hazards, and the governance mechanisms designed to mitigate those risks. By doing so, it offers broader lessons for the design of robust shared security systems across blockchain ecosystems.

At its core, ICS enables consumer chains to lease validator security from the Cosmos Hub, reducing the need to bootstrap independent validator sets. Unlike more integrated approaches, ICS preserves clear boundaries between security providers and consumer chains. Consumer chains retain full control over their tokenomics, governance, and protocol upgrades, while validators on the Cosmos Hub are economically incentivized to secure multiple networks. Unlike more integrated approaches, ICS maintains clear boundaries between provider and consumer chains. Consumer chains retain control over their protocol parameters, token economics, and governance processes, while security providers (such as the Cosmos Hub) maintain independence in validator set management. Second, the economic relationships are structured through explicit revenue-sharing agreements that distribute transaction fees, inflationary rewards, and other value capture mechanisms between the parties. Third, these arrangements often include sophisticated mechanisms for risk sharing and dispute resolution.

Several contracting hazards emerge in these relationships that require careful institutional design. The first is measurement and monitoring costs. While basic security metrics such as uptime and block production are easily verified, more complex aspects of validator performance—such as transaction ordering optimization or MEV extraction—are harder to measure and enforce. This creates potential principal-agent problems between consumer chains and validators.

A second key hazard emerges from the need to manage adaptation over time. As security requirements evolve and network usage patterns change, the original terms of security provision may need to be adjusted. However, renegotiation is complicated by bilateral dependencies: once a consumer chain has integrated with a provider's validator set, switching costs become significant. This creates risks of opportunistic behavior on both sides: providers might attempt to extract higher fees from successful consumer chains, while consumer chains might try to renegotiate terms during market downturns. Governance decisions regarding validator rewards, slashing rules, or security guarantees require coordination across multiple stakeholders, increasing negotiation costs.

Early ICS implementations demonstrate these trade-offs. One concrete example of ICS governance is the Neutron consumer chain launch in 2023. Neutron agreed to share 25% of its transaction fees (and MEV revenue) with Cosmos Hub validators, denominated in Neutron's own token (NTRN). This rate was set based on the expectation of mutual benefit: Hub stakers gain a new revenue stream, and Neutron receives top-tier security. However, community discussion acknowledged a tension: if the Hub's 25% cut is too low, ATOM stakers might not find it a "meaningful" income; if it's too high, it could stifle the growth of the consumer chain. These trade-offs are being monitored, and there is an understanding that the percentages might be revisited via governance once real data are available. Other chains have also launched, such as Stride, which proposed a more complex arrangement including revenue sharing and protocol-owned liquidity. These variations reflect different approaches to managing the inherent contracting hazards in shared security relationships.

ICS implementations have developed several important institutional mechanisms to address these hazards. Standardized revenue models create clear frameworks for fee sharing and reward distribution, which helps reduce negotiation costs and creates predictable economics for all parties. These are complemented by formal governance mechanisms that establish processes for parameter adjustments and dispute resolution, helping manage adaptation while protecting specific investments. The arrangements often include risk management tools such as insurance pools and mutual slashing protection to distribute risks more efficiently across the security provider–consumer relationship. At a technical level, protocol-level rules create credible commitments around key security parameters.

The effectiveness of these mechanisms varies based on specific implementation details and network characteristics. Consumer chains with different security needs, transaction volumes, and governance models may require distinct institutional arrangements. This variability suggests that efficient shared security arrangements must be tailored to the specific characteristics of the networks they connect.

The ICS model must contend with significant adaptation challenges (Table 2.4). Consumer chains evolve their business models, transaction volumes fluctuate, and security requirements change. The governance mechanisms for managing these changes must balance flexibility with stability. For instance, this might involve regular

Table 2.4. Potential compensation models in Cosmos ICS.

Model Type	Economic Structure	Benefits	Challenges	Risk Distribution
Revenue share	Percentage of fees, inflation, MEV	Aligned growth incentives	Payment token volatility	Shared upside/ downside
Fee for service	Fixed payment schedule	Predictable costs	May not reflect market value	Consumer bears volatility
Token swap	Cross-chain token holdings	Deep economic alignment	Complex valuation	Mutual exposure
Bond model	Yield-generating deposits	Clear security backing	Capital inefficiency	Provider holds collateral

review processes for agreement terms, mechanisms for emergency responses to security threats, structured processes for the proposition and implementation of changes, and clear procedures for dispute resolution. The effectiveness of these adaptation mechanisms will influence the sustainability of ICS relationships. Success requires governance structures that can facilitate necessary changes while protecting the interests of all participants.

2.5 The Future of Shared Security

The governance of shared security arrangements requires carefully designed institutional structures that can address the complex challenges identified in our analysis. Drawing on Williamson's (1985) framework of economic organizations, we have identified several distinct governance approaches with different strengths and limitations for coordinating security provision across blockchain networks.

The most basic approach relies on market-based governance through price signals and formal contracts. While this approach offers high-powered incentives and flexibility, it struggles to address the complex adaptation requirements inherent in blockchain security provision. The effectiveness of pure market governance depends critically on the completeness of contracts and the measurability of security outcomes, both of which are particularly challenging in the blockchain context. Our analysis suggests that market-based approaches are most suitable for standardized security services with clear performance metrics but face significant limitations for more complex security relationships.

Hybrid governance structures, which combine elements of market and hierarchical coordination, appear better suited to managing the complexity of shared security relationships. These arrangements typically involve long-term contracts supplemented by adaptive mechanisms and relational governance. The Cosmos ICS model exemplifies this hybrid approach using formal economic arrangements alongside more flexible governance processes for handling adaptation and dispute resolution. The success of hybrid governance depends crucially on the development of effective mechanisms for modifying agreements in response to changing circumstances while protecting against opportunistic behavior.

At the other end of the spectrum, hierarchical governance internalizes security provision within a single organizational framework. This approach, represented by more integrated models such as Ethereum's Layer 2 solutions, reduces certain transaction costs but sacrifices some benefits of market coordination. While hierarchical governance can effectively address adaptation challenges through authority-based decision-making, it may limit innovation in security provision and reduce the autonomy of participating networks.

Our analysis reveals several critical governance challenges that future research must address. First, the role of relational contracting in maintaining shared security arrangements requires a deeper examination. While formal contracts provide important foundations, the complexity and uncertainty of blockchain security suggest that relational elements play a crucial role in sustainable arrangements. Second, the evolution of shared security markets as more networks adopt these models remains poorly understood. Network effects and ecosystem dynamics likely influence these relationships in ways that current theoretical frameworks struggle to capture.

References

Akerlof, G. A. 1970. "The market for 'lemons': Quality uncertainty and the market mechanism." *The Quarterly Journal of Economics* 84(3): 488–500.

Allen, D. W. E., Berg, C., Markey-Towler, B., Novak, M., and Potts, J. 2020. "Blockchain and the evolution of institutional technologies: Implications for innovation policy." *Research Policy* 49(1): 103865.

Arrow, K. J. 1963. "Uncertainty and the welfare economics of medical care." *The American Economic Review* 53(5): 941–973.

Berg, C., Davidson, S., and Potts, J. 2019. *Understanding the blockchain economy: An introduction to institutional cryptoeconomics.* Cheltenham, UK: Edward Elgar Publishing.

Coase, R. H. 1937. "The Nature of the Firm." *Economica* 4(16): 386–405.

Davidson, S., De Filippi, P., and Potts, J. 2018. "Blockchains and the economic institutions of capitalism." *Journal of Institutional Economics* 14(4): 639–658.

Grossman, S. J. and Hart, O. D. 1986. "The costs and benefits of ownership: A theory of vertical and lateral integration." *Journal of Political Economy* 94(4): 691–719.

Hart, O. 1995. *Firms, Contracts, and Financial Structure.* Oxford: Clarendon Press.

Holmström, B. 1979. "Moral hazard and observability." *The Bell Journal of Economics* 10(1): 74–91. https://doi.org/10.2307/3003320.

Klein, B., Crawford, R. G., and Alchian, A. A. 1978. "Vertical integration, appropriable rents, and the competitive contracting process." *The Journal of Law and Economics* 21(2): 297–326.

Knight, F. H. 1921. *Risk, Uncertainty, and Profit.* Boston, Massachusetts: Houghton Mifflin Company.

Williamson, O. E. 1985. *The Economic Institutions of Capitalism: Firms, Markets, Relational Contracting.* New York: Free Press.

https://doi.org/10.1142/9781800618664_0004

Chapter 3

Decentralized Collaborative Action: Cryptoeconomics in Space

Murdoch J. Gabbay
MACS, Heriot-Watt University, Edinburgh, UK
m.gabbay@hw.ac.uk

Abstract
Blockchains and peer-to-peer systems are part of a trend toward computer systems based on *decentralized collaborative action*, by which we mean that they (1) run across many participants, (2) without central control, and (3) are such that qualities (1) and (2) are essential to the system's intended use cases.

We propose a notion of topological space, which we call a *semitopology*, to help us mathematically model such systems. We treat participants as *points* in a space, which are organized into *actionable coalitions*. An actionable coalition is any set of participants who collectively have the resources to collaborate (if they choose) to progress according to the system's rules, independently of the rest of the system.

Mathematicians will recognize semitopology as a generalization of the notion of point-set topology, where actionable coalitions correspond to open sets.

It turns out that much useful information about the system can be obtained *just* by viewing it as a semitopology and studying its actionable coalitions. For example, we will prove a mathematical sense in which if every actionable coalition of some point p has nonempty intersection with every actionable coalition of another point q—note that this is the negation of the famous Hausdorff separation property from topology—then p and q must remain in agreement. Remarkably, since this observation depends only on the semitopological structure, it holds for any possible concrete algorithm.

This matters because remaining in agreement is a key correctness property in many distributed systems. For example, in blockchain, participant disagreement is called *forking*, and blockchain designers try hard to avoid it.

We provide an accessible introduction to the following: the technical context of decentralized systems; why we build them and find them useful; and how they motivate the theory of semitopological spaces. We also sketch some basic theorems and applications of the resulting mathematics.

Keywords: Semitopology, Decentralized Collaborative Action, Actionable Coalition, Consensus, Decentralised Computing, Topology in Computer Science.

3.1 What Is "Cryptoeconomics"?

Let us begin by proposing a definition.

Definition 3.1.1. *Cryptoeconomics* is:

> the study of socioeconomic systems enabled by modern decentralized computer systems.

Cryptoeconomics is closely related to blockchains because a blockchain is a decentralized database, and databases store *state* (i.e., data); thus, blockchains make cryptoeconomics possible, and cryptoeconomic outcomes—real or envisaged—make blockchains useful.

There is substantial overlap between cryptoeconomics and many other fields that study aspects of decentralized and distributed systems, including:

- *economics* (the study of value and incentives),
- *game theory* (the study of optimal outcomes for players with choices),
- *social choice theory* (how to synthesize collective decisions from individual votes),
- *blockchains* (decentralized databases),
- *smart contracts* (programs that operate on blockchains), and
- *law* (the interpretation of facts into socially binding meaning).

We see from this list that, in practice, cryptoeconomics touches on nearly everything.

The description of cryptoeconomics in Definition 3.1.1 uses two adjectives: "digital" and "decentralized." Digitization is important because it enables decentralization on a historically unprecedented scale, but it is the decentralization that is most important to giving cryptoeconomics its particular character.

Concerning digitization, this has been ongoing since (at least) the digital *mainframe computers* of the 1960s—powerful central computers that acted then, and still act today, as oracles enabling organizations that can afford them to deliver services more efficiently. Note, however, that this is invisible to the end user, in the sense that the user only sees a bigger, better, faster, and possibly cheaper service. This is a substantive technological advance and is great for efficiency and profits, but it does not necessarily lead to any qualitative structural change in the economics of how the value is created.

We can date the seeds of *decentralized* digitization to the mid-1970s, when pocket digital calculators took over from slide rules, and desktop computers became available. Putting digital computation in people's pockets and on people's desks started a cascade of innovations that, along with the internet, has brought us modern miracles such as mobile banking and streaming video. Even so, a user doing mobile banking on a mobile phone or watching a video on a streaming service has something fundamental in common with the technician querying a 1960s mainframe computer using a paper card with holes punched in it: the back-end system is still centrally controlled. That mainframe computer system is still around, albeit in an immensely more sophisticated form.[1]

What makes the new breeds of modern computing systems uniquely different is that they are *radically decentralized* and heterogeneous, such that *if they were centrally controlled, then they would not even make sense*. This is the start of cryptoeconomics as intended in Definition 3.1.1, and it is new.

---

[1]In practice, the modern "mainframes" that (for example) serve banking, social media, or streaming services are usually distributed clusters of servers. But being distributed is not the same as being decentralized; see Definition 3.2.1(1).

It began with Napster (a peer-to-peer file-sharing system) in June 1999, which demonstrated how music media could be disseminated independently of (centralized) media companies (David, 2016).[2] Then, Bitcoin (January 2009) and Ethereum (July 2015) changed everything by showing that money and even contracts could be mediated (albeit imperfectly) independently of banks.

These systems—of which Napster, Bitcoin, and Ethereum are perhaps the best known but certainly not the only examples—would be meaningless and make no sense if they were implemented in a centralized manner, in much the same way that a pocket calculator or desktop computer would make no sense if it were a mainframe. The decentralization is not a quality of the thing; it is the *point* of that thing.

This tendency toward radical decentralization is often discussed in ideological terms, but compelling technical forces also exist to push technology in this direction. Being decentralized gives desirable properties, including scalability, redundancy, reliability, and resilience. Being decentralized offers unique opportunities for a network of participants to *act collaboratively* for creating value by achieving their goals. We can sum this up as follows:

$$\text{cryptoeconomics} = \text{value} + \text{decentralized collaborative action.}$$

We are only beginning to get to grips with the implications of this equation.

[2]The article itself illustrates some of the compromises involved in creating and disseminating knowledge. The article's author is an associate professor at a U.K. university. The publisher's version is behind a paywall (since the publisher makes money from publishing); an author's preprint is made freely online by his university (which makes money by employing the author to educate students); and the author most likely wrote the article in-between teaching obligations, for zero marginal cost to his employer (i.e., "for free").

To be fair, the publisher's version looks nicer than the author's preprint, and the publisher's website makes the work easy to find; the university survives, and its students get taught by a well-informed professor; the author's preprint is accessible to any reader who can dig it out; and the author enjoyed writing the article. In this sense, all parties—the author, the publisher, the students, the university, the article's readership, and science itself—benefit from the shambling compromise that is academic publishing, though they might also all complain about the division of that benefit.

3.2 What Is "Decentralized Collaborative Action"?

3.2.1 *The definition*

Decentralized collaborative action is a feature of *decentralized permissionless heterogeneous computing systems.* Let's unpack the jargon:

Definition 3.2.1.

1. A system is *decentralized* when it is *distributed* (meaning that it is composed of several distinct parts), and furthermore the system as a whole is not centrally controlled.

   Most blockchain systems and peer-to-peer networks are decentralized in this sense. The internet is also (mostly) decentralized, at least in principle.[3]
2. A system is *permissionless* (or *unpermissioned*) when participants can leave and join the system at any time.

   Nature is naturally permissionless (living things do not need permission to be born or to die). National voting systems *are* permissioned (because citizens require government certification to be allowed to vote). Peer-to-peer systems (including file sharing and blockchain protocols) are often, though not always, unpermissioned.
3. A system is *heterogeneous* when participants may legitimately be following different rules.[4]

---

[3]The internet was designed to be an information network that would be resilient to a nuclear attack. It did this by being "centrifugal"; emphasizing node-to-node actions instead of center-to-center actions. See Ryan (2010), summarized by Ars Technica (Ryan, 2011).

Note that the boundary between "distributed" and "decentralized" can be fluid. For example, should we consider a system to be decentralized when its parts can act independently most of the time, but every so often they check in with a central controller? This depends on what aspects of the system we care about, e.g., its short-term or long-term behavior. There is room for a nice discussion here, but it will not be addressed in this particular article.

[4]By "different rules," we include the situation where an algorithm (such as a consensus algorithm) is agreed upon among participants, but a critical parameter may vary substantively across them; e.g., imagine a blockchain in which some participants require more than a two-thirds majority to act, while others require only over half the votes. By "legitimate," we exclude the case of a hostile participant.

Ethereum and Tezos are decentralized and permissionless, but they are not heterogeneous in the sense we intend. If you are running a Tezos or Ethereum node, then you are not forced to follow the rules, but if you do not, then by definition you are not acting as a legitimate Tezos or Ethereum node.
In contrast, consider the combination of Tezos and Ethereum as a single system connected by a *blockchain bridge*.[5] This is heterogeneous because Tezos nodes and Ethereum nodes have different rules and different consensus mechanisms. A Tezos node is not a bad node simply because it is not following the rules of Ethereum, and vice versa, but because of the blockchain bridge, they can be considered to be operating within a single (heterogeneous) combined system.

There are many flavors of decentralized system; however, in the most general case, we have a decentralized heterogeneous permissionless system that consists of *some* participants communicating to do *something*, with no *a priori* restrictions on who, what, or how.

This scenario—with its weak well-behavedness assumptions that do not even assume all participants share a common set of rules—might seem a terrible idea which we should not allow, as it admits crazy networks with bad behavior. But here the generality is a feature, not a bug:

1. Mathematically, it can be *useful* to admit general models, including both good and bad ones, so that we can formalize their good and bad behavior[6] and express conditions to include or exclude it.
2. Surprisingly, it will turn out that there is still a lot that we can say even about the general case, and we shall see that much useful structure will emerge, even from very weak assumptions.

Therefore, granted that the generality of decentralized collaborative action is a feature and not a bug, how should we approach this mathematical generality?

---

[5]See https://ethereum.org/en/bridges/ (permalink: https://web.archive.org/web/20240324090911/https://ethereum.org/en/bridges/).

[6]. . . which will vary by application; e.g., sometimes all participants should play by the same rules, but in the case of a blockchain bridge, we specifically want to *admit* different rules.

The key is to look at how groups of participants can *progress (i.e., update) their local state.* To see this, we need to delve a bit deeper.

In a decentralized system, a participant must store the local state—if there were a global source of truth for the state, then whoever controls that truth would *de facto* control the system—and communicate with other participants to decide on how their local states evolve. There must be *some* rules about how this state should be updated, even if these rules may differ across participants in the system and even though the rules may not always be followed. It turns out that one common feature of decentralized heterogeneous permissionless systems is a notion of what in Gabbay (2024, 2025) is called an *actionable coalition*, by which we mean:

> *a set of participants who are legally entitled (but not obliged) to collaborate to progress and update their local state (possibly but not necessarily in identical ways).*

3.2.2 *Some informal examples from real life*

We consider some examples of actionable coalitions taken from real life:

1. Ethereum.
   Ethereum's consensus protocol is proof-of-stake. So, an actionable coalition on Ethereum is any group of participants who hold a majority stake of tokens (this is a bit of a simplification, but it will do).
2. Ethereum and Tezos with a blockchain bridge between them.
   Tezos's consensus protocol is also proof-of-stake. An actionable coalition in this system is either an actionable coalition of Ethereum or one of Tezos, *or* the union of sets of an actionable coalition from each, along with the bridging node (again, a simplification, but it will do).[7] We return to this in Example 3.3.6.

[7] Typically, participants can update their state if they held a majority of the stake at some time in the past (e.g., two weeks ago)—the idea being that all participants have reached agreement on, and learned, the state of the network two weeks in the past, so this can be treated as immutable common knowledge without undermining the decentralized nature of the system in the present (Goodman, 2014, Section 3.2.1, final paragraph).

3. A Tango dance evening where leaders will only dance with followers and vice versa.[8]
   An actionable coalition is any set containing equal numbers of leads and followers.
4. A set of people wishing to lift a heavy rock.
   An actionable coalition is any subset of these people who, lifting together, have enough strength to do so.

If an actionable coalition can communicate to agree on a set of local state updates; for example, if the Tango lead leads a move and the Tango follower chooses to follow it, then the participants in this coalition are entitled to update their local states accordingly. Note that local state updates need not be literally identical across participants; they only need to be mutually agreed upon and then actioned.

Some important notes:

1. The actionable coalition can progress *without* consulting the rest of the system.
2. Being in an actionable coalition does not imply control. This set describes a potential legal collaboration, but participants can choose what actionable coalition to work with, if any, and they can also choose not to follow the rules.[9]
3. If O is an actionable coalition for some participant p, and p' is another participant in O, then O is also an actionable coalition for p'. Note that this makes actionable coalitions look a bit like open sets in a topology.

So, we can now introduce our first mathematical abstraction: we identify participants as *points*, and we let *open sets* be *actionable coalitions*. An actionable coalition is a *coalition of participants with the capacity to act*. They are not obliged to act, and if they do act, then their action need not be identical across all participants, but the potential exists for this set to collaborate to progress their states.

---

[8] Many dancers can both lead and follow, including this author, but for the sake of the mathematics, we will simplify.

[9] If you put your elbow into your dance partner's eye or simply deliver a poor lead or a poor follow, then the other dancer might stop dancing with you or turn you down if you ask for another dance. But neither of you are *compelled* to dance with one another, and if you do, you are not *compelled* to dance well.

1. With reference to our example of dancing couples, an example of an actionable coalition that is not minimal is a set containing two leads and two followers. There are two ways for the participants to pair off to collaborate (i.e., dance).
2. With reference to our bridged blockchain example, an example of a set that contains an actionable coalition but is not one itself is an actionable coalition from Ethereum, along with the bridging node. The Ethereum coalition on its own is actionable, but the bridging node cannot take any action without also collaborating with an actionable coalition from Tezos.

To get a flavor of our mathematical results, consider a fundamental problem in any decentralized system: *consensus*, i.e., the problem of ensuring that participants remain in agreement for some suitable sense of "agree." To take a simple example from blockchain, if we reach a situation where half of the nodes say that we have paid for a service, and the other half say that we have not, then *everyone* has a problem because the system has become incoherent, and it is not clear how the system as a whole can restore coherence and progress.[10] This phenomenon is called *forking*, and blockchain designers really want to avoid it!

We call our mathematical abstraction of agreement, *antiseparation*. In a little more detail, antiseparation properties are coherence properties that are guaranteed to hold of a decentralized system *simply* by analyzing the structure of its actionable coalitions. It turns out that we can get surprisingly detailed information about agreement/antiseparation properties, even while working from quite weak and abstract mathematical assumptions on the actionable coalitions.

We emphasize this point: sometimes we can predict important macro properties of a system's behavior without knowing anything about its specifics, provided that we have knowledge about certain good properties of its actionable coalitions.

[10]Coherent (adj.) 1550s, "harmonious;" 1570s, "sticking together," also "connected, consistent" (of speech, thought, etc.), from French cohérent (16c.), from Latin cohaerentem (nominative cohaerens), present participle of cohaerere "cohere," from assimilated form of com "together" (see co-) + haerere "to adhere, stick" (etymologyonline: https://www.etymonline.com/word/coherent).

3.2.3 *Two formal mathematical examples*

Definition 3.2.2. We call *binary consensus* the problem of getting participants in a distributed system to announce a single value, **t** or **f**. This is the simplest possible consensus problem; however, note that by running multiple rounds of binary consensus, we can get participants to announce *bitstrings* (finite sequences of values), and arbitrary data can be serialized to bitstrings, so this consensus problem—simple as it is—is also complete for all data in a suitable sense.

Example 3.2.3. (A simple majority system). We consider a simple situation where participants are trying to solve binary consensus. Continuing the theme of simplicity, assume some finite nonempty set of participants M, and let their actionable coalitions be just any set of participants that forms a majority (so it contains strictly more than half of M, the set of all participants). Now, suppose that the participants in some actionable coalition $O \subseteq \mathsf{M}$ (where $O \subseteq \mathsf{M}$ means that O is a set of elements from M) have communicated and progressed to agree on the value $\mathbf{t}$. Because they form an actionable coalition, they are entitled to act and announce $\mathbf{t}$, and so they do. They have now all committed to this state update, and they cannot change their minds.

So, can this system fork? Consider some participant $p \notin O$ (where $p \notin O$ means that p is a participant that is not in O). If p wants to progress to decide on some value, that value must be $\mathbf{t}$. This is because all of its actionable coalitions intersect with O, and so they contain at least one participant that has already committed to $\mathbf{t}$ and cannot change its mind.

This does not mean that p has to agree on $\mathbf{t}$; it could choose not to agree with anything and not progress (i.e., not update its local state with any value), or it could break the rules. But, by definition, if p does want to make a decision legally, then the decision has been made, and it must eventually go along with the majority. Thus, we have proved that any progress that is made by one participant within the rules (...must be shared with some actionable coalition of that participant and since all such coalitions intersect it ...) must eventually be followed by any other participant that also progresses within the rules. Thus, forking is impossible.

The reader may already be familiar with Example 3.2.3, but note that this antiseparation property comes simply *from the structure of the actionable coalitions.* There is no need to consider the protocol or even how values are interpreted. It turns out that antiseparation-style behavior is common and arises even if we do not require actionable coalitions that are simple majorities. Consider the following example.

Example 3.2.4. Let participants be $\mathbb{Z} = \{0, 1, \text{-}1, 2, \text{-}2, \dots\}$, and let actionable coalitions be generated by sets of three consecutive numbers starting with an even number $\{2i, 2i{+}1, 2i{+}2\}$—so, for example, $\{0, 1, 2\}$ and $\{2, 3, 4\}$ are actionable coalitions but not $\{2\}$ or $\{1, 2, 3\}$—and suppose again that we are trying to agree on $\mathbf{t}$ or $\mathbf{f}$.

Note that unlike for Example 3.2.3, actionable coalitions need not intersect. Yet, once one triplet of participants commits to $\mathbf{t}$, the rest of the system is obliged to eventually agree if all participants play by the rules. Now, this example system is not necessarily particularly safe or desirable in practice because we can imagine that $\{0, 1, 2\}$ agree on $\mathbf{t}$, and $\{4, 5, 6\}$—acting independently but in good faith—agree on $\mathbf{f}$; then, 3 cannot legally progress because within $\{2, 3, 4\}$, 2 has announced $\mathbf{t}$ and 4 has announced $\mathbf{f}$, and 3 cannot agree with both. However, we know that *if* all participants do legally progress, then they announce the same value. So, this example illustrates how antiseparation can arise even when actionable coalitions are rather small.

The two examples above are quite different. In one, all actionable coalitions intersect, whereas in the other, they mostly do not. This suggests that a "general mathematics of (anti)separation" is possible based on the study of actionable coalitions. In a nutshell, that mathematical story is what we will develop.

3.3 What Is a Semitopology?

3.3.1 *The definition*

Let us consider what we have at a high level. Points are synonymous with participants. Further:

1. There is a notion of an *actionable coalition* (or, simply, an *open set*). This is a set $O \subseteq \mathsf{P}$ of participants with the capability,

though not the obligation, to act collaboratively to advance (i.e., update or transition) the local state of the elements in O, possibly but not necessarily in the same way for every $p \in O$.
2. The empty set $\varnothing$ (containing no points) is trivially an actionable coalition. Also, we assume that P (containing all the points) is actionable, effectively assuming that every point is a member of at least one actionable coalition.
3. A union of a set of actionable coalitions is an actionable coalition.

This leads us to the definition of a semitopology.

Definition 3.3.1. Suppose P is a set. Write $pow(\mathsf{P})$ for the power set of P (the set of subsets of P). Then, a *semitopological space*, or *semitopology* for short, consists of a pair $(\mathsf{P}, \mathsf{Open}(\mathsf{P}))$ of:

- a (possibly empty) set P of *points*, and
- a set $\mathsf{Open}(\mathsf{P}) \subseteq pow(\mathsf{P})$ of *open sets*,

such that:

1. $\varnothing \in \mathsf{Open}(\mathsf{P})$ and $\mathsf{P} \in \mathsf{Open}(\mathsf{P})$.
   In words, the empty set of points and the set of all points are both open sets.
2. If $X \subseteq \mathsf{Open}(\mathsf{P})$, then $\bigcup X \in \mathsf{Open}(\mathsf{P})$.[11]
   In words, a union of a set of open sets is an open set.

We may write $\mathsf{Open}(\mathsf{P})$ simply as Open if P is irrelevant or understood.

We recognize a semitopology as being like a *topology* (Engelking, 1989; Willard, 1970) but without the condition that the intersection of two open sets necessarily be an open set. This reflects the fact that the intersection of two actionable coalitions need not itself be an actionable coalition.

Notation 3.3.2. Suppose X and X' are sets. Then, write $X \between X'$ when X and X' are not disjoint, i.e., they have an intersection of nonempty sets: $X \cap X' \neq \varnothing$.

[11]There is a little overlap between this clause and the first one: if $X = \varnothing$, then by convention $\bigcup X = \varnothing$. Thus, $\varnothing \in \mathsf{Open}(\mathsf{P})$ follows from both clause 1 and clause 2. If desired, the reader can simply remove the condition $\varnothing \in \mathsf{Open}(\mathsf{P})$ from clause 1, and no harm would come of it.

We can now define two key antiseparation properties.

Definition 3.3.3. Suppose $(\mathsf{P}, \mathsf{Open})$ is a semitopology and $p, p' \in \mathsf{P}$. Then:

1. Write $p \between p'$, and call p and p' *intertwined* when

$$\forall O, O' \in \mathsf{Open}. p \in O \land p' \in O' \Longrightarrow O \between O'.$$

   In words, p and p' are intertwined when they do not have any pairs of disjoint open neighborhoods.
2. Write $p \between^* p'$, and call p and p' *transitively intertwined* when they are related by the transitive closure of $\between$; thus, there exists some (possibly zero length) chain $p_0, p_1, \ldots, p_{n\text{-}1}, p_n \in \mathsf{P}$ such that

$$p = p_0 \between p_1 \ldots p_{n\text{-}1} \between p_n = p'.$$

This recalls the *Hausdorff separation* property, typical in topology, that any two distinct points should have a disjoint pair of open neighborhoods. As we shall see from Theorem 3.3.4, for the study of consensus, we are particularly interested in semitopologies with antiseparation properties, of which being intertwined is a canonical property; and it is the precise negation of being Hausdorff separated.

3.3.2 *Two mathematical results*

Recall the notion of *binary consensus* from Definition 3.2.2. Now that we have built some mathematical machinery, we can represent binary consensus as the problem of defining a function $f : \mathsf{P} \to \{\mathbf{t}, \mathbf{f}\}$. We call such a function a *value assignment.*

If the value assignment is constant (so that it maps all points to only one value), then this represents system-wide consensus across all of P.

We call a value assignment *continuous* at $p \in \mathsf{P}$ when there exists an open neighborhood $p \in O \in \mathsf{Open}$ such that $\forall p' \in O. f(p) = f(p')$. The reader can check that this coincides with the usual notion of topological continuity if we give $\{\mathbf{t}, \mathbf{f}\}$ the discrete topology (so that $\{\mathbf{t}\}$ and $\{\mathbf{f}\}$ are open sets); a proof is available in Gabbay (2024, Lemma 2.2.4, p. 22). It also coincides with our intuition that if p declares some value, then it must do so in collaboration with an actionable coalition of other participants. Thus, we can write

$$\text{consensus} = \text{continuity},$$

and we can prove the following.

Theorem 3.3.4. *Suppose* $(\mathsf{P}, \mathsf{Open})$ *is a semitopology and* $p, p' \in \mathsf{P}$, *and suppose* $f : \mathsf{P} \to \{\mathbf{t}, \mathbf{f}\}$ *is a value assignment. Then:*

1. *If* p *and* p' *are intertwined and* f *is continuous at* p *and* p', *then* $f(p) = f(p')$.
2. *If* p *and* p' *are transitively intertwined and* f *is continuous at all points, then* $f(p) = f(p')$.

Proof. For part 1, suppose f is continuous at p and p', and suppose $p \between p'$. Then, by assumption, there exist open neighborhoods $p \in O \in \mathsf{Open}$ and $p' \in O' \in \mathsf{Open}$ such that f is constant on O and on O'. Since O and O' intersect, $f(p) = f(p')$.

For part 2, suppose f is continuous at every point, and suppose $p \between^* p'$. By assumption, there exists a chain of intertwinedness relations $p = p_0 \between p_1 \dots p_{n\text{-}1} \between p_n = p'$; also, by assumption, f is continuous at each of these points. By part 1 of this result, $f(p) = f(p_0) = f(p_1) = \dots = f(p_{n\text{-}1}) = f(p_n) = f(p')$. □

Simple as Theorem 3.3.4 is, it explains the consensus behavior we observed in Examples 3.2.3 and 3.2.4 via the following easy lemma.

Lemma 3.3.5. *All points in the semitopology in Example* 3.2.3 *are intertwined. All points in the semitopology in Example* 3.2.4 *are transitively intertwined.*

Proof. Left to the reader to check.[12] □

Example 3.3.6. Consider our previous example of Ethereum and Tezos, connected by a bridging node. What would this look like in abstract semitopological terms?

Assume two semitopologies $(\mathsf{E}, \mathsf{Open}(\mathsf{E}))$ and $(\mathsf{T}, \mathsf{Open}(\mathsf{T}))$ such that (for simplicity) $\mathsf{E} \cap \mathsf{T} = \varnothing$. Assume some other point $r \notin \mathsf{E} \cup \mathsf{T}$, which we call the *bridging node*. Then, define a semitopology $(\mathsf{B}, \mathsf{Open}(\mathsf{B}))$ as follows:

[12] *Hint*: check that $2i{+}1$ is intertwined with $2i$ and $2i{+}2$.

- $\mathsf{B} = \mathsf{E} \cup \{r\} \cup \mathsf{T}$.
- $\mathsf{Open}(\mathsf{B})$ is the closure under arbitrary unions of

$$\mathsf{Open}(\mathsf{E}) \cup \mathsf{Open}(\mathsf{T}) \cup \{O \cup \{r\} \cup O' \mid O \in \mathsf{Open}(\mathsf{E}), O' \in \mathsf{Open}(\mathsf{T})\}.$$

Intuitively, a quorum in the combined system is either a quorum from E or one from T, or it is a pair of quorums along with the bridging node r. The key point about this structure is that the bridging node can only make progress if it is in consensus with some quorum from E *and*, at the same time, some quorum from T. This is exactly what we would expect a bridging node to do.

Now, suppose that $(\mathsf{E}, \mathsf{Open}(\mathsf{E}))$ and $(\mathsf{T}, \mathsf{Open}(\mathsf{T}))$ are intertwined—which is what we would hope since this indicates a pair of blockchains that will not fork. Then, $(\mathsf{B}, \mathsf{Open}(\mathsf{B}))$ is *transitively* intertwined via the bridging node.

3.4 Conclusions and Open Questions

3.4.1 *Overview*

We have discussed *semitopology*, a generalization of point-set topology that removes the restriction that intersections of open sets need necessarily be open. The intuition is that points represent participants in a decentralized system, and open sets represent collections of participants who collectively have the authority to collaborate and update their local state; we call this an *actionable coalition.*

Examples of actionable coalitions include majority stakes in proof-of-stake blockchains, communicating peers in peer-to-peer networks, and even pedestrians working together to not bump into one another in the street. Where actionable coalitions exist, they have in common the following: collaborations are local (updating the states of the participants in the coalition but not immediately those of the whole system); collaborations are voluntary (up to and including breaking rules); participants may be heterogeneous in their computing power or in their goals (not all pedestrians want to go to the same place); participants can choose with whom to collaborate; and they are not assumed to be subject to permission or synchronization by a central authority.

These decentralized systems can be highly complex, and without a centralized authority to control behavior, it is not immediately obvious why they should display order. Semitopologies are a topology-flavored mathematics that offers, to some extent, explanations for how and in what circumstances they can behave well. Semitopology is also interesting in and of itself, possessing a rich and interesting theory—one which quickly deviates from standard accounts on topological spaces because the most interesting semitopologies are rather ill-behaved from the usual viewpoint, as their antiseparation properties mean that they are not Hausdorff. Various antiseparation properties—of which we have considered intertwined or transitively intertwined here, but there are many more—become central to the story, as they define participants who should decide the same value in a distributed system that tries to achieve consensus.

It is possible to construct a quite extensive theory of semitopological space based on these ideas (Gabbay, 2024, 2025) and to relate these results back to practical systems in ways that are not entirely obvious, including the following:

1. It can be proved that *any* semitopology partitions into disjoint components whose points are pairwise intertwined within each component. This provides some insight into why blockchains tend to exhibit order (Gabbay, 2024, Theorem 3.5.4, p. 32).
2. It can be proved that every semitopology has an actionable *kernel* of participants, such that if they make a decision, then all other participants must follow (Gabbay, 2024, Corollary 11.6.11, p. 152). This can be read as a distributed-systems version of Arrow's theorem (Fey, 2014) (though the proof is different).[13]
3. Semitopological logics can be constructed and used to analyze the intertwinedness properties of semitopologies (as documented in Gabbay, 2024, Chapter 20).
4. In ongoing work, we are using these logics to formally specify, reason about, and debug consensus protocols.

[13] Arrow's theorem proves that dictators exist; the semitopological result, for decentralized systems, is that dictator-*sets* exist. So, the question is whether the dictator set is small relative to the size of the whole semitopology. If so, then this serves as a measure indicating that the system may be more centralized than desired.

3.4.2 *Future work*

Semitopologies invite many questions. We mention only a few as follows:

1. What are the natural semitopological notions of path and homotopy?
2. What are the natural notions of the evolution of a semitopology over time? We ask because, in practice, actionable coalitions are not static; they evolve. Thus, it is natural to consider "deformations" of a semitopology over time.
3. Following on from the previous point, suppose we are given a semitopology all of whose points are intertwined—implying, as per Theorem 3.3.4, that all points must agree where algorithms succeed. How close is this semitopology to one such that *not* all of its points are intertwined—meaning that, as discussed, forking would be possible even where algorithms succeed? This is a question that would be of interest, for example, to users managing a blockchain to make sure it evolves safely.
4. Can logics based on semitopologies be used to accelerate development, and increase confidence in, distributed algorithms by giving new declarative descriptions of consensus algorithms?

   This is current work, and so far it has proven useful: most recently, we applied a semitopological modal logic to axiomatize the Paxos consensus algorithm (Gabbay and Zanolini, 2025), and in ongoing research, we have used a more advanced version of the logic to formally specify and identify errors in a proposed industrial protocol (*Heterogeneous Paxos*, Sheff *et al.*, 2020, 2021). We are now using the same techniques to help design its replacement.

References

David, M. 2016. "The legacy of Napster". In Nowak, R. and Whelan, A. (eds.), *Networked Music Cultures: Contemporary Approaches, Emerging Issues*. London: Palgrave Macmillan UK, pp. 49–65. DOI: 10.1057/978-1-137-58290-4_4. https://durham-repository.worktribe.com/output/1642018/ (permalink: https://web.archive.org/web/20250421093331/https://durham-repository.worktribe.com/OutputFile/1642039).

Engelking, R. 1989. *General Topology.* Sigma Series in Pure Mathematics. Berlin: Heldermann Verlag.

Fey, M. 2014. "A straightforward proof of Arrow's theorem." *Economics Bulletin* 34(3): 1792–1797.

Gabbay, M. J. 2024. *Semitopology: Decentralised Collaborative Action via Topology, Algebra, and Logic.* London, UK: College Publications.

Gabbay, M. J. 2025. "Semitopology: A topological approach to decentralised collaborative action." *The Journal of Logic and Computation.* Oxford, UK. https://doi.org/10.1093/logcom/exae050.

Gabbay, M. J. and Zanolini, L. 2025. "A declarative approach to specifying distributed algorithms using three-valued modal logic." https://arxiv.org/abs/2502.00892 (submitted for publication).

Goodman, L. M. 2014. Tezos – A Self-amending Crypto-Ledger (White Paper). https://tezos.com/whitepaper.pdf.

Ryan, J. 2010. *A History of the Internet and the Digital Future.* Reaktion.

Ryan, J. 2011. "How the atom bomb helped give birth to the internet." https://arstechnica.com/tech-policy/2011/02/how-the-atom-bomb-gave-birth-to-the-internet/ (permalink: http://web.archive.org/web/20240622221756/https://arstechnica.com/tech-policy/2011/02/how-the-atom-bomb-gave-birth-to-the-internet/) London, UK.

Sheff, I., Wang, X., van Renesse, R., and Myers, A. C. 2020. Heterogeneous Paxos: Technical Report. https://arxiv.org/abs/2011.08253.

Sheff, I., Wang, X., van Renesse, R., and Myers, A. C. 2021. "Heterogeneous Paxos." In Bramas, Q., Oshman, R., and Romano, P. (eds.), *24th International Conference on Principles of Distributed Systems (OPODIS 2020)* (Dagstuhl, Germany). Leibniz International Proceedings in Informatics (LIPIcs), Vol. 184. Schloss Dagstuhl – Leibniz-Zentrum für Informatik, pp. 5:1–5:17.

Willard, S. 1970. *General Topology.* New York, USA: Addison-Wesley, Reprinted by Dover Publications.

Part II

Real-World Assets: Digital Economic Infrastructure

https://doi.org/10.1142/9781800618664_0005

Chapter 4

The Policy Implications of Competing Digital Currencies

Huseyin Oguz Genc
The University of Tokyo, Tokyo, Japan
oguz.genc@protonmail.com

Abstract
This chapter examines the policy implications of the emerging monetary paradigm driven by the rise of private and public digital currencies based on distributed ledger technologies (DLTs). The study examines parallelism between the contemporary trend of competing currencies with previous historical contexts from the 19th and 20th centuries. The practical evidence on the adoption process and other challenges faced due to rapid developments is presented. A series of scenarios will be considered regarding the implications of a flourishing crypto Eurodollar market, such as its impact on the political economy of the United States and the financial stability implications for other economies.

Keywords: Digital Currencies, Bitcoin, Competing Currencies, Distributed Ledger Technologies (DLTs), Stablecoins, CBDCs, Cryptocurrencies, Eurodollar.

4.1 Introduction

This chapter presents past, current, and future perspectives on the rise of competing digital currencies, a trend en route to becoming one of the most critical phenomena in modern monetary history (Figure 4.1).

Fig. 4.1. Summary of trends in currency issuance and banking since the 19th century.

Starting with the gradual rise of Bitcoin as a global financial asset, the expectations regarding the role of distributed ledger technologies (DLTs) in the future of global financial systems have been of utmost significance.

Out of such expectations, a class of cryptocurrencies that has lived up to the hype has been stablecoins. Since their inception, many different stablecoin issuers have proliferated to build an industry that serves as the onramp to the DLT-based digital dollar rails. These onramps have toppled an issuance volume of $200 billion[1] and a monthly transaction volume of $750 billion,[2] becoming comparable to the total payments volume of some of the largest card processing networks.[3]

With the free experiment era approaching an end as global regulations for stablecoins are being enacted (Crisanto *et al.*, 2024), some early winner and loser use cases have emerged. Nevertheless, it has become clear that only a few stablecoins have achieved global-level adoption.

Nonetheless, to gain a thorough understanding of such developments about the competing digital currencies, one needs to have a high-level understanding of the historical events of past periods of private currency issuances, not only from 19th-century U.S. banking history but also from other examples from the rest of the world, since the parallels in the developments in the digital currency space are highly reminiscent of such previous experiences.

A high-level view of this emerging monetary paradigm in the private and public sectors is presented in the following to provide an

[1]See https://defillama.com/stablecoins.

[2]See https://visaonchainanalytics.com/transactions.

[3]Mastercard and Visa Networks' respective annual transaction volumes are $9.03 trillion and $15.68 trillion, according to the most recent data acquired from https://ycharts.com/.

orderly list of events that appear most critical for competing digital currencies' policy implications. Besides the historical context behind the rise of DLT-based digital currencies, some other key topics to be evaluated include the practical evidence of the challenges for their adoption, the flourishing crypto Eurodollar market, their implications on the global political economy, the fiscal stability of the U.S., and the financial stability implications.

4.2 The Essence of Currency Issuance in Modern History

The essence of currency digitization is the struggle over the authority for currency issuance, which is a political phenomenon rather than an economic one. Before the currency digitization process began, the most significant political economy contention in modern history was the status of the reserve currency. The current reserve currency, the U.S. dollar, was accepted at the Bretton Woods Conference in July 1944, an event that was so important that it could not even wait for the end of World War II.

At the center of the contention were the competing ideas of American and British camps regarding the design of the reserve currency or, to put it in a more straightforward context, the struggle for who would have control over its issuance. The British representation was led by John Maynard Keynes, who had deep-seated personal concerns about the international exchange regime and previous tensions due to the protectionist trade policies and competitive devaluations during the interwar period.

However, he could not triumph over the ambitions of the American delegation led by Harry Dexter White. Keynes' understanding of the dynamics of the balance of payment and how the dollar-backed Gold Standard could not be sustainable is arguably one of the most prescient approaches to avoid imbalances, which he believed to be the key issue to achieving long-lasting peace. Nonetheless, his proposition for a global reserve currency controlled by an international monetary institution never came to fruition.[4]

[4]For a brief account of the events during the creation and the aftermath of the Bretton Woods system, see https://www.federalreservehistory.org/essays/bretton-woods-created.

The Bretton Woods system lasted about 30 years and met its fate due to the imbalances caused by the reserve currency status of the U.S. dollar, as Keynes had predicted. This issue will be revisited later in this chapter at various times, as it is of utmost importance to the dynamic between financial stability and competing currencies.

Nonetheless, before the collapse of the Bretton Woods system, the Eurodollar market was born, becoming one of the most dramatic financial innovations in the post-war period (Schenk, 1998).

The inception of the Eurodollar market is disputed to date by either one of two events. The first one is the People's Republic of China (PRC) moving its dollar assets to a Soviet-owned bank in France due to fears of sanctions by the U.S. by the end of the 1950s (Balaban, 2024), while the second one is the Soviet Union moving its dollar assets to an account in the United Kingdom (U.K.) due to similar motivations after its occupation of Hungary by the mid-1950s (Schenk, 1998).

France and the U.K. emerged as rivals for the center of offshore banking of the Bretton Woods system and had no problem collaborating with communist regimes during the Cold War to gain a competitive advantage in this rivalry between themselves. There are undoubtedly important lessons in these events, including what may be coming soon due to the growth of the crypto Eurodollar market.

The movement of assets between the U.S. and European accounts was possible due to the abundance of dollars in the European market, thanks to the occurrence of structural imbalances, as Keynes had predicted. After the sudden growth of the Eurodollar market, Triffin (1961) also reasserted a similar prediction that the trade imbalances were unsustainable in a theory now known as the Triffin dilemma.[5]

While it took about a decade after Triffin's prediction until the Bretton Woods system's collapse, its demise coincidentally overlapped with the rise of a new financial technology. By 1977, SWIFT became operational as a computerized messaging network, heralding a new era of globalization for international trade payments.[6] As international trade grew with the help of digitalization, globalization

[5]For a detailed account of the Triffin dilemma, see Bordo and McCauley (2019).

[6]For a detailed account of the establishment of the SWIFT network, see Scott and Zachariadis (2012).

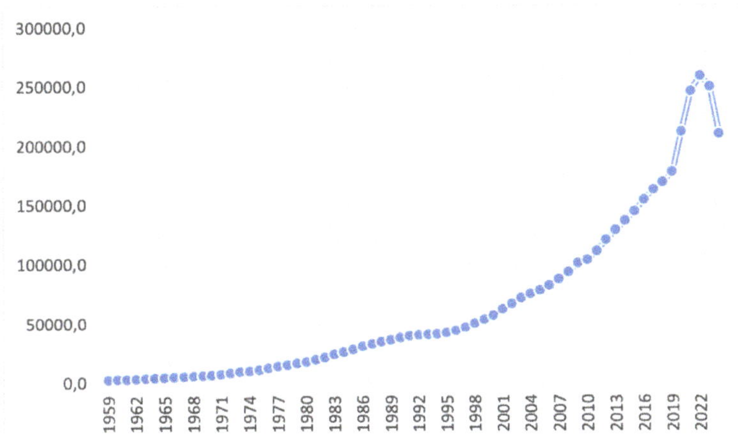

Fig. 4.2. Seasonally adjusted monthly M2 data (billions of dollars) (M2SL: open-source data from the Federal Reserve Economic Data, Federal Reserve Bank of St. Louis).

grew with an increasingly stronger momentum, coupled with everlasting growth in the global money supply (Figure 4.2).

Fast forward to contemporary times: starting with COVID-19, the extreme increase in the money supply, followed by the Russia–Ukraine War and several other geopolitical security events, led to an inflationary environment yet to be normalized.

Like the growth of the Eurodollar market during the 1950s due to the tensions between the U.S. and the Soviet Union and PRC, these recent shock events are leading to the birth of a crypto Eurodollar market that has proven to continue seeing higher user adoption despite the high-interest environment (Hampl *et al.*, 2024; Kreuzer *et al.*, 2024).

Therefore, a brief introduction to the history of the centralization process of currency issuance is also highly relevant to the current proliferation of private and public currencies due to the significant parallelism between these phenomena.

4.2.1 *A short background of currency issuance centralization*

One can adopt a deductive approach from the existing core vectors of currency decentralization to provide a more fundamental basis for the political struggle underlying the competition between public and private currencies. Since the central actor of currency digitization is the U.S., a simple approach would be surveying the ideological background of competing currencies in modern American history.

Deep within the center of the debate lie two camps, the first spearheaded by Alexander Hamilton, the first Secretary of the Treasury of the U.S., who championed a strong central government. The primary goals were reestablishing commerce and industry, repaying war debt, restoring the currency's value, and lowering inflation. Hamilton used the Bank of England charter as the basis of his plan, and the First Bank of the United States was founded with a twenty-year charter in 1791.[7]

The opposition to this approach was led by Thomas Jefferson, the third president of the U.S., famous for fundamentally disagreeing with the idea of a central bank on various grounds, such as the jeopardy of centralization of power, as well as his argument that the Constitution did not grant the authority to the government to establish such a bank. Although a second charter was issued mainly due to the war with Great Britain, President Andrew Jackson, who shared similar views with Jefferson, prevented the extension of the second charter, opening the doors for a highly experimental phase for decentralized banking in the U.S.

After the expiration of the Second Bank's federal charter in 1836, American banks began issuing currency with no centralized federal oversight for almost three decades. This era is often called the "free banking" era in the U.S., although it is regarded as a misconception by free banking experts since there were state-level regulations that (mis)governed such banks, while the free banking system is attributed to operating without special government regulations or restrictions (Selgin, 2020). Although banks would issue currency that is supposed to be redeemable against some species, fraud was rampant due to a lack of regulatory oversight, leading to the adoption of the infamous name "wildcat banking" for the referred era.

[7]For a brief account of the establishment of the First Bank of the United States, see https://www.federalreservehistory.org/essays/first-bank-of-the-us.

In short, the relevance of the disagreement between the two camps with the scope of competing can be summarized in two aspects: opposing views on establishing a central bank and collateral preference for currency issuance.

Other decentralized banking and currency issuance experiments took place in the 19th century, such as in Ireland (Selgin & White, 1987) and Switzerland (Bordo, 2017), demonstrating a stable currency competition environment without a central bank. Nevertheless, the Federal Reserve Bank was established after tumultuous banking crises, starting from the American Civil War to the early 20th century,[8] and central banking became the norm worldwide over the following years. Nevertheless, the intellectual debate on alternative banking systems and currency issuance remained relevant, particularly gaining momentum after the collapse of the Bretton Woods system, with some of the most prominent intellectual and philosophical works that aimed to create a breakthrough for the practical adoption of competing currencies being drafted. Perhaps the most influential one remains Hayek (1990), who even admitted that private currencies could not rival public currencies under the existing monetary tools of the late 20th century. The triumph of centralized currency issuance was undisputed by the end of the 20th century.

At the advent of the Global Financial Crisis of 2008, Bitcoin was introduced, marking a similar trend to the collapse of the Bretton Woods system. The systemic instability exhibits a more evident presence in the post-COVID-19 era, where wars are omnipresent, and trade protectionism and disruption are becoming more rampant. The fact that new financial technology is seeing higher adoption with each passing day is highly reminiscent of significant historical events from the 19th and 20th centuries, while American history remains at the center stage of these debates per se.

Upon covering the historical background of the dispute between opponents and proponents of currency issuance (de)centralization,

[8]For a short introduction on the banking panics prior to the establishment of the FED, see https://www.federalreservehistory.org/essays/banking-panics-of-the-gilded-age.

a brief classification of the digital currencies within the scope of this study is presented in the following section.

4.3 A Simple Classification of Competing Digital Currencies

There have been several attempts to classify digital currencies. An early taxonomy by van der Merwe (2021) looks at crypto assets from a broader perspective, including stablecoins. While stablecoins issued via smart-contract-powered protocols are named "cryptocurrency-backed stablecoins," other stablecoins such as Tether's USDT are categorized as "fiat-backed stablecoins," as their primary collateral is U.S. treasuries and other cash equivalents that can cumulatively be called real-world assets (RWAs). Minting and burning of such stablecoins are centralized and kept as exclusive privileges for authorized clients.[9]

Ito *et al.* (2020) expand the collateral classification by adding commodity-backed and unbacked stablecoins. Others offer a similar taxonomy but exclude commodity-backed stablecoins due to their insignificance while referring to unbacked stablecoins as *algorithmic stablecoins*, which have become the terminological standards over the years (Chanson and Senner, 2022; Fiedler and Ante, 2023).

Moin *et al.* (2020) present a taxonomy of the stablecoin design mechanisms from multiple axes, such as the collateral types, collateralization amount, peg mechanism, and price data input. Such a taxonomy focuses on the technical aspects of stablecoin classification. While a typical risk of such taxonomies is the changing landscape of the stablecoin industry, the collateral categorization of stablecoin taxonomies has become a standard practice over recent years.

The most significant centralized stablecoin issuer, Tether, releases quarterly reports to announce collaterals. According to the most recent audit results, the company keeps nearly $85 billion in U.S. treasuries and another $40 billion in other cash-equivalent assets, corporate bonds, precious metals, Bitcoin, and other investments.[10]

---

[9] *See* https://tether.io/news/tether-issuance-primer/ as an example for the issuance process of centralized stablecoins.

[10] See Independent Auditor's Report on Consolidated Financial Figures and Reserves Report from 30 September 2024, at https://tether.to/en/transparency/?tab=reports.

Therefore, this category can also be named *permissioned* or *custodial* stablecoins.

Other than the centralized permissioned custodial stablecoins, another market for stablecoins has emerged thanks to the unique issuance mechanism through the technical capabilities offered by smart contracts, where issuance can be minimized to the custodianship of the individual through collateralization of one's crypto assets. This issuance mechanism is *permissionless* and may have significantly enhanced technical properties of censorship resistance, possibly becoming immutable against the political preferences of sovereign states. These stablecoins can interchangeably be named *permissionless* or *non-custodial* stablecoins.

However, not all permissionless non-custodial stablecoins have such attributes, thus requiring further classification between them. This classification can be denominated based on their levels of decentralization, which is a highly convoluted and nuanced topic that depends on different parameters such as technical, asset-related, and political factors. Therefore, it should be the topic of future studies.

However, focusing on the collateral of permissionless non-custodial stablecoins, it is known that some use RWAs as collateral, such as treasuries and centralized stablecoins, or a mixture of those assets with more decentralized cryptocurrencies like BTC and ETH. Meanwhile, others can only stick to decentralized crypto assets for enhanced censorship resistance attributes.

A primary differentiator for this classification would be the collateral type. Therefore, regardless of whether the issuance is non-custodial (at the individual level), the decentralization of the issued stablecoin depends on the type of underlying collateral. If this collateral is limited to digital currencies that are censorship-resistant commodities, then the stablecoin can be decentralized at the collateral level. If the collateral consists of RWAs, such as digital assets with inbuilt blacklist functions in their smart contracts, then such stablecoins cannot be deemed as decentralized at the collateral level.

A seminal example is the DAI stablecoin of Maker DAO (now Sky Protocol), the most significant permissionless non-custodial stablecoin issuance protocol known by the categorical name of Collateralized Debt Position (CDP) protocol. The essence of this issuance method is displayed in Figure 4.3, along with a comparison with the permissioned custodial stablecoin issuance mechanism.

Consequently, the agent of issuance is fundamentally decentralized for CDP protocols. However, the same cannot be said for collaterals. Maker decided to diversify its collateral base from the Ethereum Network's token ETH to centralized RWA-backed stablecoins, such as USDC.[11] This event marks a significant turning point since censorable collaterals can and practically do violate the censorship-resistant nature of the protocol.

A more fundamentally decentralized stablecoin issuance mechanism in terms of collateral is offered by Liquity, another CDP protocol inspired by Maker. Besides being non-custodial, Liquity V1 only

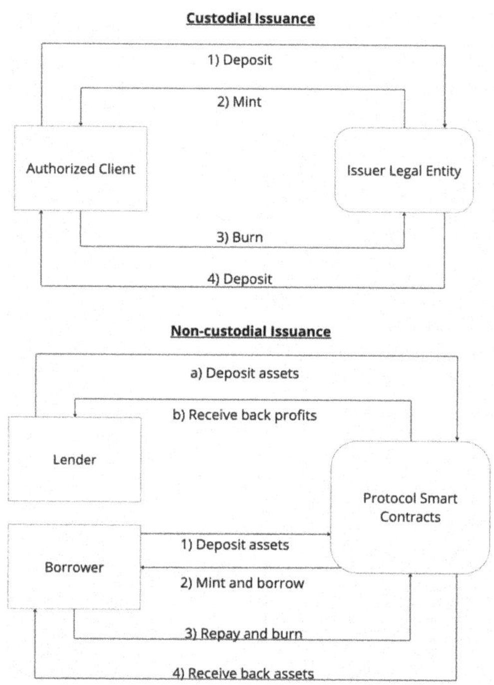

Fig. 4.3. Comparison of issuance mechanisms for custodial vs. non-custodial stablecoins.

---

[11]In 2020, Maker's governance voted for accepting USDC as a collateral, marking a dramatic shift from usage of conventional collaterals such as ETH. See https://blog.makerdao.com/usdc-approved-by-maker-governance-as-the-third-collateral-type-of-the-maker-protocol/ .

allows ETH as collateral, thus making it much more censorship-resistant at the collateral asset level.

Another type of collateral classification for stablecoins is utilized for algorithmic stablecoins. This classification includes two categories known as exogenous and endogenous collaterals. In simple terms, an exogenous collateral is an asset that would not lose its intrinsic value in the event of a bank run for the main stablecoin. In contrast, an endogenous collateral would typically also experience a similar deterioration in value under similar circumstances. The most famous example is Terra USD (UST), which saw significant adoption yet ended up in a death spiral as it defies the simple principles of the impossible trinity (Liu *et al.*, 2023).

Table 4.1 displays the categorization of stablecoins based on their issuance types, collateral types, collateral ratios, and proximate legal definitions, while no comparison is made regarding decentralization due to the convoluted nature of the topic.

On the other hand, since the currency digitization trend is not limited to private space, public digital currencies are also of interest

Table 4.1. A simple classification of stablecoins.

Issuance Type	Collateral Type	Collateral Ratio	Legal Definition[12]	Stable Currency
Custodial	Real-world assets (RWAs)	≥100%	E-money token; Asset referenced token	USDT, USDC; Libra, PAX
Non-custodial	RWAs; exogenous	≥100%	Crypto-collateralized token	DAI, LUSD, RAI
Non-custodial	Endogenous	≥100%	Crypto-collateralized token	Stability primitives
Non-custodial	Endogenous	≤100%	Algorithmic token	UST

[12]Varies depending on jurisdiction.

to this study. Geva and Muraj (2024) provide a more comprehensive taxonomy, combining cryptocurrencies, stablecoins, and CBCDs. Nonetheless, as an upgrade to the national monetary networks, CBDCs are not collateralized, shifting the research focus of their classification based on their design choices, which are divided into several axes (Genc and Takagi, 2024).

After introducing some relevant past stories about competing currencies and presenting a simplified and updated classification, the following section investigates the current adoption trends of stablecoins.

4.4 Adoption Trends of Competing Digital Currencies

The adoption trends of competing digital currencies are one of the best objective sources regarding the demand for currency digitalization. After the monumental bank run on FTX, one of the largest centralized cryptocurrency exchanges at the time, the cryptocurrency market entered an elongated bear market, further depressed by the restrictive monetary policies adopted in most parts of the world. The same period also corresponded with a clampdown on cryptocurrency investments in China due to financial stability concerns (Shin, 2022), leading to a perfect storm of stagnating adoption for digital currencies.

However, stablecoins have removed themselves from this function as the sole asset class that attracted further adoption despite many other limitations, such as the highly hostile banking policy toward the crypto-friendly banks in the U.S. during previous administrations.

In particular, policies during the Biden administration are highly questionable, such as the infamous Operation Chokepoint 2.0, which led to the bankruptcy of a series of crypto-friendly banks (Gannon *et al.*, 2024). This event caused USDC, the largest on-shore stablecoin in the U.S., to decouple from its peg to the U.S. dollar, which also caused DAI to temporarily lose its peg due to the protocol's utilization of USDC as collateral (Sarkar, 2023). Subsequently, U.S. regulators also enforced a seizure of issuance for Binance's stablecoin, BUSD, by Paxos, a regulated stablecoin issuer in the U.S. (Roth, 2023). The timing of the decision could not be worse, as the market was still feeling the shock from the collapse of FTX. Meanwhile, it was one of the most self-evident events regarding the preferential treatment of the U.S. government for competing stablecoins.

Nonetheless, there has been a clear trend of increased adoption of USDT, particularly within jurisdictions with high financial instability (Castle Island Ventures and Brevan Howard Digital, 2024). An important trend to underscore regarding this adoption has been the volume of data per blockchain network. Tron Network has been the leader,[13] suggesting that many users may prefer a cheaper and faster but more centralized network.

A critical event regarding the rivalry between Tron and Ethereum within the realm of stablecoin issuance also appeared, when Circle abruptly stopped the issuance of USDC on the Tron Network, stating that the decision is "aligned with its efforts to ensure that USDC remained trusted, transparent and safe." (Wilson, 2024). Nonetheless, despite all such adverse events, stablecoin adoption has surged.

Simultaneously, another global trend has occurred with the stablecoin market, as the pegging currency has undisputedly been the U.S. dollar since its inception, with approximately 99% of existing stablecoin volume being pegged to the U.S. dollar (Castle Island Ventures and Brevan Howard Digital, 2024). This situation will likely remain the same for several reasons, such as the increasing dominance of the U.S. dollar as a global unit of account (Rolfe, 2024).

Meanwhile, looking at the Euro-pegged stablecoin market, there are multiple reasons to speculate that it may not see the same level of adoption as USD-pegged stablecoins in the short term. One reason is that stablecoin adoption occurs in financially strained economies outside the Eurozone (Castle Island Ventures and Brevan Howard Digital, 2024). The second reason is the regulatory landscape of Europe, which has seen the introduction of significant limitations for stablecoins from early on (Hansen & Bauer, 2024). A third reason is the lack of sovereign debt in the Eurozone, which limits the ability to control the supply of the currency from a central authority, thus limiting the growth of the financial account. This situation also does

[13]See https://defillama.com/stablecoin/tether.

not provide a favorable environment for the international adoption of the euro as a reserve currency.

Nevertheless, while such adoption trends can be valid for custodial stablecoins, non-custodial stablecoin issuance has not been as fortunate. One of the most significant projects in the early boom stage of DeFi in 2021 was Liquity, which has provided one of the market's most decentralized stablecoin issuance mechanisms that lacked any governance mechanism to upgrade its smart contracts. However, this deterministic logic had its trade-offs.

Liquity V1 is designed to only charge 0.5% in stablecoin or collateral terms (ETH) when opening and closing a debt position. The interest rate is unilaterally 0% for all debt positions. By the early days of DeFi's boom, global interest rates were low, and deflationary trends were prevalent, which made the 0% interest policy a viable option. However, the highly expansionary monetary policies of the COVID-19 era returned to inflation after 2022.

While other ventures in DeFi were able to adapt to the macroeconomic norms and offer higher yields for users, Liquity V1's lack of adaptability led to the natural result of a sharp drop in the volume of its stablecoin (LUSD) due to lenders abandoning the protocol, as displayed in Figure 4.4. Eventually, the protocol released a new version, which adopted a *laissez-faire* ethos by allowing lenders and borrowers to set the market rate in an open market. The results of this experiment will be observed in the next cycle.

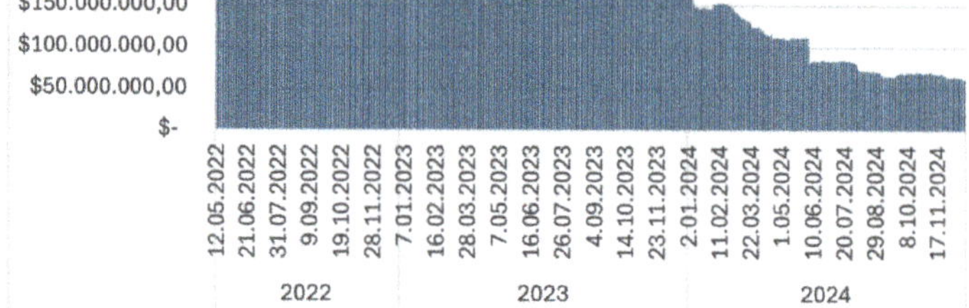

Fig. 4.4. Total LUSD circulating.
Source: Open-source data from DefiLlama.

Meanwhile, the most significant non-custodial stablecoin issuance protocol, Maker DAO, experienced an identity crisis when deciding between becoming a centralized RWA-backed stablecoin issuer or remaining committed to its original position as a champion of decentralized finance. The founder of Maker eventually spearheaded a significant effort to rebrand the protocol[14] and pivot the stablecoin issuance strategy by separating centralized and decentralized stablecoin issuance more straightforwardly. The result of this pivot is yet to be seen, but some important lessons for permissionless non-custodial stablecoin issuance have been prevalent.

4.4.1 *Why do permissioned custodial stablecoins have significant competitive advantages?*

Custodial stablecoin issuers have various competitive advantages. First and foremost, they have higher liquidity due to having onramps to the banking system. Second, they are part of what can rather be regarded as the fintech ecosystem. Various embedded finance-type applications have surged recently, providing a dollar account for their users and a savings account where users can quickly gain yield on their dollar savings. Embedded finance also requires KYC/AML checks that fundamentally contradict the decentralization ethos. Therefore, the lack of compliance tools prevents non-custodial stablecoins from scaling further. On top of these, off-ramp solutions, thanks to card issuance, are also available for embedded finance applications that support custodial stablecoins, completing a neo-bank-type experience for users in a regulated environment.

On the other hand, non-custodial stablecoins typically serve as agents for leveraged trading, an important use case in DeFi, yet they lack the use case for implementing traditional financial applications such as payments and remittances.

4.4.2 *Why have CBDCs failed to reach adoption thus far?*

While some scholars believe that CBDCs will supplant private currencies in the long term (Peneder, 2022), as it currently stands,

[14]For a detailed account of the rebranding plans of the Maker DAO into Sky Protocol, see https://forum.sky.money/t/the-5-phases-of-endgame/20830.

CBDCs are yet another group of digital currencies struggling to see any meaningful adoption.

Although more minor-scale experiments are also present, China and Nigeria have been the most extensive-scale experiments thus far (Dowd, 2024). While several academic arguments were made in favor of e-CNY (Allen *et al.*, 2022; Lee *et al.*, 2021; Li & Huang, 2021), evidence shows that such benefits already exist without a CBDC network (Genc and Takagi, 2024). Despite significant government efforts in a jurisdiction with the highest adoption rate of cashless payments globally, alongside Sweden, the adoption of e-CNY has been a failure so far (Dowd, 2024).

Meanwhile, another mass-scale CDBC experiment took place in Nigeria. With significant turmoil in its macroeconomic environment, Nigerian officials took dramatic measures, including limiting cash circulation and temporarily banning cryptocurrencies to enforce the usage of the e-Naira (Anthony, 2023). This attempt backfired dramatically, pushing society to the brink of a mass-scale social upheaval (Anthony, 2023), accompanied by a simultaneous surge in the adoption of dollar-pegged stablecoins,[15] while the Nigerian government blamed Binance and its citizens for the failure of e-Naira (Anthony, 2024).

The cases of China and Nigeria provide important lessons about the CBDC experiment, showing that regardless of the efforts of a government in what may look like an ideal setup for adoption, CBDCs are not demanded by the citizens.

A recent survey showing the lack of enthusiasm among U.S. citizens (Ekins and Gigi, 2024) was probably why President Trump promised not to allow a CBDC during his term in office. Such opposition to a CBDC in the U.S. can also be strengthened due to the ideological roots overviewed in a previous chapter. Thus, the currency digitization stage is set for private enterprises that receive preferential treatment from the U.S. government, providing a controlled environment for competing currencies again, but this time in a highly globalized and connected world through the internet, where the U.S. dollar is becoming a global unit of account.

[15]For recent data on increased stablecoin adoption in Nigeria during the crypto bear market, see https://www.chainalysis.com/blog/subsaharan-africa-crypto-adoption-2024/.

4.5 Policy Implications of Competing Digital Currencies

The policy implications of competing digital currencies can be divided into two parts. These are simply the implications for public digital currencies against private ones. Since practical implications are more imminent on the private currencies side, the focus will remain in the private realm despite the implications being largely theoretical.

4.5.1 *Policy implications of public digital currencies (CBDCs)*

A simple comparison of the supposed benefits and risks of CBDCs is provided in Table 4.2. The benefits are purported to be extensive, such as more flexible monetary policy tools for central banks, better tax collection, a more robust security setup for the banking system, and various social benefits, including improved financial inclusion and cross-border settlements. Meanwhile, the risks may be extensive and must be weighed against the benefits based on the practical evidence from existing CBDC experiments.

The main issue with the socioeconomic benefits is that competing currencies, such as custodial stablecoins, already offer all the benefits CBDCs can offer while providing a more stable medium of exchange and store of value than most sovereign currencies. Another disadvantage of CBDCs in this regard is that stablecoins have a significant comparative head start in adoption, thus making it even less likely for the CBDC-centered banking system to rival them.

Table 4.2. Generic risks and benefits of CBDCs.

Benefits	Flexible monetary policy
	Broader tax base
	Increased efficiency in payments
	Payment system backstop
	Improved financial inclusion
Risks	Disintermediation of financial institutions
	Miscalibration of government involvement
	Financial risks due to a lack of regulatory expertise and capacity
	Technological vulnerabilities or entrenched design mistakes
	Loss of privacy

Source: Genc and Takagi (2024).

Nonetheless, a primary advantage of CBDCs over custodial stablecoins is that they can act as a lender of last resort. However, since all significant stablecoins are over-collateralized, the lender-of-last-resort argument also becomes questionable regarding the marginal benefits it may introduce.

Regarding improved taxation and more robust banking security, it is impossible to provide empirical evidence to suggest that such improvements will be achieved thanks to CBDC adoption. Some studies provide empirical evidence on the impact of cashless payments on improving tax collection (Immordino & Russo, 2018), but this outcome has already been achieved without CBDCs, while the results depend on the dynamics of each jurisdiction. There is contradictory evidence that increased digitalization causes the cash-based shadow economy to shift toward digital currencies (Berdiev *et al.*, 2024), which logically makes sense since the highest adoption rates are seen in countries with significant financial instability (Castle Island Ventures and Brevan Howard Digital, 2024).

On the other hand, a secure private permissioned blockchain ledger with the necessary privacy, compliance, and scalability features has yet to be realized at the government scale, not to mention smart contract risks being a significant threat to DLT-based financial systems (Zhang, 2024), which is the main reason why the European Commission has enacted the EU Data Act that requires kill switches for blockchain networks to be compliant (Preiss, 2023). With reputable banks experimenting with Layer 2 solutions (Nijerk, 2024), it may seem like central banks are also coming closer to such implementations. However, no evidence suggests that CBDCs provide a more robust security system thanks to DLTs.

The most apparent improvement of CDBCs is considered the ability of central banks to implement negative interest rates (Xin & Jiang, 2023), which would serve as a true novelty from the central banking perspective. However, negative interest rates are unlikely to resolve the critical issue of savings and investment imbalances, as there are strong arguments that the lack of investment is not due to a constraint in savings (Klein & Pettis, 2020).

Notwithstanding, implementing a negative interest policy through CBDCs requires eliminating cash, a highly questionable policy objective from a privacy perspective (Wenker, 2022). Meanwhile, although CDBC systems are dubiously claimed to improve the security of the national payment systems, eliminating cash would be an ultimate downgrade to overall security. Therefore, it is almost impossible to justify this supposed benefit of CDBCs without any empirical evidence due to the dramatic requirement of eliminating cash, which is very different from encouraging a higher proportion of cashless transactions.

4.5.2 *Policy implications of private digital currencies*

Policy implications of private currencies are much more diverse and practically imminent than those of public currencies. Since stablecoins are a phenomenon of a growing crypto Eurodollar market, the most crucial jurisdiction for policy implications is the U.S., as the growth of stablecoins will probably have various strategic importance for American policymakers. Simultaneously, there will be financial stability implications due to the dramatic increase in the globalization of the monetary system, which will be covered as another significant policy implication.

4.5.2.1 *Policy implications from the U.S. perspective*

While all matters regarding the growing stablecoin market could be interesting as a part of the U.S. national security interests, a simplified list of such interests is provided as follows as a more systematic presentation:

- Impact of stablecoins on the fiscal policy of the U.S.
- Impact of the growing Eurodollar market on balance of payments.
- Impact of the growing Eurodollar market on sanctions policies.
- Impact of the growing Eurodollar market on the reserve currency status of the U.S. dollar.

For starters, the most apparent benefit for the growth of the crypto Eurodollar market is the long-term sustainability of the U.S. fiscal debt. The dramatic growth in the debt of the U.S. is a financial stability risk for the entire world. However, the foreign holdings of U.S. treasuries have been continuously declining since 2008, from over 50% to around 30% of the marketable U.S. treasuries held by the public.[16] Simultaneously, Tether is about to become one of the top 20 holders of U.S. treasuries,[17] marking a significant event for the stablecoin market.

Increased stablecoin adoption provides a perfect instrument for the U.S. to socialize its debt by enabling the rest of the world to save and invest in dollars. After a dramatic increase in the tokenization of U.S. treasuries, the world may witness a widespread adoption of dollar accounts thanks to a low entry barrier for users and significant advancements in embedded finance applications.

Such a trend will probably fortify the skew in the balance of payments, which has led the rest of the world to export its savings glut into the U.S. Nevertheless, it is too early to conclude, although the trend requires expert scrutiny.

One main reason for doubt is that there is no guarantee that the growing Eurodollar market will dramatically fortify the reserve currency status of the U.S. dollar. If Bitcoin emerges as a significant alternative in the long term, it could be the ultimate agent for the rest of the world to diversify from exporting excess savings to U.S. financial markets while simultaneously using U.S. dollars as a medium of exchange and a new form of commodity, such as Bitcoin, as a store of value. Thus, there is no guarantee that the excess savings will flow into the U.S. financial account with increased momentum.

Lastly, there is growing concern that a crypto Eurodollar market could cause a loss of political power for the U.S. and the rest of the Western bloc as stablecoins enable sanctions avoidance (Fantacci and Gobbi, 2024; Travkina *et al.*, 2022). While this may be true, on-chain transactions are much easier to trace than the existing cash market for dollars and euros, which serves as a significant unaccountable shadow economy for avoiding sanctions. Therefore, a crypto Eurodollar market would be a more effective tool for critical policy objectives, such as preventing terror financing. A bottom line to achieve such a policy goal would be dissuading users from privacy tools, which has already been a part of the agenda of the U.S. prosecutors despite such policy objectives being hard to justify on legal grounds (De, 2024).

---

[16]See https://sgp.fas.org/crs/misc/RS22331.pdf/.

[17]See https://www.statista.com/statistics/246420/major-foreign-holders-of-us-treasury-debt/.

4.5.2.2 *Financial stability implications*

Scholars have extensively researched the potential financial stability implications of the crypto Eurodollar market. A significant concern is the stability of the stablecoins themselves. Grobys *et al.* (2021) observe the impact of Bitcoin volatility on the price stability of stablecoins, finding a significant correlation. Meanwhile, stablecoins have been subject to shocks from significant market events, such as the collapse of several banks that served the cryptocurrency industry in the U.S., which impacted the peg of stablecoins like USDC and DAI.

Nonetheless, evidence shows that the leading actor in the banking panic, Silvergate Bank, could withstand up to 70% of withdrawals and eventually decided to voluntarily wind up services after experiencing sustained pressure from U.S. regulators.[18] Hence, looking at the recovering pegs in the aftermath of the crypto-banking panic and the momentary resilience of the banking system, the financial stability regarding crypto banking and price stability is strong for stablecoins. Nonetheless, there are important lessons for the rest of the world regarding the nation-state-level attack on centralized RWA-backed stablecoin issuers.

Another significant financial stability concern is dollarization or currency substitution, depending on the preference for terminology. As seen in the example of Nigeria, currency substitution can be a real problem for local authorities, as the institutions fail to instill trust in their competence to recover confidence in local currency.

Similar situations have led to different policy responses in G-20 countries such as Turkey and Argentina. Turkey has taken early action to ban crypto payments. Although public reasoning was not offered, financial stability and currency substitution risks are likely the reason. Meanwhile, Argentina has endorsed dollarization after the recent presidential election, offering a perfect environment for stablecoin adoption, which is already at one of the highest levels in the world (Partz, 2024).

The future is vague regarding currency substitution, but it would not be an exaggeration to claim that there is a chance of dollarization

[18]Evidence based on the testimony of a senior officer of Silvergate Bank. See https://cases.stretto.com/public/x353/13020/PLEADINGS/1302009182480000000098.pdf.

happening on a more global scale if the geopolitical environment remains inflationary in the long term. The simple reason for this risk is that the citizens of vulnerable economies now have access to a dollar account outside the banking system of their jurisdiction, which forces the hands of regulators into implementing stablecoins into the banking systems or facing further loss of trust from the public.

In such a case, many economies could pay for the American public debt for relatively much higher financial stability, while Americans could print dollars to buy the next reserve currency. This idea is perhaps behind the meaning of President Trump's statement that America might pay off its debt with Bitcoin.

Finally, even if dollarization happens at a large scale, it is hard to imagine many nations endorsing a stablecoin like USDT or USDC, as neither provides the necessary decentralization to guarantee the independence of the technical infrastructure from the sphere of interest of the U.S. regulators. That is why commodity-backed stablecoins on sovereign networks such as Layer 2s built on a credibly neutral network could have significant room for adoption if dollarization seems inevitable.

4.6 Limitations and Future Research

There are two main limitations of this study. The first is the lack of empirical research for many theories around stablecoins and CBDCs. The latter limitation is due to the volatile nature of the cryptocurrency industry, which has seen many shocking events since its inception. There is no guarantee that the most significant stablecoin of the current date will not become insignificant within the next 10 years. While the ossification of industry winners seems more likely than ever, the history of money is full of surprises.

Meanwhile, future research calls for a debate on the decentralized currency issuance infrastructure, which could be the best bet for nations considering dollarization. However, the money supply is limited by the savings amount (either in foreign currency or the commodity collateral) in this setting, which radically differs from the conventional banking system, where banks primarily create money depending on consumer demand that policy rates set by central banks directly impact (McLeay *et al.*, 2014).

The potential role of currency boards, the trade-offs between foreign exchange or digital commodities as collateral of future money issuance settings, and the custodial setting of future currency systems will define the demand for such monetary networks from the public's perspective, which seems to be the differentiator for adoption success, as seen from the CBDC experiments.

4.7 Conclusion

Competing currencies will define the next chapter of the global monetary paradigm. The history of currency issuance and the transformation of the banking system starting from the 19th century provides a great prelude to current events unfolding in global finance. The most important policymaker in the space is the U.S., as it has historically been since Bretton Woods.

There is no denying that private currencies have the upper hand against CBDCs for several reasons. Like its historical position, the U.S. has the most political influence on this trend by adopting a rhetoric that prefers private currencies over public ones. However, the policies adopted by the U.S. are convoluted and vague, which makes them difficult to decipher systematically. At the same time, there is no reason to expect unconditional friendly policymaking from any administration, as stablecoin issuance practically equals the power of dollar issuance.

There is a chance that the growing U.S. fiscal debt becomes more sustainable to service if global dollarization occurs. This strategy would give an asymmetric advantage to the U.S. in the medium to long term by allowing it to acquire more time for policymaking in its interests.

Meanwhile, the growing Eurodollar market causes financial stability risks for vulnerable economies, primarily as an increasing risk for currency substitution. A good hedge under such circumstances is working on the best technical standards for setting up sovereign networks to issue USD-pegged stablecoins.

However, the solution that would gain the public's trust for long-term adoption does not easily intersect with the best interests of policymakers, who, in most cases, will want to imbue the network with censorship tools. Nonetheless, if competing stablecoins do not proliferate, many nations may risk falling into a political economy paradigm that may allow even more significant economic influence of the U.S. than before.

References

Allen, F., Gu, X., and Jagtiani, J. 2022. "Fintech, cryptocurrencies, and CBDC: Financial structural transformation in China." *Journal of International Money and Finance* 124: 102625. https://doi.org/10.1016/j.jimonfin.2022.102625.

Anthony, N. 2023. "Nigerians' rejection of their CBDC is a cautionary tale for other countries." *Cato Institute*, December 22, 2023. https://www.cato.org/commentary/nigerians-rejection-their-cbdc-cautionary-tale-other-countries.

Anthony, N. 2024. "Nigeria's government is blaming Binance for its own mismanagement." *Cato Institute*, December 22, 2024. https://www.cato.org/commentary/nigerias-government-blaming-binance-its-own-mismanagement.

Balaban, I. A. 2024. "The establishment of the Eurodollar market in Paris and the failure of regulation and reform, 1959–1964." *Business History* 66(7): 1735–57. https://doi.org/10.1080/00076791.2023.2202909.

Berdiev, A. N., Goel, R. K., and Saunoris, J. W. 2024. "Global cryptocurrency use, corruption, and the shadow economy: New insights into the underlying linkages." *The American Journal of Economics and Sociology* 83(3): 609–29. https://doi.org/10.1111/ajes.12566.

Bordo, M. D. 2017. "Currency competition in Switzerland." *Universität St.Gallen, Schweizerisches Institut Für Aussenwirtschaft Und Angewandte Wirtschaftsforschung (SIAW-HSG)* 68(1): 101–108.

Bordo, M. D. and McCauley, R. N. 2019. "Triffin: Dilemma or myth?" *IMF Economic Review* 67(4): 824–51. https://doi.org/10.1057/s41308-019-00088-y.

Castle Island Ventures and Brevan Howard Digital. 2024. "Stablecoins: The emerging market story." Castle Island Ventures, November 19, 2024. https://castleisland.vc/writing/stablecoins-the-emerging-market-story/.

Chanson, M. and Senner, R. 2022. "Stablecoins' quest for money: Who is afraid of credit?" *The Journal of FinTech* 02(01n02): 2250002. https://doi.org/10.1142/S270510992250002X.

Crisanto, J. C., Ehrentraud, J., and Garcia Ocampo, D. 2024. "Stablecoins: Regulatory responses to their promise of stability." *BIS Financial Stability Institute* 57: 1–26.

De, N. 2024. "Distilling the tornado cash and Samourai suits." *CoinDesk*, April 30, 2024. https://www.coindesk.com/policy/2024/04/30/distilling-the-tornado-cash-and-samourai-suits/.

Dowd, K. 2024. "So far, central bank digital currencies have failed." *Economic Affairs* 44(1): 71–94. https://doi.org/10.1111/ecaf.12621.

Ekins, E. and Gygi, J. 2023. "Poll: Only 16% of Americans support the government issuing a central bank digital currency." *Cato Institute*, December 19, 2023. https://www.cato.org/survey-reports/poll-only-16-americans-support-government-issuing-central-bank-digital-currency.

Fantacci, L. and Gobbi, L. 2024. "Stablecoins, central bank digital currencies and US dollar hegemony: The geopolitical stake of innovations in money and payments." *Accounting, Economics, and Law: A Convivium* 14(2): 173–200. https://doi.org/10.1515/ael-2020-0053.

Fiedler, I. and Ante, L. 2023. "Stablecoins." In Baker, H. K., Benedetti, H., Nikbakht, E., and Smith, S. S. (eds.), *The Emerald Handbook on Cryptoassets: Investment Opportunities and Challenges*. Bingley, UK: Emerald Publishing Limited, pp. 93–105.

Gannon, S. T., Bonici, M., Davis, E. L., and Rovira, K. 2024. "'Operation chokepoint 2.0': De-banking policies and the adverse use of reputational risk in bank supervision." *Davis Wright Tremaine Financial Services Law Advisor*, December 21, 2024. https://www.dwt.com/blogs/financial-services-law-advisor/2024/12/debanking-crypto-regulation-trump-andreessen-sacks.

Genc, H. O. and Takagi, S. 2024. "A literature review on the design and implementation of central bank digital currencies." *International Journal of Economic Policy Studies* 18(1): 197–225. https://doi.org/10.1007/s42495-023-00125-9.

Geva, B. and Muraj, M. 2024. "The digitization of money: Stablecoins and CBDC." *Banking & Finance Law Review* 40(1): 115–141.

Grobys, K., Junttila, J., Kolari, J. W., and Sapkota, N. 2021. "On the stability of stablecoins." *Journal of Empirical Finance* 64: 207–223. https://doi.org/10.1016/j.jempfin.2021.09.002.

Hampl, F., Vágnerová Linnertová, D., and Horváth, M. 2024. "Crypto havens during war times? Evidence from the Russian invasion of Ukraine." *The North American Journal of Economics and Finance* 71: 102093. https://doi.org/10.1016/j.najef.2024.102093.

Hansen, P. and Bauer, H. 2024. "MiCA's significance regime for stablecoins - A sledgehammer to crack a nut?" *SSRN Electronic Journal*. https://doi.org/10.2139/ssrn.4699043.

Hayek, F. A. von. 1990. *Denationalisation of Money: The Argument Refined; an Analysis of the Theory and Practice of Concurrent Currencies*. 3rd ed. London: Institute of Economic Affairs.

Immordino, G. and Russo, F. F. 2018. "Cashless payments and tax evasion." *European Journal of Political Economy* 55: 36–43. https://doi.org/10.1016/j.ejpoleco.2017.11.001.

Ito, K., Mita, M., Ohsawa, S., and Tanaka, H. 2020. "What is stablecoin?: A survey on its mechanism and potential as decentralized payment systems." *International Journal of Service and Knowledge Management* 4(2): 71–86. https://doi.org/10.52731/ijskm.v4.i2.574.

Klein, M. C. and Pettis, M. 2020. *Trade Wars Are Class Wars: How Rising Inequality Distorts the Global Economy and Threatens International Peace.* New Haven, CT: Yale University Press.

Kreuzer, C., Laschinger, R., Priberny, C., and Benninghoff, S. 2024. "Cryptocurrencies as a vehicle for capital exodus: Evidence from the Russian–Ukrainian crisis." *Finance Research Letters* 69: 106191. https://doi.org/10.1016/j.frl.2024.106191.

Lee, D. K. C., Yan, L., and Wang, Y. 2021. "A global perspective on central bank digital currency." *China Economic Journal* 14(1): 52–66. https://doi.org/10.1080/17538963.2020.1870279.

Li, S. and Huang, Y. 2021. "The genesis, design and implications of China's central bank digital currency." *China Economic Journal* 14(1): 67–77. https://doi.org/10.1080/17538963.2020.1870273.

Liu, J., Makarov, I., and Schoar, A. 2023. *Anatomy of a Run: The Terra Luna Crash.* NBER Working Paper No. w31160. Cambridge, MA: National Bureau of Economic Research. https://doi.org/10.3386/w31160.

McLeay, M., Radia, A., and Thomas, R. 2014. "Money creation in the modern economy." *Bank of England Quarterly Bulletin* 54(1): 14–27.

Moin, A., Sekniqi, K., and Sirer, E. G. 2020. "SoK: A classification framework for stablecoin designs." In Bonneau, J. and Heninger, N. (eds.), *Financial Cryptography and Data Security, Lecture Notes in Computer Science.* Cham: Springer International Publishing, pp. 174–197.

Nijerk, M. 2024. "Deutsche Bank's L2 Blockchain to Be 'Public and Permissioned,' Says Tech Partner." *CoinDesk*, December 18, 2024. https://www.coindesk.com/tech/2024/12/18/deutsche-banks-l2-blockchain-to-be-public-and-permissioned-says-tech-partner.

Partz, H. 2024. "Argentina overtakes Brazil in crypto inflows — Chainalysis." *Cointelegraph*, December 22, 2024. https://cointelegraph.com/news/argentina-leads-latin-america-crypto-inflows.

Peneder, M. 2022. "Digitization and the evolution of money as a social technology of account." *Journal of Evolutionary Economics* 32(1): 175–203. https://doi.org/10.1007/s00191-021-00729-4.

Preiss, I. 2023. "EU data bill threatens to upend smart contracts in potential blow for DeFi." *DL News*, August 27, 2023. https://www.dlnews.com/articles/regulation/eu-rules-on-smart-contracts-could-damage-defi-if-not-changed/.

Rolfe, A. 2024. "The Dollar's share of global payments surges to 49.1%." *Payments Cards & Mobile*, December 20, 2024. https://www.paymentscardsandmobile.com/the-dollars-share-of-global-payments-surges-to-49-1/.

Roth, E. 2023. "Crypto firm paxos ordered to stop issuing binance stablecoin." *The Verge*, February 13, 2023. https://www.theverge.com/2023/2/13/23597539/crypto-paxos-order-sec-binance-usd-stablecoin.

Sarkar, A. 2023. "Circle's USDC instability causes domino effect on DAI, USDD Stablecoins." *Cointelegraph*, March 11, 2023. https://cointelegraph.com/news/circle-s-usdc-instability-causes-domino-effect-on-dai-usdd-stablecoins.

Schenk, C. R. 1998. "The origins of the Eurodollar market in London: 1955–1963." *Explorations in Economic History* 35(2): 221–238. https://doi.org/10.1006/exeh.1998.0693.

Scott, S. V. and Zachariadis, M. 2012. "Origins and development of SWIFT, 1973–2009." *Business History* 54(3): 462–482. https://doi.org/10.1080/00076791.2011.638502.

Selgin, G. 2020. "Modeling the legend, or, the trouble with diamond and Dybvig: Part I." *Cato Institute*, December 19, 2020. https://www.cato.org/blog/modeling-legend-or-trouble-diamond-dybvig-part-i.

Selgin, G. A. and White, L. H. 1987. "The evolution of a free banking system." *Economic Inquiry* 25(3): 439–57. https://doi.org/10.1111/j.1465-7295.1987.tb00752.x.

Shin, F. 2022. "What's behind China's cryptocurrency ban?" *World Economic Forum*, January 21, 2022. https://www.weforum.org/stories/2022/01/what-s-behind-china-s-cryptocurrency-ban/.

Travkina, E. V., Fiapshev, A. B., and Belova, M. T. 2022. "Stablecoin-based digital trading and investment platforms and their potential in overcoming sanctions restrictions." *Economies* 10(10): 246. https://doi.org/10.3390/economies10100246.

Triffin, R. 1961. *Gold and the Dollar Crisis: The Future of Convertibility.* New Haven, CT: Yale University Press.

van der Merwe, A. 2021. "A taxonomy of cryptocurrencies and other digital assets." *Review of Business* 41(1): 1–34.

Wenker, K. 2022. "Retail central bank digital currencies (CBDC), disintermediation and financial privacy: The case of the Bahamian sand dollar." arXiv:2204.01535. https://doi.org/10.48550/ARXIV.2204.01535.

Wilson, T. 2024. "Crypto firm circle to end support for USDC stablecoin on tron blockchain." *Reuters*, February 21, 2024.

Xin, B. and Jiang, K. 2023. "Economic uncertainty, central bank digital currency, and negative interest rate policy." *Journal of Management Science and Engineering* 8(4): 430–52. https://doi.org/10.1016/j.jmse.2023.04.001.

Zhang, Z. W. 2024. "CBDC Security." In Huang, K., Parisi, C., Tan, L. J., Ma, W., and Zhang, Z. W. (eds.), *Web3 Applications Security and New Security Landscape*. Cham: Springer Nature Switzerland, pp. 73–92.

https://doi.org/10.1142/9781800618664_0006

Chapter 5

Wallets as End-User Universal Access Devices

Kim Peiter Jørgensen
TecMinho, University of Minho, Guimaraes, Portugal
kimpeiter@proton.me

Abstract
Wallets are access points for value creation in the digital economy. Wallets for blockchains store the end-users' cryptographic keys for administering their digital assets and enable access to blockchain/Web3 systems. Web3 delivers new service opportunities. This chapter focuses on the Web3-enabled release of value through the lens of wallets. Wallets may be implemented as software apps on smartphones, web apps on desktops, or hardware devices. Wallet users request high security, ease of use, and relevant access from their wallets. Increasing connectivity, functionality, autonomy, personal support, and offline capability make the wallet the user's universal access device for any digital asset. Through wallet-based services, the owner obtains enhanced digital empowerment. The new Web3 solution areas—identity and decentralization—enable considerable societal effects, and wallets are an integral part of these. One example is self-sovereign identity solutions combined with wallet-borne AI for personalized support, empowering the end-user beyond anything previously known. Improved welfare is foreseen globally through enlarged markets with collaborative services and drastically lowered transaction costs compared to today; the expected vastly increased levels of automation in society necessitate enhanced end-user protection. As wallets are considered a weak spot for security, improving overall security through blockchains is essential.

Keywords: Blockchain Wallets, Self-Sovereign Identity (SSI), Universal Wallets, User Empowerment, Interoperability, Decentralization, Digital Assets, Ease of Use.

5.1 Introduction

Digital wallets are already well known from Web2 systems such as Facebook, Amazon, and Google services. Wallets for blockchain systems are devices, typically dApp software on smartphones, that connect to blockchain systems (Jørgensen & Beck, 2022). Wallets store the end-user's cryptographic keys for administering their digital assets and enable access to blockchain/Web3 systems. Even if they resemble the wallets of Web2 systems, blockchain wallets are fundamentally different. Based on Web3, they enable entirely new service opportunities we can hardly imagine today, combined with a much higher overall security for the end user (Cai *et al.*, 2018). The paradigms behind blockchain were early described by Swan (2019) and Swan and de Filippi (2017).

It should be noted that any of the following examples can be constructed outside of Web3; it is simply far more effective, safe, and easy to develop these as Web3 solutions. Decentralization and identity are well-known core capabilities enabled by Web3. Other Web3 aspects include drastically improved interoperability (Park *et al.*, 2023) and the use of metaverse technologies.

We describe the world of wallets through brief narratives to illustrate realized roles and upcoming solutions. We first take a traditional look at wallets for Web3/blockchains as appendages to the blockchain systems, examining how their implementation brings benefits and some limitations of existing solutions. Then, we inspect recent developments for ease of use and security, and we analyze some of the opportunities created by the technology with digital identity and decentralized services providing user empowerment, system and societal interconnection, and trustworthy services. We also consider examples of civic solutions where wallets are already contributing to society. What is coming? The wallet's increased ability to act independently creates entirely new solutions and services with wallets in other roles than those traditionally expressed and utilized.

Finally, we discuss some of the overall economic and societal implications of Web3 perspectives and summarize our findings as takeaway conclusions.

5.2 Wallets for Blockchain Systems

5.2.1 *A traditional look*

According to Popchev *et al.* (2023), "A blockchain wallet is a mechanism (device, physical medium, software, or a service), operating through cryptographic key pairs, that enables users to interact with a variety of blockchain-based assets and serves as an individual's interface to blockchain networks." Wallets place the user at the center of focus (Voskobojnikov *et al.*, 2021). The user becomes empowered vastly beyond what is possible from today's digital wallets.

In short, wallets are end-user access points for value creation in the digital economy (Jørgensen & Beck, 2022), as illustrated in the use case for identities by Degen and Teubner (2024). Here, the digital service becomes available to what has been called the "access economy." The literally thousands of wallets for blockchain systems available cover many usage areas. Although the vast majority focus on cryptocurrencies, the wallet functionality has expanded drastically in recent years. On top of the cryptocurrency solutions are new types of tokens such as non-fungible tokens (NFTs), real-world assets (RWAs), upcoming identity solutions, and Verifiable Credentials with large-scale use cases covering everyday life in the European Blockchain Services Infrastructure (EBSI).

In the following, a few examples of current wallet functionality and solutions are presented. Through a wallet, users can manage their digital assets, including their personal key, and manage access by governing which systems are accessed and which data are transferred, with whom, and when. These two areas—access and asset management—can be considered the core wallet functionalities. Several auxiliary services exist to make the end user's lives easier, offering extra storage or enhanced security functionality (Hyperledger Indy, 2024) to wallets accessing their applications.

5.2.2 *Recent wallet developments*

Further to the above core functions, the wallet fulfills several specific functions dependent on the blockchain system it accesses. With developments within digital identity, such as self-sovereign identity

(SSI), wallet holders can govern and use generalized digital identities in completely new service types. Such solutions are being launched on a large scale across the EU with specific identity wallets (EUIDs) (European Commission, 2025).

5.2.2.1 *Ease of use and usability*

Ease of use is a priority for end users. Usability is so essential for the success of any device or service that it should be considered a given, together with high security and a well-performing platform for services. Currently, end users are insufficiently shielded from the complexities of blockchain technology by not being presented with a simplified, easy-to-use interface (Voskobojnikov *et al.*, 2021). The need for intuitive use will increase as the types of assets managed through wallets extend beyond finance-like identities (Sartor *et al.*, 2022) into other societal areas with Verifiable Credentials and other digital tokens (Tan *et al.*, 2023). We need an easy-to-navigate and understandable user-centric wallet interface (Hart, 2023), avoiding technical jargon while providing precise and helpful error messages to guide users.

The importance of this is illustrated through the connection between ease of use and reduced digital divide (Loo & Ngan, 2012). The wallet should work seamlessly across different devices and blockchain systems as part of ease-of-use. Users wish to avoid being bothered by accessing many apps, hence the need for universal wallets (Jørgensen & Beck, 2022). This should be contrasted with today's purpose-specific wallets, which function as end-user interfaces to a set of specific applications. In the Far East, there is a development around super-apps (Minghai *et al.*, 2023), involving essentially the same argument we make here for universal wallets, where all the functionality requested by the user is made available via a single app.

To reach enough end users and citizens to achieve the intended benefits and usage, authorities and corporations need to plan how to incorporate wallets as the access vector to their digital services (Viriyasitavat *et al.*, 2019). Albayati *et al.* (2021) find ease of use and the relevance of services—for example, that the wallet adapts to the user's interactions and can provide personalized experiences and security (Yu *et al.*, 2024)—to be the highest priorities among the analyzed users.

5.2.2.2 *Security*

Security is one of the key "abilities" blockchain systems offer (Goyal, 2023). Users need to feel safe using their wallets. The wallet is often considered the weak link in highly safe blockchain solutions (Houy *et al.*, 2023; Marella *et al.*, 2020) precisely because they have access to the blockchain without being one. It should be noted that good security needs to be closely linked with user-friendliness to avoid end users making security-compromising errors (Sambin, 2023). Security risks (Erinle *et al.*, 2023) are well understood, with a rich literature (Houy *et al.*, 2023). Following penetration, there is a risk of losing the private keys (Erinle *et al.*, 2023), which irreversibly locks the assets governed by that wallet.

Other risks are more subtle. A risk that users should always consider is data framing. For example, anyone can send data segments to any current wallet. These segments might contain incriminating data being planted to discredit the holder.

A key security consideration for Web3 wallets is who controls (owns) the user's keys. Wallet recovery methods are key to user confidence. There are two types of custody for wallets. The first is a custodial wallet, where a third party (often a crypto exchange) manages your private keys. If one loses or forgets one's keys, access can be recovered. The other type of custody is called non-custodial wallets (Vadlamani & Sharma, 2023). With a non-custodial wallet, the end user alone has complete control over the wallet's key and digital access (Perdana & Hu, 2023). "Non-custodial" also means there is no safety net for the user. If the keys are lost, there is no way to contact the assets connected to the wallet (Takei & Shudo, 2024). This becomes relevant for people who may have been but can no longer administer their digital wallets (den Breeijen *et al.*, 2022). Examples of both types of custody could be Metamask (https://metamask.io/), a custodial-type wallet service that also offers a non-custodial wallet. Binance (https://www.binance.com/en/square) is another example of a custodial construct with its Trust Wallet as a highly reputed non-custodial, open-source offering (https://trustwallet.com/).

The custodial situation is quite different for institutional users, who need to be fully backed up in case of inability. Anchorage (https://www.anchorage.com/), for example, offers custodial solutions as a necessity, which also means other security solutions are available for recreating keys if lost. Here, continuous operation is a key criterion rather than a user's privacy.

5.2.2.3 *Wallet categories*

Wallets may be categorized into three wallet categories according to the medium of their implementation: software, hardware, and paper. The most popular wallets for blockchains are software wallets. They come as solutions on the web, desktop, or mobile. Some software wallets are easy to use, inexpensive or free, and capable of managing a large number of assets. An internet connection is an obvious attack vector because they are connected to their assets through the internet via so-called “hot” wallets. Several approaches increase security for software wallets such as multi-sig wallets, which require multiple authorizing signatures, adding control and reducing fraudulent transaction risks. An interesting software wallet providing very high levels of security is INTMAX (https://www.intmax.io/), which claims to achieve similar levels of protection as hardware wallets (Rybakken *et al.*, 2023) through the use of homomorphic encryption.

Hardware wallets are physical devices; the private keys they store on a secure device cannot be transferred out of the device in plaintext. They are considered the most secure and are often used for asset storage. Even though crypto-wallet hardware stores keys separately from exchanges, they still interact with Web3 and may inadvertently be used to sign malicious smart contracts that send assets to a hacker. Most hardware wallets are not very user-friendly; they are not free, and—most importantly—they introduce a single point of failure: they can be lost, stolen, or damaged. Dabrowski *et al.* (2021) consider “hardware wallets the new single point of failure.” Cold wallets are considered the most secure type of crypto wallets because they operate entirely offline and do not have Web3 interaction. However, they can be and have been hacked.

The wallet category paper wallets provide offline (“cold”) storage of private keys. Along with the private and public key pairs are associated QR codes. In printed form, these enable receiving or spending digital assets. Paper wallets were popular when first introduced, but users soon realized they could be lost, stolen, or damaged.

5.2.3 *Web3 technology raises several new opportunities*

Web3 technology raises several new opportunities. The most significant initial change in system paradigms from these new classes of digital services, not least combined with the proliferation of smart devices (Büttgen *et al.*, 2021), will be the introduction of SSI into society (de Amorim, 2024), building upon Web3 identity tokens, Verifiable Credentials (W3C, 2024), and Decentralized Identifiers (DIDs) (W3C, 2022). Unlike the several VC-specialized wallets for the non-blockchain world, these tokens are built for transferability from the outset and do not present challenges for blockchain wallets. The wallet is key for success in this new environment, as it facilitates user access to and interaction with these services.

5.2.3.1 *Identity*

Identity wallets (Podgorelec *et al.*, 2022) are a rapidly growing market transforming technological potential into value (World Economic Forum, 2024). The interest in improving digital identity has been growing for 20 years. A key paper by Cameron (2005) proposed a new way of thinking about digital identity, placing the user in charge. Several countries and organizations have initiated digital identity drives, with the PRC, India, and the EU mentioned here as the currently most significant in volume and impact. The EU is based upon the eIDAS2.0 regulation, launching EU-wide identity systems for which all EU countries need to develop an EUID wallet solution and enable EU citizens to operate their credentials from their country of origin within all other EU countries by 2026 (European Parliament, 2024). This is spurring a number of services which interact with Verifiable Credentials and DIDs (Sedlmeir *et al.*, 2021). These digital identity drives are of key interest to the financial and banking industry, providing much-improved know-your-customer (KYC) and anti-money laundering (AML) services. This Web3 proliferation, with identity and decentralization as key elements, enables local decentralized digital services with potentially ultra-low transaction costs, as these services oust expensive current bank and credit card solutions.

5.2.3.2 *The decentralization paradigm*

The decentralization paradigm is fundamental to original blockchain thinking. With DIDs (W3C, 2022), a standard way of referring to an identity is described by a set of transactions conducted locally. DIDs are already used in hospitality and travel (Identity Foundation, 2023), the clothing industry (Guth-Orlowski & Sabadello, 2023), and, together with Verifiable Credentials, in the upcoming digital product passports in the EU (Garcia *et al.*, 2020).

Web3 greatly improves interoperability among IT systems (Park *et al.*, 2023; Liu *et al.*, 2022), often by interconnecting blockchains through the use of smart contracts (Khan *et al.*, 2021). This approach also lets a blockchain govern non-blockchain applications. Popchev *et al.* (2023) mention wallets using smart contracts to secure and automate wallet operations. As it can be quite cumbersome to interconnect blockchains directly, using wallets (Schlatt *et al.*, 2023) can simplify cross-blockchain connections, at least at the end-user level. Such solutions demonstrate the possibility of managing more asset types than cryptocurrencies across domain areas such as healthcare, smart cities, supply chains, and gaming.

5.2.3.3 *Trust*

The end users' trust in the digital solutions is crucial to fully adopting a digital lifestyle (Marella *et al.*, 2020). Credible decentralized structures, including wallets, must be interwoven into the Web3 architecture (Bambacht & Pouwelse, 2022). Another element in trust is availability. We trust that the services we need are available when needed. With increasing levels of automation, the availability of functionality becomes critical for the functioning of individuals and society. Several solutions for interim offline capability have been proposed (Igboanusi *et al.*, 2021).

5.3 Civic Solutions Where Wallets Are Already Contributing to Changing and Improving Human Society

An essential aspect of Web3 is an opportunity to spread individual empowerment through SSI and the general use of Verifiable Credentials, enabling greater transparency, accountability, and security. These opportunities for participatory citizenship are already expressed in several activities where wallets contribute to transforming and improving human society. For example, agriculture in Kenya (Bolt, 2019) and Ghana (Glavanits & Szabo, 2024) is viewed by Asare *et al.* (2024) as a sector in which blockchain technology may serve as a catalyst for transformation in Africa. These projects utilize the technical opportunities to address solutions other than those found prior to Web3, with the wallet playing a key role precisely where the end user is involved. Such civic solutions are initiated across the world with wallets constructed to handle tokens created for use locally by the local community (Balbo *et al.*, 2020).

5.3.1 *Decentralization*

A key point for understanding the wallet perspective in civic or democratic blockchain projects is blockchain's fundamentally decentralized approach. We have seen how wallets with blockchains enable the user to safely participate in a broader range of digital activities than is currently possible. "Disciplined initiative" (Alexander, 2020) states that the person in a given situation has the most precise perspective of what is needed and what is doable within the plans and resources available. Blockchain wallets' user-centric and empowering approach also allows for transactional optimization, which is crucial to reducing the overall transactional costs of decentralized systems. Examples of socioeconomic participation and interactions are reported from local communities (Viano *et al.*, 2022) and smart cities (Kassen, 2021). Social coins, e.g., tokens with some value attached, are found as loyalty tokens in various shopping platforms, gaming, and social gatherings (Abbas & Alkhzaimi, 2024), as well as potential interchange with fiat money. Viano *et al.* (2023) provide an example of community wallets with a token-based decentralized economy.

This local societal participation can be an element in the democratic process, including voting (Ghazinoory *et al.*, 2024), and opens new ways of accessing and participating in society. The range of blockchain solutions targeting community applications in China warrants closer examination (Kshetri, 2023).

5.3.2 *Including marginalized groups*

A further example of the community solutions mentioned above are the many solutions developed for refugees in refugee camps (Garazha, 2024).

5.3.3 *The digital divide*

The growing split between those who can and do use available digital systems and those outside these categories has become more critical with increasing levels of automation. As wallets cover an increasing amount of each person's digital life activities, it becomes critical to actively reduce the digital divide. One reason for this split is unequal access to digital technology, including smartphones and devices needed to connect to the services. Another is that society is changing with the many new systems being implemented. A person cannot participate anymore without being connected to societal systems (Helsper, 2021). The reservations of many people not currently using systems are often related to security and privacy; one could say they lack trust in the system, hence the importance of the self-sovereignty concept and, generally, the security and protection of users' assets and privacy in a decentralized environment.

One of the key activities needed to bridge this gap is extensive education to prepare and train the population for these new societal practices (Vassilakopoulou & Hustad, 2023). It is not sufficient simply to provide instructions on how to use the latest systems; the concept of using a wallet as an access and management tool to participate as a digital citizen is new to a high percentage of the population. This is demonstrated in the Portuguese Blockchain Agenda (2022), where a nationwide blockchain-based set of societal solutions is developed. Here is a clear need for a strong focus on end-user training to make people use the wallets and new services efficiently and securely. Substantial online training seems the only realistic way to achieve this.

5.3.3.1 *Access for people with disabilities*

In a highly automated society where all users become highly dependent on their wallets, a key question is how to integrate users who cannot use these facilities. Previously, we have pointed to custodial solutions for people who, for certain reasons, are mentally unable to use their wallets and the relevant system. Physical impairment also prevents citizens from using the systems. Of the many areas of impairments and practical solutions to mitigate these, we mention one: visual impairment (Zhou *et al.*, 2023).

Anti-crime activities are already being realized, with successful anti-corruption drives reported from the public sector (Olalekan, 2024) and accounting and auditing from the private sector (Kaplan, 2021), as well as successful anti-trafficking activities (Enrile & Aquino-Adriatico, 2024).

5.4 What Is Coming?

What is coming? Wallets are also becoming the wallet-carrier's process coordinator, where smart contracts may provide an easy way to coordinate processes among solutions on different IT platforms as an interconnectivity device. The wallet is not a blockchain; this can be exploited for enhanced interconnection with legacy and non-blockchain systems. That is needed because most systems accessed by end users today are still non-blockchain systems, further to the blockchain systems already in place. Such interconnectivity can be developed into an actual collaboration between several parties exploiting the abilities of Web3 solutions. This is key for local and rural development of community solutions.

Wallets are developing in roles other than traditionally expressed, with drastically increasing levels of automation and the necessarily associated automation of security procedures such as sign-on and continuous validation. The platform also enables far more personal support from decentralized AI directly on the wallet platform. Kin is an early example of this (https://mykin.ai/), and Apple is expected to follow suit, establishing customer bots (Birch, 2023). This demonstrates the proliferation of areas where wallets will cover increasing aspects of digital services and support for the end user. Are wallets becoming agents? Barresi and Zatti (2020) point to the logical development of the wallet as the universal access device for financial services. Generalizing this, Büttgen *et al.* (2021) point to the need for autonomous, proactive wallets to access the drastically increasing number of digital services that will become available to each person in the future, as well as increased levels of services using smart devices. The universal wallet is a key access and digital asset mechanism in all these examples. The Web3 technology stack represents the next leap forward in institutional technology: crypto technologies facilitate trust and lower the costs of economic coordination. This innovation enables elements to "talk" to each other, as the wallets may cooperate in swarms, communicating wallet-to-wallet. Note that these multi-agent systems could behave as a decentralized artificial superintelligence even without the individual elements of the network necessarily being intelligent (Ponomarev & Voronkov, 2017). So, even before a general spread of AI to wallets, the system could behave intelligently (Shammar *et al.*, 2024). Such a solution has already been launched to enhance security (Strobel *et al.*, 2023).

The wallet will be developed and refined with the progress of society and as more systems are rethought as decentralized systems to obtain drastically lowered transaction and intermediation costs (Chen & Bellavitis, 2020) and to enable enhanced types of services made possible through Web3-enabled interaction.

5.4.1 *Future directions of wallet platforms*

Smartphone-based wallets are by far the most prevalent and commonly used today. Their functionality could be ported to platforms that are more convenient for use, such as Heads Up Computing. The number of wearable devices is rapidly expanding (Ometov *et al.*, 2021), differentiating from smartphones (Zhao *et al.*, 2023) by offering seamless computing support for humans' daily activities as the next milestone. The wallet and many other devices are logical devices delivering specific functionality for access and asset management and some potentially collaborative interconnectivity. Such new processing platforms fit into current IoT, and smart devices are soon to be superseded by really smart devices that are expected to increase in number in the coming years. These smart devices will need faculty to decide what to access and how to administer the relevant assets within their realm. For this, they will need wallet functionality. Such embedded wallets already exist (Watanabe *et al.*, 2024). With autonomous and proactive solutions (Santana & Albareda, 2022), the wallet may operate on entirely new solutions and services of its own creation, introducing functionalities that were previously considered unthinkable.

The above wallet functionalities are conceptualized in Figure 5.1.

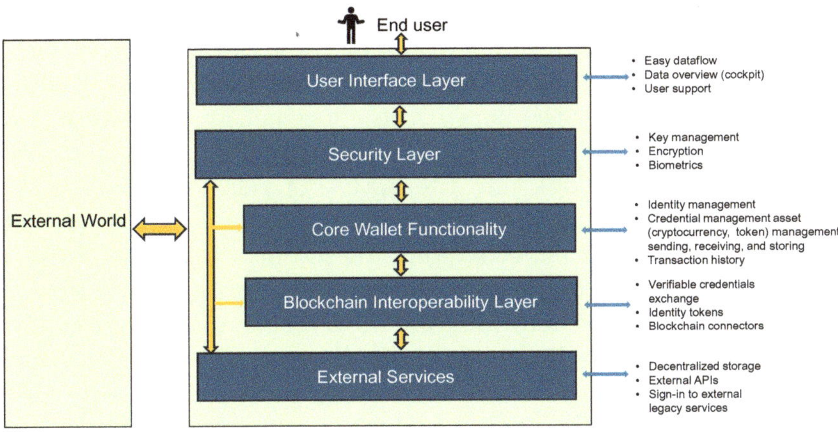

Fig. 5.1. Conceptual blueprint for end-user wallets.

5.5 Economic and Societal Implications: Who Benefits?

Blockchain wallets represent several interesting aspects of delivering the benefits presented here. The benefits from a transactional economic perspective are not difficult to estimate. The wallet's initial role as governance and operating devices around cryptocurrencies, with the spread of crypto assets into general tokens such as NFTs and RWAs, are examples fitting into classical business models where value buildup is identifiable.

Web3 services such as digital identity and particularly SSI empower users to maintain control over the information associated with their identity, increasing security and reducing data leakage. With increased functionality and security, improved ease of use, reduced transaction costs, and a significantly increased number of new services and new types of digital assets to manage, the end-user can enter the digital world as a self-sovereign individual with the wallet as the direct interface to a vast number of new services. The wallet carrying digital identity files may provide far more streamlined and secure digital services than those currently known. With the proliferation of identity wallets—such as EUID—some of the described benefits are classical, including slim-lined payments and direct benefits from improved KYC and AML, with an expected reduction in data theft and other fraudulent activities amounting to annual savings of trillions of dollars and euros. In all these cases, there are direct transactional benefits. Furthermore, some are like insurance, where you do not directly see the benefit if the mechanism works or if theft or fraud is avoided.

It is necessary to look into the nature of value projection. This includes questions of who benefits and whether the benefits materialize at the microeconomic, ecosystem, meso-, or macro-level. Wallets are of direct importance as user-access points for individual systems (a microeconomic consideration) and at the economic ecosystem level since the systems are interconnected. Expanding its use into new industries will provide network effects at the meso level. Finally, there is a much larger national/global context (a macroeconomic consideration), as including a more significant percentage of the population as wallet users will enhance the productivity of society as a whole. The wallet, as an essential element and a site of value creation in the rapidly growing software-based access economy, is rarely considered in the above scenarios. Value creation in wallets should be viewed within the context of wallets being connectable to many services, not merely the marginal value of each wallet connection summed up across all systems.

Having a large number of active wallet users provides a better digitally trained population and cumulative benefits from digitization. A parallel is the welfare state, where the certainty of support makes life easier, more predictable, and less expensive for the individual user to the benefit of the individual, the local community, and the nation. The actual beneficiaries of value creation from wallets are thus partly society, the end user, and the digital services involved. This argument is key in this chapter; a well-designed wallet could benefit everyone in society, though in different ways.

A list of benefits for key high-level groups is given as follows:

Individual citizens: Greater security, easier access to services, and increased financial and social inclusion benefit individuals across all socioeconomic groups. Blockchain wallets can provide access to financial services for those currently excluded from the traditional banking system, empowering them to participate more fully in the economy (Rosli *et al.*, 2022).

Businesses: New markets and opportunities could emerge soon, initially in the technology and finance sectors but increasingly in other areas of society, covering and developing new opportunities that enable collaboration, security, and ease of use.

Governments: More efficient service delivery, reduced fraud, and improved citizen satisfaction are potential benefits for governments.

Society as a whole: A long-term outcome could be a more inclusive, secure, and efficient society with reduced inequality. While blockchain technology is safe, widespread adoption will require robust safeguards against new threats that may emerge. As it is almost impossible to tamper with blockchain data, a high degree of trust is provided. There is value in data being resilient in society. The risk of surveillance, whether conducted by private or governmental bodies, is a key concern for users' trust (Torres *et al.*, 2023).

5.5.1 *Some societal benefits*

Reduced data theft: Enhanced security could protect sensitive personal and financial information, benefiting all citizens but particularly vulnerable groups, often being targets of fraud and exploitation, thus reducing social tension.

Increased access to services: Easier access to online services, such as government assistance programs, could streamline processes and reduce bureaucratic hurdles for those needing them most. Custodial and non-custodial wallets were previously treated. The key question is, how does society provide the necessary support in the social system for recovery mechanisms, custodial care, and general support for the public in maintaining their data throughout their life cycle?

Automation and efficiency: Blockchain technology can automate processes, facilitate inter-organizational automation, and reduce administrative costs.

5.5.2 *Challenges*

Digital literacy and access are prerequisites for success. Ensuring everyone has the skills needed to use blockchain wallets is crucial. Mass education is necessary to mitigate this divide. As presented here, the wallet concept can be regarded as a societal infrastructure, far more than individual blockchains. It also pays to optimize for the user rather than only for the specific blockchain system, as is standard today.

It is also evident that value generated by wallets shifts significantly if one takes the wallet's end-user perspective from creating value in the specific ecosystem of the requested digital service to the multiplicative effects of values from many elements, as we find in network economic models. An important societal point is often missed: an overall stable society with a high number of services available is generally wealth-generating and beneficial. Think of the Pax Romana.

In regionwide implementations, as currently conducted in the EU, the wallet is key to success "in this new tech/social/regulatory disruptive environment" (de Amorim, 2024), reflecting the user's access to and interaction with these services. Large tech companies have successfully launched wallets that access their Web2 applications and have significant market shares that federated identity structures have already achieved. Apple is negotiating with the EU about launching its well-functioning, non-eIDAS-compliant Digital Driver's License solution in the EU. Many politicians (personal communication with MEP) and decision-makers understand why eIDAS compliance is important. A benefits realization model seems much needed here to evaluate the benefits' significance and understand the consequences of the various flavors of proposals.

The EU's launch of identity solutions and a large set of Verifiable Credential-based solutions is an interesting innovation regarding societal value generation. The concept of using a wallet as an access and management tool to participate as a digital citizen for a high percentage of the population is a new development.

New business models are necessary to enhance work on developing decentralized business models. Currently, the focus is on local decentralized digital services with ultra-low transaction costs. However, we need to understand and calculate the benefits, even if they spread at many levels of society and across industries and nations. How do we develop business models while also ensuring a collaborative aspect for nation- and international-wide benefit-generating systems, such as wallet services, that can interest the average institutional investor? An interesting aspect is the many well-functioning blockchain solutions provided without a direct profit/loss perspective. This unmonetization could explain the difficulty of financing such solutions even as they generate net value. There is a need for better business models that incorporate these new functionalities and demonstrate to investors where realizable benefits are generated. One example is local functionality, such as a wallet-borne personal AI. This recent and exciting area is in the early stages of development for local implementation. It will be possible to offer highly personalized and context-related just-in-time support and education programs to the end user's wallet. Even before AI functionality becomes fully available locally, it can be offered as a web-based service or a local functionality using traditional tools. These will further empower the end user and open up entirely new services and markets.

Trust in the overall digital solutions is critical for end users' acceptance of the solutions, enabling them to fully embrace a digital lifestyle. The wallet itself can significantly minimize the digital footprint—but it cannot verify if data sent from or via the wallet has been eavesdropped. When you are requested at a border to download everything from your laptop or mobile, you'll simply do it—or not enter.

Risks are present as with all systems. One generated by the nationwide perspective promoted here is the need for continuous availability of these systems, which are becoming critical national infrastructure. The blockchain architecture is probably our closest current architecture for continuously available services. Similar performance should be demanded of all service vendors offering nation-critical services.

Also, there is an increasing need for offline functionality. With the increasing digital service density in society, these services must be available anytime and anywhere. The current blockchain wallet solutions presume increasingly available network services, although shorter or longer offline situations are relevant for many application areas. Examples illustrating the breadth of these cases are healthcare, homecare, construction sites, military expeditions, and refugee empowerment (Garazha, 2024).

New services to assist and empower the end user will be created, triggering completely new industries from possibilities such as vastly enhanced storage, e.g., the interplanetary file system (IPFS). This is needed with the much larger responsibilities placed upon each user. With the new expectations that we all take charge of our total datasets throughout our lifetime, many practical burdens are placed on the end user. How does one find a specific data item from when one was 12 years old? What to do in case of doubt? A call to a support person will typically be too expensive. Automated services must be developed to provide end users with the services known from data centers for tracking and restoring problematic data.

Empirical studies on the above and studies examining user experiences with different wallet types are needed to illustrate user preferences, security concerns, and usability challenges, as well as how to educate users better about risks and management strategies, especially in addressing vulnerabilities specific to non-custodial wallets. Exploring practical security implementations for wallets as well as how to develop more inclusive wallet designs that address the needs of diverse user groups, including those with disabilities or limited digital literacy, is essential for success. Future research might investigate the development of industry standards for the highly important interoperability among wallets and blockchain applications, facilitating a smoother user experience and more in-depth analysis of the long-term societal implications of widespread wallet adoption, particularly in terms of economic equity and the impacts on marginalized communities. By addressing these areas in future work, the discussion can evolve to clarify and enhance the security, accessibility, and societal impact of digital wallets in an increasingly digital world.

5.6 Conclusion

The role of wallets in the blockchain/Web3 ecosystem is crucial and often underestimated or not properly understood, particularly when it comes to precise value-creation estimates. As wallets are the gateway to the end user's access and interaction with the new digital world, they enable blockchain solutions focusing on end users to reach their market (Rifkin, 2002), allowing for an access economy. Further, as the wallets may be enabled to access the digital services currently embedded in legacy systems, their value increases even more. The universal blockchain wallets transform how we interact with the digital world, allowing users to delve deeper into a digital lifestyle that is self-governed and self-sovereign. By prioritizing usability and accessibility, we can unlock the power of this technology for everyone. Of course, there are challenges and risks in Web3. However, the overall opinion is that Web3 technology provides orders of magnitude higher security and safety than what is currently seen on the market. The dangers are in society as a whole, from drastically increased levels of automation and dependence on our systems. We have deliberately focused on concrete examples of benefits, as they are the drivers for venturing into new projects, and since Web3 solutions often cover new areas from various angles and offer opportunities for connecting to everything rather than the isolated silo approaches of traditional IT solutions. The economic considerations are somewhat qualitative and indicative, as our current understanding of some of the most significant potentials is just dawning. We relied heavily on inference in the discussion. That is necessary when going beyond the current frontline; a firmer deductive discussion may come when our models have covered new ground. Thus, we have here attempted to establish the anatomy of value generation in decentralized networked systems.

Of course, wallets are not everything. However, hopefully, the above chapter has demonstrated that blockchain wallets are the end users' access point to digital services in the Web3 world and the key to releasing value from Web3/blockchain systems and connecting the end user to the digital world, blockchain, Web3, and legacy systems. These possibilities open several quite interesting paths to new areas. All this makes it worthwhile to consider the wallet as a sound foundation for creating and utilizing digital services now and in the future.

References

Abbas, C. and Alkhzaimi, H. 2024. "Transforming economies and societies: The potential of social coins." SSRN Working Paper. https://doi.org/10.2139/ssrn.5022944.

Albayati, H., Kim, S. K., and Rho, J. J. 2021. "A study on the use of cryptocurrency wallets from a user experiences perspective." *Human Behavior and Emerging Technologies* 3(5): 720–738.

Alexander, M. R. P. 2020. *Mission Command: The Need for Disciplined Initiative.* Fort Leavenworth, KS: School of Advanced Military Studies, US Army Command and General Staff College.

Asare, M. T., Damoah, D. D., Doe, M., Amponsah, R. A., Okoe, E. A., and Amoako, P. Y. O. 2024. "Blockchain technology: A catalyst for transformation in Africa." In *2024 IEEE SmartBlock4Africa.* IEEE, pp. 1–5.

Balbo, S., Boella, G., Busacchi, P., Cordero, A., De Carne, L., Di Caro, D., Guffanti, A., Mioli, M., Sanino, A., and Schifanella, C. 2020. "CommonsHood: A Blockchain-based wallet app for local communities." In *2020 IEEE International Conference on Decentralized Applications and Infrastructures (DAPPS)*. IEEE, pp. 139–144.

Bambacht, J. and Pouwelse, J. 2022. "Web3: A decentralized societal infrastructure for identity, trust, money, and data." arXiv:2203.00398.

Barresi, R. G. and Zatti, F. 2020. "The importance of where central bank digital currencies are custodied: Exploring the need of a universal access device." SSRN Working Paper. https://doi.org/10.2139/ssrn.3691263.

Birch, D. 2023. "Identity, Innovation And Very Smart Wallets." *Forbes*, October 11, 2023. https://www.forbes.com/sites/davidbirch/2023/10/11/buterin-innovation-and-very-smart-wallets/.

Bolt, J. S. 2019. *Financial resilience of Kenyan smallholders affected by climate change, and the potential for blockchain technology.* CGIAR Research Program on Climate Change, Agriculture and Food Security (CCAFS).

Büttgen, M., Dicenta, J., Spohrer, K., Venkatesh, V., Raman, R., Hoehle, H., De Keyser, A., Verbeeck, C., Zwienenberg, T. J., Jørgensen, K. P., and Beck, R. 2021. "Blockchain in service management and service research—developing a research agenda and managerial implications." *Journal of Service Management Research* 5(2): 71–102.

Cai, W., Wang, Z., Ernst, J. B., Hong, Z., Feng, C., and Leung, V. C. 2018. "Decentralized applications: The blockchain-empowered software system." *IEEE Access* 6: 53019–53033.

Cameron, K. 2005. "The laws of identity." Microsoft Corporation White Paper 12: 8–11.

Chen, Y. and Bellavitis, C. 2020. "Blockchain disruption and decentralized finance: The rise of decentralized business models." *Journal of Business Venturing Insights* 13: e00151.

Dabrowski, A., Pfeffer, K., Reichel, M., Mai, A., Weippl, E. R., and Franz, M. 2021. "Better keep cash in your boots—hardware wallets are the new single point of failure." In *Proceedings of the 2021 ACM CCS Workshop on Decentralized Finance and Security*, pp. 1–8.

de Amorim, A. P. and Sousa, R. D. 2024. "The Neutrality and Dichotomy of Self-Sovereign Identity: An Exploratory Study." In *Proceedings of the 31st Mediterranean Conference on Information Systems (MCIS)*. https://aisel.aisnet.org/mcis2024/50/.

Degen, K. and Teubner, T. 2024. "Wallet wars or digital public infrastructure? Orchestrating a digital identity data ecosystem from a government perspective." *Electronic Markets* 34(1): 50.

Den Breeijen, S., van Dijck, G., Jonkers, T., Joosten, R., and Zimmermann, K. 2022. "Self-Sovereign Identity and Guardianship in Practice." *European Journal of Law and Technology* 13(3).

Enrile, A. and Aquino-Adriatico, G. 2024. "Technology Innovations in Fighting Slavery and Human Trafficking." In *The Palgrave Handbook on Modern Slavery.* Cham: Palgrave Macmillan, pp. 179–203.

Erinle, Y., Kethepalli, Y., Feng, Y., and Xu, J. 2023. "SoK: Design, vulnerabilities and defense of cryptocurrency wallets." arXiv:2307.12874.

European Commission. 2025. "EU Digital Identity Wallet Home." https://ec.europa.eu/digital-building-blocks/sites/display/EUDIGITALIDENTITYWALLET/EU+Digital+Identity+Wallet+Home.

European Parliament. 2024. "Revision of the eIDAS Regulation—European Digital Identity (EUid)." In *A Europe Fit for the Digital Age.* https://www.europarl.europa.eu/legislative-train/spotlight-JD22/file-eid.

Garazha, A., Merz, C., Schwabe, G., and Zavolokina, L. 2024. "Resilience in Times of Crisis: Empowering Refugees with Self-Sovereign Identity." Working Paper.

Ghazinoory, S., Mardani, A., Maddah-Ali, M. A., and Montazer, G. A. 2024. "A blockchain-powered e-cognocracy model for democratic decision making." *Information Systems and e-Business Management*: 1–38.

Glavanits, J. and Szabo, T. 2024. "FinTech solutions supporting sustainable agriculture? Lessons from Africa." *Proceedings of the Central and Eastern European eDem and eGov Days 2024*: 97–103.

Goyal, A. 2023. "Blockchain wallet for secure transactions." *Kilby* 100: 7. https://doi.org/10.2139/ssrn.4487894.

Guth-Orlowski, S. and Sabadello, M. 2023. "Resolving Digital Product Passports." Medium, October 11, 2023. https://medium.com/@susi.guth/resolving-digital-product-passports-f08ac8f11b5a.

Hart, S. U. 2024. "From promise to practice: A cross-institutional analysis of design trends, enablers and challenges in blockchain-enabled cash and voucher delivery." *International Journal of Disaster Risk Reduction* 100: 104129.

Helsper, E. 2021. *The Digital Disconnect: The Social Causes and Consequences of Digital Inequalities.* London: SAGE Publications.

Houy, S., Schmid, P., and Bartel, A. 2023. "Security aspects of cryptocurrency wallets—A systematic literature review." *ACM Computing Surveys* 56(1): 1–31.

Hyperledger Indy. 2024. "Wallet Storage Design." https://hyperledger-indy.readthedocs.io/projects/sdk/en/latest/docs/design/003-wallet-storage/README.html.

Identity Foundation. 2023. "Hospitality and Travel SIG Specification." https://identity.foundation/Hospitality-and-Travel-SIG/spec/.

Igboanusi, I. S., Dirgantoro, K. P., Lee, J. M., and Kim, D. S. 2021. "Blockchain side implementation of pure wallet (pw): An offline transaction architecture." *ICT Express* 7(3): 327–334.

Jørgensen, K. P. and Beck, R. 2022. "Universal wallets." *Business & Information Systems Engineering*: 1–11.

Kaplan, A. 2021. "Cryptocurrency and corruption: Auditing with blockchain." In *Auditing Ecosystem and Strategic Accounting in the Digital Era: Global Approaches and New Opportunities*. Cham: Springer International Publishing, pp. 325–338.

Kassen, M. 2021. "Understanding decentralized civic engagement: Focus on peer-to-peer and blockchain-driven perspectives on e-participation." *Technology in Society* 66: 101650.

Khan, S., Amin, M. B., Azar, A. T., and Aslam, S. 2021. "Towards interoperable blockchains: A survey on the role of smart contracts in blockchain interoperability." *IEEE Access* 9: 116672–116691.

Kshetri, N. 2023. "Blockchains with Chinese characteristics." In *Blockchain in the Global South: Opportunities and Challenges for Businesses and Societies*. Cham: Springer Nature Switzerland, pp. 83–111.

Liu, Z., Xiang, Y., Shi, J., Gao, P., Wang, H., Xiao, X., Wen, B., Li, Q., and Hu, Y. C. 2021. "Make web3.0 connected." *IEEE Transactions on Dependable and Secure Computing* 19(5): 2965–2981.

Loo, B. P. and Ngan, Y. L. 2012. "Developing mobile telecommunications to narrow digital divide in developing countries? Some lessons from China." *Telecommunications Policy* 36(10–11): 888–900.

Marella, V., Upreti, B., Merikivi, J., and Tuunainen, V. K. 2020. "Understanding the creation of trust in cryptocurrencies: The case of Bitcoin." *Electronic Markets* 30(2): 259–271.

Minghai, Y., Wenqing, L., Khan, W. A., and Nurhalim, W. 2023. "The SuperApp implementation in business: Revolutionizing business operations for a seamless future." *Bincang Sains dan Teknologi* 2(03): 118–123.

Olalekan, O. A. 2024. "Blockchain technology and anti-corruption measures in the setting of public administration in Nigeria." Working Paper.

Ometov, A., Chukhno, O., Chukhno, N., Nurmi, J., and Lohan, E. S. 2021. "When wearable technology meets computing in future networks: A road ahead." In *Proceedings of the 18th ACM International Conference on Computing Frontiers*, pp. 185–190.

Park, A., Wilson, M., Robson, K., Demetis, D., and Kietzmann, J. 2023. "Interoperability: Our exciting and terrifying Web3 future." *Business Horizons* 66(4): 529–541.

Perdana, A. and Hu, E. I. 2023. "Decentralized Finance (DeFi), Strengths Become Weaknesses: a Literature Survey." *Jurnal RESTI (Rekayasa Sistem dan Teknologi Informasi)* 7(2): 397–404.

Podgorelec, B., Alber, L., and Zefferer, T. 2022. "What is a (digital) identity wallet? a systematic literature review." In *2022 IEEE 46th Annual Computers, Software, and Applications Conference (COMPSAC)*. IEEE, pp. 809–818.

Ponomarev, S. and Voronkov, A. E. 2017. "Multi-agent systems and decentralized artificial superintelligence." arXiv:1702.08529.

Popchev, I., Radeva, I., and Dimitrova, M. 2023. "Towards blockchain wallets classification and implementation." In *2023 International Conference Automatics and Informatics (ICAI)*. IEEE, pp. 346–351.

Portuguese Blockchain Agenda. 2022. "Portuguese Blockchain Agenda." https://www.inesc-id.pt/blockchainpt/.

Rifkin, J. 2001. *The age of access: The new culture of hypercapitalism, where all of life is a paid for experience*. New York: J. P. Tarcher.

Rosli, M. S., Saleh, N. S., Md. Ali, A., and Abu Bakar, S. 2023. "Factors determining the acceptance of E-wallet among gen Z from the lens of the extended technology acceptance model." *Sustainability* 15(7): 5752.

Rybakken, E., Hioki, L., and Yaksetig, M. 2023. "Intmax2: A ZK-rollup with Minimal Onchain Data and Computation Costs Featuring Decentralized Aggregators." *Cryptology ePrint Archive*.

Sambin, G. 2023. *Usability of Safety Critical Applications in Enterprise Environments: Defining Guidelines for Error Preventing UI/UX Patterns and Improving Existing Interfaces*. Doctoral dissertation, Politecnico di Torino.

Santana, C. and Albareda, L. 2022. "Blockchain and the emergence of Decentralized Autonomous Organizations (DAOs): An integrative model and research agenda." *Technological Forecasting and Social Change* 182: 121806.

Sartor, S., Sedlmeir, J., Rieger, A., and Roth, T. 2022. "Love at first sight? A user experience study of self-sovereign identity wallets." In *ECIS 2022 Proceedings*.

Schlatt, V., Sedlmeir, J., Traue, J., and Völter, F. 2023. "Harmonizing sensitive data exchange and double-spending prevention through blockchain and digital wallets: The case of e-prescription management." *Distributed Ledger Technologies: Research and Practice* 2(1): 1–31.

Sedlmeir, J., Smethurst, R., Rieger, A., and Fridgen, G. 2021. "Digital identities and verifiable credentials." *Business & Information Systems Engineering* 63(5): 603–613.

Shammar, E., Cui, X., and Al-qaness, M. A. 2024. "Swarm learning: A survey of concepts, applications, and trends." arXiv:2405.00556.

Strobel, V., Pacheco, A., and Dorigo, M. 2023. "Robot swarms neutralize harmful Byzantine robots using a blockchain-based token economy." *Science Robotics* 8(79): eabm4636.

Swan, M. 2019. "Blockchain economic networks: Economic network theory—Systemic risk and blockchain technology." In *Business Transformation through Blockchain: Volume I*, pp. 3–45.

Swan, M. and De Filippi, P. 2017. "Towards a philosophy of blockchain." *Metaphilosophy* 48: 603–619.

Takei, Y. and Shudo, K. 2024. "Pragmatic Analysis of Key Management for Cryptocurrency Custodians." Working Paper.

Tan, E., Lerouge, E., Du Caju, J., and Du Seuil, D. 2023. "Verification of education credentials on European Blockchain Services Infrastructure (EBSI): Action research in a cross-border use case between Belgium and Italy." *Big Data and Cognitive Computing* 7(2): 79.

Torres, C. F., Willi, F., and Shinde, S. 2023. "Is your wallet snitching on you? An analysis on the privacy implications of web3." In *32nd USENIX Security Symposium (USENIX Security 23)*, pp. 769–786.

Vadlamani, A. and Sharma, S. 2023. "Bridging the Divide between DeFi and Regulators: Showcasing Decentralized Autonomous Governance as the Future for Self-Custody Wallet Regulation." *University of Illinois Journal of Law, Technology & Policy*: 373–394.

Vassilakopoulou, P. and Hustad, E. 2023. "Bridging digital divides: A literature review and research agenda for information systems research." *Information Systems Frontiers* 25(3): 955–969.

Viano, C., Avanzo, S., Cerutti, M., Cordero, A., Schifanella, C., and Boella, G. 2022. "Blockchain tools for socio-economic interactions in local communities." *Policy and Society* 41(3): 373–385.

Viano, C., Avanzo, S., Boella, G., Schifanella, C., and Giorgino, V. 2023. "Civic Blockchain: Making blockchains accessible for social collaborative economies." *Journal of Responsible Technology* 15: 100066.

Viriyasitavat, W., Da Xu, L., Bi, Z., and Pungpapong, V. 2019. "Blockchain and internet of things for modern business process in digital economy—the state of the art." *IEEE Transactions on Computational Social Systems* 6(6): 1420–1432.

Voskobojnikov, A., Wiese, O., Mehrabi Koushki, M., Roth, V., and Beznosov, K. 2021. "The u in crypto stands for usable: An empirical study of user experience with mobile cryptocurrency wallets." In *Proceedings of the 2021 CHI Conference on Human Factors in Computing Systems*, pp. 1–14.

W3C. 2022. "Decentralized Identifiers (DIDs) v1.0 Core architecture, data model, and representations." W3C Recommendation, July 19, 2022. https://www.w3.org/TR/2022/REC-did-core-20220719/.

W3C. 2024. "Verifiable Credentials Overview." W3C Group Note, July 6, 2024. https://www.w3.org/TR/2024/NOTE-vc-overview-20240706/.

Watanabe, H., Ichihara, K., and Aita, T. 2024. "VELLET: Verifiable Embedded Wallet for Securing Authenticity and Integrity." arXiv:2404.03874.

World Economic Forum. 2024. "How universal wallets can help businesses unleash the full potential of digital identity." February 2024. https://www.weforum.org/agenda/2024/02/how-businesses-could-use-universal-wallets-to-unleash-potential-of-digital-identity/.

Yu, Y., Sharma, T., Das, S., and Wang, Y. 2024. "Don't put all your eggs in one basket: How Cryptocurrency Users Choose and Secure Their Wallets." In *Proceedings of the CHI Conference on Human Factors in Computing Systems*, pp. 1–17.

Zhao, S., Tan, F., and Fennedy, K. 2023. "Heads-up computing moving beyond the device-centered paradigm." *Communications of the ACM* 66(9): 56–63.

Zhou, Z., Sharma, T., Emano, L., Das, S., and Wang, Y. 2023. "Iterative design of an accessible crypto wallet for blind users." In *Nineteenth Symposium on Usable Privacy and Security (SOUPS 2023)*, pp. 381–398.

Part III

Protocol Institutions: The Economic Future of Institutions

https://doi.org/10.1142/9781800618664_0007

Chapter 6

DeSci and DeScAI: Distributed Epistemic Economies

Sasha Shilina
Lomonosov Moscow State University, Moscow, Russia
sasha@episteme.ac

Abstract
This chapter seeks to articulate a conceptual framework for decentralized science (DeSci) economic theory, positing how decentralized technologies are set to transform the structural foundations of the scientific ecosystem, reshaping its governance, funding, and collaboration mechanisms. The theory is built upon three key pillars: first, the ontological nature of economics as a discipline that addresses scarcity and coordination, wherein decentralized systems introduce novel efficiencies in resource allocation for research; second, the economics of science, which confronts the intrinsic public-good nature of knowledge and the inherent challenges in its incentivization and production; and third, DeSci's unique innovation in leveraging blockchain technology to forge transparent, equitable ecosystems for scientific inquiry. Through the integration of smart contracts, AI-driven agents, and decentralized autonomous organizations (DAOs), DeSci facilitates peer-to-peer funding, autonomous proposal evaluation, and distributed governance—establishing an open, auditable, and trustless record of scientific contributions. These components not only optimize coordination but also foster global collaboration and dynamic responsiveness. Ultimately, the chapter positions DeSci as a catalyst for a paradigm shift in how humanity approaches knowledge creation and dissemination—one shaped by the convergence of decentralized technologies and artificial intelligence—a synthesis we

term "DeScAI." In this emerging model, science is no longer bound by centralized gatekeepers but evolves within a borderless, self-organizing, and machine-augmented epistemic infrastructure.

Keywords: Decentralized Science (DeSci), DeScAI (Decentralized Science + Artificial Intelligence), Tokenized Research, Scientific Incentives, Knowledge Commons, Open Science.

6.1 Introduction

Science has catalyzed human progress, yet its funding, publication, and evaluation remain remarkably centralized. A handful of decision-making bodies still dictate research priorities, and restrictive paywalls sequester over half of peer-reviewed literature (Björk *et al.*, 2010; Brembs, 2018; Larivière *et al.*, 2015; Piwowar *et al.*, 2018; Romero, 2019). The effects are most severe in lower-income regions: high-income countries control roughly 65% of global R&D spending (UNESCO, 2021), entrenching dependence and suppressing local innovation.

A growing reproducibility crisis compounds these inequities: large fractions of published findings cannot be replicated (Baker, 2016; Ioannidis, 2005). "Publish or perish" incentives favor incremental work, and U.S. scientists spend approximately 40% of their time writing grants instead of performing experiments (Powell, 2016). Women still represent only one-third of the global research workforce (UNESCO, 2021).

In light of these challenges, decentralized technologies offer a bold alternative. Decentralized science (DeSci) leverages blockchain protocols (Nakamoto, 2008; Swan, 2015), smart contracts, and decentralized autonomous organizations (DAOs) to distribute the governance of research funding and data sharing. Through peer-to-peer funding, transparent decision-making, and immutable data verification, DeSci endeavors to realign incentives toward collaboration, reproducibility, and equity. The parallel rise of artificial intelligence (AI) accelerates this shift: large-language-model (LLM) agents automate hypothesis generation, AI-mediated peer review, and on-chain governance analytics, creating an adaptive DeScAI ecosystem.

This chapter builds a conceptual framework for DeSci economics around three philosophical pillars: (1) the ontology of economics, emphasizing decentralized coordination over centralized resource allocation; (2) the economics of science, highlighting the public-good nature of knowledge and the inherent difficulty of incentivizing its production; and (3) the promise of decentralized infrastructures to create dynamic, inclusive, and transparent models for science. Taken together, these elements illuminate an alternative vision of scientific progress—one in which knowledge generation transcends traditional silos and global collaboration is rewarded rather than impeded.

We seek to answer three interrelated research questions: (1) How can decentralized technologies reshape the economics of scientific production? (2) What specific economic mechanisms underlie DeSci systems? (3) What are the implications of DeSci and decentralized science + AI (DeScAI) for scientific governance, funding, and reproducibility?

The analysis employs an interdisciplinary conceptual approach, synthesizing economic theory, philosophy of science, and blockchain–AI studies through an integrative literature review.

6.2 Defining DeSci

Integrating decentralized technology, cryptoeconomic incentives, and community-driven governance models, DeSci is an emerging framework that seeks to reshape the scientific process. Unlike traditional systems of scientific research—often characterized by hierarchical funding bodies, closed-access publishing, and opaque peer review—DeSci aspires to create a more inclusive, transparent, and collaborative environment for knowledge creation (Shilina, 2023; Weidener & Spreckelsen, 2024). It builds upon both historical and contemporary insights in philosophy, economics, and information science, blending classical liberal ideals with modern distributed ledger technologies (Table 6.1).

At its core, DeSci channels values of open inquiry and public discourse. Immanuel Kant (1784) emphasized the necessity of free exchange for intellectual progress, while Karl Popper (1959) highlighted falsifiability and critique. DeSci enacts these through open-access data, transparent funding, and immutable records on decentralized networks (Buterin, 2014), enabling scholars and citizen scientists alike to build upon each other's work beyond centralized barriers.

Philosophically, DeSci resonates with Michael Polanyi's (1962) "Republic of Science," where openness and mutual authority

Table 6.1. Core principles of DeSci.

Core Principle	Description	Foundation	Implementation
Openness and transparency	Open protocols, open access, and verifiable research data	Kant (public reason), Popper (falsifiability)	Blockchain records, open-access journals
Community governance	Distributed decision-making among diverse stakeholders	Hayek (distributed knowledge), Arendt (action)	DAOs, voting mechanisms, participatory development
Incentive alignment	Token-based rewards to align individual and collective goals	Smith (invisible hand), Ostrom (commons), Hurwicz (mechanisms)	Tokens for peer review, data sharing, and reputation

guide inquiry. It replaces hierarchical structures with distributed governance inspired by Friedrich Hayek's (1945) dispersed knowledge and Hannah Arendt's (1958) collective action, affirming the role of pluralistic participation in shaping shared realities. DeSci also aligns with Elinor Ostrom's (1990) vision of commons-based knowledge, promoting open licensing, transparent repositories, and token incentives that support collaboration and equitable access.

Moreover, DeSci's emphasis on cryptoeconomic systems (Zamfir, 2015; Voshmgir & Zargham, 2020) derives from mechanism design (Hurwicz, 1973; Maskin, 1999; Myerson, 1999) that studies how rules and incentives can be engineered to align individual actions with socially optimal outcomes. Within the context of DeSci, smart contracts and reputation tokens can reward constructive contributions—such as peer reviewing, data validation, and reproducibility efforts—thereby incentivizing behaviors that improve the quality and reliability of the overall scientific corpus.

On the other hand, DeSci builds on the economic rationale of blockchain (Davidson, De Filippi & Potts, 2016). Therefore, decentralized solutions are becoming increasingly cost-effective compared to centralized systems due to exponential cost reductions in computation (Moore's law), storage (Kryder's law), and bandwidth (Nielsen's law). The potential of DeSci reflects a Schumpeterian process of "creative destruction," wherein centralized systems face substitution by decentralized counterparts. This substitution is non-linear, influenced by network effects (Metcalfe, 2013), switching costs, and regulatory barriers. Such dynamics are visible in the transition from traditional closed-access publishing and centralized funding bodies to decentralized platforms, open-access repositories, and tokenized incentive systems. The recent integration of AI into DeSci—here termed "DeScAI"—further amplifies this transformation, introducing autonomous agents into decentralized epistemic infrastructures.

Although foundational work has defined DeSci's architecture and values (Weidener *et al.*, 2024), empirical research remains limited. DeScAI is even less studied: while DeSci and AI have each garnered academic and technical interest, their convergence remains underexplored. Cross-disciplinary research combining economics, AI ethics, and science and technology studies (STS) will be critical to evaluating the transformative potential of these frameworks.

6.3 Ontological Nature of DeSci Economics

Economics, though framed as a practical discipline of resource production and allocation, nevertheless rests on deeper philosophical assumptions about scarcity, human relationships, and collective action. These ontological foundations shape how we understand reality, agency, and social order through economic systems.

6.3.1 *Scarcity and the human condition*

Scarcity—central to economic thought—posits that finite resources (time, talent, capital, and data) cannot satisfy infinite human wants. This idea masks deeper ontological questions about being, material relations, and socially constructed needs. DeSci re-examines this concept by proposing mechanisms that aim to democratize access and reduce artificially imposed constraints on knowledge creation.

Philosophers and economists have long debated whether scarcity is purely a natural phenomenon or, rather, shaped by historical and social contexts. In classical economics, scarcity tends to be treated as an immutable aspect of reality: Adam Smith and Thomas Malthus, for instance, posited that the material world places inherent constraints on human existence (Smith, 1776; Malthus, 1798). Smith's classical view highlights scarcity as a motivation for innovation and specialization. In his framework, limited resources stimulate the division of labor, thereby enhancing productivity and efficiency (Smith, 1776/1976). DeSci builds upon this perspective by enabling more open collaboration within scientific research. Through decentralized platforms, scientists across borders can share expertise and data, forming specialized communities that collectively produce and disseminate knowledge. Rather than relying solely on market exchanges to mitigate scarcity, DeSci leverages token-based incentives and open-source principles, offering global participation and spurring new solutions. By distributing research tasks among a broader community, DeSci intensifies the specialization Smith advocated, yet it does so through decentralized protocols that minimize friction in collaboration.

Yet, Smith's interpretation has been challenged on philosophical and sociological grounds. Karl Marx interpreted scarcity not only as a result of limited resources but also as a condition shaped by inequitable economic structures. In capitalist systems, ownership and control of resources are concentrated in the hands of a few, perpetuating scarcity for the majority (Marx, 1867/1976). DeSci responds to this critique by proposing mechanisms for redistributing scientific resources, such as decentralized funding and shared data repositories. Community-driven DAOs enable collective ownership of research initiatives, effectively bypassing traditional gatekeepers such as large publishing houses or institutional funders. This mode of organization aims to reduce "artificial scarcity" by ensuring that data, research tools, and funding streams remain accessible to a wider community. DeSci thus alters power structures around knowledge production, encouraging a more equitable access to and distribution of scientific outputs.

In neoclassical models, scarcity is addressed by rational agents making decisions based on opportunity costs (Walras, 1874/1954). DeSci upholds this rationale but enriches it with blockchain-mediated mechanisms. On-chain voting, token incentives, and reputation systems guide researchers and stakeholders in allocating limited funds and deciding which projects to prioritize. Here, the rational-choice framework is preserved: participants weigh costs and benefits when contributing to or funding a research project. However, decentralized protocols introduce additional variables—token price fluctuations, trustless verification processes, and distributed data curation—that influence how scientists calculate opportunity costs. By integrating these blockchain-based instruments into the rational-choice paradigm, DeSci offers a novel lens through which economic decision-making and scientific collaboration can be viewed. Mechanisms such as quadratic funding amplify community-backed contributions, directing resources to niche fields and underserved communities. Retroactive public goods funding further rewards creators after their work has proven valuable, reinforcing impact over prestige.

Anthropologist Marshall Sahlins argued that scarcity is not solely a material condition but also a cultural construct: societies define what constitutes "enough" based on communal values (Sahlins, 1972). DeSci expands upon this anthropological perspective by fostering open-data norms and reproducibility standards that redefine the value of research outputs. In these decentralized communities, shared grants, open-access repositories, and collaborative networks can reduce the perceived scarcity of findings and resources. Instead of hoarding data or maintaining paywalls, DeSci encourages cultures of openness, where contribution to the common good, such as publishing raw datasets for community validation, is highly prized and incentivized. This cultural shift from privatized knowledge to shared repositories effectively reconfigures the boundaries of scarcity within scientific inquiry.

Contemporary economics views intangibles such as time, attention, and data as scarce resources. DeSci formalizes these as tokenized contributions by using AI and blockchain to allocate attention toward reproducible, high-impact work. Platforms like VitaDAO and Episteme exemplify how smart algorithms route funds and attention—core to the emerging DeScAI stack.

6.3.2 *Coordination and the nature of order*

If scarcity frames the existential relationship between humans and resources, coordination addresses the question of how societies organize themselves to meet needs and desires within those constraints. Debates around coordination illuminate ontological perspectives on human agency, freedom, and the shape of social order. Friedrich Hayek famously argued that markets function as spontaneous orders, emerging from the local knowledge and self-interested actions of individuals (Hayek, 1945). Markets, in this view, express human freedom through choice and preference revelation. Hayek's view aligns closely with the ontology of DeSci, where decentralized networks facilitate scientific collaboration without the need for central control. Blockchain-based protocols enable researchers to self-organize, contribute resources, and share findings across borders. Smart contracts and decentralized marketplaces for research funding exemplify Hayek's vision of fluid adaptive coordination.

The same type of argument—evolution toward complexity (Kauffman, 1993; Potts, 2000)—extends across computation (open-source networks), governance (democracy), law (common law), and communication (social media). In DeSci, the market transcends funding and collaboration, becoming a medium of scientific freedom. Researchers bypass traditional gatekeepers, participating directly in decentralized protocols that foster dynamic, community-driven contributions to global knowledge.

In contrast, centralized coordination—such as state-sponsored research or institutional funding—while effective in crisis management, can entrench power, inefficiencies, and inequities. Michel Foucault critiqued centralized authority for limiting autonomy (Foucault, 1975), and Marx decried capitalism's alienation of workers from their labor, echoing how academia often alienates researchers from their contributions (Marx, 1867/1976). DeSci counters these paradigms by adopting participatory governance models, DAOs, and token-weighted voting, reclaiming researcher agency over resource allocation and enabling equitable systems.

Game theory provides valuable insights into the challenges of coordination in decentralized systems. Models such as the Prisoner's Dilemma and Nash equilibria demonstrate how individual rationality may conflict with collective welfare (von Neumann & Morgenstern, 1944; Nash, 1950). DeSci introduces mechanisms that reward cooperative behavior: smart contracts incentivize peer review, reproducibility, and data sharing. AI agents within DeScAI environments further optimize coordination by triaging proposals, detecting statistical flaws, and aligning resource allocation with collective interests.

Building on the insights of Douglass North, DeSci recognizes the importance of institutions—both formal protocols and informal norms—as the scaffolding for decentralized coordination (North, 1990). Blockchain systems encode formal rules, while

DAO culture reflects community values—transparency, inclusion, and adaptability. These institutions don't merely coordinate; they embody shared epistemic ethics. For instance, open review systems reflect commitments to mutual accountability and decentralized trust.

From an economic philosophy standpoint, DeSci treats scientific knowledge as a public good, addressing the "tragedy of the commons" (Hardin, 1968). Elinor Ostrom's (1990) work on self-governed resource management informs DeSci's use of smart contracts and tokenized governance to sustain open data and pooled research funds. Transparent ledgers ensure fairness and mitigate free-rider issues, aligning individual efforts with collective goals (Davidson, De Filippi, & Potts, 2018). In parallel, DeScAI agents can dynamically monitor access patterns, contribution histories, and coordination efficiency.

Mainly, this emergent architecture can challenge Kuhn's (1962) structure of scientific revolutions, suggesting that rapid, community-driven shifts might replace the insular paradigm cycles that have historically dictated the pace of change in academic fields.

6.3.3 *The problem of human agency*

The interplay between scarcity and coordination ultimately revolves around questions of agency: How free are individuals to shape their economic and social reality, and to what extent do existing structures constrain or empower them? DeSci brings these questions to the forefront by challenging traditional power structures in knowledge production and emphasizing individual and collective agency.

Anthony Giddens's theory of structuration emphasizes that structures both enable and limit individual actions, creating a dynamic interplay where agents shape and are shaped by their contexts (Giddens, 1984). Blockchain protocols, DAOs, and token-based systems provide new structures for scientific collaboration that empower researchers to act independently of centralized gatekeepers. Yet, these structures are also co-constituted by the community, continuously evolving as participants make choices and adapt to the system, which highlights the inherently adaptive nature of DeSci, where agency and structure exist in a reciprocal relationship.

DeSci reflects Amartya Sen's emphasis on human capabilities by reframing economics as an ethical endeavor focused on expanding freedoms (Sen, 1999). By removing access barriers, redistributing funding, and tokenizing overlooked contributions (e.g., peer review), DeSci unlocks latent potential. Within DeScAI, autonomous agents further extend this empowerment: by automating laborious tasks, they allow researchers to focus on creativity and critical thinking.

Modern complexity theories complement this view by treating economies and systems such as DeSci as evolving networks shaped by feedback loops, emergent behavior, and nonlinear dynamics (Arthur, 1994). This aligns with process philosophy, as articulated by Alfred North Whitehead, which views reality as a continuous process of becoming (Whitehead, 1929/1978). In DeSci, the interplay of decentralized agents, smart contracts, and dynamic governance creates an ecosystem that resists static equilibrium, instead flourishing through adaptation and innovation. Such adaptive capacity highlights the potential to navigate systemic challenges of funding inequities, lack of reproducibility, or inefficiencies in knowledge dissemination. DeScAI captures this adaptability through self-learning agents and responsive infrastructure, enabling rapid realignment of goals and incentives.

Moreover, the question of agency in DeSci intersects with issues of inclusivity and participation. While DeSci lowers barriers for traditionally excluded groups to contribute to scientific knowledge, challenges remain in ensuring equitable representation and access to its systems.

Finally, DeSci amplifies a fundamental ontological question in economic and social theory: are systems inherently deterministic, or can human agency drive transformative change? By decentralizing control and embedding participatory mechanisms, DeSci suggests a model where human creativity and collective action are the primary drivers of systemic evolution, offering a vision of science that is both more equitable and dynamic in its pursuit of knowledge (Table 6.2).

6.4 The Economics of Science

6.4.1 *Theoretical foundations and the potential of DeSci*

The economics of scientific knowledge treats scientific activity as driven by incentives, constraints, and institutional structures, with scientists conceptualized as economic agents who seek to maximize forms of utility such as prestige, funding, or intellectual fulfillment

Table 6.2. Ontological nature of DeSci economics.

Aspect	Key Concept	Foundation	DeSci/DeScAI Implication
Scarcity	Finite resources shaped by social contexts	Smith (division of labor), Marx (artificial scarcity), Sahlins (cultural constructs)	Tokenized funding, open data, AI-driven allocation of scarce attention and expertise
Coordination	Decentralized systems for resource allocation	Hayek (spontaneous order), Foucault (power hierarchies), Ostrom (commons governance)	DAOs and smart contracts, and AI agents for adaptive, participatory coordination
Agency	Structures constrain and empower individuals	Giddens (structuration), Sen (capabilities), Whitehead (process philosophy)	Permissionless participation, AI-augmented peer review, and dynamic governance mechanisms

(Dasgupta & David, 1994; Boumans & Davis, 2010). In this view, science can be likened to a market-like system in which knowledge is produced, disseminated, and utilized under the influence of both competitive and cooperative dynamics. Traditionally, researchers have employed various theoretical models to understand these dynamics.

The *neoclassical* approach applies standard economic principles of rational choice, efficiency, and equilibrium to the realm of science (Arrow, 1962). Scientists are assumed to be rational agents who respond to incentives such as grants, career advancements, or patent rights. According to this view, knowledge possesses public-good characteristics (non-rival and often non-excludable) (Arrow, 1962; Nelson, 1959), yet private rewards—such as intellectual property—can motivate innovation. Dasgupta and David (1994) characterize scientific research as involving a tension between openness and proprietary interests, conceptualizing a dual economy in which a public domain fosters open knowledge exchange while a private domain incentivizes discoveries with proprietary protections. Although these models provide clarity on how economists think incentive structures shape research outputs, neoclassical assumptions can be too narrow, neglecting factors such as curiosity, ethical considerations, and disciplinary norms (Merton, 1973). DeSci addresses these gaps by tokenizing behaviors that foster collaboration and innovation. Through DAO funding, smart contract marketplaces, and reputation systems, DeSci realigns incentives to reward openness and integrity (Buterin, 2013; Nakamoto, 2008; Pandey *et al.*, 2023). DeScAI takes this further: AI agents can triage proposals, evaluate prior research, and suggest funding distributions based on reproducibility and collective interest, thereby lowering the cost of rational decision-making at scale.

Game-theoretic approaches, by contrast, emphasize strategic interaction among scientists. Under this view, each scientist or research team is a strategic player who must anticipate the actions of others when deciding, for example, whether to share data or race to publish first (Kitcher, 1993). This perspective is particularly useful for analyzing phenomena such as priority races, in which the "winner-take-all" structure of scientific credit can encourage secrecy or duplication, and collaboration dilemmas, where the fear of being "scooped" may inhibit open sharing. While game-theoretic models illuminate competitive and cooperative equilibria, they often assume perfect rationality and complete information, thus underrepresenting the importance of biases and institutional regulations that shape real-world decisions (Simon, 1957). In this framework, DeSci offers innovative solutions. It intervenes by automating shared attribution through on-chain timestamps and smart contracts. Collective reward structures (Weyl & Buterin, 2019) enable multiple contributors to gain shared recognition. AI-enhanced platforms track co-authorship networks and automate credit distribution, reducing incentive misalignment.

Recognizing the complexities of previous models, the *behavioral* or *bounded rationality* approach incorporates insights from psychology, sociology, and organizational studies to account for scientists' cognitive and institutional constraints. Bounded rationality posits that scientists, facing time pressure and uncertainty, frequently satisfice rather than optimize, using heuristics and routines to guide decisions (Simon, 1957). Moreover, norms identified by Merton (1973)—communalism, universalism, disinterestedness, and organized skepticism—highlight how non-economic factors can significantly influence peer review processes or the selection of research questions. DeSci leverages blockchain transparency to reduce uncertainty and encode ethical practices. DeScAI can model normative behavior patterns, flag statistical anomalies, and suggest replicability checks—turning bounded rationality into calibrated decision support.

The *information-theoretic* approach views science as an information ecosystem (Stigler, 1961), focusing on how the production, exchange, and use of knowledge affect the rate and direction of research. Knowledge travels through journals, conferences, and informal networks, but information asymmetries can arise if researchers withhold crucial data or findings. Such asymmetries may distort funding decisions or lead to fragmented efforts. Meanwhile, open access mandates and other policies aimed at reducing barriers to information flow can accelerate the cumulative nature of scientific progress. These models trace the flow of knowledge within scientific communities but often overlook the intricate dynamics of personal motivation, disciplinary culture, and institutional norms that influence what is shared and how. DeSci minimizes information asymmetries through decentralized repositories, ensuring research outputs are accessible on open platforms (Bartling & Fecher, 2017). Transparent funding flows enabled by on-chain tracking provide real-time insights into grant allocations and project progress. Additionally, token-based incentives promote timely data sharing, streamlining knowledge dissemination (Davidson, De Filippi, & Potts, 2018). Besides, AI algorithms optimize knowledge flow, reducing fragmentation and accelerating cumulative insight.

Furthermore, the *transaction costs* approach, grounded in institutional economics (Coase, 1937; Williamson, 1985), highlights the costs of coordinating scientific "transactions," such as sharing data, publishing results, or forming collaborations. High transaction costs can discourage otherwise beneficial partnerships, particularly in research fields that require extensive coordination and expensive equipment (Guston, 2000; Martin, 2003). Conversely, robust institutional arrangements or formal consortium agreements can lower coordination burdens, making large-scale, multi-institutional projects feasible. A further consideration is whether researchers opt for proprietary or open science models—decisions influenced by

Table 6.3. Scientific knowledge approaches and contributions from DeSci/DeScAI.

Approach	Focus	Key Feature	Limitation	DeSci/DeScAI Contribution
Neoclassical	Incentives and efficiency	Rational agents; public-private knowledge tension	Ignores curiosity, ethics, and norms	Token systems for balanced openness and proprietary protections
Game-theoretic	Strategic interactions	Priority races and collaboration dilemmas	Assumes perfect rationality	Smart contracts + AI moderation to encourage open collaboration
Behavioral	Cognitive and institutional limits	Heuristics, norms, and bounded rationality	Limited formal modeling	Blockchain for transparency; AI agents reduce decision complexity
Information-based	Knowledge flow and bottlenecks	Focus on asymmetries in data sharing	Overlooks cultural factors	Open ledgers + AI-enhanced discovery, routing attention to underexplored data
Transaction costs	Coordination costs	Costs of collaboration and IP management	Downplays individual agency	Smart contracts & AI cut overhead for complex projects

balancing the administrative and legal overhead of maintaining intellectual property against the benefits of broad collaboration. While this perspective excels at identifying how institutional architectures shape coordination, it may underemphasize other drivers, including individual agency and sociocultural factors (Benkler, 2002). DeSci has the potential to reduce overhead with smart contract automation for agreements and milestones, streamline peer review through decentralized protocols, and simplify large-scale collaboration via DAO-based governance with transparent, on-chain rules. DeScAI further reduces friction by streamlining peer review workflows, modeling network externalities, and automating low-trust coordination (Table 6.3).

6.5 Decentralized Innovations for Science

Leveraging Web3 technologies, DeSci seeks to address systemic inefficiencies in traditional science and transform the structures underpinning research. Decentralizing funding, governance, and knowledge dissemination, DeSci challenges hierarchical and non-transparent systems.

6.5.1 *Funding mechanisms*

Decentralized systems bypass traditional intermediaries, enabling researchers to concentrate on their work while offering investors direct opportunities to fund and share in groundbreaking projects. Through mechanisms like DAO-driven crowdfunding, DeFi, and quadratic funding, DeSci revolutionizes research funding, creating a more equitable and efficient landscape for scientific innovation.

Therefore, DAOs provide a transparent and community-centric framework for funding and governing research (Bischof *et al.*, 2022; Fantaccini *et al.*, 2024). They enable token holders to collectively decide on project funding, aligning individual incentives with broader community goals. Platforms such as VitaDAO allow community members to purchase tokens to support longevity research while earning governance rights and potential revenue from successful outcomes (Golato & Kohlhaas, 2021). Similarly, BIO Protocol acts as a launchpad, facilitating global collaboration to fund and govern research initiatives from universities, researchers, and companies. Its ecosystem includes specialized DAOs such as HairDAO (targeting hair loss), CerebrumDAO (boosting brain health), ValleyDAO (synthetic biology), AthenaDAO (women's health), and CryoDAO (cryogenics). By integrating liquidity and incentive mechanisms, BIO Protocol accelerates the commercialization of science while fostering decentralized governance.

Furthermore, DeFi introduces sustainable funding models for scientific research. Platforms such as Gitcoin Grants leverage DeFi strategies to maximize matching funds for public goods, creating consistent funding streams. Quadratic funding enhances this model by matching smaller donations with larger institutional grants based on the square of contributor numbers, ensuring that projects with broad community support receive a fair share of resources. As demonstrated by Gitcoin and CLR.fund, quadratic funding democratizes resource allocation, fostering inclusivity and equity in funding (Weiss, 2022). While these models have shown significant success in public goods and open-source initiatives, their application in scientific research is still evolving and offers considerable potential for growth.

6.5.2 *Collaboration and governance*

DeSci redefines collaboration and governance by harnessing distributed networks, DAOs, and advanced voting systems to create a global, community-driven ecosystem. It facilitates cross-border participation, incorporates diverse perspectives, and employs transparent smart contracts to automate decision-making, resource distribution, and IP management.

VitaDAO and LabDAO projects exemplify how token-based ecosystems can collectively fund and govern research. VitaDAO allows token holders to vote on funding proposals while managing IP collaboratively. LabDAO expands this concept into computational life sciences, providing tools to make BioML research more accessible and clinically relevant. Through funding facilitation, collaboration tools, and research resources, these platforms demonstrate the potential of decentralized governance to unlock scientific progress (DeFrancesco & Klevecz, 2022). DAOs such as AthenaDAO and ValleyDAO extend decentralized governance into specialized areas, including women's health and synthetic biology. Advanced voting tools such as Snapshot and Tally enhance blockchain governance. However, challenges such as token concentration, reputation bias, and Sybil attacks persist. Emerging solutions such as Proof-of-Humanity and Humanode address these issues, promoting fairness and resilience (James, 2021; Kavazi *et al.*, 2021).

6.5.3 *Peer review and validation*

Decentralized peer review platforms are transforming traditional models by embedding transparency, accountability, and financial incentives into the process (Trovò & Massari, 2021). For instance, ResearchHub compensates contributors with cryptocurrency for providing high-quality feedback, offering a practical alternative to the unpaid labor commonly expected in academia. Highlighted by *Nature*, ResearchHub pays reviewers an average of $150 per review, creating meaningful financial opportunities for contributors (Else, 2024). Mainly, by incentivizing reviewers and creating a transparent record of feedback, decentralized systems are building a more inclusive way to validate scientific research.

6.5.4 *Tokenized research outputs*

Intellectual property non-fungible tokens (IP-NFTs) are redefining IP management in DeSci by granting researchers ownership, monetization opportunities, and the freedom to share their work. Unlike conventional IP systems, which can be costly and favor large institutions, IP-NFTs represent scientific discoveries, data, or protocols on the blockchain, streamlining transactions, ensuring transparent provenance, and unlocking new funding avenues (Bamakan *et al.*, 2022; Shilina, 2023).

Platforms like Molecule connect researchers and funders through tokenized IP, allowing investors to purchase fractional ownership—an approach especially useful for bridging funding gaps in areas such as drug discovery. VitaDAO manages IP tokens (IPTs) such as VitaRNA and VITA-FAST, representing stakes in gene therapies and autophagy research. Similarly, AthenaDAO, in partnership with Gero, launched OVARIA to explore groundbreaking treatments for ovarian aging, giving token holders governance rights and fostering community-driven research. By embedding smart contracts in IP-NFTs, royalties and usage rights are automated, reducing disputes and simplifying collaboration.

6.5.5 *Reproducibility and data sharing*

Community-driven and multi-governmental initiatives, such as the European Open Science Cloud, are developing centralized, non-blockchain-based data storage infrastructures aimed at providing universal access to research data for all researchers (Budroni *et al.*, 2019). In DeSci, platforms such as IPFS and Arweave are central to enhancing reproducibility and data sharing. IPFS leverages cryptographic hashes for tamper-proof data storage, ensuring integrity and easy verification of research files (Benet, 2014). Arweave provides permanent data availability through a one-time payment model, guaranteeing long-term access to research outputs (Williams *et al.*, 2018). By embedding immutable data storage, DeSci fosters a transparent and mutual ecosystem. Researchers can confidently share their findings and methodologies, allowing others to reproduce results and build upon existing work—ultimately accelerating innovation across scientific disciplines.

6.5.6 *Community involvement and incentivization*

A core principle of DeSci is broadening scientific participation beyond academic circles to anyone capable of contributing. This democratization taps into diverse expertise and ideas, spurring novel solutions and heightened engagement. Platforms such as Pump.science illustrate this approach by turning longevity research into a tokenized prediction market, where users can invest in experimental regimens and trade based on real-time data streams. Similarly, Episteme envisions scientific hypotheses as tradable tokens, further gamifying research. Bio Protocol's "bio/acc rewards" program showcases another incentive model, rewarding community members with tokens for their contributions in expertise, financing, or ideation.

Beyond conventional mechanisms, DeSci embraces meme tokens and AI agents to spark wider interest. For example, tokens such as DRUGS (Big Pharmai) aim to disrupt traditional pharmaceutical monopolies, while GIRLE, issued by AthenaDAO, aims to support and normalize research. This gamified, meme-driven culture has generated significant buzz within the DeSci field in late 2024. Ultimately, such incentive models exemplify how DeSci leverages community-driven structures, playful engagement, and open access to fuel a more inclusive, efficient, and vibrant ecosystem for scientific discovery.

6.5.7 *The rise of DeScAI (decentralized science + AI)*

The convergence of decentralized technologies and AI—DeScAI—marks a profound shift in the architecture of scientific inquiry. While DeSci lays the foundation for open, transparent, and self-governing research, AI introduces automation, scalability, and adaptivity at unprecedented levels. DeScAI is not merely a technological synthesis but a transformation in how knowledge is produced, verified, and governed.

AI amplifies DeSci mechanisms across funding, validation, and governance. In grant allocation, machine learning can prioritize proposals by analyzing historical performance, citation networks, and community signals, making decentralized funding more efficient and inclusive. In peer review, AI tools evaluate methodological rigor and reproducibility, easing bottlenecks and bias. Platforms now integrate algorithmic moderation and reward systems, with agents such as Elicit, SciPhi, and others capable of hypothesis generation, literature synthesis, and experimental design at a superhuman scale.

When embedded in decentralized networks, these agents become real-time oracles, verifying hypotheses, updating prediction markets, and informing governance. DeScAI thus becomes a recursive engine: AI doesn't simply coordinate scientific communities; it becomes a co-producer of knowledge.

Crucially, DeSci doesn't merely use AI; it decentralizes it. GPU-sharing and model-staking networks such as Bittensor, Golem, and Akash unlock siloed compute and data for the global research commons. AI, in turn, enables DeSci to scale by curating open corpora, detecting fraud, and routing capital toward under-replicated findings in real time. Without decentralized rails, AI risks falling into cloud-based oligopolies; without AI, DeSci cannot navigate petabyte-scale epistemic flows. Each is the other's substrate: together, they form a self-reinforcing DeScAI stack.

In essence, DeScAI accelerates, democratizes, and reconfigures scientific progress. It envisions science not as a centralized institution but as a self-organizing, continually learning, and radically inclusive process—redefining the social contract of knowledge creation for the 21st century (Table 6.4).

Table 6.4. Comparing traditional science with DeSci and DeScAI.

Aspect	Traditional Science	DeSci	DeScAI
Funding models	Centralized, favors established disciplines	Decentralized via DAOs and quadratic funding, DAOs, quadratic funding, tokenized incentives	AI-curated proposals, algorithmic funding prioritization
Grant processes	Bureaucratic, slow, and biased	Transparent and efficient tokenized funding	AI-assisted triage and reviewer assignment
Transparency	Opaque peer review and publishing processes	Blockchain-based transparent governance	AI agents flag bias, fraud, and reproducibility gaps
Access to research	Paywalled and limited accessibility	Open access via IP-NFTs and Creative Commons	AI-curated open corpora, personalized retrieval
Intellectual property	Costly, complex, and restrictive	Tokenized IP for collaboration and monetization	Smart-contract royalties + AI-assisted IP valuation
Research metrics	Emphasis on quantity over impact	Decentralized, impact-based reward systems	AI-powered impact analytics + real-time credit systems
Reproducibility	Low replication due to bias and poor design	Immutable data storage ensures reproducibility	AI checks for statistical rigor, flags anomalies
Global participation	Favors elite institutions; high barriers for low-income regions	DAOs reduce barriers and promote global collaboration	AI lowers language/data barriers, supports low-resource researchers
Public engagement	Isolated from the public	Gamified and tokenized public participation	AI chat agents, predictive interfaces, public hypothesis generation
Institutional structures	Rigid hierarchies discourage innovation	Inclusive, flat hierarchies via DAO governance	Dynamic, adaptive structures co-evolving with AI moderation
Interdisciplinary collaboration	Silos dominate research landscapes	Open platforms foster cross-field collaboration	AI bridges domains, synthesizes cross-disciplinary knowledge
Adaptability	Slow to adopt new methods and technologies	Agile with smart contracts and token incentives	Real-time optimization via learning systems
Reward systems	Seniority and publications valued over impact	Transparent, contribution-focused rewards	AI tracks micro-contributions and automates fair compensation

6.6 Discussion

While DeSci is making its first steps toward revolutionizing traditional scientific systems (Golato & Kohlhaas, 2021; Shilina, 2023; Weiss, 2022), it faces economic hurdles. Regulatory ambiguity complicates taxation and IP enforcement (Yadav*et al.*, 2022), market volatility diverts long-term investment (Buterin, 2021), and scalability remains daunting for resource-intensive projects (Chauhan *et al.*, 2018). The absence of gatekeepers also raises quality-control and reputation challenges (Battah, Iraqin & Damiani, 2020); entrenched academic norms slow adoption.

Equitable access to advanced AI compute is both an obstacle and an opportunity. Concentration among a few cloud providers risks recentralizing epistemic power. Decentralized AI networks tokenize shared GPUs and models, converting scarce compute into a public good (Ding *et al.*, 2022; Wang & Ding, 2022). In return, AI agents slash coordination costs by triaging grant proposals, detecting statistical errors, and matching reviewers. This mutual dependence—AI needs decentralized rails to avoid oligopoly lock-in, while DeSci needs AI to govern petabyte-scale data—creates a self-reinforcing DeScAI stack whose ultimate trajectory hinges on governance choices (Ohlhaver, Weyl & Buterin, 2022).

Despite these hurdles, regulatory clarity, stable market mechanisms, and integration with existing institutions can unlock DeSci's promise of a more resilient and inclusive knowledge economy.

6.7 Conclusion

DeSci signals the dawn of a new paradigm in scientific discovery—one that dissolves entrenched boundaries of funding, governance, and access. By weaving decentralized technologies directly into the fabric of research, DeSci reconfigures core economic mechanisms of resource distribution, incentivization, and collaboration. Leveraging tokenized rewards, DAOs, and open-access protocols, it reframes knowledge as a public good and aligns individual incentives with collective advancement. Drawing on classical, behavioral, and game-theoretic insights, DeSci dismantles longstanding bottlenecks—from funding monopolies and data hoarding to opaque peer review—while forging more efficient, transparent paths to discovery.

6.7.1 *Key findings and contributions*

This chapter presents one of the first integrated conceptual frameworks for DeSci economic theory and its AI-augmented extension, DeScAI. It shows how decentralized infrastructures:

1. mitigate scarcity through tokenized public-goods funding (quadratic and retroactive models) that channels resources to underfunded regions and early-career researchers;
2. solve coordination challenges via DAO governance and immutable ledgers that create transparent, participatory decision-making processes and auditable provenance for research outputs;
3. expand researcher agency by enabling permissionless participation, diversifying IP management through IP-NFTs, and rewarding "invisible" labor such as peer review, data validation, and replication;
4. accelerate adaptability with AI, where DeScAI agents triage proposals, detect statistical errors, and optimize funding allocation and reputation metrics, thus lowering transaction costs without reinstating centralized gatekeepers.

Together, these mechanisms outline a testable economic blueprint for a self-organizing, globally inclusive, and dynamically responsive scientific ecosystem. Future empirical work can validate—and iterate on—these design principles, ensuring that the next era of knowledge production remains both decentralized and ethically aligned.

References

Arendt, H. 1958. *The Human Condition.* Chicago: University of Chicago Press.

Arrow, K. J. 1962. "Economic welfare and the allocation of resources for invention." In *The Rate and Direction of Inventive Activity: Economic and Social Factors.* Princeton, NJ: Princeton University Press, pp. 609–626.

Arthur, W. B. 1994. *Increasing Returns and Path Dependence in the Economy.* Ann Arbor: University of Michigan Press.

Baker, M. 2016. "1,500 scientists lift the lid on reproducibility." *Nature* 533(7604): 452–454. https://doi.org/10.1038/533452a.

Bamakan, S. M., Nezhadsistani, N., Bodaghi, O., and Qu, Q. 2022. "Patents and intellectual property assets as non-fungible tokens; key technologies and challenges." *Scientific Reports* 12(1): 1–13. https://doi.org/10.1038/s41598-022-05920-6.

Bartling, S. and Fecher, B. 2017. "Blockchain for science and knowledge creation: Promises and potentials of distributed ledger technology in knowledge exchange." Medium. https://doi.org/10.31235/osf.io/5ujd8.

Battah, A., Iraqi, Y., and Damiani, E. 2020. "Blockchain-Based Reputation Systems: Implementation Challenges and Mitigation." *Electronics* 10(3): 289. https://doi.org/10.3390/electronics10030289.

Benet, J. 2014. "IPFS-Content addressed, versioned, P2P file system." (arXiv:1407.3561). arXiv. https://arxiv.org/abs/1407.3561.

Benkler, Y. 2002. "Coase's Penguin, or Linux and the nature of the firm." *The Yale Law Journal* 112(3): 369–446.

Bischof, E., Botezatu, A., Jakimov, S., Suharenko, I., Ostrovski, A., Verbitsky, A. *et al.* 2022. "Longevity foundation: Perspective on decentralized autonomous organizations for special-purpose financing." *IEEE Access* 10: 33048–33058. https://doi.org/10.1109/ACCESS.2022.3161392.

Björk, B.-C., Welling, P., Laakso, M., Majlender, P., Hedlund, T., and Guðnason, G. 2010. "Open Access to the scientific journal literature: Situation 2009." *PLoS ONE* 5(6): e11273.

Boumans, M. and Davis, J. B. 2010. *Economic Methodology: Understanding Economics as a Science*. London: Palgrave Macmillan.

Brembs, B. 2018. "Prestigious science journals struggle to reach even average reliability." *Frontiers in Human Neuroscience* 12: 37. https://doi.org/10.3389/fnhum.2018.00037.

Budroni, P., Burgelman, J.-C., and Schouppe, M. 2019. "Architectures of knowledge: The European Open Science Cloud." *ABI Technik* 39(2): 130–141. https://doi.org/10.1515/abitech-2019-2006.

Buterin, V. 2013. "Ethereum: A next-generation smart contract and decentralized application platform [White paper]." https://ethereum.org/content/whitepaper/whitepaper-pdf/Ethereum_Whitepaper_-_Buterin_2014.pdf.

Buterin, V. 2014. "A next-generation smart contract and decentralized application platform." Ethereum Whitepaper.

Buterin, V. 2021. "Moving beyond coin voting governance." Vitalik Buterin's Blog, August 16, 2021. https://vitalik.ca/general/2021/08/16/voting3.html.

Coase, R. H. 1937. "The nature of the firm." *Economica* 4(16): 386–405.

Chauhan, A., Malviya, O. P., Verma, M., and Mor, T. S. 2018. "Blockchain and scalability [Preprint]." ResearchGate. https://www.researchgate.net/publication/327000219_Blockchain_and_Scalability.

Dasgupta, P. and David, P. A. 1994. "Toward a new economics of science." *Research Policy* 23(5): 487–521.

David, P. A. 2004. "Understanding the emergence of 'open science' institutions: Functionalist economics in historical context." *Industrial and Corporate Change* 13(4): 571–589.

Davidson, S., De Filippi, P., and Potts, J. 2016. "Economics of blockchain." SSRN. https://ssrn.com/abstract=2744751.

Davidson, S., De Filippi, P., and Potts, J. 2018. "Blockchains and the economic institutions of capitalism." *Journal of Institutional Economics*, 14(4): 639–658. https://doi.org/10.1017/S1744137417000200.

DeFrancesco, L. and Klevecz, A. 2022. "Decentralized investor communities gain traction in biotech." *Nature Biotechnology* 40(9): 1310–1315. https://doi.org/10.1038/s41587-022-01459-z.

Ding, W., Hou, J., Li, J., Guo, C., Qin, J., Kozma, R., and Wang, F. 2022. "DeSci based on Web3 and DAO: A comprehensive overview and reference model." *IEEE Transactions on Computational Social Systems* 9: 1563–1573. https://doi.org/10.1109/TCSS.2022.3204745.

Else, H. 2024. "'Getting paid to review is justice': Journal pays peer reviewers in cryptocurrency." *Nature*. https://doi.org/10.1038/d41586-024-04027-4.

Fantaccini, S., Grassi, L., and Rampoldi, A. 2024. "The potential of DAOs for funding and collaborative development in the life sciences." *Nature Biotechnology* 42(4): 555–562. https://doi.org/10.1038/s41587-024-02189-0.

Foucault, M. 1975. *Discipline and Punish: The Birth of the Prison*. New York, NY: Pantheon Books.

Giddens, A. 1984. *The Constitution of Society: Outline of the Theory of Structuration*. University of California Press.

Golato, T. and Kohlhaas, P. 2021. "VitaDAO whitepaper (Version 1.0)." VitaDAO. https://raw.githubusercontent.com/VitaDAO/whitepaper/master/VitaDAO_Whitepaper.pdf.

Guston, D. H. 2000. "Retiring the social contract for science." In *Science and Technology in Society: From the Policy Perspective to the Cultural Meaning of Science and Technology*, pp. 75–94.

Hardin, G. 1968. "The tragedy of the commons." *Science* 162(3859): 1243–1248.

Hayek, F. A. 1945. "The use of knowledge in society." *The American Economic Review* 35(4): 519–530.

Hurwicz, L. 1972. "On Informationally Decentralized Systems." In *Decision and Organization*. Amsterdam: North-Holland.

Ioannidis, J. P. A. 2005. "Why most published research findings are false." *PLoS Medicine* 2(8): e124.

James, S. 2021. “Proof of humanity: An explainer on how to register for Proof of Humanity and use the platform.” Kleros Blog.

Kauffman, S. A. 1993. *The Origins of Order: Self-organization and Selection in Evolution*. Oxford University Press. https://doi.org/10.1093/oso/9780195079517.001.0001.

Kant, I. 1991. “An answer to the question: What is enlightenment?” (H. B. Nisbet, Trans.). In Reiss, H. S. (ed.), *Political writings* (2nd ed., pp. 54–60). Cambridge: Cambridge University Press. (Original work published 1784).

Kavazi, D., Smirnov, V., Shilina, S., Li, M., Contreras, R., Gajera, H., and Lavrenov, D. 2021. “You are [not] a bot.” arXiv:2111.13189. https://arxiv.org/abs/2111.13189.

Kitcher, P. 1993. *The Advancement of Science: Science Without Legend, Objectivity Without Illusions*. New York, NY: Oxford University Press.

Kuhn, T. S. 1962. *The Structure of Scientific Revolutions*. Chicago: University of Chicago Press.

Larivière, V., Haustein, S., and Mongeon, P. 2015. “The oligopoly of academic publishers in the digital era.” *PLoS ONE* 10(6): e0127502. https://doi.org/10.1371/journal.pone.0127502.

Malthus, T. R. 1798. “An essay on the principle of population.” J. Johnson.

Martin, B. R. 2003. “The changing social contract for science and the evolution of the university.” In Geuna, A., Salter, A. J., and Steinmueller, W. E. (eds.), *Science and Innovation: Rethinking the Rationales for Funding and Governance*. Edward Elgar, pp. 7–29. https://doi.org/10.4337/9781781950241.00011.

Marx, K. 1976. *Capital: A Critique of Political Economy* (Vol. 1). London: Penguin Books. (Original work published 1867).

Maskin, E. 1999. “Nash equilibrium and welfare optimality.” *Review of Economic Studies* 66(1): 23–38. https://doi.org/10.1111/1467-937X.00075.

Merton, R. K. 1973. *The Sociology of Science: Theoretical and Empirical Investigations*. Chicago, IL: University of Chicago Press.

Metcalfe, R. M. 2013. “Metcalfe's law after 40 years of Ethernet.” *Computer*, 46(12): 26–31. https://doi.org/10.1109/MC.2013.374.

Myerson, R. B. 1999. “Nash equilibrium and the history of economic theory.” *Journal of Economic Literature*, 37(3): 1067–1082. https://doi.org/10.1257/jel.37.3.1067.

Nakamoto, S. 2008. “Bitcoin: A peer-to-peer electronic cash system.” Bitcoin White Paper.

Nash, J. 1950. “Equilibrium points in n-person games.” *Proceedings of the National Academy of Sciences* 36(1): 48–49. https://doi.org/10.1073/pnas.36.1.48.

Nelson, R. R. 1959. "The simple economics of basic scientific research." *Journal of Political Economy* 67(2): 297–306.

North, D. C. 1990. *Institutions, Institutional Change and Economic Performance*. Cambridge, England: Cambridge University Press.

Ohlhaver, P., Weyl, E. G., and Buterin, V. 2022. "Decentralized society: Finding Web3's soul." SSRN Working Paper. https://doi.org/10.2139/ssrn.4105763.

Ostrom, E. 1990. *Governing the Commons: The Evolution of Institutions for Collective Action*. Cambridge, England: Cambridge University Press.

Pandey, R., Gurung, I., Adhikari, S., Marouane, A., Dhakal, S., & Maskey, M. 2023. Exploring blockchain to support open science practices. Paper presented at IGARSS 2023 (IEEE International Geoscience and Remote Sensing Symposium), Pasadena, CA. NASA NTRS. https://ntrs.nasa.gov/citations/20230009029.

Piwowar, H., Priem, J., Orr, R. *et al.* 2018. "The state of OA: A large-scale analysis of the prevalence and impact of Open Access articles." *PeerJ* 6: e4375.

Polanyi, M. 1962. "The republic of science: Its political and economic theory." *Minerva* 1(1): 54–73.

Popper, K. 1959. *The Logic of Scientific Discovery*. London: Hutchinson.

Potts, J. 2000. *The New Evolutionary Microeconomics: Complexity, Competence and Adaptive Behaviour*. Edward Elgar.

Powell, K. 2016. "Young, talented and fed-up: Scientists tell their stories." *Nature* 538(7624): 446–449.

Romero, F. 2019. "Philosophy of science and reproducibility crisis." *Synthese* 196(8): 3067–3086.

Sahlins, M. 1972. *Stone Age Economics*. Chicago, IL: Aldine de Gruyter.

Sen, A. 1999. *Development as Freedom*. Oxford, England: Oxford University Press.

Shilina, S. 2023. "Decentralized science (DeSci): Web3-mediated future of science." Paradigm Research. https://medium.com/paradigm-research/decentralized-science-desci-web3-mediated-future-of-science-2547f9a88c40.

Shilina, S. 2023. "Intellectual property (in science): The potential & advantages of NFTs." Research Gate Preprint. https://doi.org/10.13140/RG.2.2.10291.50729/1.

Simon, H. A. 1957. *Models of Man: Social and Rational*. New York: Wiley.

Smith, A. 1976. *An Inquiry into the Nature and Causes of the Wealth of Nations*. Chicago: University of Chicago Press. (Original work published 1776).

Stigler, G. J. 1961. "The economics of information." *Journal of Political Economy* 69(3): 213–225.

Swan, M. 2015. *Blockchain: Blueprint for a New Economy.* Sebastopol, California: O'Reilly Media.

Trovò, B. and Massari, N. 2021. "Ants-Review: A protocol for incentivized open peer-reviews on Ethereum." ArXiv. https://doi.org/10.1007/978-3-030-71593-9_2.

UNESCO. 2021. *UNESCO Science Report: The Race Against Time for Smarter Development.* Paris, France: UNESCO Publishing.

von Neumann, J., and Morgenstern, O. 1944. *Theory of Games and Economic Behavior.* Princeton University Press.

Voshmgir, S. and Zargham, M. 2020. "Foundations of Cryptoeconomic Systems." WU Vienna University of Economics and Business Working Paper Series, Institute for Cryptoeconomics, Interdisciplinary Research No. 1. https://doi.org/10.57938/10d8b646-3266-4ec9-b94d-810b528c40a9.

Walras, L. 1954. *Elements of Pure Economics.* Trans. W. Jaffé. London: Allen & Unwin. (London, England: Original work published 1874).

Wang, F.-Y., Ding, W., Wang, X., Garibaldi, J., Teng, S., Rudas, I., and Olaverri-Monreal, C. 2022. "The DAO to DeSci: AI for free, fair, and responsibility sensitive sciences." *IEEE Intelligent Systems* 37: 16–22. https://doi.org/10.1109/MIS.2022.3167070.

Weidener, L., Greilich, K., and Melnykowycz, M. 2024. "Adapting Mintzberg's organizational theory to DeSci: The decentralized science pyramid framework." *Frontiers in Blockchain* 7: 1513885. https://doi.org/10.3389/fbloc.2024.1513885.

Weidener, L. and Spreckelsen, C. 2024. "Decentralized science (DeSci): Definition, shared values, and guiding principles." *Frontiers in Blockchain* 7: 1375763. https://doi.org/10.3389/fbloc.2024.1375763.

Weiss, K. 2022. "Gitcoin grants – Quadratic funding for the world." Gitcoin. https://gitcoin.co.

Wennerås, C. and Wold, A. 1997. "Nepotism and sexism in peer-review." *Nature* 387: 341–343.

Weyl, E. G. and Buterin, V. 2019. "Liberation through radical decentralization." Working Paper.

Whitehead, A. N. 1978. *Process and Reality.* Corrected edition, edited by David Ray Griffin and Donald W. Sherburne. New York: Free Press. (Original work published 1929).

Williams, S., Diordiiev, V., Berman, L., Raybould, I., and Uemlianin, I. 2018. "Arweave: A protocol for economically sustainable information permanence." Arweave White Paper.

Williamson, O. E. 1985. *The Economic Institutions of Capitalism.* New York, NY: Free Press.

Yadav, S. P., Agrawal, K. K., Bhati, B. S., Al-Turjman, F., and Mostarda, L. 2022. "Blockchain-based cryptocurrency regulation: An overview." *Computational Economics* 59(4): 1659–1675.

Zamfir, V. 2015. *What is Cryptoeconomics?* Paper presented at Cryptoeconomicon 2015. Mountain View, CA.

https://doi.org/10.1142/9781800618664_0008

Chapter 7

Protocols and Institutions

Michael Zargham[*,‡] **and Ilan Ben-Meir**[*,†,§]

[*] *BlockScience*
[†] *Brown University, Providence, Rhode Island, USA*
[‡] *zargham@block.science*
[§] *ilan@block.science*

Abstract
This chapter explores the relationship between protocols and institutions through the lens of control systems engineering. Cross-referencing concepts from institutional economics, cybernetics, control theory, and market design, we define institutions mathematically by correspondence to stability (in the sense of Lyapunov), demonstrating that behavior can be enduringly and predictably patterned without resorting to coercive control. Grounded in engineering practice, we emphasize field surveys as prerequisites for formal modeling, avoiding purely theoretical constructs. Aligning our terminology with control engineering's canonical forms enables us to direct readers to a broad suite of practical methods while highlighting emerging work on institutional design through protocolization.

Keywords: Institutions, Protocols, Lyapunov Stability, Control Systems Engineering, Cybernetics, Institutional Engineering.

7.1 Introduction

In recent years, the claim that societal institutions are breaking down has matured from a provocation into a truism. The growing consensus that our institutions are dysfunctional, however, has not yet produced an actionable discourse on *how to fix them* that is commensurate with the complexity of the problem. This deficit is due, at least in part, to the lack of clarity surrounding our understanding of what institutions are and (therefore) what characterizes their failure. Answering these questions rigorously makes it possible to think about institutions and their failure through the lens of control systems engineering, thus enabling us to apply methods and insights drawn from that discipline to the urgent but achievable work of revitalizing them.

7.2 Institutions

The natural starting point for our inquiry is the field of institutional economics, where the academic study of institutions *as such* is concentrated. At the foundation of that ongoing conversation, one finds Douglass North's definition: "Institutions are the rules of the game in a society or, more formally, are the humanly devised constraints that shape human interaction. In consequence, they structure incentives in human exchange, whether political, social, or economic" (North, 1990). In North's telling, "[t]he major role of institutions in a society is to establish a stable (but not necessarily efficient) structure to human action." Elinor Ostrom sounds a similar note in *Governing the Commons: The Evolution of Institutions for Collective Action*, explaining that "'[i]nstitutions' can be defined as the sets of working rules" (Ostrom, 1990) that govern interactions within a particular context. "Working rules are those actually used, monitored, and enforced when individuals make choices about the actions they will take," Ostrom elaborates, explaining that when it comes to institutions, "all rules are nested in another set of rules that define how the first set of rules can be changed." This "nesting of rules within rules at several levels is similar to the nesting of computer languages at several levels," she goes on to suggest, and helps institutions to realize their purpose insofar as it reinforces "the stability of mutual expectations among individuals interacting according to a set of rules." Ostrom and North thus appear to agree: institutions are the rules that human beings develop in order to provide stable structures for our interactions.

Ostrom seems to have revised her understanding of institutions, however, during the five-year interval separating the release of *Governing the Commons* and the publication of "A Grammar of Institutions" (co-authored with Sue E. S. Crawford). The latter paper begins with a declaration that it "is based on a view that institutions are enduring regularities of human action in situations structured by rules, norms and shared strategies, as well as by the physical world" (Crawford and Ostrom, 1995). Here, "institutions" are no longer the "rules, norms, and shared strategies" that structure the "situations" in which human beings interact; instead, they have become the "enduring regularities of human action" that are *produced by* or *emerge from* the interactions that take place in such situations. In fact, Crawford and Ostrom's definition of institutions as "enduring regularities of human action in situations structured by rules, norms, and shared strategies, as well as the physical world" involves no fewer than *four* distinct concepts:

1. The "rules, norms, and shared strategies" that make up the "humanly constituted elements of institutions."
2. The "physical world" that, along with these "humanly constituted elements," structures the "situations" in which institutions can be found.
3. The "situations" that are "structured by" both the "components of institutions" and the "physical world."
4. The "enduring regularities of human action" that are found "in [such] situations."

Insofar as Crawford and Ostrom intend for their proposed "Institutional Grammar" to provide "a theoretical structure for analysis of the humanly constituted elements of institutions (i.e., rules, norms, and shared strategies)," it must also be read as explicitly acknowledging a *difference* between these "humanly constituted elements of institutions" (which Crawford and Ostrom also call "the components of institutions") and the institutions into which they are composed.

Institutional economics (as a discipline) is still engaged in the work of litigating precisely how these four concepts relate to one another, along with the related task of *assigning each a distinct (and consistent) name.* While North, for example, identifies "[a] crucial distinction ... between institutions and organizations" corresponding to the separation of "the rules from the players" of a given game, his characterization of "organizations" collapses the conceptual distinction between the loci of activity that Crawford and Ostrom call "situations" and the "physical world" in which various organizational "bodies" (North, 1990) concretely interact. Furthermore, Geoffrey M. Hodgson convincingly argues that the imprecision of North's terminology means that "even by North's own definition, organizations must be regarded as a type of *institution*" (Hodgson, 2006).

We thus conclude that it is necessary to look beyond its borders to find clarity about institutions, as well as terminology that is precise enough to facilitate both their description and their design.

7.3 Protocols and Purposive Systems

Although his language often appears to coincide with that of Ostrom and North, the understanding of institutions put forth by Stafford Beer in *Designing Freedom* offers tools for untangling the conceptual confusions opened up by the institutional economics literature.

As Beer explains, "institutions ... are not just things, entities we recognize and label. They are instead *dynamic and surviving systems* ... they consist of related parts, and the relations—the connexions—between those parts [... in] a particular organization which produces particular outputs" (Beer, 1974). The "specific modes of organization" in which these parts and their relations are *realized* are concrete systems—not merely *specifications* but particular *implementations*.

Institutions, Beer notes, "are actually *outputs* of this system. They are what they are because the system is organized in the way that it is, and this organization produces an inescapable kind of behavior." Translating Beer's famous acronymic aphorism "POSIWID" (The Purpose of a System is What it Does) to the context at hand, one could say that "the purpose of an organization is the behavior that it *realizes*" (Beer, 2002).

Beer thus makes it clear that the "enduring regularities of human action"—that Crawford and Ostrom identify as "institutions"—are more precisely understood as *the stable emergent properties* (or the system-level behavior) of the concrete systems that Beer calls *organizations*. These realized systems correspond to both the "physical world" and the *implementations* of any "rules, norms, and shared strategies," thus overlapping both item (1) and item (2) in Crawford and Ostrom's definition of "institutions." The "situations structured by" this physical world (and its interplay with the organization's existing "rules, norms, and shared strategies"), meanwhile, correspond to such systems' *states.* While at first glance it may be confusing that "rules, norms, and shared strategies" are represented in both the *organization* and in the *situation*, this simply means we are dealing with a "second-order system." Second-order dynamical systems have state variables, which represent the way other state variables change (Khalil, 2001; Sontag, 1999). This complexity is necessary to accurately represent the ways that an organization's "rules, norms, and shared strategies" both *influence* and *are influenced by* the actions of its actors, albeit along different temporal horizons.

Beer's work helps us to refine our model by mapping three of the four concepts in Crawford and Ostrom's definition to a (second-order) dynamical system. What remains is to find a suitable term for the "rules, norms, and shared strategies" *themselves.*

7.3.1 *Protocols*

What do "rules, norms, and shared strategies" have in common *other than* their structural relationship to institutions? The answer is that all three are means of patterning behavior which can be grouped together under a single category: they are all types of *protocols.*

Derived from the Greek *protokollon* (from *protos*, meaning "first,"and *kolla*, meaning "glue"), the first protocols were cover sheets attesting to the provenance (and thus the authenticity or validity) of the documents to which they were attached, thereby operating as "an early techno-social system of administration that has functional equivalents from Antiquity up until today" (Beuster *et al.*, 2022). Eventually, the term expanded to refer to regularizing practices in areas as diverse as the sciences or international diplomacy—sets of common constraints that function to produce interoperability despite difference, "often independent from time and place." In contemporary usage, "protocol" has also taken on a particular technical meaning (albeit one highly consonant with its broader sense): "a cascade of formalized standards or agreements to be implemented as control regimes for flexible material and/or semiotic organization [... that] predictably structures in an often layered, sometimes hierarchical way the behaviors of data and objects [such that they are able] to participate in infrastructural networks."

The close conceptual association that has formed between the concept of "protocols" and digital technology is not accidental; protocols are, essentially, "distributed algorithms" (Lynch, 1996) (the title of Nancy A. Lynch's 1996 textbook describing the protocols underlying the then-emerging internet), or *control mechanisms for the flow of information through decentralized systems.* In *Protocol: How Control Exists After Decentralization*, Alexander Galloway thus identifies protocol as "the principle of organization native to computers in distributed networks" (Galloway, 2004). Galloway connects the contemporary technical meaning of "protocol" to its historical antecedents, explaining that inasmuch as both usages refer to "conventional rules that govern the set of possible behavior patterns within a heterogeneous system ... protocol is a technique for achieving voluntary regulation within a contingent environment ... a distributed management system that allows control to exist within a heterogeneous material milieu."

If protocols are mechanisms that control the flow of information (or that structure the substrate by way of which information, matter, energy, and thus also action flow), then the field of *control systems engineering* can be understood as a rigorous and formal study of the interplay between the physical world, specified protocols, and realized behavior of the assemblage thereof, thus equipping us with the machinery needed to engineer the stabilization of institutions at all scales, from micro-markets to the most vital functions of a healthy society.

7.3.2 *Control systems engineering*

Design and analysis of control systems is accomplished by representing these assemblages via dynamical systems. In the context of multi-agent systems, control engineering explores how locally defined and locally implemented rules interact within dynamic environments to generate emergent behaviors that are both stable and predictable at the system level—in other words, how the protocols that constrain behavior *within* an organization can be composed in order to induce stable properties in the emergent system-level behavior *of* that organization (Kia *et al.*, 2019; Uchiyama *et al.*, 2022).

Cooperative Control of Distributed Multi-Agent Systems, edited by Jeff S. Shamma, provides a detailed look at the methods (which is to say, the protocols and collections of interrelated protocols) that contemporary control systems use to compose complex assemblages where individual agents, operating with access to only local information and retaining autonomy over their decisions, collaboratively produce emergent, higher-level patterns of behavior (Shamma, 2007). These stabilized patterns are not static but instead represent the system's capacity to dynamically and continuously solve complex constrained resource allocation problems in changing environments, all without any agent accessing global information.

7.3.3 *Cybernetics*

The cybernetics literature extended the (then-contemporary) practices of control systems engineering to assemblages other than human-made systems. As Norbert Wiener explains in the introduction to the volume that christened the field, "[w]e have decided to call the entire field of control and communication theory, whether in the machine or in the animal, by the name Cybernetics, which we form from the Greek $\chi\upsilon\beta\epsilon\rho\nu\eta\tau\eta\varsigma$ or *steersman*" (Wiener, 1949). In *Designing Freedom*, Beer revises Wiener's definition, asserting that "[c]ybernetics is the science of effective organization"—or, we might say, of how to organize systems in order to produce specific desired effects. Beer pays particular attention to "the conditions [organizations] must meet in order to remain stable yet adaptive." These latter properties are what is meant by the second part of Beer's definition of institutions as "*dynamic and surviving systems.*" In the context of a dynamic system, "survival" is best understood as persistence of function rather than prevention of demise.

As Beer explains, "[t]he number of possible states of a system is called its *variety*," and "[i]n order to regulate a system, we have to absorb its variety. If we fail in this, the system becomes unstable" (1974). He proceeds to invoke "the Law of Requisite Variety—named Ashby's law, after its discoverer," which asserts that "only variety can absorb variety"; the implication of Ashby's law, Beer explains, is that "[i]f varieties in a regulatory system are disbalanced, the system cannot attain stability. Assuming that the regulator has the smaller variety, there are only two ways of meeting the demand of Ashby's law. One is to attenuate variety in the system, the other is to amplify variety in the regulator." Beer is careful to note that "these strategies can be mixed," but in both cases, "[t]he mode of organization adopted for the system is its variety controller." In other words, the *stability* of a dynamical system depends on that system's *adaptive capacity*, which is in turn a function of its "mode of organization," or *the way that its organization is structured.*

Crucially, the characterizations by both Ashby and Beer are implicitly dependent on a "second-order" model, wherein an organization can adapt its own structure.

7.3.4 *Dynamic stability*

In control systems engineering, "stability" has a precise technical meaning: it refers to the system's ability to maintain consistent and predictable behavior in the face of disturbances. Importantly, stability does not necessarily imply returning to a fixed, unchanging state; rather, the equilibrium of a system can itself be a dynamic behavior—such as a pattern of oscillation or a stimulus–response pair—as long as the defining properties of that behavior remain stable over time. For a system to be stable, any deviations from this dynamic equilibrium must either decay over time (asymptotic stability) or remain within a bounded region where the system continues to exhibit the same characteristic behavior.[1] These dynamic equilibria manifest as "enduring regularities" in the system-level behaviors of organizations—which is to say, as *institutions*, "patterns of behavior" (Beer, 1974) that persist despite variations in individual behavior or shocks from the environment. The "failure" of an institution occurs when this dynamic stability is lost.[2]

[1]This characterization of stability is also consistent with the work of Robert Axelrod, who studied the emergence and stabilization of equilibria over norms in his seminal work *The Evolution of Cooperation* (Axelrod, 1984). Notably, Axelrod's models placed the norms that agents used to make their decisions within the state of his models, allowing them to change over time via turnover in the agent population. It is also related to stability in population games, as developed extensively by Sandholm in *Population Games and Evolutionary Dynamics* (Sandholm, 2010). Population games study strategic interactions in large populations where individual agents have negligible influence but collectively shape system-level behavior.

[2]This perspective aligns closely with the thesis of Acemoglu and Robinson's *Why Nations Fail*, in which they argue that the long-term success or failure of nations hinges on the inclusiveness and adaptability of their institutions (Acemoglu and Robinson, 2012). In this view, the nation itself is the organization, and its "institutions" constitute the protocols that contour its potential system-level behavior. Nations whose institutions co-regulate each other in a stable and productive way succeed (that is, themselves become institutions), whereas nations whose institutions lack stabilizing feedback loops fail.

In Beer's time, the ability to apply cybernetics to practical problems was limited—both technically and politically. The methods of implementation required access to expensive computational resources and a mandate from centralized authorities. The discipline's methods reflected these constraints. In recent years, however, significant advances in technology and mathematics have relaxed both the technical and political constraints. Advances in distributed optimization and multi-agent control provide the basis for a political shift toward "ceding control in favor of coordination" (as per Zargham *et al.*, summarizing Swann) (Swann, 2020; Zargham *et al.*, 2023). The rise of open-source software development (particularly peer-to-peer protocols which constitute large public networks) demonstrates the realizability of a shift from top-down cybernetics toward bottom-up (or at least middle-out) alternatives (Voshmgir and Zargham, 2020)—from the *command and control* cybernetics of the 1980s to a techno-politics whose watchwords are *protocolize and govern.*

7.3.5 *Engineered institutions*

The field of market design offers a glimpse into the future of emerging institutions constituted by protocols that have been carefully engineered to produce reliable behavior. In his seminal work "The Economist as Engineer: Game Theory, Experimentation, and Computation as Tools for Design Economics," Alvin E. Roth discusses how economists can design and implement protocols to create reliable and efficient market behaviors (Roth, 2002). The canonical example is the development of kidney exchange programs, where incompatible patient–donor pairs are matched through carefully engineered algorithms to facilitate life-saving transplants. These protocols ensure that the exchanges are both efficient and fair, maximizing the number of successful transplants while adhering to ethical standards (Roth *et al.*, 2004).

Another example of an engineered economic system is a platform economy, which provides software and serves as an intermediary to facilitate exchanges between users. Rochet and Tirole's research on platform competition in two-sided markets highlights how these platforms are designed to efficiently match supply and demand, often employing sophisticated algorithms to clear transactions (Rochet and Tirole, 2003). While academically market design focuses on efficiency and fairness, it is important to critically examine these platforms through the lens of Beer's POSIWID principle: despite their stated goals, many platform economies appear empirically to optimize for profit extraction, benefiting shareholders while only questionably serving users and often inducing other negative externalities (Srnicek, 2017). This observation suggests a need for further scrutiny to ensure that these engineered markets serve the broader public interest (Shorish, 2023).

7.4 An Approach to Institutional Engineering

Supplementing the insights of institutional economics with the rigor and precision of control systems engineering gives us the necessary materials to lay out a general yet *practical* approach for institutional engineering; that is, one that can be *applied* by those creating or governing concrete organizations with specific purposes, insofar as these purposes can be understood as desired "patterns of behavior" which must be rendered "stable" (in the control-theoretic sense) through the design, implementation, and governance of protocols. Despite our use of formal methods, we acknowledge the fundamental subjectivity in the act of representation, as well as the inevitable influence such representations have on the systems they represent. Our confidence that methods of control engineering are appropriate for addressing challenges in institutional engineering emanates from the fact that control systems engineers have successfully integrated economic mechanism design methods into cyber-physical systems, such as transportation networks and power grids (Chremos and Malikopoulos, 2024).

A fundamental challenge in designing systems meant to *pattern* (and, thus, to *regulate*) human behavior stems from the need to preserve individual autonomy even as one seeks to stabilize desirable properties in system-level behavior. Inevitably, governance decisions, i.e., those which act on an organization's protocols, create winners and losers; "the questions of central relevance to governance of impersonal organizations are those surrounding disagreement or dispute among members," as Eric Alston writes in "Governance As Conflict" (Alston, 2022). In "Aligning Decentralized Autonomous Organizations to Precedents in Cybernetics," Zargham and Nabben adapt the phrase "control surface" to describe the "governance surface" through which decentralized organizations evolve their structures by modifying their protocols—both technically, via smart contract code, and socially, via community covenant documents (Zargham and Nabben, 2023).

7.4.1 *Institutions as dynamical systems*

In "A State-Space Modeling Framework for Engineering Blockchain-Enabled Economic Systems," Zargham *et al.* introduce two key ideas: (1) blockchain networks can be understood as second-order dynamical systems; (2) Lyapunov-like value functions can be used to encode and preserve desirable properties within crypto-economic systems (Zargham *et al.*, 2018). In "Foundations of Cryptoeconomic Systems," Voshmgir and Zargham argue that cryptoeconomic systems are fundamentally a governance technology and can be approached like cyber-physical systems (Voshmgir and Zargham, 2020). Zargham and Shorish build on this intuition in "Generalized Dynamical Systems: Foundations," generalizing the state-space framework presented in "A State-Space Modeling Framework for Engineering Blockchain-Enabled Economic Systems" to control systems with non-numerical state spaces and relaxing the control conditions by restricting admissible actions rather than specifying a unique control action (Zargham and Shorish, 2022).

This innovation—replacing the control law with a restriction on admissible actions—provides the basis for engineering institutions through the design of protocols. Figure 7.1 demonstrates the intuition for reasoning about governance in terms of second-order dynamical systems.

The framing allows us to reason about the systems as a differential inclusion. Let $z = \begin{bmatrix} \dot{x} \\ x \end{bmatrix}$. Then, the dynamics $\dot{z} = \begin{bmatrix} \ddot{x} \\ \dot{x} \end{bmatrix}$ are given by

$$\dot{z} \in \{F(z, u) | u \in U_{x(z)}\},$$

where the set of admissible actions $U_x(z)$ are still state-dependent in the full state z. The resulting system is non-deterministic but is nonetheless *structured by* the "organization," and it realizes behavior in the form of a sequence of values u and z. Such a system potentially

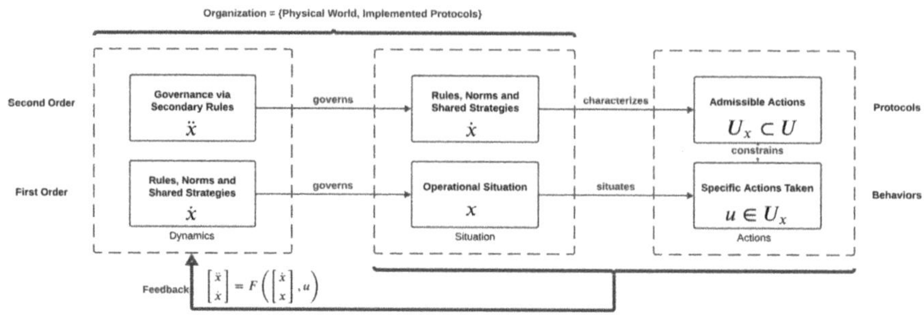

Fig. 7.1. Control framework for governance, rules, norms, and actions. The system evolves dynamically through feedback and constraints. For simplicity, *laws of motion* representing the physical world are compressed into the differential topology characterized by $F : Z \times U \to \partial Z$.

has many stable properties, despite the variation in time and non-determinism; these stable properties can be described via Lyapunov-like value functions V, as long as those functions can be thought of as "loss functions" (to borrow a concept from machine learning), and the properties they encode are oriented at their zero value. We are then interested in how the protocol regulates the differential of the loss function:

$$\dot{V} \in \nabla V(z)^\top F(z, u), \quad \forall u \in U_{x(z)};$$

ultimately, we can claim the property represented by the value function or loss function V encodes a stable emergent property only if

$$\sup_{u \in U_{x(z)}} \nabla V(z)^\top F(z, u) \leq 0.$$

That is to say, if even without knowing the individual choices u, the introduction of the protocol into the organization stabilizes the property encoded by V, in the sense of Lyapunov.

7.4.2 *Institutional dynamics*

The intuition is presented in continuous time because the dynamical systems canon is developed for continuous systems. Our work on protocols and institutions, however, is more naturally situated in discrete-event systems for two reasons: (1) the protocols we have studied are implemented as computer software, which is natively discrete; (2) organizations adapt themselves through discrete changes to their protocols, i.e., passing governance proposals and/or merging updated code into production environments. Therefore, for the remainder of this chapter, we use the discrete-time characterization from "Generalized Dynamical Systems: Foundations" (Zargham and Shorish, 2022). Furthermore, while we retain the assumption that our model is second-order—that is, a state contains within itself the rules, norms, and shared strategies that determine actors' admissible action sets—we collapse our notation to simply denote that state $x \in X$, with the discrete-event dynamics represented as $f : X \times U \to X$.

Let an *organization* be the concrete action-situation, structured by *implemented* protocols and the physical world, in which actors take actions, and the consequences of those actions are realized as changes to that organization's state. We *represent* the organization as a generalized dynamical system (GDS):

$$x^+ = f(x, u),$$

where $x \in X$ represents the state of the organization, $u \in U$ represents the actions taken by actors, and $x^+ \in X$ represents the state of the organization resulting from the actions u. The unconstrained U represents the set of all the *physically possible* actions u, which must be distinguished from the set U_x representing the *admissible* actions in any given state—those that satisfy the organization's already-implemented norms, rules, and shared strategies.[3] For such a dynamical system, there is realization

$$(x_0, u_0), (x_1, u_1), (x_2, u_2), \ldots, (x_t, u_t), \ldots,$$

which may exhibit desirable (or undesirable) patterns of behavior. Some of the patterning is attributable to the structure of the organization (which we have represented as $f(x, u)$), but some of the patterning is attributable to regularities in the choices of u given x and knowledge or beliefs *about* $f(x, u)$. In control engineering, one asserts a control law $u = g(x)$ with the purpose of achieving a property represented as $V(x_t) \leq \epsilon$. This is accomplished by learning or

[3]While some systems, such as cryptographically enforced peer-to-peer networks, can strictly enforce their protocols, we do not assume perfect compliance in practice. Rather, we rely on control-theoretic techniques for *bounding the consequences of non-compliance.*

deriving a model of "the plant"—in our case, the "organization"—and then ensuring the control rule satisfies the condition that

$$V(x^+) = V(f(x, g(x))) \leq V(x).$$

Although our model $f(x, u)$ is surely an imperfect representation, and our control action is imperfectly translated into the world, these representations help us to create the circumstances under which the organization exhibits the property $V(x) \leq \epsilon$. Put differently, each of

$$V(x_0), V(x_1), V(x_2), \ldots, V(x_t), \ldots$$

satisfies the property $V(x) \leq \epsilon$ and that we expect the property to be satisfied in the foreseeable future.

Let us define an *institution* to be an enduring regularity in the behavior of an organization. In our framework, the institution is a property $V(x) \leq \epsilon$ for an organization represented by $x^+ = f(x, u)$. We do not, however, wish to "control" the behavior of the actors within the organization, so we will not assert a control law $g(x)$ that the actors within that organization are commanded to abide.

But how, then, can we ensure the stability of the property $V(x) \leq \epsilon$. Are we simply at the whim of the actors' choices? We are—*unless* we institute a *Protocol.* A protocol is a set of constraints introduced into an organization to induce a desirable property; in other words, it is a state-dependent subset $U_x \subset U$ that offers our property-preserving guarantee:

$$\Delta V(x) = V(f(x, u)) - V(x) \leq 0 \quad \forall u \in U_x, \, \forall x \in X.$$

This expression does not guarantee a reduction in $V(x)$ if we cannot guarantee $u \in U_x$, but it sets us up to write supermartingale and Lyapunov drift-based stability proofs if we can bound the nature, frequency, and/or magnitude of violations of the protocols within a particular organization being modeled. Control theory gives us the necessary tools to achieve stability of the desired properties in the concrete system *because* it recognizes that there is never a perfect correspondence between a model's abstractions and the realized behavior of the system being modeled; therefore, it offers machinery that enables us to take this asymmetry into account.

7.4.3 *Ontology*

We define the following key concepts that form the basis of our approach:

- **Individual behavior** ($u \in U$): Individual actors make their own choices based on factors that are not known or knowable to system modelers or designers. These choices influence the evolution of the organization but are not strictly determined by any external control.
- **Pattern of behavior** ($g : X \to U$): A representation of *observed patterns* in individual actions as state-dependent policies. This captures how individual behavior tends to correlate with specific states of the organization.
- **Situation** ($x \in X$): The *state of the organization* at a given time. Actors take their concrete choices with *partial awareness* of the system's state and dynamics. They have beliefs but not full knowledge of the consequences of their actions.
- **Dynamics** ($f : X \times U \to X$): A representation of how the organization's *state evolves* as a result of the actions taken by individuals. It models the transition process from one situation to another.
- **Protocol** ($U_x \subset U$): A set of *humanly constructed rules, norms, or shared strategies* that specify a subset of actions available to individuals in a given situation, thereby coordinating individual behavior.
- **Property** ($V : X \to \mathbb{R}_+$): A function that can be understood as a *loss function encoding a pattern* in the system's state. It provides a measure of how well the system aligns with some desired or undesired behavior.
- **Institution** ($\Delta V(x) \leq 0$): An *enduring pattern of behavior* where $V(x)$ remains stable (in the sense of Lyapunov) over time, indicating that the system maintains certain properties despite variations in specific situations and individual actions.

7.4.4 *Implications of this approach*

The precise innovation of GDS is the observation that, mathematically, it is not necessary to assert a control law $g(x)$ to produce a desirable property; it suffices to introduce a protocol that limits actions *just enough* to ensure the property of interest. It is worth noting that although institutional economists often identify patterns in $g(x)$ as institutions, we can use $V(x)$ without loss of generality simply by defining $V(x)$ as a loss function expressing the deviation of the $V(x_t) = \|u_t - u_t^*\|^2$, where u_t is the observed behavior and $u_t^* = g(x_t)$ is the expected behavior.

The benefit of building on the control engineering literature to develop this approach is that doing so gives us the composing and nesting properties of control systems practically for free. For general results, see Jan C. Willems's "The Behavioral Approach to Open and Interconnected Systems" (Willems, 2007). For a GDS-specific discussion of composability, see "Block Diagrams for Categorical Cybernetics" (Zargham and Shorish, 2023).

While this method provides a clear path for the analysis of institutions as persistent patterns in the behavior exhibited by organizations, as well as for the design of protocols via control-theoretic methods in order to modify or stabilize those institutions, it also invites important questions regarding the degrees of restriction to be tolerated, relative to the benefits of the desired stable properties.

As shown in "A State-Space Modeling Framework for Engineering Blockchain-Enabled Economic Systems" (Zargham *et al.*, 2018), users of the Bitcoin Network tolerate the restriction "no double-spends" to induce the global property of a stable total supply of 21 million Bitcoin. Cryptographically secured software systems, however, are significantly more susceptible to this type of formal analysis than organizations where the *rules in use* may deviate significantly from the *rules in form* (Ostrom *et al.*, 1994).

Furthermore, some of our most important institutions emerge from organizations in which the choices actors make with their degrees of freedom contribute meaningfully to the institution. Markets, for example, do not exist to *set* prices; they clear transactions and *discover* prices. In "Economic Games as Estimators," Zargham *et al.* show that a particular set of protocols implemented in automated market makers have the property of being "price estimators"; the price estimate is realized when individual actors exercise their freedoms within the protocol (Zargham *et al.*, 2020). In the kidney exchange example from Roth, the key properties are fairness and efficiency, but there is no notion of price (Roth *et al.*, 2004).

In practice, organizations are heterogeneous and distributed—entangled with each other such that we, as modelers, must make choices about what is in and out of scope. Modeling involves subjective decisions, such as how to divide stakeholders into groups with similar action-situations, as well as similar incentives and preferences.[4] Continuing with our control engineering approach, suppose the actors are denoted $i \in S$ and that each actor has a set of observables $y_i \in Y_i$ and controllables $u_i \in U_i$, representing what they *can see* and what they *can do*, respectively. The realized behavior at any time is the Cartesian product of all the individual actor behavior $U = \bigotimes_{i\in S} U_i$, as informed by their observables and constrained by their respective controllables. This consideration attends to North's insistence on the separation of the actors from the rules of the game; it also provides the basis for the dynamics to be distributed across local action situations k, such that $f(x, u) = [\ldots, f_k(x, u), \ldots]$ to be set up in a manner that represents complex and varied local actuation-situations, including topologies with non-trivial power disparities between actor groups. The topology of the network can take on arbitrary causal patterns such as those described in multi-agent influence diagrams (MAIDs) (Koller and Milch, 2003). Furthermore, modeling overlapping action-situations within such a representation, $f(x, u)$, provides a more formal perspective on what Vincent and Elinor Ostrom's work refers to as *polycentricity* (Ostrom, 2010; Ostrom *et al.*, 1961)—if we also introduce a plethora of distinct $V_j(x)$ representing a range of dynamically entangled properties, consistent with North's "institutional matrix" and with Abigail Devereaux's work in "Multiple Games Analysis: A Petri Dish for Growing Polycentric Orders" (Devereaux, 2019).

Equipped with these additional concepts, we can turn our attention to developing models of organizations that enable us to explore the impact of potential protocols on those organizations' system-level behaviors. Leaping directly to modeling, however, would be akin to building a house without blueprints or a stable foundation; instead,

---

[4]While the use of advanced modeling techniques can sometimes be viewed as problematic for questions in political science, we appeal to Primo and Clark's "A Model Discipline" for the argument that models are an integral part of the political science (Primo and Clarke, 2012). Keeping with an engineering ethos, we strive to use models as tools in service to the public, rather than as a means of manipulation. Our engineering-informed approach to modeling is documented in "Method for Functional Decomposition of Organizations and Their Environments" (Zargham and Ben-Meir, 2023).

a rigorous and responsible engineering process must begin by surveying the field and mapping the critical loci at which meaningful interventions might be designed.

7.5 Conclusion

Rehabilitating society's institutions is not merely about fixing what is broken; it is also about designing for a future where stability, variety, and adaptability coexist. Historically, organizations have been controlled through document-based policy paradigms, where governance relied on formalized rules, laws, and regulations (Stone, 2011). Today, we are witnessing a shift toward a data-driven, software-mediated protocol paradigm, where intra- and inter-organizational processes are increasingly embedded in digital systems, algorithms, and automated governance mechanisms (Zargham and Nabben, 2023). This transformation offers both opportunities and risks, as it reconfigures how institutions stabilize behavior while allowing for adaptive evolution.

"Science," for example, can be understood as a distributed organization whose system-level behavior of producing and disseminating reliable shared knowledge is stabilized by that organization's defining protocol: the scientific method. Science has entered the digital era in an *ad hoc* manner, leaning heavily on digital publishers, citation metrics, and algorithmic evaluation measures that have arguably destabilized, rather than reinforced, its core epistemic properties. Promising endeavors such as NumFOCUS's "OpenSource Science Initiative" and decentralized scientific infrastructures such as the DeSci Network, however, suggest that a more deliberate and constructive transition is possible (NumFOCUS, n.d.; Zargham *et al.*, 2024).

The distributed organization "engineering" is similarly characterized by *its* defining protocol, the engineering design process, which stabilizes the system-level behavior of transforming knowledge into practical, safe, and reliable systems that meet human needs. Engineering has confronted the challenges of digital transformation with model-based systems engineering (MBSE), successfully integrating system design into digital workflows, executable models, and dynamic document generation (Delp *et al.*, 2013; Karban *et al.*, 2016).

Meanwhile, open-source software communities are pioneering governance mechanisms using git protocol-based coordination tools. These approaches offer compelling templates for protocol-driven institutional design, where modularity, version control, and transparency can enhance institutional resilience.

At the frontiers of institutional design, we find work that challenges us to think beyond the constraints of legacy governance models. Kei Kreutler's exploration of designing for unprecedented situations urges us to engineer institutions that can function in radically novel environments (Kreutler, 2024). Ellie Rennie's ethnographic study of SourceCred introduces the concept of "terraforming" organizations and shows how new protocols can reconstitute economic landscapes and redefine value coordination (Rennie, 2023). Rennie and Potts extend this line of inquiry with their theory of contribution goods, where value is dictated by protocols of production and exchange, rather than traditional market pricing (Rennie and Potts, 2024). In a similar vein, Austin Wade Smith conceptualizes ecological institutions, whose explicit function is to stabilize the fragile and visibly unhealthy (and unstable) relationship between human society and ecological systems.

These emerging frameworks suggest that protocolization provides a unifying lens for institutional design. By decomposing institutions into their constituent protocols, we can pinpoint failure points, reinforce stability, and enhance adaptability in a modular, recursive fashion. This shift from monolithic structures to dynamic, reconfigurable systems enables organizations to respond to complex challenges, including climate change, public health crises, and the digitization of civic engagement—without becoming brittle or obsolete.

We began this chapter by reviewing literature from institutional economics, cybernetics, and other related fields. We then presented a control-theoretic approach to institutional design that focuses on stabilizing desirable properties via the introduction of protocols. Finally, we extrapolated the digitalization trend to hypothesize that a control-theoretic approach to designing and governing institutions via protocols is not only possible but necessary, given the complexity of our society and the severity of its issues.

In the end, we believe that our conception of institutions enables a more rigorous approach to their design and opens up new possibilities for their renovation. We have found that top-down control and rigid rules are not required in order to implement organizations that can withstand shocks while supporting diverse forms of local and regional action; the urgent (but achievable) work of re-stabilizing our institutions can be accomplished with *protocols*. By aligning organizations with their intended purposes while embedding adaptability at their core, we can lay the groundwork for a society that is resilient, cooperative, and capable of thriving amid uncertainty.

References

Acemoglu, D. and Robinson, J. A. 2012. *Why Nations Fail: The Origins of Power, Prosperity, and Poverty.* New York: Crown Business.

Alston, E. 2022. "Governance as conflict: Constitution of shared values defining future margins of disagreement." *MIT Computational Law Report.* https://law.mit.edu/pub/governanceasconflict.

Axelrod, R. 1984. *The Evolution of Cooperation.* New York, NY: Basic Books. https://www.basicbooks.com/titles/robert-axelrod/the-evolution-of-cooperation/9780465005642/.

Beer, S. 1974. *Designing Freedom.* London: John Wiley & Sons.

Beer, S. 2002. "What is cybernetics?" *Kybernetes* 31(2): 209–219. DOI: 10.1108/03684920210417283.

Beuster, G., Leistert, O., and Röhle, T. 2022. "Protocol." *Internet Policy Review* 11(1). DOI: 10.14763/2022.1.1651, https://doi.org/10.14763/2022.1.1651.

Chremos, I. V. and Malikopoulos, A. A. 2024. "Mechanism design theory in control engineering: A tutorial and overview of applications in communication, power grid, transportation, and security systems." *IEEE Control Systems Magazine* 44(1): 57–78. DOI: 10.1109/MCS.2023.3329919, https://ieeexplore.ieee.org/document/10384599/.

Crawford, S. E. S. and Ostrom, E. 1995. "A grammar of institutions." *American Political Science Review* 89(3): 582–600.

Delp, C., Lam, D., Fosse, E., and Lee, C.-Y. 2013. "Model based document and report generation for systems engineering." In *2013 IEEE Aerospace Conference*, pp. 1–11. DOI: 10.1109/AERO.2013.6496926.

Devereaux, A. 2019. "Multiple games analysis: A petri dish for growing polycentric orders." *SSRN Electronic Journal.* DOI: 10.2139/ssrn.3477461, https://papers.ssrn.com/sol3/papers.cfm?abstract_id=3477461.

Galloway, A. R. 2004. *Protocol: How Control Exists after Decentralization.* Cambridge, MA: MIT Press.

Hodgson, G. M. 2006. "What are institutions?" *Journal of Economic Issues* 40(1): 1–25. DOI: 10.1080/00213624.2006.11506879.

Karban, R., Dekens, F. G., Herzig, S., Elaasar, M., and Jankevičius, N. 2016. "Creating system engineering products with executable models in a model-based engineering environment." In Angeli, G. Z. and Dierickx, P. (eds.), *Modeling, Systems Engineering, and Project Management for Astronomy VII*, Vol. 9911. Bellingham, WA: SPIE, p. 99110B. DOI: 10.1117/12.2232785, https://doi.org/10.1117/12.2232785.

Khalil, H. K. 2001. *Nonlinear Systems.* 3rd edn. Upper Saddle River, NJ: Prentice Hall.

Kia, S. S., Van Scoy, B., Cortes, J., Freeman, R. A., Lynch, K. M., and Martinez, S. 2019. "Tutorial on dynamic average consensus: The problem, its applications, and the algorithms." *IEEE Control Systems Magazine* 39(3): 40–72. DOI: 10.1109/MCS.2019.2900783.

Koller, D. and Milch, B. 2003. "Multi-agent influence diagrams for representing and solving games." *Games and Economic Behavior* 45(1): 181–221.

Kreutler, K. 2024. "How to repair a spaceport: A metaphor for our technological present." *Folklore* (blog), Mirror. https://folklore.mirror.xyz/6Lm7xORHWDb-YoVtqv3Vc2G7dT73xiKws5pJBv9ADZE. Accessed: 2025 January 26.

Lynch, N. A. 1996. *Distributed Algorithms.* San Francisco: Morgan Kaufmann.

North, D. C. 1990. *Institutions, Institutional Change and Economic Performance.* Cambridge, UK: Cambridge University Press.

NumFOCUS, n.d. "Open source science initiative (OSSci)." https://numfocus.org/open-source-science-initiative-ossci Accessed: 2025 January 29.

Ostrom, E. 1990. *Governing the Commons: The Evolution of Institutions for Collective Action.* Cambridge, UK: Cambridge University Press.

Ostrom, E. 2010. "Beyond markets and states: Polycentric governance of complex economic systems." *American Economic Review* 100(3): 641–672. DOI: 10.1257/aer.100.3.641, https://www.aeaweb.org/articles?id=10.1257/aer.100.3.641.

Ostrom, E., Gardner, R., and Walker, J. 1994. *Rules, Games, and Common-Pool Resources.* Ann Arbor: University of Michigan Press. DOI: 10.3998/mpub.9739.

Ostrom, V., Tiebout, C. M., and Warren, R. 1961. "The organization of government in metropolitan areas: A theoretical inquiry." *American Political Science Review* 55(4): 831–842. DOI: 10.2307/1952530, https://www.jstor.org/stable/1952530.

Primo, D. M. and Clarke, K. M. 2012. *A Model Discipline: Political Science and the Logic of Representations.* New York, NY: Oxford University Press. https://global.oup.com/academic/product/a-model-discipline-9780195382204.

Rennie, E. 2023. "The CredSperiment: An ethnography of a contributions system." *SSRN Electronic Journal.* DOI: 10.2139/ssrn.4570035, https://ssrn.com/abstract=4570035.

Rennie, E. and Potts, J. 2024. "Contribution systems: A new theory of value." *SSRN Electronic Journal.* DOI: 10.2139/ssrn.4754267, https://ssrn.com/abstract=4754267.

Rochet, J.-C. and Tirole, J. 2003. "Platform competition in two-sided markets." *Journal of the European Economic Association* 1(4): 990–1029. DOI: 10.1162/154247603322493212, https://academic.oup.com/jeea/article/1/4/990/2280902.

Roth, A. E. 2002. "The economist as engineer: Game theory, experimentation, and computation as tools for design economics." *Econometrica* 70(4): 1341–1378. DOI: 10.1111/1468-0262.00335, https://onlinelibrary.wiley.com/doi/abs/10.1111/1468-0262.00335.

Roth, A. E., Sönmez, T., and Ünver, M. U. 2004. "Kidney exchange." *The Quarterly Journal of Economics* 119(2): 457–488. DOI: 10.1162/0033553041382157.

Sandholm, W. H. 2010. *Population Games and Evolutionary Dynamics.* Cambridge, MA: MIT Press. https://mitpress.mit.edu/9780262195874/population-games-and-evolutionary-dynamics/.

Shamma, J. S. (ed.). 2007. *Cooperative Control of Distributed Multi-Agent Systems.* Chichester, UK: Wiley. ISBN: 9780470060315.

Shorish, J. 2023. "Market design lessons for 'safety first' institutional engineering." https://blog.block.science/market-design-lessons-for-safety-first-institutional-engineering/. Accessed: 2025 January 29.

Smith, A. W. 2024. "Ecological institutions → Protocols to grow autonomous and convivial ecological actors." Austin Wade Smith (blog), Mirror. https://mirror.xyz/austinwadesmith.eth/tv9z1XXrtqQxDIxE8FygZ_W39NpkQJkVfrtjCtdbzA8. Accessed: 30 January 2025.

Sontag, E. D. 1999. *Mathematical Control Theory: Deterministic Finite Dimensional Systems.* 2nd edn. New York, NY: Springer-Verlag. https://link.springer.com/book/10.1007/978-1-4757-3048-7.

Srnicek, N. 2017. *Platform Capitalism.* Cambridge, UK: Polity Press. https://www.politybooks.com/bookdetail/?isbn=9781509504862.

Stone, R. W. 2011. *Controlling Institutions: International Organizations and the Global Economy.* New York, NY: Cambridge University Press. https://www.cambridge.org/core/books/controlling-institutions/AB18F080C5212E9D145223144E286EA5.

Swann, T. 2020. *Anarchist Cybernetics: Control and Communication in Radical Politics.* Bristol, UK: Bristol University Press (2020). https://bristoluniversitypress.co.uk/anarchist-cybernetics.

Uchiyama, H., Ishii, H., and Sakurama, K. 2022. *Emergent Behavior Detection and Task Coordination for Multiagent Systems.* Cham, Switzerland: Springer Nature. DOI: 10.1007/978-3-030-86896-3, https://link.springer.com/book/10.1007/978-3-030-86896-3.

Voshmgir, S. and Zargham, M. 2020. "Foundations of cryptoeconomic systems." *Research Institute for Cryptoeconomics Working Paper Series.*

Wiener, N. 1949. *Cybernetics: Or Control and Communication in the Animal and the Machine.* Cambridge, MA: MIT Press.

Willems, J. C. 2007. "The behavioral approach to open and interconnected systems." *IEEE Control Systems Magazine* 27(6): 46–99. DOI: 10.1109/MCS.2007.906923.

Zargham, M. and Ben-Meir, I. 2023. "Method for functional decomposition of organizations and their environments." *SSRN Electronic Journal.* DOI: 10.2139/ssrn.4606672, https://papers.ssrn.com/sol3/papers.cfm?abstract_id=4606672.

Zargham, M. and Nabben, K. 2023. "Aligning 'decentralized autonomous organization' to precedents in cybernetics." *MIT Computational Law Report.* https://law.mit.edu/pub/dao-precedents-cybernetics.

Zargham, M., Paruch, K., and Shorish, J. 2020. "Economic games as estimators." In Pardalos, P., Kotsireas, I., Guo, Y., and Knottenbelt, W. (eds.), *Mathematical Research for Blockchain Economy.* Cham, Switzerland: Springer Nature, pp. 125–142.

Zargham, M. and Shorish, J. 2022. "Generalized dynamical systems: Foundations." *WU Vienna University of Economics and Business. Working Paper Series.* Pre-publication Working Paper.

Zargham, M. and Shorish, J. 2023. "Block diagrams for categorical cybernetics." *SSRN Electronic Journal.* DOI: 10.2139/ssrn.4569037, https://ssrn.com/abstract=4569037.

Zargham, M., Sisson, D., Vandevoorde, C., and Ben-Meir, I. 2024. "Digital public infrastructure for decentralized science." Technical Report, DeSci Labs. https://nodes.desci.com/dpid/275/v4/root/DeSci_Labs_Report___9_27_24.pdf.

Zargham, M., Zartler, J., Nabben, K., Goldberg, R., and Emmett, J. 2023. "Disambiguating autonomy." *Zenodo.* DOI: 10.5281/zenodo.8239311, https://doi.org/10.5281/zenodo.8239311.

Zargham, M., Zhang, Z., and Preciado, V. 2018. "A state-space modeling framework for engineering blockchain-enabled economic systems." *arXiv preprint* https://arxiv.org/abs/1807.00955.

https://doi.org/10.1142/9781800618664_0009

Chapter 8

Agentic Learning DAOs for Sustainable Energy Transition

Rumy Narayan[*,‡] **and Annika Laine-Kronberg**[†,§]

[*] *University of Vaasa, Vaasa, Finland*
[†] *Åbo Akademi University Human and Social Sciences, School of Business and Economics, Turku, Finland*
[‡] *rumy.narayan@uwasa.fi*
[§] *annika.laine-kronberg@abo.fi*

Abstract

This chapter proposes an adaptive, AI-enhanced blockchain framework for incentivizing research on sustainable energy systems. Building on the *multi-level perspective (MLP), institutional theory, and learning organization* paradigm, the model couples *blockchain-based digital autonomous organizations* (for transparent, tokenized rewards and on-chain governance) with *artificial intelligence (AI) agents* (for data-driven evaluation, adaptive rule setting, and automated verification). Within the *MLP*, the AI–blockchain niche challenges incumbent research regimes by rapidly funding high-risk, high-impact projects and learning from outcomes in real time. *Institutional theory* clarifies how smart-contract rules and AI monitoring can realign academic norms—prioritizing open data, replication, and interdisciplinary collaboration—while providing the legitimacy and accountability needed for wider adoption. The *learning organization* lens frames the DAO community as a reflexive system, where blockchain supplies immutable feedback loops, and AI agents convert those loops into continuous improvements of incentive parameters and strategic direction. Together, these technologies create a decentralized yet intelligent incentive architecture that overcomes siloed structures, accelerates knowledge diffusion, and fosters collective problem-solving. The chapter argues that such AI–blockchain integration offers a viable pathway to transform research incentives, mobilizing diverse actors and speeding sociotechnical transitions toward global sustainable energy transitions.

Keywords: Blockchain Integration, Decentralized Autonomous Organizations (DAOs), Tokenized Research Incentives, Sustainability Transitions, Institutional Theory, Learning Organization, Socio-Technical Transition.

8.1 Introduction

This chapter adopts problematization as its method (Alvesson & Sandberg, 2011; Laguerre, 2023) to interrogate the assumptions behind today's research-incentive regimes and ask a focal question: ***how can we design incentives that genuinely reward and nurture inquiry into sustainable energy systems?*** Any new scheme must continuously align with contemporary social priorities as they evolve while spurring transformative work on the planet's most urgent problems.

The chapter discusses how university research systems could be transformed by incentivizing research toward sustainable energy systems. It does so by integrating the multi-level perspective (MLP) on sociotechnical transitions, institutional theory, and the learning organization paradigm. The MLP is used to develop a framework for transitions, and blockchains serve as an institutional technology integrated with artificial intelligence (AI) to form a new class of agents (Potts, 2025) that could be leveraged for transforming university research systems through incentives into decentralized yet integrated adaptive intelligent learning organizations with polycentric governance (Ostrom, 2010). Learning organizations are critical as the global transition from industrial to information economy takes shape, thus emphasizing the role and significance of digital institutions (Banon & Potts, 2024). As money and energy are intrinsically linked through complex interactions and relationships (Ayres *et al.*, 2013; Pollitt & Mercure, 2018; Galvin, 2020), designing such learning organizations requires a deeper understanding of how the nexus of energy, information, and matter works (Hoke *et al.*, 2021). Currently, our theories focus on the role of matter as a resource and energy, which typically ignores how the same matter can have other important effects as a carrier of information or a modifier of the environment (Marleau *et al.*, 2020; Little *et al.*, 2022). Potts and Dopfer (2024) have noted that we have a new class of problems that are an outcome of centuries of industrial activities, lending a level of complexity that involves a formidable assemblage of knowledge resources. This chapter acknowledges this task, with the objective of opening a discursive process to take a first step toward articulating how such a learning trajectory could take shape. By embedding AI agents alongside human experts within blockchain-based decentralized autonomous organizations (DAOs), it is possible to create incentive structures that remain decentralized and tamper-proof while also becoming genuinely adaptive and intelligent (Chahar *et al.*, 2025; Weidener & Boltz, 2025). Such Decentralized Science (DeSci) DAOs aim to contribute meaningfully to the production of scientific knowledge by leveraging AI (Weidener & Boltz, 2025). AI learns from past outcomes, makes context-aware adjustments, and offers real-time analytics, while humans contribute judgment, domain insight, and values. Together they can continuously fine-tune funding flows, co-evaluate research proposals, and exchange rapid feedback with project teams by collectively steering sustainable-energy research toward more meaningful and accountable results. It could potentially help balance innovation and rigor within collaborative structures (Weidener & Boltz, 2025).

The second section of the chapter introduces the need for energy transition and the MLP's role in transition research (Smith *et al.*, 2005; Geels, 2019), then problematizes the current incentive structure (Grey, 2010; Kanger, 2020), and finally offers how blockchain as an institutional technology (Swan, 2015; Berg *et al.*, 2019; Allen *et al.*, 2020; Frolov, 2021; Potts *et al.*, 2021; Davidson & Potts, 2022) could contribute to creating networks of learning organizations through purpose-driven tokens (Voshmgir & Zargham, 2020; Rennie & Potts, 2024). The third section presents the methodology that describes how problematization has been used to select relevant literature, along with a short longitudinal case study of a university in transition. The fourth section presents a general incentive model; this is followed by the fifth and final section offering discussions and conclusions.

8.2 The Energy-Information Nexus

8.2.1 *Energy systems: The lifeline of modern existence and the case for interdisciplinarity*

Energy underpins cultural norms, daily practices, and artifacts, shaping how societies engage with nature and reconfiguring their ecological setting (Syvitski *et al.*, 2020; Cederlöf, 2021; Garrett *et al.*, 2022). Given that shelter, mobility, food, and clothing all hinge on energy use, redirecting the actors embedded in these practices is vital for any transition (Geels, 2021; Kump, 2023). Transitions research therefore investigates long-term technological change and offers tools to steer it (Genus & Coles, 2008). The field's principal lens is the MLP (Geels, 2020), which explains change through the interplay among niche innovations, stabilized regimes, and the wider landscape (Rip & Kemp, 1998; Geels, 2002, 2005; Sovacool & Hess, 2017; Kanger, 2021). Alignment across these levels allows niches to scale, landscape pressures to unsettle regimes, and systems to reconfigure, while newer studies incorporate social-practice insights (Keller *et al.*, 2022) and broaden knowledge on low-carbon transitions (Hansmeier *et al.*, 2021; Andersen & Markard, 2024; Geels, 2024).

Yet gaps persist. Researchers call for theories that capture dominant and "under-the-radar" systems (Kangar, 2020), relational dynamics across sectors (Andersen *et al.*, 2020; Malhotra *et al.*, 2019), multi-system interactions (Rosenbloom, 2020), and micro-level events within broader trajectories (Poole & Van de Ven, 1989; Köhler *et al.*, 2019). Empirical evidence also demonstrates that diffusion can precede system alignment, and the early internet is a classic case (Abbate, 1999; Kanger & Schot, 2016; Zuboff, 2023).

Meeting these challenges demands interdisciplinary inquiry fit for complex systems (Repko, 2008; Menken & Keestra, 2016). General systems theory and cybernetics supply such integrative lenses (Von Bertalanffy, 1972; Wiener, 1950; Barkley Rosser, 2010) and have influenced thinkers such as Hayek (Lange, 2014; Oliva, 2016). Sustainable energy transitions are essential for tackling pressing global problems (Smith *et al.*, 2005; Geels, 2019) and entail orchestrating uncertain, path-dependent systems (Van Lente *et al.*, 2003; Cherp *et al.*, 2011; Binz & Truffer, 2017; Kivimaa *et al.*, 2019; Kangar, 2021; Marsiglio & Tolotti, 2024). Universities can accelerate this agenda by realigning research toward systems change (Wolf *et al.*, 2021).

8.2.2 *Incentive gaps: Bridging research stagnation and technological opportunity*

Universities are strategically positioned and could catalyze climate action, yet bureaucratic inertia stalls their own pledges (Bookbinder *et al.*, 2024). Scholarly production is itself in crisis (Hanitzsch *et al.*, 2024; Knöchelmann, 2024; Fernández-Cano, 2021; Grimes *et al.*, 2018), and sustainability-transition research too often stays within normal-science boundaries (Hopkins *et al.*, 2020; Kuhn, 1996). Alternative theoretical traditions are therefore underused (Hopkins *et al.*, 2020).

Path dependency is reinforced by tenure metrics, elite journals, and gatekeeping networks (Grey, 2010; Kanger, 2020), shrinking intellectual diversity (Alvesson & Sandberg, 2013; Delbridge & Fiss, 2013) and sidelining dissent, even though dissent sparks new paradigms (Kanger, 2020). Likewise, discipline-bound, competitive models curb transformative learning, thus necessitating transdisciplinary, action-oriented platforms (Loorbach & Wittmayer, 2024).

Institutional change arises from co-evolving learning actors (Almudi *et al.*, 2024). The research university already behaves like a knowledge firm (Etzkowitz, 2003), and in the United States, this has evolved bottom-up into an entrepreneurial growth engine (Soete, 2002). Knowledge now drives the economy but also produces ecological, social, and economic crises that appear as what has been described as "hyperobjects" (Potts, 2025; Garrett *et al.*, 2020; Harman, 2010, 2018; Morton, 2011, 2013).

Yet incentives lag, and the tenure-publication logic generates anxiety (Hanitzsch *et al.*, 2024; Knöchelmann, 2024; Fernández-Cano, 2021; Grimes *et al.*, 2018). This echoes neoclassical views of static knowledge (Dopfer & Potts, 2008). Universities themselves risk becoming a hyperobject (Peim & Stock, 2023), while incremental technological fixes perpetuate rebound effects (Van den Bergh *et al.*, 2011).

Technology's meaning, once understood as "industrial art" and now as "applied science," has been collapsed into deterministic invention stories (Schatzberg, 2006). Reframed analytically, it illuminates transition paradoxes across planetary and everyday scales (Agar, 2019; Callon, 1987). Here, Beck's "world risk society," in capturing the twin promise and peril of such progress (Beck, 1992; Latour, 2003), re-problematizes future dangers that can unsettle capitalism, law, consumerism, and science (Beck, 2015) and reopen debate on externalities (Callon, 1998).

Integrating science-based technologies into economic models has been long overdue (Freeman & Soete, 1997). As multinational hierarchies fade, university-orchestrated firm clusters could rise, leveraging the potential knowledge commons these clusters embody by deploying AI through reticular networks, such as the internet, and governed by blockchains. They offer possibilities for enabling decentralized, ecologically attuned reorganization (Stiegler, 2018b, 2019; Vergne, 2020; Heikkurinen *et al.*, 2021; Featherstone, 2020), representing assemblages offering multiple paths for aligning incentives with planetary boundaries.

8.2.3 *Blockchains and AI for governing complex assemblages*

Tsing's "assemblages" are open-ended commons that carry stories of progress, yet remain shot through with precarity, indeterminacy, and surprise (Tsing, 2015). Technologies through innovative social practices weave into these commons. The internet has become the fabric into which diverse life stories are stitched (Castells, 2016), just as language, the quintessential social technology, that acts as an extension of the mind (Clark & Chalmers, 1998), giving communities a collective tool for steering imagination (Dor, 2017). The internet's discursive logic traces back to post-war cybernetics, the art of steering sociotechnical systems composed of humans and machines (Wiener, 1948, 1954; Simon, 1947; Vallée, 2009). Unlike an automated device that repeats a task, the internet is a recursive medium that integrates contingency, thus extending cybernetics beyond a purely mechanical worldview (Hanseth & Lyytinen, 2016).

Blockchain represents the latest turn in this lineage of decentralized institutional technologies (Swan *et al.*, 2019). Paired with AI, it opens fresh organizational possibilities and unpredictable complex dynamics (Potts, 2025; Weidener & Boltz, 2025; Ahl *et al.*, 2020, 2022; Sánchez, 2022; Wu *et al.*, 2022). This is evident in the evolving metaphors for the firm, from "organization-as-computer" to "organization-as-network" and now to "peer-to-peer networks of computers" (Vergne, 2020). It shifts focus from top-down command-and-control toward seeing the entire planet as an interconnected cybernetic system that must be actively redesigned, not merely adapted (Hui, 2017; Allen *et al.*, 2020; Stiegler, 2018a, 2018b). For sustainable-energy research, blockchains can hardwire distributed or polycentric governance (Ostrom, 2010) and incentive mechanisms across heterogeneous actors (Allen *et al.*, 2020) through DAOs. Yet, incentives must recognize that greener energy alone does not resolve all sustainability challenges; for instance, token lifecycles and proof-of-work energy demand can create rebound effects (de Vries, 2019). Hence, reward systems should illuminate the hidden links in production–consumption chains and privilege configurations aimed at environmental regeneration, democratic redistribution, and value plurality (Howson, 2021). Blockchains already coordinate collective work and expose legitimacy gaps (Osipenko & Sørensen, 2022; Curry, 2024).

Research on commons shows why. Blockchain foundations can internalize externalities by supplying high-quality public goods (Potts *et al.*, 2021). Building on the ethnography of blockchain initiatives, Rennie & Potts (2024) outline a novel calculus of value in which property rights emerge through algorithmic consensus, somewhat like an economic computation performed via rules rather than prices. Code establishes order and security, while markets channel capital.

DAOs translate these insights into practice. Built on smart contract platforms, DAOs allow token holders to govern transparently and immutably (Fantaccini *et al.*, 2024; Unfried, 2024). In a sustainable-energy context, an "Energy DAO" could issue tokens that finance research, timestamp every contribution, and automatically release additional rewards when milestones, such as independent replication, are met. VitaDAO, devoted to longevity science, already shows how communities can pool funds and co-own resulting intellectual property (Fantaccini *et al.*, 2024).

Tokenization alone, however, scales poorly if human voting must parse ever-growing information loads. To overcome information fragmentation and enable scalable participation, DAOs need a modular, multi-agent AI coordination layer. One with interoperable agents dedicated to governance, onboarding, science communication, and community support that share memory, run on controlled reasoning pipelines, and preserve explicit data provenance (Weidener & Boltz, 2025). AI agents can augment DAO governance by filtering proposals, detecting synergies, and executing parameter tweaks, thus reducing friction without reinstating hierarchy (Benedict *et al.*, 2022). Together, blockchain's transparency and AI's adaptive capacity offer a path for research incentives that are reflexive, equitable, and oriented toward rapid learning in the pursuit of sustainable energy futures.

8.3 Methodology

Many of today's most significant challenges are not inherently economic issues but rather the consequences of solutions implemented to address past economic problems (Potts & Dopfer, 2024). Therefore, solutions to these challenges demand a different approach. They require us to question assumptions and explore new ideas through strategies guided by problematization principles for generating research questions (Alvesson & Sandberg, 2011). The problematization method encourages an evaluation of underlying assumptions of the existing constructs and theoretical perspectives to bring about practices related to introspection and scientific self-examination (Laguerre, 2023).

This objective lies at the core of this research process, which began with the exploration of a small university situated in a highly literate, sparsely populated Northern European country with strong and deep economic and cultural ties to the city in which it is located. The university's transition process began decades ago, initially focusing on energy, primarily developing general research on energy markets. This background enabled it to quickly pivot toward a sustainable energy transition pathway aligned with a larger European agenda for sustainability. Based on this background, a longitudinal study has been underway for the past eight years, spanning six workshops and thirty interviews involving a diverse set of stakeholders.

The findings of the interim report explore the transition toward sustainable energy systems within the university context, employing the MLP to analyze the interactions between different societal levels, including industry, technology, markets, policy, culture, and civil society. It highlights the university's evolving role in these transitions, emphasizing its potential as a path creator in shaping and influencing socio-technical configurations. The report attempts to bridge the gap in transition literature by focusing on the university's role, often overlooked, in facilitating these co-evolutionary dynamics and fostering new economic opportunities aligned with environmental and socioeconomic goals. The report provided an empirical lens on how transition processes at a university can unfold, influenced by the interaction of various actors and the application of path creation as an analytical tool to capture these dynamic processes.

It also revealed the limitations of what is possible within the existing framework. This report was then used as a problem statement to locate literature that could explain why this transition process is fraught with obstacles for the path creators, many of whom are early-career researchers. The literature review was done using an innovative rhizomatic approach to evidence and literature (Fox, 2024). The evidence from the case was relatable to the different framings emerging from literature. These included highly specific issues such as how tenures are decided and publication metrics are valued and how these are linked to an interconnected system that understands the need for change but uses its current structures of power to prevent any meaningful changes.

Figure 8.1 illustrates the research process.

The results of this process were used to problematize the organization of current research on transitioning toward sustainable energy systems and to propose a model for transitioning. The following section presents the proposed model.

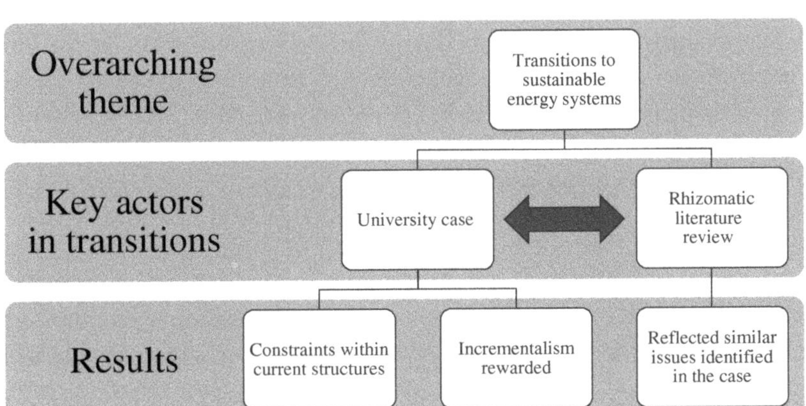

Fig. 8.1. The research process.

8.4 Human–AI-Governed Blockchain Commons for Sustainable Energy Research

Drawing on Rennie and Potts (2024) and Potts (2025), this section presents a design for a blockchain-based incentive mechanism that is enhanced through integration with AI agents for transforming sustainable energy research. Sustainable energy innovation is a complex, multi-stakeholder endeavor that requires coordinating vast data, diverse expertise, and long-term goals under conditions of uncertainty. Governing such hyperobject challenges that are distributed, large-scale, and complex defies traditional governance and oversight (Potts, 2025; Garrett *et al.*, 2020; Harman, 2010, 2018; Morton, 2011, 2013). This is why conventional top-down institutional mechanisms struggle to manage such systems, which span across vast spatial, temporal, and organizational scales.

In this context, AI-enhanced, blockchain-based institutions are uniquely suited to govern these hyperobject-like systems. Rather than attempting external control, they enable embedded co-governance, where the rules and decision-making processes reside within the system's digital fabric, continuously interacting with the system's state. Here, Potts' (2025) concept of an agentic commons—a shared computational infrastructure governed by a community and participating in its own governance via built-in rules, autonomous agents, and feedback mechanisms—gains relevance. The institutional ecosystem (through AI agents and smart contracts) senses and responds to changes, making adjustments in real time alongside human participants. This dynamic, cybernetic form of commons blurs the line between the governing and governed systems. It effectively blends human and machine agency in collective governance, as seen in emerging contribution systems where decentralized agents coordinate to maintain digital resources.

Such infrastructures are decentralized and participatory by design, co-produced by humans and AI agents, and they demand new models of incentives and strategies to function. Crucially, they embrace the scale and unpredictability of hyperobjects instead of being undermined by them. By leveraging an agentic commons model, a sustainable energy research commons can remain resilient and responsive in the face of the unknown unknowns inherent in climate and energy systems (Rennie & Potts, 2024). In this way,

AI–blockchain institutions align well with distributed, large-scale challenges, as they are capable of coordinating action and learning across networks without a centralized controller, exactly the kind of adaptive governance a hyperobject like the global energy transition requires (Potts, 2025).

Blockchain ledgers provide an immutable, shared record of research contributions, funding, and decisions, enhancing trust and accountability in collaborative projects (Bookbinder *et al.*, 2024). This transparency helps align stakeholders by making information and progress openly visible. AI further complements this by processing large data streams and detecting patterns or inefficiencies that humans might miss. Integrated AI agents can assist in decision-making, which might involve prioritizing project proposals or optimizing resource allocation, based on real-time data and learned insights. Together, these technologies create an adaptive decision system that can autonomously execute agreed rules (via smart contracts) while learning from outcomes. This means the organization not only follows predefined protocols but also refines them over time through embedded feedback loops (Curry, 2024). By continuously monitoring performance and incorporating new information, the blockchain–AI commons behaves as a learning ecosystem that evolves with emerging sustainability challenges rather than remaining static.

Developing such an operational mechanism through a digital blockchain foundation that operates as a DAO would address the challenging bureaucratic and operational structures and contexts within universities that resist change (Bookbinder *et al.*, 2024). The process of developing and designing a DAO could be a learning experience in itself for all actors. A process of introduction to the technology could serve as an important organizational learning mechanism that is not geared toward making people within the current bureaucratic setup redundant, but rather toward making them aware of the challenges and inviting them to be part of the transition process through dialogues and discussions. This could also contribute toward creating legitimacy and building trust, an aspect that has been highlighted in experiments in the public sector (Curry, 2024). Such a process will not only introduce the technology but also allow actors to understand its potential for social coordination and behavioral recalibration (Rennie & Potts, 2024). In understanding the social value, actors can then leverage it as a tool for addressing challenges that hold back critical changes needed for transition. Implementing smart contracts to automate and enforce outcomes through a process of democratic decision-making could enable the streamlining of operations and ensure transparency.

Incorporating the MLP within the mechanism design of the foundation or DAO involves providing an established framework to work with. Incorporating the MLP could help in understanding how transitions occur, what the state of the art is, and use this knowledge to address transitions at various levels, from niche innovations to regime shifts and landscape-level changes. The development process of the DAO itself could provide a rich empirical setting for understanding the micro ideas, decisions, actions, or events in the larger developmental episodes that have remained somewhat underdeveloped within the MLP framework (Geels, 2020). The conceptual framework for such a foundation could incorporate a recursive learning model. As it targets niche-level innovations, encourages regime-level transitions, and leverages landscape-level changes through various mechanisms, it could experiment with this model within its own structure. For niche-level innovations, it could use targeted token grants where the token distribution is designed specifically to incentivize novel and challenging ideas, which could be tested as the foundation itself takes shape. Doing this would allow the foundation or DAO to remain alert to what could work and learn about what could be possible as it engages with a wider ecosystem of stakeholders. These could include collaborative research projects that study systems that are not directly connected yet have an impact on sustainability transitions (Kangar, 2020) or those that develop the relational dynamics of industrial transformations and sustainability transitions (Andersen *et al.*, 2020).

The design of the token distribution could offer insights into how the incentive system could be improved to encourage better collaboration and coordination. This could lead to regime-level facilitation of the formation of consortiums geared toward transition objectives. Distributing performance parameters would help address the institutionalized structures that evaluate research by prioritizing publications and academic specializations led by norms dictated by

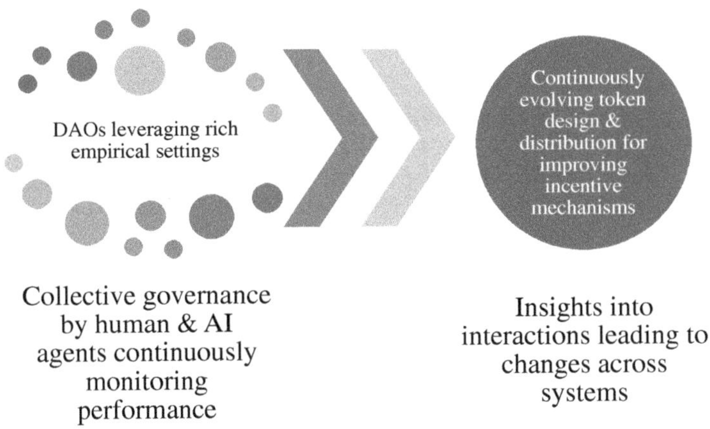

Fig. 8.2. Human–AI-governed blockchain commons for sustainable energy research.

influential academics (Grey, 2010; Kanger, 2020). Figure 8.2 offers a snapshot of the human–AI-governed blockchain commons for the sustainable energy research model (Table 8.1).

The foundation or DAO could invite global organizations and networks to strategically partner with them and help them develop their own tokens and could offer insights into how to bridge theories, develop novel methodologies, and orchestrate multi-system interactions (Hansmeier *et al.*, 2021; Kanger, 2021; Andersen & Markard, 2024; Geels, 2024). Transitions impact multiple systems (Kangar, 2020; Rosenbloom, 2020) and tokens could act as guides that offer insights into the interactions leading to changes across systems. For instance, releasing new tokens to highlight important milestones in terms of positive and negative feedback could offer critical learning for the growing group of actors.

This organizational design leverages blockchain and AI technologies and a DAO structure to create a dynamic, responsive, and transparent mechanism for fostering sustainable energy research. By aligning with the MLP framework and incorporating a robust learning model, it aims to drive advances in sustainable energy systems, encouraging innovation at all levels and facilitating a holistic approach to energy transitions.

Table 8.1. Functioning of a proposed learning organization.

Component	Role in the Blockchain–AI Commons Model
Core governance	Decentralized, community-driven governance implemented through a DAO on blockchain. Decision rights are distributed among researchers, funders, and other stakeholders via tokenized voting or reputation systems, ensuring inclusive control. This polycentric governance (Ostrom, 2010) fosters legitimacy and trust because rules and contributions are transparent to all members (Bookbinder *et al.*, 2024). AI agents monitor compliance and suggest rule adjustments when needed (e.g., new voting methods if participation drops under an adaptive-bylaws logic). Thus, the framework evolves with community feedback and data rather than remaining fixed.
Operational mechanisms	Day-to-day functions are managed by smart contracts and AI automation. Funding, resource allocation, and task coordination run on blockchain smart contracts that execute when milestones or deliverables are met. Sensors and data oracles feed real-time performance data to AI models for objective evaluation. When anomalies or new opportunities appear, the AI either flags them for governance review or adjusts operational parameters within approved limits (Curry, 2024). This cuts administrative overhead and bias while enabling rapid response to changing conditions. All transactions and decisions are recorded on-chain for full auditability, letting contributors trace how their funds, data, or ideas are used—reinforcing accountability.
Multi-level perspective (MLP) alignment	The commons is designed to bridge sociotechnical levels in line with the MLP on sustainability transitions. At the *niche* level, it shelters radical energy experiments (e.g., community microgrids). Through a transparent ledger, successful niches share results with the *regime* level and invite industry or government actors to observe or join (Curry, 2024). Over time, proven standards can diffuse into mainstream practice. Meanwhile, the model stays alert to *landscape* pressures (climate policy shifts and economic shocks) and can redirect collective effort quickly. This cross-scale alignment enables knowledge transfer and scaling, accelerating the wider shift to sustainable energy (Rennie & Potts, 2024).

Table 8.1. (*Continued*)

Component	Role in the Blockchain–AI Commons Model
Learning structure	Continuous learning is embedded in the organization, making it a genuine learning organization. Every project or decision is an experiment whose outcomes are logged on the blockchain. Through recursive feedback loops, the community and AI agents analyze successes and failures, then update protocols, priorities, or even DAO code (Potts, 2025). If one funding model outperforms others, smart contract logic can amplify it in future rounds. This "double-loop" learning questions underlying assumptions as evidence evolves. Open proposal submission allows for constant entry of fresh ideas and participants. Over time, the organization "learns how to learn," boosting its capacity to navigate complexity and surprises—crucial in fast-changing sustainability contexts. By design, the blockchain–AI commons remains open to feedback and innovation, avoiding the rigidity that hampers traditional institutions (Curry, 2024; Bookbinder *et al.*, 2024).

8.5 Conclusions and Discussions

Research on transitions has expanded over the years to cover broad themes involving understanding and governing transitions, civil, social, and cultural movements, business and industries, transitions in practice, the geography of transitions, ethics, and methodologies; however, grand challenges related to sustainability remain unsolved (Köhler *et al.*, 2019). This is because the highly complex class of problems spawned by more than a century of concentrated industrial activity demands a new level of coordination of vast and diverse knowledge resources (Potts & Dopfer, 2024). In this chapter, we argue for designing a learning organization based on a blockchain–AI commons model. Such a model with a decentralized governance structure will be primed for continuous learning and adaptation, innovation tracking through incentivization, enhanced collaboration, dynamic role and project allocation, transparency in decision-making, and continuous feedback and performance analysis. This could potentially enhance wider research collaboration, streamline intellectual property management, facilitate secure data sharing, improve resource allocation and funding, democratize access to research opportunities, and enable global participation in research activities.

Through this architecture, the blockchain–AI commons model acts as a strategic learning tool for sustainable energy research. It is recursive (monitoring and adjusting its own processes in light of outcomes), adaptable (able to pivot focus or methods as new challenges emerge), and open to novelty (welcoming new contributors, ideas, and technologies). These qualities echo key principles of learning organizations, where structures thrive on continuous improvement and creative adaptation but now enabled at scale by decentralized technology. In practical terms, this means the institution can rapidly integrate breakthroughs and respond to crises because it does not rely on rigid hierarchies or outdated protocols for decision-making. Instead, it harnesses the collective intelligence of humans and AI agents in a transparent, trust-minimized environment. By drawing on Potts's (2025) agentic commons paradigm and the real-world success of DeSci initiatives (Fantaccini *et al.*, 2024; Unfried, 2024), this model embodies an active, evolutionary approach to governance. It draws upon the lessons from the university case, complemented by the rhizomatic literature review, to argue that sustainable energy research should not be approached as a static problem to be solved once, but as a dynamic and ongoing process of learning and adaptation. In doing so, a blockchain–AI-powered commons can drive innovation faster and more collaboratively than legacy institutions, helping society navigate the unpredictable journey toward sustainable energy futures. This convergence of blockchain and AI is more than a technical solution; it is a governance innovation that turns the research enterprise itself into a learning commons for sustainability.

Integrating blockchain and AI technologies for the governance and coordination of sustainable energy initiatives offers the potential for rethinking how these systems are organized. By fostering an environment that reduces transaction costs and enhances coordination, such blockchain–AI commons could help create a learning environment that would continuously strive for sustainability.

Sustainability transitions, which reallocate resources, opportunities, and power among stakeholders, frequently lead to disputes and conflicts. For the general public, there is significant interest in reconciling environmental objectives with socioeconomic priorities, including job creation and economic growth. Therefore, the legitimacy of transition policies can be enhanced by linking these transitions to the generation of new economic opportunities. The evolution of economic theories concerning industrial dynamics, technological change, and innovation introduces a modern perspective on the role of institutional technologies, such as blockchain and AI (Potts & Dopfer, 2024; Potts, 2025). The proposed design of the incentive structure for promoting transitions to sustainable energy systems research leverages the blockchain–AI commons to facilitate a process of institutional evolution, characterized by new forms of governance and coordination dedicated to learning and adaptation.

The blockchain–AI commons can be a pivotal tool in this context by providing a transparent, secure, and efficient way to manage and verify a vast amount of data related to societal energy needs and usage, carbon footprints, and renewable energy sources, without the traditional constraints of centralized systems. It can facilitate smoother transitions by enabling more agile responses to shifting regulations, market demands, and technological advancements (Dóci *et al.*, 2015; Geels, 2018).

Thus, by fostering a research environment through the blockchain–AI commons, we can create a more conducive landscape for developing a sustainable energy research environment. This environment would inherently challenge the status quo, encouraging the adoption of new technologies and practices that align with broader sustainability goals, ultimately leading to more resilient and adaptive energy systems.

References

Abbate, J. 2000. *Inventing the Internet.* Cambridge, MA: MIT Press.

Agar, J. 2019. "What is technology? Technology: Critical history of a concept, by Eric Schatzberg, Chicago and London, University of Chicago Press, 2018." *Annals of Science* 76(1): 1–6.

Ahl, A., Goto, M., Yarime, M., Tanaka, K., and Sagawa, D. 2022. "Challenges and opportunities of blockchain energy applications: Interrelatedness among technological, economic, social, environmental, and institutional dimensions." *Renewable and Sustainable Energy Reviews* 166: 112623.

Ahl, A., Yarime, M., Goto, M., Chopra, S. S., Kumar, N. M., Tanaka, K., and Sagawa, D. 2020. "Exploring blockchain for the energy transition: Opportunities and challenges based on a case study in Japan." *Renewable and Sustainable Energy Reviews* 117: 109488.

Allen, D. W., Berg, C., Markey-Towler, B., Novak, M., and Potts, J. 2020. "Blockchain and the evolution of institutional technologies: Implications for innovation policy." *Research Policy* 49(1): 103865.

Almudi, I., Fatas-Villafranca, F., Foster, J., and Potts, J. 2024. "Coevolution and dynamic processes: an introduction to this issue and avenues for future research." *Review of Evolutionary Political Economy* 5: 1–25.

Alvesson, M. and Sandberg, J. 2011. "Generating research questions through problematization." *Academy of Management Review* 36(2): 247–271.

Alvesson, M. and Sandberg, J. 2013. "Has management studies lost its way? Ideas for more imaginative and innovative research." *Journal of Management Studies* 50(1): 128–152.

Andersen, A. D. and Markard, J. 2024. "Multi-system dynamics in sustainability transitions: Introduction and outlook." *Environmental Innovation and Societal Transitions* 50: 100781.

Andersen, A. D., Steen, M., Mäkitie, T., Hanson, J., Thune, T. M., and Soppe, B. 2020. "The role of inter-sectoral dynamics in sustainability transitions: A comment on the transitions research agenda." *Environmental Innovation and Societal Transitions* 34: 348–351.

Ayres, R. U., Campbell, C. J., Casten, T. R., Horne, P. J., Kümmel, R., Laitner, J. A. *et al.* 2013. "Sustainability transition and economic growth enigma: Money or energy?" *Environmental Innovation and Societal Transitions* 9: 8–12.

Banon, J. and Potts, J. 2024. "Digital institutions create wealth by increasing economic computational complexity." SSRN Working Paper. https://doi.org/10.2139/ssrn.4693478.

Beck, U. 1992. "From industrial society to the risk society: Questions of survival, social structure and ecological enlightenment." *Theory, Culture & Society* 9(1): 97–123.

Beck, U. 2015. "Emancipatory catastrophism: What does it mean to climate change and risk society?" *Current Sociology* 63(1): 75–88.

Benedict, G., Sullivan, C., and Gill, A. 2022. "Governance challenges of AI-enabled decentralized autonomous organizations: Toward a research agenda." In *Proceedings of the International Conference on Information Systems (ICIS 2022)*, Paper 1184. Atlanta, GA: Association for Information Systems.

Berg, C., Davidson, S., and Potts, J. 2019. *Understanding the Blockchain Economy: An Introduction to Institutional Cryptoeconomics.* Cheltenham, UK: Edward Elgar Publishing.

Binz, C. and Truffer, B. 2017. “Global Innovation Systems—A conceptual framework for innovation dynamics in transnational contexts.” *Research Policy* 46(7): 1284–1298.

Bookbinder, R., Mdee, A., and Roelich, K. 2024. “The possibility of a theory of change to tackle the climate crisis in a UK university.” *International Journal of Sustainability in Higher Education* 25(8): 1571–1588.

Callon, M. 1987. “Society in the making: the study of technology as a tool for sociological analysis.” In *The Social Construction of Technological Systems: New Directions in the Sociology and History of Technology*, pp. 83–103.

Callon, M. 1998. “Introduction: the Embeddedness of Economic Markets in Economics.” In Callon, M. (ed.), *The Laws of the Markets.* Oxford: Blackwell.

Castells, M. 2016. “Networks of Outrage and Hope: Social Movements in the Internet Age.” In *Democracy.* New York: Columbia University Press, pp. 433–435.

Cederlöf, G. 2021. “Out of steam: Energy, materiality, and political ecology.” *Progress in Human Geography* 45(1): 70–87.

Chahar, S., Kaur, K., Kaswan, K. S., and Dhatterwal, J. S. 2025. “Explainable AI in Blockchain System for Decentralized Governance.” In *2025 International Conference on Pervasive Computational Technologies (ICPCT).* IEEE, pp. 725–729.

Cherp, A., Jewell, J., and Goldthau, A. 2011. “Governing global energy: Systems, transitions, complexity.” *Global Policy* 2(1): 75–88.

Clark, A. and Chalmers, D. 1998. “The extended mind.” *Analysis* 58(1): 7–19.

Curry, D. 2024. “Limitations of trust and legitimacy in blockchain: Exploring the effectiveness of decentralisation, immutability and consensus mechanisms in blockchain governance.” *International Journal of Public Sector Management* 37(6): 618–635.

Davidson, S. and Potts, J. 2022. “Institutional cryptoeconomics.” In *The Economics of Blockchain and Cryptocurrency.* Cheltenham, UK: Edward Elgar Publishing, pp. 1–12.

de Vries, A. 2019. “Renewable energy will not solve bitcoin’s sustainability problem.” *Joule* 3(4): 893–898.

Delbridge, R. and Fiss, P. C. 2013. “Editors’ comments: Styles of theorizing and the social organization of knowledge.” *Academy of Management Review* 38(3): 325–331.

Dóci, G., Vasileiadou, E., and Petersen, A. C. 2015. “Exploring the transition potential of renewable energy communities.” *Futures* 66: 85–95.

Dopfer, K. and Potts, J. 2008. *The General Theory of Economic Evolution.* London: Routledge.

Dor, D. 2017. "From experience to imagination: Language and its evolution as a social communication technology." *Journal of Neurolinguistics* 43: 107–119.

Etzkowitz, H. 2003. "Research groups as 'quasi-firms': The invention of the entrepreneurial university." *Research Policy* 32(1): 109–121.

Fantaccini, S., Grassi, L., and Rampoldi, A. 2024. "The potential of DAOs for funding and collaborative development in the life sciences." *Nature Biotechnology* 42(4): 555–562.

Featherstone, M. 2020. "Stiegler's ecological thought: The politics of knowledge in the anthropocene." *Educational Philosophy and Theory* 52(4): 409–419.

Fernández-Cano, A. 2021. "Publish, publish... cursed!" *Scientometrics* 126(4): 3673–3682.

Fox, N. J. 2024. "Rhizomatic review: A materialist minor science approach to research evaluation." *Qualitative Research* 24(5): 1101–1120.

Freeman, C. and Soete, L. 1997. *The Economics of Industrial Innovation.* Cambridge, MA: MIT Press.

Frolov, D. 2021. "Blockchain and institutional complexity: An extended institutional approach." *Journal of Institutional Economics* 17(1): 21–36.

Galvin, R. 2020. "What is money? And why it matters for social science in energy research." In *Inequality and Energy.* London: Academic Press, pp. 31–51.

Garrett, T. J., Grasselli, M., and Keen, S. 2020. "Past world economic production constrains current energy demands: Persistent scaling with implications for economic growth and climate change mitigation." *PLoS One* 15(8): e0237672.

Garrett, T. J., Grasselli, M. R., and Keen, S. 2022. "Lotka's wheel and the long arm of history: How does the distant past determine today's global rate of energy consumption?" *Earth System Dynamics* 13(2): 1021–1028.

Geels, F. W. 2002. "Technological transitions as evolutionary reconfiguration processes: A multi-level perspective and a case-study." *Research Policy* 31(8–9): 1257–1274.

Geels, F. W. 2005. *Technological Transitions and System Innovations: A Co-Evolutionary and Socio-Technical Analysis.* Cheltenham, UK: Edward Elgar Publishing.

Geels, F. W. 2018. "Disruption and low-carbon system transformation: Progress and new challenges in socio-technical transitions research and the Multi-Level Perspective." *Energy Research & Social Science* 37: 224–231.

Geels, F. W. 2019. "Socio-technical transitions to sustainability: A review of criticisms and elaborations of the Multi-Level Perspective." *Current Opinion in Environmental Sustainability* 39: 187–201.

Geels, F. W. 2020. "Micro-foundations of the multi-level perspective on socio-technical transitions: Developing a multi-dimensional model of agency through crossovers between social constructivism, evolutionary economics and neo-institutional theory." *Technological Forecasting and Social Change* 152: 119894.

Geels, F. W. 2021. "From leadership to followership: A suggestion for interdisciplinary theorising of mainstream actor reorientation in sustainability transitions." *Environmental Innovation and Societal Transitions* 41: 45–48.

Geels, F. W. 2024. "The multi-level perspective on sustainability transitions: Background, overview, and current research topics." *Environmental Innovation and Societal Transitions* 50: 100778.

Genus, A. and Coles, A. M. 2008. "Rethinking the multi-level perspective of technological transitions." *Research Policy* 37(9): 1436–1445.

Grey, C. 2010. "Organizing studies: Publications, politics and polemic." *Organization Studies* 31(6): 677–694.

Grimes, D. R., Bauch, C. T., and Ioannidis, J. P. 2018. "Modelling science trustworthiness under publish or perish pressure." *Royal Society Open Science* 5(1): 171511.

Hanitzsch, T., Markiewitz, A., and Bødker, H. 2024. "Publish and perish: Mental health among communication and media scholars." *Journal of Communication* 74(3): jqae012.

Hanseth, O. and Lyytinen, K. 2016. "Design theory for dynamic complexity in information infrastructures: The case of building internet." In *Enacting Research Methods in Information Systems.* Cham: Palgrave Macmillan, pp. 104–142.

Hansmeier, H., Schiller, K., and Rogge, K. S. 2021. "Towards methodological diversity in sustainability transitions research? Comparing recent developments (2016-2019) with the past (before 2016)." *Environmental Innovation and Societal Transitions* 38: 169–174.

Harman, G. 2010. "Technology, objects and things in Heidegger." *Cambridge Journal of Economics* 34(1): 17–25.

Harman, G. 2018. *Object-Oriented Ontology.* London: Penguin UK.

Heikkurinen, P., Clegg, S., Pinnington, A. H., Nicolopoulou, K., and Alcaraz, J. M. 2021. "Managing the Anthropocene: Relational agency and power to respect planetary boundaries." *Organization & Environment* 34(2): 267–286.

Hoke, K. L., Zimmer, S. L., Roddy, A. B., Ondrechen, M. J., Williamson, C. E., and Buan, N. R. 2021. "Reintegrating biology through the nexus of energy, information, and matter." *Integrative and Comparative Biology* 61(6): 2082–2094.

Hopkins, D., Kester, J., Meelen, T., and Schwanen, T. 2020. "Not more but different: A comment on the transitions research agenda." *Environmental Innovation and Societal Transitions* 34: 4–6.

Howson, P. 2021. "Distributed degrowth technology: Challenges for blockchain beyond the green economy." *Ecological Economics* 184: 107020.

Hui, Y. 2017. "On cosmotechnics: For a renewed relation between technology and nature in the anthropocene." *Techne: Research in Philosophy and Technology* 21(2/3): 319–341.

Kanger, L. 2020. "Neglected systems and theorizing: A comment on the transitions research agenda." *Environmental Innovation and Societal Transitions* 34: 352–354.

Kanger, L. 2021. "Rethinking the multi-level perspective for energy transitions: From regime life-cycle to explanatory typology of transition pathways." *Energy Research & Social Science* 71: 101829.

Kanger, L. and Schot, J. 2016. "User-made immobilities: A transitions perspective." *Mobilities* 11(4): 598–613.

Keller, M., Sahakian, M., and Hirt, L. F. 2022. Connecting the multi-level-perspective and social practice approach for sustainable transitions. *Environmental Innovation and Societal Transitions* 44: 14–28.

Kivimaa, P., Boon, W., Hyysalo, S., and Klerkx, L. 2019. "Towards a typology of intermediaries in sustainability transitions: A systematic review and a research agenda." *Research Policy* 48(4): 1062–1075.

Knöchelmann, M. 2024. "Formal authorship in the wake of uncertain futures: The narrative of publish or perish in the humanities." *Research Evaluation* 33(6): rvae044.

Köhler, J., Geels, F. W., Kern, F., Markard, J., Onsongo, E., Wieczorek, A. *et al.* 2019. "An agenda for sustainability transitions research: State of the art and future directions." *Environmental Innovation and Societal Transitions* 31: 1–32.

Kuhn, T. S. 1996. *The Structure of Scientific Revolutions.* 3rd ed. Chicago: University of Chicago Press.

Kump, B. 2023. "Lewin's field theory as a lens for understanding incumbent actors' agency in sustainability transitions." *Environmental Innovation and Societal Transitions* 46: 100683.

Laguerre, R. 2023. "Challenging assumptions in research and practice using problematization principles." *Industrial and Organizational Psychology* 16(1): 101–104.

Lange, O. 2014. *Introduction to Economic Cybernetics.* Amsterdam: Elsevier.

Latour, B. 2003. "Is re-modernization occurring-and if so, how to prove it? A commentary on Ulrich Beck." *Theory, Culture & Society* 20(2): 35–48.

Little, C. J., Rizzuto, M., Luhring, T. M., Monk, J. D., Nowicki, R. J., Paseka, R. E. *et al.* 2022. "Movement with meaning: Integrating information into meta-ecology." *Oikos* 2022(8): e08892.

Loorbach, D. A. and Wittmayer, J. 2024. "Transforming universities: Mobilizing research and education for sustainability transitions at Erasmus University Rotterdam, The Netherlands." *Sustainability Science* 19(1): 19–33.

Malhotra, A., Schmidt, T. S., and Huenteler, J. 2019. "The role of inter-sectoral learning in knowledge development and diffusion: Case studies on three clean energy technologies." *Technological Forecasting and Social Change* 146: 464–487.

Marleau, J. N., Peller, T., Guichard, F., and Gonzalez, A. 2020. "Converting ecological currencies: Energy, material, and information flows." *Trends in Ecology & Evolution* 35(12): 1068–1077.

Marsiglio, S. and Tolotti, M. 2024. "Complexity in low-carbon transitions: Uncertainty and policy implications." *Energy Economics* 138: 107803.

Menken, S. and Keestra, M. 2016. *An Introduction to Interdisciplinary Research: Theory and Practice.* Amsterdam: Amsterdam University Press.

Morton, T. 2011. "Here comes everything: The promise of object-oriented ontology." *Qui Parle: Critical Humanities and Social Sciences* 19(2): 163–190.

Morton, T. 2013. *Hyperobjects: Philosophy and Ecology After the End of the World.* Minneapolis: University of Minnesota Press.

Oliva, G. 2016. "The road to servomechanisms: the influence of Cybernetics on Hayek from the sensory order to the social order." In *Research in the History of Economic Thought and Methodology.* Bingley, UK: Emerald Group Publishing Limited, pp. 161–198.

Osipenko, S. and Sørensen, C. 2022. "Tokens matter." In Venkatesh, V., Hui, K.-L., and Böhmann, T. (eds.), *The 2022 International Conference on Information Systems (ICIS 2022).* Copenhagen: Association for Information Systems.

Ostrom, E. 2010. "Beyond markets and states: Polycentric governance of complex economic systems." *American Economic Review* 100(3): 641–672.

Peim, N. and Stock, N. 2023. "Education after the end of the world. How can education be viewed as a hyperobject?" In *Education for Sustainable Development in the 'Capitalocene'.* London: Routledge, pp. 28–39.

Pollitt, H. and Mercure, J. F. 2018. "The role of money and the financial sector in energy-economy models used for assessing climate and energy policy." *Climate Policy* 18(2): 184–197.

Poole, M. S. and Van de Ven, A. H. 1989. "Toward a general theory of innovation processes." In *Research on the Management of Innovation: The Minnesota Studies*, pp. 637–662.

Potts, J. 2025. "Governing hyperobjects – new economics of AI regulation." In Stocker, V., Schrepel, T., and Kuenzler, A. (eds.), *Network Law Review* (special symposium issue). Conference paper presented at The Law, Technology, and Economics of AI Regulation conference, Hong Kong, May 22–23, 2025.

Potts, J., Allen, D. W. E., Berg, C., Davidson, S., and MacDonald, T. 2021. "An economic theory of blockchain foundations." SSRN Working Paper. https://doi.org/10.2139/ssrn.3842281.

Potts, J. and Dopfer, K. 2024. "New evolutionary economics." SSRN Working Paper. https://doi.org/10.2139/ssrn.4837360.

Rennie, E. and Potts, J. 2024. "Contribution systems: A new theory of value." SSRN Working Paper. https://doi.org/10.2139/ssrn.4754267.

Repko, A. 2008. *Interdisciplinary Research: Process and Theory.* Thousand Oaks, CA: Sage.

Rip, A. and Kemp, R. 1998. "Technological change." In *Human Choice and Climate Change: Vol. II, Resources and Technology.* Columbus, OH: Battelle Press, pp. 327–399.

Rosenbloom, D. 2020. "Engaging with multi-system interactions in sustainability transitions: A comment on the transitions research agenda." *Environmental Innovation and Societal Transitions* 34: 336–340.

Rosser Jr, J. B. 2010. "Is a transdisciplinary perspective on economic complexity possible?" *Journal of Economic Behavior & Organization* 75(1): 3–11.

Sánchez, M. A. 2022. "A multi-level perspective on financial technology transitions." *Technological Forecasting and Social Change* 181: 121766.

Schatzberg, E. 2006. "'Technik' comes to America: Changing meanings of 'Technology' before 1930." *Technology and Culture* 47(3): 486–512.

Simon, H. 1997. *Administrative Behavior: A Study of Decision-Making Processes in Administrative Organization.* 4th ed. New York: Macmillan. (Original work published 1947).

Smith, A., Stirling, A., and Berkhout, F. 2005. "The governance of sustainable socio-technical transitions." *Research Policy* 34(10): 1491–1510.

Soete, L. 2002. "The challenges and the potential of the knowledge-based economy in a globalised world." In *New Knowledge Economy in Europe: A Strategy for International Competitiveness and Social Cohesion*, pp. 28–53.

Sovacool, B. K. and Hess, D. J. 2017. "Ordering theories: Typologies and conceptual frameworks for sociotechnical change." *Social Studies of Science* 47(5): 703–750.

Stiegler, B. 2018a. *The Neganthropocene.* Ed. and Trans. D. Ross. Ann Arbor, MI: Open Humanities Press.

Stiegler, B. 2018b. "Artificial stupidity and artificial intelligence in the anthropocene." Lecture delivered November 23, 2018 at the Institute of Ereignis, Shanghai.

Stiegler, B. 2019. "For a neganthropology of automatic society." In Pringle, T. and Koch, G. (eds.), *Machine.* Lüneburg: Meson Press, pp. 25–47.

Swan, M. 2015. *Blockchain: Blueprint for a New Economy.* Sebastopol, CA: O'Reilly Media.

Swan, M., Potts, J., Takagi, S., Witte, F., and Tasca, P. (eds.). 2019. *Blockchain Economics: Implications Of Distributed Ledgers-Markets, Communications Networks, And Algorithmic Reality* (Vol. 1). Singapore: World Scientific.

Syvitski, J., Waters, C. N., Day, J., Milliman, J. D., Summerhayes, C., Steffen, W. *et al.* 2020. "Extraordinary human energy consumption and resultant geological impacts beginning around 1950 CE initiated the proposed Anthropocene Epoch." *Communications Earth & Environment* 1(1): 32.

Tsing, A. L. 2015. *The Mushroom at the End of the World: On the Possibility of Life in Capitalist Ruins.* Princeton, NJ: Princeton University Press.

Unfried, M. 2024. "Advancing longevity research through decentralized science." *Frontiers in Aging* 5: 1353272.

Vallée, R. 2009. "History of cybernetics." *Systems Science And Cybernetics* 3: 22–33.

Van den Bergh, J. C., Truffer, B., and Kallis, G. 2011. "Environmental innovation and societal transitions: Introduction and overview." *Environmental Innovation and Societal Transitions* 1(1): 1–23.

Van Lente, H., Hekkert, M., Smits, R., and Van Waveren, B. A. S. 2003. "Roles of systemic intermediaries in transition processes." *International Journal of Innovation Management* 7(03): 247–279.

Vergne, J. P. 2020. "Decentralized vs. distributed organization: Blockchain, machine learning and the future of the digital platform." *Organization Theory* 1(4): 2631787720977052.

Von Bertalanffy, L. 1972. "The history and status of general systems theory." *Academy of Management Journal* 15(4): 407–426.

Voshmgir, S. and Zargham, M. 2020. "Foundations of cryptoeconomic systems." WU Vienna University of Economics and Business Working

Paper Series, Institute for Cryptoeconomics, Interdisciplinary Research No. 1.

Weidener, L. and Boltz, L. 2025. "Challenges of DAOs in decentralized science: A qualitative analysis of expert interviews." SSRN Working Paper. https://doi.org/10.2139/ssrn.5239018.

Wiener, N. 1948. *Cybernetics: Control and Communication in the Animal and the Machine.* Cambridge, MA: MIT Press.

Wiener, N. 1950. "Cybernetics." *Bulletin of the American Academy of Arts and Sciences* 3(7): 2–4.

Wiener, N. 1954. *The Human Use of Human Beings Cybernetics and Society.* New York: Avon Books.

Wolf, P., Harboe, J., Sudbrack Rothbarth, C., Gaudenz, U., Arsan, L., Obrist, C., and van Leeuwen, M. 2021. "Non-governmental organisations and universities as transition intermediaries in sustainability transformations building on grassroots initiatives." *Creativity and Innovation Management* 30(3): 596–618.

Wu, Y., Wu, Y., Cimen, H., Vasquez, J. C., and Guerrero, J. M. 2022. "Towards collective energy Community: Potential roles of microgrid and blockchain to go beyond P2P energy trading." *Applied Energy* 314: 119003.

Zuboff, S. 2023. "The age of surveillance capitalism." In *Social Theory Re-wired.* London: Routledge, pp. 203–213.

Part IV

Digital Network Economies

https://doi.org/10.1142/9781800618664_0010

Chapter 9

A Theory of Chaordic Economics: How Artificial Intelligence and Blockchain Transform Businesses, Economies, and Societies

Horst Treiblmaier

School of International Management,
Modul University Vienna, Vienna, Austria
horst.treiblmaier@modul.ac.at

Abstract

Dee Hock, the founder of Visa, coined the term "chaordic" to describe simultaneously chaotic and ordered systems. Based on his reasoning, we introduce the theory of chaordic economics to explain how economic systems are transformed by two disruptive technologies: artificial intelligence and blockchain. Artificial intelligence can generate novel output through algorithmic yet rather unpredictable processes. Blockchain creates deterministic results without central authorities and relies on elaborated protocols that prescribe how consensus can be reached within a network of peers. The amalgamation of chaos and order produces chaordic economic systems and can yield hitherto unimaginable economic structures.

Keywords: Chaordic Economics, Blockchain, Artificial Intelligence, Theory Development.

9.1 Introduction

For better or worse, the evolution of humankind is invariably linked to the governance structures it creates to organize economic and social endeavors. This pertains to the exchange of goods and services (mainly in the private sector) and the mechanisms for establishing organizational and societal governance (in the public and private sectors). The emerging structures are fundamentally determined by the underlying technological means, especially in relation to the flow and processing of information needed to understand what is happening in remote locations and act accordingly. Due to the lack of sophisticated information technologies, relatively simple social hierarchies prevailed in the Stone Age and were restricted to small and controllable areas. From 550 BC onward, great empires emerged (e.g., in Persia, China, Rome, Byzantium, and India), sustained by a combination of military force, economic incentives, cultural integration, and administrative innovations. As these empires have disappeared, others have followed, and today's world is characterized by the political and economic dominance of a relatively small number of nation-states, only a handful of which control the world's economy, together with multinational corporations governed by intricate mechanisms that have evolved over centuries.

In the 1960s, motivated by his ongoing quest to shape organizations from how they are to how they ought to be, Dee Hock launched an international payment system, later branded "Visa", as a deliberately decentralized organization. He was also the one who coined the term "chaordic" since he concluded that traditional approaches would not suffice to facilitate the growth needed for his envisioned worldwide organization (Hock, 2005). "Chaordic" is a portmanteau illustrating the need to balance flexibility or unpredictability (chaos)[1] with a clear structure (order) and to allow an organization to innovate and thrive while remaining resilient in turbulent environments.

Academic research has highlighted the relevance of chaordic systems and their implications for organizational and social structures.

[1]Various definitions of chaos and order exist. In this chapter, we take a rather broad approach and view chaos as unpredictability and order as predictability, leading to unstructured and structured outcomes, respectively.

For example, van Eijnatten and Putnik (2004) propose that learning organizations might evolve into "chaordic enterprises" capable of self-organization and transformative change. Edwards (2014) evaluates and summarizes the literature on chaordic systems thinking applied to organizational transformation and identifies several so-called metatheoretical lenses that can be used in chaordic systems thinking, including connectivity, emergence, indeterminacy, open systems, agency-communion, dialogue, holarchy, dissipation, consciousness, and the individual versus collective lens.

However, academia still lacks an overarching theory on chaordic systems that scrutinizes the impact of disruptive technologies and, importantly, provides a theoretical explanation for how technological transformation allows the reorganization of existing structures, potentially fostering economic growth and welfare. This is understandable since Dee Hock's original ideas were driven by practical needs rather than academic inquiry. To better understand the implications of modern technologies for economic and societal change and to raise awareness of forthcoming transformations, we postulate that it is the available tools that initially determine the capabilities and that these capabilities, in turn, determine the structures. We consider information technology, specifically tools for the collection, storage, processing, transfer, and use of information, as an essential driver of change and, consequently, claim that advances in information technology ultimately transform structures at various levels by creating new possibilities. In this day and age, when light travels through fiber optic cables at about 200,000 km/s, decentralized ledgers facilitate consensus and create trust among entities who do not know each other, and AI-powered systems take mere seconds to process more information than a human could contemplate in a lifetime; it is time to question whether the structures and processes that worked considerably well during the industrial revolution[2] are still the best available means to organize work and life in the 21st century.

[2]They have worked well to foster innovation and economic progress on a national level in industrialized nations using standard economic metrics. If the ecological consequences and the implications for the subjugated nations and the working classes were considered, the final assessment would be a different one.

In this chapter, we propose and logically justify the theory of chaordic economics that specifically considers two important and presumably complementary technologies: artificial intelligence (AI) and blockchain. We argue that both can not only lead to unpredictable and chaotic outcomes but also help to create orderly and structured systems. Together, they can provide the basis for a new economic order and yield hitherto impossible structures for organizations, economies, and societies.

9.2 Theories on Chaos and Order

Numerous existing theories can be applied to analyze, explain, and predict the emergence of chaos versus order and identify relevant driving factors. In this chapter, we focus on a handful of theories that strive to explain economic outcomes. To start with, information theory is rooted in the seminal work by Shannon (1948), in which he mathematically formalized the core elements of communication and developed the concept of information entropy, expressed as the unpredictability of information content. From an organizational, economic, and societal perspective, entropy can be used to quantify the amount of uncertainty in a system, with organizations operating somewhere on a spectrum ranging from predictable (low-entropy) to unpredictable (high-entropy) environments. Information theory also elucidates the interplay between information flows and organizational structures, with hierarchical structures generally featuring clearly defined flows, while emergent structures are characterized by rather unstructured, decentralized interactions. From the viewpoint of information theory, self-organization can occur through unplanned interactions and patterns, allowing structure and order to emerge.

Chaos theory emerged as a branch of mathematics that investigates how minor variations in initial states lead to vastly different outcomes. Empirically discovered through meteorology (Lorenz, 1963), it has found widespread application in fields such as mathematics, physics, biology, medicine, computer science, the social sciences, and economics. At the core of this theory is the assumption that complex systems that appear to be chaotic may have an underlying order and can even have a deterministic foundation.

In this regard, deterministic chaos describes a situation in which order (i.e., deterministic rules) and chaos (i.e., unpredictable outcomes) coexist. From an organizational, economic, and social perspective, this implies that even seemingly ordered systems might contain the potential for unpredictable change.

Cybernetics is a transdisciplinary field that investigates systems in which outputs become inputs, resulting in feedback loops that can regulate the overall system, adapt to changes, and help to achieve desired goals. It originates from the work of Wiener (1948), who combined ideas from mathematics, biology, and engineering to design systems of control and communication. From a cybernetic perspective, systems become chaotic when control mechanisms are inadequately designed or fail, as is the case with insufficient governance or inappropriate policies. Conversely, it is also possible that order emerges from chaos, as happens when markets reach a new equilibrium or communities self-regulate during times of crises. In short, communication, feedback, and control can help to stabilize systems through efficient information flows, dynamic adjustment, and coordinated regulation.

The focus of game theory lies in the analysis of strategic interactions among agents, which can include individuals, organizations, or other economic entities. These agents make decisions in scenarios that can be modeled as games in which the choices and outcomes depend not only on their own actions but also on the actions of others, such that strategic action often requires consideration of mutual expectations. Similar to the theories discussed above, the origins of game theory can be found in mathematics, with the seminal works of John von Neumann and Oskar Morgenstern laying the foundation. The initial ideas were later refined by Nash (1951), who extended von Neumann's work to non-cooperative games by introducing the concept of the Nash equilibrium. He provided a theoretical framework to understand the outcome of games in which players make decisions independently. In a nutshell, it is the nature of the interactions that leads either to conflict, which often implies chaos, or to order enabled by structured cooperation.

At the heart of network theory lies the study of interactions between networked nodes, which could be individuals or organizations, and how information flows among them. Its origins can be traced back to the works of the mathematician Leonard Euler, who laid the foundation for graph theory in the 18th century and inspired significant work in that area, including the Erdős–Rényi model of random graphs, which fostered an understanding of how networks grow and evolve. Albert and Barabási (2002) introduced the concept of scale-free networks and the preferential attachment model, in which they illustrate that many real-world networks, such as the internet and social networks, follow a power-law degree distribution, with only a few highly connected nodes. In such networks, local interactions can serve both as the foundation of order and a source of instability. Further developments include economic network theory (Swan, 2019), which indicates that the widespread adoption of distributed ledgers can help mitigate systemic risks in financial networks.

When it comes to the emergent organization of the economic sector, Coase (1937) posed the fundamental question of why firms exist in the first place. He concluded that the so-called transaction costs (i.e., expenses for search and information, negotiations, enforcement, and compliance) ultimately determine a firm's boundaries. Simply put, firms will grow if conducting transactions internally is cheaper than on the open market. Environments characterized by uncertainty and complexity tend to yield hierarchies that can cope with outside conditions and foster hierarchical structures for control.

Austrian economics represents a school of thought that emphasizes the role of individual decision-making, subjective value, and the importance of free markets to foster economic coordination and growth (von Mises, 1949). The core concepts were developed and refined by numerous economists, including Carl Menger, Ludwig von Mises, Friedrich Hayek, and Murray Rothbard. They postulate that it is primarily interference with free market mechanisms that leads to the emergence of chaos since the natural flow of information, as expressed by prices in voluntary exchanges, becomes distorted. Consequently, they routinely blame governmental interventions for causing such distortions. On the other hand, they claim that an economic order can be established by allowing decentralized decision-making and letting individuals pursue their self-interests.

In stark contrast to the Austrian economists, John Maynard Keynes (1936) concentrates on the roles of aggregate demand fluctuations, general uncertainty, and wrong policy decisions in creating chaotic economic environments. He postulates that market inefficiencies can be corrected and stable economic conditions ensured by focusing on the management of demand through controlled governmental interventions, including counter-cyclical policies using monetary and fiscal measures.

Finally, proponents of behavioral economics focus on the understanding of how humans make economic decisions. They deviate from the underlying assumptions of unbounded rationality and pure self-interest by identifying cognitive biases, emotions, and social influences as important determinants of decision-making processes. From an individual's perspective, gains and losses are not evaluated objectively but are rather compared to a subjective reference point (Kahneman and Tversky, 1979). According to this theory, chaos in economic systems can be explained by (objectively) irrational human behavior leading to unpredictable, inconsistent, or destabilizing outcomes. These behaviors, aggregated across individuals or institutions, can disrupt market equilibria, amplify volatility, and create systemic instability. While individual behaviors may appear irrational when viewed in isolation, behavioral economics demonstrates that these behaviors are often systematic and predictable. When aggregated, they form structured patterns that explain market trends, policy outcomes, and social dynamics.

In Table 9.1, we summarize these different perspectives on the drivers of order and chaos, focusing on the important role of information in shaping the emergent organizational, economic, and societal structures.

9.3 Artificial Intelligence and Blockchain as Drivers of Order and Chaos

Russell and Norvig (1995) understand AI as the study of rational agents that optimize the expected outcome of their actions, classifying the concept into four categories: (1) thinking humanly, (2) thinking rationally, (3) acting humanly, and (4) acting rationally. The first and third categories follow a humanistic approach, whereas the second and fourth follow a rationalist approach. Blockchain is defined as a "digital, decentralized and distributed ledger in which transactions are logged and added in chronological order with the goal of creating permanent and tamperproof records" (Treiblmaier, 2018, p. 547).

Academic researchers have already recognized the important interplay between blockchain and AI. For example, Adel *et al.* (2023)

Table 9.1. Theoretical perspectives on chaos and order.

Theory/Framework	Chaos	Order
Information theory	Information entropy as disorder	Self-organization through unplanned interactions
Chaos theory	Ordered systems can exhibit unstable and unpredictable behavior	Identification of conditions that yield ordered systems
Cybernetics	Inadequate or broken control mechanisms	Stabilization through communication, feedback, and control
Game theory	Cooperation yields order	Conflict yields chaos
Network theory	Local interactions as a predictor for global disorder	Local interactions as the foundation of self-organization and hierarchy
Transaction cost economics	Uncertainty and complexity	Hierarchical structures for internal coordination and cost control
Austrian economics	Imbalances caused by external distortions and disruptions of natural market processes	Decentralized decision-making yields ordered economic activity
Keynesianism	Uncertainty and inadequate responses can increase instability	Creation of order through strategic interventions
Behavioral economics	Individual irrational behavior	Aggregate effects of irrational behavior can create predictable structures

analyzed 2,615 peer-reviewed journal articles published between 2017 and 2023 to identify eight emerging themes in which AI and blockchain work together. These include machine learning applications, price prediction of digital currencies, federated learning, industry applications (e.g., in supply chain management), reinforcement learning, and Industry 4.0. Enhancing blockchain through AI can yield better security (e.g., through anomaly and fraud detection), improve smart contracts (e.g., code creation and bug detection), improve consensus mechanisms, and optimize auctions and smart grids (Ressi *et al.*, 2024). Contrariwise, blockchain can serve as an enabler for autonomous AI in digital native economic and financial institutions by allowing AI agents to autonomously interact with blockchain-based institutions through the use of private keys (Nguyen Thanh *et al.*, 2024). Blockchain can also be used to verify knowledge generated through AI. Decentralized knowledge graphs can be used to address challenges related to biases, hallucinations, intellectual property rights, and data ownership (TraceLabs, 2024).

In the following sections, we use the theoretical angles introduced above to investigate how these different yet complementary technologies can impact business, the economy, and society. We start with a brief investigation of how they impact information flows, processing, and entropy. We then focus on topics related to organizational structure and processes before, finally, investigating broader implications related to markets, economies, and societies. These perspectives were conceptually derived from a compilation of the main aspects covered in the aforementioned theories.

9.3.1 *Artificial intelligence*

AI exhibits features that can contribute to chaos (i.e., unpredictability) and order (i.e., predictability). Generative AI, in particular, is capable of producing unpredictable output through complex processes. However, behind the apparent chaos lie well-defined algorithms and mathematical models. From an information perspective, AI can potentially enhance chaos through the creation and propagation of misinformation, which, from the viewpoint of entropy, increases uncertainty and noise in the available information. However, the application of AI can also have the opposite effects on information, through efficient filtering, fact-checking, and structuring, as well as enhancing the flow of information through constant monitoring and analysis. In this context, pattern recognition and compression help to reduce the amount of information entropy.

When it comes to decision-making, AI can yield chaos by amplifying existing biases and generating unpredictable and unverifiable results. Contrariwise, it can also be argued that the decisions taken by AI are driven by data rather than potentially irrational human reasoning and thus help to create order based on rationality. From the perspective of structure and organization, AI can create chaos when the emerging structures are misaligned with systemic or human needs, which can happen if the restructuring is done without taking into account important goals (humanitarian or organizational) or if the tools are implemented without proper integration. Order can be created by optimizing processes, streamlining tasks through automation, and providing support for decision-making. AI can also drive chaos in control mechanisms if it increases the unpredictability of control, reduces the influence of humans, or poses a risk for malicious manipulation. Simultaneously, it can lead to order through the automation of control mechanisms and potentially yield more equitable decisions. From the viewpoint of centralization versus decentralization, AI can create chaotic situations by suggesting conflicting priorities and power imbalances, but it can also help to align interests between central authorities and local autonomies. Emerging situations can lead to either cooperation or conflict, which can be exacerbated by the creation of information asymmetries and misinformation or mitigated by the improvement of collaboration.

On a market level, the introduction of AI can lead to destabilization of existing systems, for example through the creation and spreading of misinformation and an amplification of risks. On the positive side, algorithms might be capable of allocating scarce resources more efficiently and stabilizing markets. Consequently, emerging economies can be either plagued by a disruption of the existing workforce and increasing economic inequalities or aided by a more efficient allocation of resources and the streamlining of workflows. Finally, social structures might be plunged into chaos through restructuring, which exacerbates inequalities; conversely, the application of AI may yield more efficient and fair governance processes and foster inclusivity. In Table 9.2, we summarize the different perspectives on how AI can contribute to the emergence of chaos and order from different angles.

9.3.2 *Blockchain*

Blockchain can induce unpredictability in information processing through fragmented systems that lack interoperability and the complexity of smart contract code. It can also promote order since the execution of these contracts is deterministic, and the transactions can be traced on a transparent ledger. In this respect, the "Internet of Contracts" can completely transform the way in which legal contracts are created, enforced, and regulated (Noto La Diega, 2022).

Table 9.2. Artificial intelligence as a driver of chaos and order.

	Chaos	Order
Information processing	Creation of misinformation	Filtering, fact-checking, and structuring
Information flow	Propagation of misinformation	Monitoring and analyses in real time
Information entropy	Increasing uncertainty and noise	Pattern recognition and information compression
Decision-making processes	Amplification of biases and unpredictability	Data-driven and organized decisions
Organizational structures	Misalignment with systemic and human needs	Process optimization, task automation, and decision support
Control mechanisms	Increasing unpredictability, removal of human oversight, or manipulation	Task automation and fairness
Centralization vs. decentralization	Conflicting priorities and the creation of power imbalances	Alignment of central authority with the interests of local autonomies
Cooperation vs. conflict	Creation of information asymmetries and misinformation	Improved collaboration
Market processes	Destabilization of existing systems and amplification of risks	Improving resource allocation and market stabilization
Economic activities	Disruption of the workforce and economic inequality	Efficient resource allocation and streamlining workflows
Social structures	Changing power structures and the creation of inequality	Supporting governance and decision-making and inclusivity

Information flows might be negatively impacted by unregulated dissemination and the amplification of feedback loops caused by real-time transaction processing and feedback. In chaordic and non-linear systems, such loops might result in unpredictable dynamics. However, the traceability of the transactions also stabilizes the system and improves transparency and trust. From an information entropy perspective, blockchain can enhance chaos, defined as unpredictability, by increasing data redundancy (a defining characteristic of distributed ledgers), decentralization, introducing inconsistencies caused by forks, and potentially also information silos due to the proliferation of different blockchains. At the same time, distributed ledgers reduce the amount of entropy through standardized protocols, improved reliability since previous transactions cannot be altered, and increased security through the application of cryptographic procedures.

When it comes to decision-making processes in chaordic economics, blockchain can induce chaos through its reliance on decentralized authorities, which implies interactions between entities with potentially conflicting goals. Depending on the decision-making process, certain groups of actors may be able to take over by acquiring a significant amount of governance tokens, with or without malicious intentions. At the same time, achieving consensus within a network of peers is transparent and based on clearly specified mechanisms such as Proof-of-Work (PoW) or Proof-of-Stake (PoS). Compliance can be enforced via rewards, and decisions are final and can be trusted. The effects on existing structures of transitioning to a blockchain-based system can also be twofold: While it is possible that decentralization of control and power raises conflicts between stakeholders and makes it hard to govern, the rules for governance also become more transparent and the relationships between the various stakeholders are clarified.

In terms of control mechanisms, the introduction of blockchain-based governance can increase complexity due to the decentralization of authority and weaken existing control structures. This might be mitigated or compensated by the introduction of clear incentives for the creation of orderly structures, the provision of mechanisms that help to resolve conflicts, and the easy enforcement of accountability. In terms of (de)centralization, Blockchain can foster chaos through conflicts between centralized and decentralized authorities, which might be aggravated by the emergence of centralized structures within decentralized systems (e.g., disproportionate mining power in PoW systems or unequal token distribution in PoS blockchains). However, such systems can also exhibit greater flexibility, which strengthens their resilience in complex and ever-changing environments. The introduction of decentralized autonomous organizations (DAOs) can also disrupt well-established conflict resolution mechanisms, thus leading to increased chaos, as expressed, for example, by the forking of blockchains. The same tools can also have the opposite effect and create a stable foundation for cooperation by building trust that is based on the transparency of protocols and transactions, which, in turn, leads to a better alignment of goals.

When it comes to markets, blockchain can increase chaos by leading to increased fragmentation that splits markets into competing ecosystems. The "tokenization of everything" can potentially lead to a hyper-financialization that yields speculative bubbles and increases volatility. Simultaneously, stabilizing effects can be expected from the transparency of blockchain, which not only allows transactions to be easily audited but can also increase overall market efficiency. On an economic level, well-established structures might be displaced by rather untested economic models, which can increase speculation and volatility and make regulation and oversight more complex. On the other hand, ordered systems might emerge that automatically enforce regulatory compliance and promote the optimized allocation of resources to provide sufficient security for long-term planning.

The introduction of blockchain can have chaotic effects on social structures and lead to the erosion of well-established hierarchies, the introduction of (new) inequalities, and an overreliance on protocols that have not been adequately tested on a large scale. Stabilizing effects on societal structures can be expected from introducing protocols that ensure the fair distribution of value, improve the overall accountability of decision makers (which can be protocols), and streamline the resolution of conflicts. Table 9.3 summarizes the roles of blockchain as a driver of chaos and order from numerous perspectives.

9.4 Chaordic Economics: Blurring Boundaries and Emerging Structures

We introduce the theory of chaordic economics as a theoretical framework to analyze, explain, and predict current and future transformations that affect businesses, economies, and societies. Chaordic economics is based on the transformative force of disruptive technologies such as AI and blockchain and characterizes an adaptive state in which economic systems (including societal structures) operate

Table 9.3. Blockchain as a driver of chaos and order.

	Chaos	Order
Information processing	Fragmentation and complexity	Deterministic execution, transparency, and traceability
Information flow	Unregulated information dissemination and amplification of feedback loops	Increased transparency and trust
Information entropy	Redundancy, uncertainty, and inconsistencies	Standardization, reliability, and security
Decision-making processes	Decentralized authority, goal conflicts, and malicious interference	Consensus mechanisms, compliance, and finality
Organizational structures	Decentralization of control and power, lack of governance, and stakeholder conflict	Transparent governance and clarification of stakeholder relationships
Control mechanisms	Increased complexity, decentralized authority, and loss of traditional control structures	Incentives for order, mechanisms for conflict resolution, and enforcement of accountability
Centralization vs. decentralization	Conflict of interests between centralized and decentralized authorities, centralization tendencies	Increased flexibility and resilience
Cooperation vs. conflict	Disruption of existing conflict resolution mechanisms	Transparency-based trust and shared goals
Market processes	Emergence of fragmented ecosystems and amplification of volatility	Efficient and transparent processed
Economic activities	Disruption of well-established structures and proliferation of untested economic models	Predictable economic frameworks, efficient allocation of resources, and built-in regulation
Social structures	Erosion of traditional hierarchies, inequality, and overreliance on technology	Fair value distribution, improved accountability, and streamlined dispute resolution

efficiently and effectively. In the following sections, we first outline the key determinants that characterize the theory of chaordic economics, followed by a high-level visualization of how the underlying technological drivers transform organizational structures, interorganizational relations and macroeconomic processes, and societal structures.

9.4.1 *Key characteristics*

We postulate that organizations, economies, and societies that transform into a chaordic state exhibit several critical characteristics that distinguish them from traditional mechanistic and hierarchical structures.

9.4.1.1 *Self-organization and emergence*

In chaordic systems, various forms of economic transactions and structures emerge from the interactions of numerous individual agents (which can be humans but also machines) rather than from rigid top-down control. This corresponds to the idea of a spontaneous order in free markets but also recognizes the need for guiding principles to prevent destructive states of disorder. Such principles could be encoded into smart contracts.

9.4.1.2 *Adaptability and resilience*

By nature, chaordic economic systems are designed to be resilient, adaptive, and flexible. Decentralized approaches enable such systems to adapt to disruptions, such as technological changes, environmental disasters, or economic shocks. This is achieved through feedback loops, which help the systems develop and adjust their structure to be able to cope with external events.

9.4.1.3 *Nonlinearity*

The complex interplay between chaos and order can yield unpredictable behaviors that expose nonlinear outcomes. Feedback loops and tipping points create emerging patterns that cannot be explained by traditional linear models and necessitate broad systemic thinking and an increased focus on adaptability.

9.4.1.4 *Balance between chaos and order*

Chaordic economies exhibit a balance where structure exists to provide stability, but sufficient flexibility is granted to allow for innovation and adaptability. The extreme endpoints are avoided, recognizing that a rigid and hierarchical order can prevent growth and innovation, while uncontrolled chaos can lead to instability.

9.4.1.5 *Decentralized control*

Chaordic economics does not rely on central planning or *laissez-faire* approaches but is based on a balanced middle ground in which general guidelines and principles steer behavior without rigid control. This encourages market-driven open innovation while simultaneously ensuring stability through shared principles, values, and, if needed, regulations.

9.4.1.6 *Stakeholder integration*

Chaordic economic systems are open to diverse stakeholders, including individuals, businesses, local communities, and governments. Rather than focusing entirely on competition to foster development, chaordic economics emphasizes collaboration and the alignment of potentially diverse interests. From this perspective, economies and societal structures are seen as interconnected ecosystems that evolve together and influence each other.

9.4.1.7 *Complexity*

Chaordic economics considers the interconnected and rather unpredictable nature of economies. It deviates from reductionist thinking, which implies that systems can be best understood if broken down into parts, and acknowledges that economic outcomes result from complex and frequently nonlinear interactions. This acknowledges that our world is characterized by increasing technological, economic, and social complexity.

9.4.1.8 *Sustainability*

An integrative view of sustainability incorporates environmental, economic, and social aspects. In this regard, chaordic economics integrates flexible and self-organizing processes that follow the principles of the circular economy while simultaneously considering economic and social disparities. Such an approach favors long-term stability over short-term gains, leveraging feedback loops and emergent behaviors to align economic goals with sustainable practices.

9.4.2 *Integrative theoretical framework*

Figure 9.1 depicts the blurring boundaries between organizational structures, economic conditions (shown as inter-organizational relationships and macroeconomic conditions), and societal structures. In a chaordic economic system, the boundaries between centralization and decentralization, as well as private and public, become permeable, as is shown by the two-headed arrows. Based on our reasoning, as outlined above, the direction of a specific development is hard to predict, but in general, chaordic systems tend to be more decentralized and autonomous than existing hierarchical structures. Private

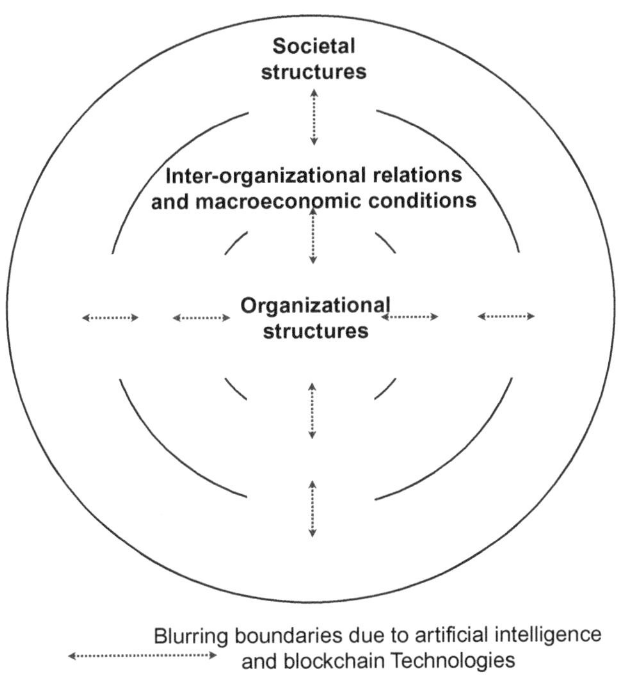

Fig. 9.1. Blurring of boundaries in chaordic economics.

organizations or DAOs can take over social tasks (e.g., related to governance or voting), and governing structures will evolve into self-organizing autonomous systems.

9.5 Discussion

Existing economic and social structures, established over centuries under fundamentally different conditions from today, no longer pose the most effective and efficient ways to manage organizations, steer economies, and govern societies. In this chapter, we postulate that if the underlying conditions and technological means have changed, it is reasonable to assume that new structures and processes will emerge that will alter all levels of economic and social activity. In this regard, we build on seminal literature and emphasize the need for systematic thinking rather than analyzing individual parts in isolation (Meadows, 2008). Our reasoning is based on the assumption that information is the key to governing organizations (Laudon and Laudon, 2020) and societies (Beniger, 1986). As a starting point, we use numerous existing theories to gain a better understanding of how chaos and order emerge in different kinds of systems. In addition to these classic theories, new approaches, such as smartnetwork field theory (Swan and dos Santos, 2020), have already indicated that novel technologies, including blockchain and AI, can yield disruptive and autonomously operating networks that lead to new economic equilibria and explain how such developments can be explained from the viewpoint of the natural sciences.

The proposed theory of chaordic economics is a grand theory outlining broad and fundamental aspects that need to be further broken down into smaller components and frameworks, labeled as middle-range theories, which lend themselves to rigorous academic inquiry. This will help to analyze, explain, and predict how systems emerge, change, and adapt that are partially chaotic in that they exhibit adaptive and decentralized structures and are partially ordered since they are determined and controlled by underlying protocols and algorithms following predetermined rules. Over time, self-organizing networks (e.g., DAOs) exhibiting the core characteristics outlined in this chapter emerge.

Table 9.4. Research questions for the theory of chaordic economics.

Theory Type	Questions
Analysis and exploration	What are the core characteristics of chaordic economics?
	How are the core characteristics of chaordic economics related to each other?
	How do external factors (e.g., technology, regulation, and culture) shape the emergence of chaordic economics?
	What are the fundamental values underlying the theory of chaordic economics?
Explanation	Why does a specific type of behavior emerge in chaordic economics?
	How can emergent behavior be modeled in chaordic economics?
	How do businesses adapt to chaordic economics?
	What role do feedback loops play in the shaping of chaordic economics?
Prediction	How will chaordic economic systems evolve if the environmental conditions change?
	What factors predict the success or failure of chaordic economics?
Design and action	How can systems be designed that follow the principles of chaordic economics?
	How can systems be deployed that follow the principles of chaordic economics?
	How can systems be controlled that follow the principles of chaordic economics?

Following the classification by Gregor (2006), we suggest theory-based inquiries for the proposed theory of chaordic economics. Table 9.4 shows exemplary research questions as starting points for rigorous academic research. Ideally, and in line with the multidisciplinary nature of chaordic economics, these questions are tackled by multidisciplinary teams, bringing insights from economics, sociology, computer science, information systems, systems science, and business administration. These questions are meant to analyze existing systems transitioning into a chaordic state, explain the occurrence of specific events and transformations, and predict future developments based on technological developments. Additionally, the theory of chaordic economics can be used as a guiding framework (i.e., a worldview) to design and implement systems that exhibit desired properties and to steer future developments.

From a practitioner's point of view, the theory of chaordic economics provides multiple angles for managers and policymakers to investigate and better understand current economic and social transformations and to act accordingly. A comprehensive systemic perspective allows them to simultaneously consider disruptive forces and acknowledge the complex behavior of emerging systems. Allowing better systems to emerge might imply that policymakers relinquish control, which, presumably, will be a huge mental hurdle for those in power. In this regard, it has to be acknowledged that the theory of chaordic economics has a strong normative component, originating in Dee Hock's initial quest to find out how organizations *ought* to be. Furthermore, it is crucial to emphasize that all important components must be considered simultaneously, and the neglect of fundamental underlying values (e.g., the right to privacy) cannot be justified by exclusively focusing on parts of the whole, such as economic efficiency.

9.6 Conclusion, Limitations, and Further Research

In this chapter, we have proposed the theory of chaordic economics, which is based on the fundamental assumption that the flow, processing, and use of information are changing and that this development will significantly affect businesses, economies, and societies. Global economic and societal systems are not static but constantly evolving, and technologies are major enablers and drivers in this development. We postulate that this will lead to the emergence of chaordic systems, which can adjust to external changes through adaptation and self-organization while concurrently maintaining stability and structure. Chaordic economics helps to establish adaptive businesses, economies, and societies that can thrive in constantly changing environments and can adjust to technological, market, and political changes.

Despite promising economic and societal gains, this transformation will presumably face powerful and stubborn opponents. Individuals in command will strive to control the uncontrollable, and technology-enhanced supervision capabilities can support them to remain in power. The devastating effects of futile administration and compulsive control are by no means new phenomena and have been explained decades ago pointedly and humorously by Parkinson (1958). He described how strict hierarchies cause a lack of innovation and how overburdened bureaucracies stifle innovation and employees' motivation by creating useless work and control structures with no purpose other than bolstering the egos of those in control. Parkinson used the example of the British Royal Navy, in which bureaucracy increased over time even though the actual fleet size and the number of sailors decreased. His warnings are even more relevant during times when mindless Excel sheets can serve no purpose other than cementing existing power structures. In this regard, we believe that chaordic systems represent a development that has long begun and will be hard to stop.

Our conceptual research faces a couple of limitations that present a roadmap for future research. First, we acknowledge that technologies other than AI and blockchain might also play an important role in shaping future developments. For example, the Internet of Things, robotics, or quantum computing might also serve as disruptive technological drivers. Second, numerous criticisms and challenges exist regarding AI and blockchain, both individually and in their interplay. For example, both technologies can be notoriously energy-intensive (in the case of blockchain, this pertains mainly to the use of PoW as a consensus mechanism), but there are also other issues such as scalability, interoperability, security, privacy, and potentially regulatory issues, calling for extensive and structured future investigations (Treiblmaier *et al.*, 2021).

In summary, we suggest that the theory of chaordic economics presents a promising starting point for researchers and practitioners who wish to better understand existing systems, their transformations, and the potential to shape them in a way that fosters humanity rather than simply remaining outside observers of these developments.

References

Adel, K., Elhakeem, A., and Marzouk, M. 2023. "Blockchain and artificial intelligence: Scientometric analysis and visualization." *IEEE Access* 11:137911–28. https://doi.org/10.1109/ACCESS.2023.3339752.

Albert, R. and Barabási, A.-L. 2002. "Statistical mechanics of complex networks." *Reviews of Modern Physics* 74(1): 47–97. https://doi.org/10.1103/RevModPhys.74.47.

Beniger, J. R. 1986. *The Control Revolution: Technological and Economic Origins of the Information Society*. 1st edn. Cambridge, Mass.: Harvard University Press.

Coase, R. H. 1937. "The nature of the firm." *Economica* 4(16): 386–405.

Edwards, M. G. 2014. "A metatheoretical evaluation of chaordic systems thinking." *Systems Research and Behavioral Science* 31(2): 160–80. https://doi.org/10.1002/sres.2193.

Gregor, S. 2006. "The nature of theory in information systems." *MIS Quarterly* 30(3): 611–42.

Hock, D. 2005. *One from Many: VISA and the Rise of Chaordic Organization*. 2nd edn. San Francisco, CA: Berrett-Koehler Publishers.

Kahneman, D. and Tversky, A. 1979. "Prospect theory: An analysis of decision under risk." *Econometrica* 47(2): 263–291.

Keynes, J. M. 1936. *The General Theory of Employment, Interest and Money*. London, Great Britain: Macmillan. https://shapero.com/en-us/products/keynes-general-theory-employment-1936-first-edition-109128.

Laudon, K. and Laudon, J. 2020. *Management Information Systems: Managing the Digital Firm*. 16th edn. Harlow: Pearson.

Lorenz, E. N. 1963. "Deterministic nonperiodic flow." *Journal of the Atmospheric Sciences* 20(2): 130–141.

Meadows, D. H. 2008. *Thinking in Systems: A Primer*. White River Junction, Vermont: Chelsea Green Publishing. https://www.amazon.com/Thinking-Systems-Donella-H-Meadows/dp/1603580557.

Mises, L. V. 1949. *Human Action: A Treatise on Economics*. New Haven, Connecticut: Yale University Press.

Nash, J. 1951. "Non-cooperative games." *Annals of Mathematics* 54(2): 286–95. https://doi.org/10.2307/1969529.

Nguyen Thanh, B., Son, H. X., and Vo, D. T. H. 2024. "Blockchain: The economic and financial institution for autonomous AI?" *Journal of Risk and Financial Management* 17(2): 54. https://doi.org/10.3390/jrfm17020054.

Noto La Diega, G. 2022. "The internet of contracts." In La Diega, G. N. (ed.), *Internet of Things and the Law: Legal Strategies for Consumer-Centric Smart Technologies*. London, UK: Routledge, pp. 117–83. https://doi.org/10.4324/9780429468377-4.

Parkinson, C. N. 1958. *Parkinson's Law or the Pursuit of Progress*. 1st edn. London, UK: John Murray.

Ressi, D., Romanello, R., Piazza, C., and Rossi, S. 2024. "AI-enhanced blockchain technology: A review of advancements and opportunities."

Journal of Network and Computer Applications 225(May): 103858. https://doi.org/10.1016/j.jnca.2024.103858.

Russell, S. J. and Norvig, P. 1995. *Artificial Intelligence: A Modern Approach*. Upper Saddle River, NJ: Prentice-Hall. https://en.wikipedia.org/w/index.php?title=Artificial_Intelligence:_A_Modern_Approach&oldid=1257746703.

Shannon, C. E. 1948. "A mathematical theory of communication." *The Bell System Technical Journal* 27(3): 379–423. https://doi.org/10.1002/j.1538-7305.1948.tb01338.x.

Swan, M. 2019. "Blockchain economic networks: Economic network theory—Systemic risk and blockchain technology." In Treiblmaier, H. and Beck, R. (eds.), *Business Transformation through Blockchain I*. Cham, Switzerland: Palgrave Macmillan, pp. 3–45.

Swan, M. and dos Santos, R. P. 2020. *Smart Network Field Theory: The Technophysics of Blockchain and Deep Learning*. London, United Kingdom: World Scientific. http://arxiv.org/abs/1810.09514.

TraceLabs. 2024. "Verifiable Internet for Artificial Intelligence: The Convergence of Crypto, Internet and AI." https://origintrail.io/documents/Verifiable_Internet_for_Artificial_Intelligence_whitepaper_v3_pre_publication.pdf.

Treiblmaier, H. 2018. "The impact of the blockchain on the supply chain: A theory-based research framework and a call for action." *Supply Chain Management: An International Journal* 2(6): 545–59.

Treiblmaier, H., Swan, M., de Filippi, P., Lacity, M. C., Hardjono, T., and Kim, H. 2021. "What's next in blockchain research?—An identification of key topics using a multidisciplinary perspective." *ACM SIGMIS Database: The DATABASE for Advances in Information Systems* 52(1): 27–52. https://doi.org/10.1145/3447934.3447938.

van Eijnatten, F. M. and Putnik, G. 2004. "Chaos, complexity, learning, and the learning organization: Towards a chaordic enterprise." *The Learning Organization* 11:418–29. https://doi.org/10.1108/09696470410548782.

Wiener, N. 1948. *Cybernetics or Control and Communication in the Animal and the Machine*. 1st edn. New York, NY, US: The Technology Press/Wiley.

https://doi.org/10.1142/9781800618664_0011

Chapter 10

Flow Dynamics: Advanced Network Science for Supply and Cryptocurrency Remittance Networks

Hiroko Yamano[*,‡] **and Takayuki Mizuno**[†,§]
[*]*Institute for Future Initiatives, The University of Tokyo, Tokyo, Japan*
[†]*National Institute of Informatics, Tokyo, Japan*
[‡]*yamano@ifi.u-tokyo.ac.jp*
[§]*mizuno@nii.ac.jp*

Abstract
The increasing complexity and uncertainty of the global marketplace underscore the need to view supply chains not merely as linear chains of supplier–customer relationships but as complex networks that include both direct and indirect distant linkages. As efforts to build resilient supply chains advance, understanding the non-trivial impact of distant transaction partners and their influence within these long and complex supply networks becomes critical. This chapter analyzes flows within supply and cryptocurrency remittance networks to develop a network control model for detecting and mitigating unethical transactions hidden within the routes. By examining the expanding scale of corporate strategy and the potential of blockchain technology in supply networks, this study proposes an advanced network science perspective to navigate long-distance supply networks and foster socially responsible markets in the face of ongoing global challenges.

Keywords: Supply Chain, Inter-Firm Networks, Financial Ecosystem, Illicit Transactions.

10.1 Introduction

Supply chains are shaped by corporate decisions on sourcing materials and components essential for production. Firms strategically optimize procurement, quality management, and distribution to enhance competitiveness. The pursuit of efficiency and cost minimization—through access to inexpensive labor and facilities—has driven the expansion of long-distance global supply chains, enabled by technological advances in international transportation. However, such optimization strategies rely on relatively stable market conditions, and recent crises have highlighted their vulnerability in the face of unforeseen market fluctuations and exogenous shocks (OECD, 2021; White_House, 2023). For instance, the COVID-19 pandemic caused severe supply chain disruptions, demonstrating how factory shutdowns and delays in one region could ripple across industries on a global scale. Similarly, the Great East Japan Earthquake highlighted how supply chain collapse can have widespread economic consequences, affecting not only companies in disaster areas but also their direct and indirect trading partners (Carvalho *et al.*, 2021). These cases underscore the risks embedded in highly intertwined supply chains and the need to monitor and enhance supply chain resilience to mitigate unexpected market shocks.

Recent sustainability concerns and policy changes related to trade, environment, and human rights, coupled with increasing unpredictable exogenous shocks such as natural disasters, pandemics, and geopolitical crises, are increasing supply uncertainty. In the United States, the Uyghur Forced Labor Prevention Act of 2021 prohibits the importation of products mined, produced, or manufactured in the Xinjiang Uyghur Autonomous Region. In addition, in 2022, the European Commission published a proposal for a Directive on Corporate Sustainability Due Diligence, which would require large companies in the EU that meet certain revenue and employee thresholds to conduct due diligence to identify and prevent adverse human rights and environmental impacts. This directive was further extended in 2024 to include companies outside the EU that meet the same revenue criteria in order to prevent adverse impacts arising along their chain of activities (The European Parliament and the Council of the European Union, 2024). Notably, these policies target not only direct suppliers but also indirect suppliers within the supply chain.

In addition to these international regulatory updates, changes in national trade policies have had a significant impact on supply chains. Through policies such as trade blocking, tariff increases, and the elimination of preferential treatment, supply chains can be used as a weapon in international trade disputes. Some links are dominated by suppliers in one country, increasing interdependencies and risks to economies. In particular, weak links in the complex network are difficult to detect and may only become apparent after a threat occurs (Farrell & Newman, 2022).

The global expansion of complex and highly fluctuating supply chains is exposing the limitations of traditional linear pipeline models of supply chain management, which assume direct trading relationships between upstream and downstream orders (Papert *et al.*, 2024; Stevens & Johnson, 2016). A shift is underway to view supply chains as multi-tiered supply networks that include indirect links across higher-order tiers, reflecting broader business perspectives and collaborative management (Stevens & Johnson, 2016). The problem, however, is that the impact of distant trading partners in supply networks is not immediately apparent, and this has become more acute with the growing concern and focus on building resilient trading relationships, as described above. Most companies know little more than their direct suppliers and, in some cases, their suppliers' suppliers, i.e., second-tier suppliers (European Commission *et al.*, 2020; Farrell & Newman, 2022; Pichler *et al.*, 2023; Shao *et al.*, 2018). While companies may be aware of their business partners several hops ahead in the supply network, this knowledge remains limited to the scope of an ego network centered around a focal company (Ahuja, 2000; Lavie, 2006; Vanhaverbeke *et al.*, 2009), so the influence between higher-tier suppliers is largely unknown. Thus, while exogenous risk factors can be identified, it is not clear how they propagate through the network or what roles and functions the connectivity patterns play.

This chapter first outlines the theoretical perspectives on long-distance supply chains, expanding from the micro to the macro scale. We then highlight the increased risks posed by long-distance operations, i.e., unintended involvement in illicit transactions hidden in the long chains, in addition to intentional attacks targeting users and cash. We discuss how these risks can be effectively managed by capturing flows in the networks. By analyzing the structural positioning of unethical accounts in cryptocurrency and supply networks, we propose a network-based approach to detect and mitigate hidden illicit transactions, offering a solution to improve the health of financial ecosystems.

10.2 Expanding Scales in Corporate Strategies

10.2.1 *Theories on corporate resource locations: From internal capabilities to network advantages*

Corporate competitive strategies have expanded their scale from the pursuit of the advantages of a single firm's internal resources to strategies that consider relationships between firms and wider networks as resources. The resource-based view (RBV), which seeks the source of competitive advantage in the resource heterogeneity owned by a single company, emphasized core competencies that are unique capabilities of a company and are not easily transferable (Barney, 1986; Peteraf, 1993; Prahalad & Hamel, 1990; Wernerfelt, 1984). Unlike the RBV theory, which focuses on the accumulation and differentiation of internal resources within individual companies, the relational view considers critically important resources to be located beyond the boundaries of companies. The resources and capabilities held by partner companies change over time, and mutual dependencies are formed through co-evolution via inter-firm collaborations. Although relational theory regards the relationships between firms themselves as assets, emphasizing the external knowledge and complementary resources that become accessible through connections with partner firms, it focuses on the direct dyadic links between firms, or, in other words, the microscopic structure of the network.

Network resource theory (NRT) further extends the RBV by considering direct and indirect links between companies as resources that serve as a medium for knowledge (Gulati, 1999; Lavie, 2006). Effective information exchange between firms occurs not only through immediate network ties of direct trading partners but also through indirect ties via shared partners or two-step leverage of common neighbors (Gulati, 1999). NRT focuses on the macroscopic structure of networks, such as network density, structural holes, and core-periphery structures, demonstrating that the unique structural patterns in which firms are situated within the network provide inimitable resources that generate competitive advantages (Gulati *et al.*, 2000). While relational theory focuses on the quality of individual inter-firm relationships, NRT emphasizes the values of the entire network properties, capturing a wider and more complex connectivity of inter-firm networks.

According to NRT, the cultivation of close and long-term relationships with other companies can yield benefits, such as fostering trust. However, it should be noted that there are also arguments that suggest excessive embeddedness in networks can lead to negative lock-in, impeding the capacity to generate innovation (Grabher, 1993; Gulati, 1995; Gulati *et al.*, 2000; Uzzi, 1996, 1999). Supply chain flexibility and agility have a positive impact on firm performance, such as growth, market share, and technological exploration and deepening (Ambulkar *et al.*, 2015; Chan *et al.*, 2017; Choi *et al.*, 2001; Vickery *et al.*, 1999; Zhou & Wu, 2010). Agile supply chains have been shown to outperform less agile competitors in turbulent business environments (Christopher & Peck, 2004; Erol *et al.*, 2010; Yusuf *et al.*, 2014). By increasing supply chain agility and building in the redundancy and flexibility of networks that enable alternative trading partners to be secured, companies can gain rapid recovery capabilities (resilience) (Hohenstein *et al.*, 2015; Sheffi & Jr., 2005). As knowledge specialization and diversification increase, loosely coupled network connections that bring in external knowledge become more important. In today's open business environment, companies tend to innovate not in isolation, but by integrating and sharing knowledge from both internal and external resources. As a result, organizations need to go beyond managing internal knowledge and develop capabilities to capture and disseminate insights by leveraging assets that serve as potential sources of information (Chesbrough & Haas, 2006; Chesbrough, 2003).

10.2.2 *Revisiting externalities: Beyond firm-level strategies to ecosystems*

Given the recognition that the source of innovation is shifting toward clusters that facilitate knowledge exchange and technology transfer among different actors, innovation research must shift its focus from the microstructures of individual firm resources and inter-firm relationships to the larger units of networks (O'Reilly & Tushman, 2013).

The "external" sources of knowledge and technology range from "weak signals at the periphery" of the organization (Day & Schoemaker, 2000; Day & Schoemaker, 2005), "non-redundant" alliance partners (Vanhaverbeke *et al.*, 2009), and "external information" outside the firm (Cohen & Levinthal, 1990) to "extra-cluster knowledge" (Giuliani & Bell, 2005) and "distant knowledge" (Enkel & Heil, 2014; Gassmann *et al.*, 2011; Jansen *et al.*, 2006; Kalogerakis *et al.*, 2010; March, 1991), discussed across various scales. Collaboration across heterogeneous fields is often the result of "long-distance partnerships" (Nishiguchi, 2007), which are different from existing business relationships and can be a catalyst for structural change and value creation within industries. Intermediaries in supply chains facilitate these long-distance relationships between different firms and clusters, which were previously difficult to realize, by leveraging external knowledge for market exploration and cluster evolution (Yamano & Sakata, 2022).

The increasing unpredictability of external shocks, such as natural disasters, pandemics, and international conflicts, has served as a stark reminder of the growing global interdependencies in supply chains. Growing global concerns over issues such as global warming and human rights have led to changes in international regulations aimed at building sustainable supply chains, prompting a shift toward supply network strategies based on broader business perspectives and collaborative management. In this context, the concept of business ecosystems, in which firms interact and co-evolve (Moore, 1993, 2006), has gained renewed attention in recent years. This approach contrasts with individual firm strategy models based on competitive advantage, such as the RBV, which focuses on a firm's unique core competencies; relational theories, which emphasize the complementarity of inter-firm relationships; and NRT, which emphasizes a wider range of network characteristics. The business ecosystem perspective emphasizes the unique roles of firms based on their heterogeneous capabilities and highlights the interdependencies within a network of firms. It suggests that critical competition occurs not between individual firms, but across networks of firms as ecosystems based on the symbiotic relationship of a community of firms sharing a common fate, competing and cooperating with each other (Iansiti & Clark, 1994; Iansiti & Levien, 2004; Moore, 1993). This ecosystem-based strategy is being revisited as a leading vision for building new supply chain models. It responds to global trends such as the digitization and virtualization of supply chains, along with increasing awareness of sustainability, facilitated by the advancement of enabling information technologies such as blockchain (Papert *et al.*, 2024).

10.3 Approaches to Mitigate the Risks of Increasing Distance in Transaction Networks

10.3.1 *Risks in long-distance supply chains*

The transition from localized production and sourcing to highly interconnected, long-distance supply networks has enabled firms to optimize resource allocation, diversify suppliers, and enhance competitive advantage. Theoretical perspectives on corporate strategy have evolved from internal resource management to network-based advantages and business ecosystems, highlighting how firms leverage both direct and indirect inter-firm relationships to maximize value creation. However, while inter-firm networks and business ecosystems provide firms with strategic flexibility and knowledge externalities, they also introduce vulnerabilities that arise from the increasing complexity and opacity of multi-tiered relationships.

Long-distance supply chains are a double-edged sword that can amplify both positive and negative fluctuations along their paths (Acemoglu & Tahbaz-Salehi, 2024). The impact of production technology improvements by individual firms can propagate through network flows via multiplier effects and thus be amplified as the supply chain expands, accelerating the reduction of product prices and the pace of national growth (McNerney *et al.*, 2022). On the other hand, it also amplifies negative shocks, such as the disruption of trading relationships due to disasters (Acemoglu & Tahbaz-Salehi, 2024; Carvalho *et al.*, 2021). Long-distance supply chains are vulnerable to exogenous shocks and attacks and are also associated with high management costs. The recent tightening of international due diligence requirements further exacerbates this problem. In addition, as the development of fine-grained global supply chain data is still underway (Pichler *et al.*, 2023), it is currently a challenge to accurately track the actual flows between distant companies connected in the network.

10.3.2 *Blockchain applications for supply chain management*

Due to their intricate and expansive nature, along with the growing need to address sustainability issues, modern supply chains are increasingly difficult to manage and control. Blockchain technology has the potential to tackle this issue by transforming supply chain management practices, leveraging its distributed digital ledger to ensure transparency, traceability, and security (Cole *et al.*, 2019; Treiblmaier, 2018; Wang *et al.*, 2019). It can be seen as a foundational technology for the business ecosystem that requires gradual adoption (Iansiti & Lakhani, 2017). While still in its infancy, various applications of blockchain in supply chain management have been explored, including its potential to reduce transaction costs and track supply chain flows (Cole *et al.*, 2019; Iansiti & Lakhani, 2017; Upadhyay *et al.*, 2021).

The transparency and traceability of blockchain, which creates an immutable digital record of transactions and is shared among multiple parties, is one of the main reasons for its application as a solution to address long-distance supply chains (Ahmed *et al.*, 2023). Blockchain can take over the role of third-party logistics distribution tasks, which increases supply chain complexity by adding external stakeholders and reducing transparency (Tiwari *et al.*, 2023). It has the potential to reduce the need for intermediaries or sub-suppliers, which facilitates operations in international sourcing and complex product flows by enabling direct communication through peer-to-peer transmissions (Cole *et al.*, 2019; Iansiti & Lakhani, 2017). By monitoring product flows in supply chains, blockchain technology can support the circular economy and contribute to cleaner production (Upadhyay *et al.*, 2021), increase resilience through collaboration via smart contracts (Lohmer *et al.*, 2020), and improve visibility to mitigate the risk of supply chain disruptions (Dong *et al.*, 2022).

10.3.3 *Risks hidden in the path of blockchain and supply chain*

While blockchain has the potential to track supply chain flows and improve accountability, the risks associated with long-distance networks are not limited to supply chain management. The decentralized nature of blockchain also poses challenges for financial transactions in virtual asset networks. The longer the cryptocurrency transaction paths, the greater the risk that illicit users may be present somewhere along the way. Several types of crimes have been reported in decentralized finance based on blockchain technology, ranging from direct attacks on users and cash exploitation of DeFi vulnerabilities (L. Zhou *et al.*, 2023) to indirect phishing attacks by intermediaries impersonating legitimate users (Carpentier-Desjardins *et al.*, 2023; Phillips & Wilder, 2020). The anonymity of peer-to-peer allows transactions to occur without intermediaries, which can lead to uncontrolled money laundering and financial crime (Wronka, 2023). However, there are also risks that are not related to such intentional attacks, i.e., the risks of being indirectly involved in illicit transactions within the networks. Despite the fact that blockchain technology guarantees transparency and traceability, in reality, connections with distant users are rarely considered in actual cryptocurrency transactions. This situation is similar to problems in supply chain management, where companies rarely have a comprehensive understanding of their upper-tier or deep-tier suppliers (Dong *et al.*, 2022). In recent years, as accountability for all flows along the supply chain is demanded, these types of unintended involvement risks are among the most urgent to address.

In the following sections, we present two practical solutions to these unintended risks posed by long-distance transaction networks: an approach that detects and mitigates unethical transactions hidden in the routes of virtual currency remittance networks and supply chains.

10.4 Unethical Transactions Hidden in Virtual Currency Remittance Networks

10.4.1 *Overview of Bitcoin and unethical remittance routes*

Bitcoin is a decentralized digital currency proposed in 2008 by Satoshi Nakamoto, characterized by its operation without a central authority. Bitcoin transactions are recorded on a blockchain, making tampering difficult. However, as the real owner information of the sender and receiver is not recorded, a certain degree of anonymity is maintained. While this anonymity increases the freedom of remittances, it also creates possibilities for misuse, such as illegal transactions and money laundering carried out under the cloak of anonymity. Furthermore, even if a typical, well-intentioned account never directly transacts with an illegal account, there may be cases where their transaction partners secretly deal with illegal accounts, leaving no way to discover this fact and resulting in inadvertent involvement in illicit financial flows.

For example, consider a user making a legitimate payment on a shopping website using Bitcoin. Subsequently, the site operator may use part of the funds for an online casino, and the casino might then send some of that money to an illegal marketplace such as Silk Road. Even if some of the funds ultimately end up flowing to an illegal account, the original user remains unaware of this. Thus, in the Bitcoin remittance network, legal transactions can unintentionally support unethical activities.

In this chapter, we introduce a part of the study by Jun *et al.* (2025), which analyzes the behavior of specific account groups using Bitcoin transaction data from 2009 to 2018. This research focuses on accounts related to online casinos and darknet markets like Silk Road, tracing the flow of Bitcoin to these accounts to uncover how routes for sending funds to unethical accounts are formed.

10.4.2 *Construction of the remittance network*

First, we construct the remittance network based on Bitcoin transaction history. In Bitcoin, it is common for a single user to manage multiple wallet addresses. Analyzing address-to-address relationships alone would not yield an accurate network. Therefore, we begin by applying methods to aggregate wallets presumed to belong to the same user. Specifically, we use two heuristics: (1) the multi-input heuristic (Reid & Harrigan, 2013; Ron & Shamir, 2013) and (2) the change address heuristic (Meiklejohn *et al.*, 2013). The former assumes that multiple addresses used together as inputs in a single transaction belong to the same user; the latter exploits the mechanism by which change is sent back to the sender's address—or a different one—during a transaction.

After applying these heuristics, we construct the remittance network. In this network, nodes represent users and edges represent remittance relationships between users. The edges have direction, indicating that Bitcoin was sent from one user to another. We assign each edge a weight corresponding to the ratio of the amount sent from one node to another relative to the sender node's total remittances over the observation period, thereby accounting for variations in individual nodes' remittance amounts. Based on this network, we analyze how Bitcoin flows and examine the characteristics of particular communities.

In this study, we used a dataset comprising the top 90% of remittance amounts in January 2017. The dataset is aggregated at the user level. The network consists of 5,750,237 nodes and 11,623,645 edges, forming an extensive remittance network. This large-scale dataset allows for a detailed analysis of how Bitcoin transactions are conducted and how funds are exchanged among different users.

10.4.3 *Community detection with Infomap*

Infomap (also known as the Map Equation) is a community detection algorithm based on information theory. It identifies community structures by optimally compressing the paths of a random walker moving through the network (Rosvall & Bergstrom, 2008). The algorithm uses information entropy to minimize the description length of the random walker's path through the network.

Concretely, it encodes the random walker's trajectory on the network, and by minimizing the average code length of this trajectory, the algorithm detects the network's community structure. By suitably partitioning the network into communities, the random walker tends to remain within particular communities for extended periods, which leads to more efficient encoding.

Infomap expresses the average code length of a network partition M as follows:

$$L(M) = q_{\curvearrowright} H(\mathcal{Q}) + \sum_{i=1} p^{i}_{\circlearrowright} H(\mathscr{P}^{i}), \tag{10.1}$$

where $q_{\curvearrowright}$ is the inter-community transition probability, $H(\mathcal{Q})$ is the entropy of inter-community transitions, $p^{i}_{\circlearrowright}$ is the intra-community transition probability, and $H(\mathscr{P}^i)$ is the entropy of intra-community transitions.

The first term of the equation corresponds to the average information required to encode transitions between communities, and the second term represents the sum of the average information required to encode transitions within each community. By minimizing these terms, Infomap maximizes the overall encoding efficiency for the network, thereby obtaining an optimal community partition.

The Infomap algorithm begins by assigning each node to its own community and then iteratively merges adjacent nodes or communities if this merging reduces the average code length. Repeating this process converges on a solution that yields the optimal community structure.

A key advantage of Infomap is that it naturally handles directed and weighted edges in a network. This is particularly effective in directed networks with monetary flows, such as remittance networks, where direction and weight capture the flow of funds. While modularity-based methods are better suited to undirected, unweighted networks, Infomap excels in analyzing directed, weighted networks.

For these reasons, we adopt the Infomap algorithm for community detection in the remittance network. The algorithm's capacity to consider the flow of funds through the network enables us to examine community structures in a way that helps reveal how unethical users are concentrated in specific communities.

10.4.4 *Distribution of unethical accounts and statistical analysis*

In this section, we statistically analyze the distribution of users involved in unethical transactions within the Bitcoin remittance network, demonstrating that such users are concentrated in particular communities. Here, "unethical users" refers to those who either sent money to or received money from online casinos.

The operation or use of online casinos is illegal in roughly one-third of countries worldwide, and in many other countries, it occupies a gray area due to a lack of regulatory oversight. To obtain account information for online casinos, we crawled two major Bitcoin-related sites—BitcoinTalk (BitcoinTalk, 2022) and WalletExplorer (WalletExplorer, 2022)—and identified 306 distinct users associated with online casinos. As of January 2017, 194,358 users conducted transactions (either sending or receiving) with these online casinos.

As a comparison group, we also gathered user data from typical shopping sites. Using WalletExplorer, we identified 93 shopping site accounts and a total of 433,362 users who utilized these sites. We then analyzed Bitcoin transaction histories and extracted community structures to determine how these users are distributed across the network and how they relate to each other.

Using the Infomap algorithm, we detected a total of 382,896 communities within the remittance network. Among these, 278 communities contain over 600 users. Within these communities, the share of online casino users is 1.7% of all nodes, whereas the share of shopping site users is 4.4% of all nodes.

These users are not uniformly distributed across the network but instead cluster in specific communities. For instance, some communities have extremely high concentrations of online casino users—96.0%, 88.5%, and 69.1%—while others show similarly high concentrations of shopping site users—57.6%, 64.6%, and 71.1%. The likelihood of these extreme concentrations occurring under a Poisson process assumption is each less than 0.000001%, signifying statistically significant clustering.

To statistically test the clustering tendencies of online casino users and shopping site users, we compared the proportions of the two user types within each community. The correlation coefficient between these two user proportions was 0.027, indicating that they are distributed in the remittance network without correlation, clustering independently in different communities.

From these findings, it is evident that unethical users in the Bitcoin remittance network do not appear randomly but tend to aggregate in specific communities. Such communities imply strong internal transactional links among unethical users and fewer connections to external networks, suggesting that community-based strategies could be effective in promoting a healthier remittance environment.

10.4.5 *Conclusion and measures to enhance the health of remittance networks*

In Section 10.4, we analyzed the Bitcoin remittance network and statistically demonstrated that unethical users are concentrated in particular communities. Because numerous types of users coexist within the same connected component, even those acting in good faith could indirectly supply funds to unethical users via complex transaction paths. This poses a challenge inherent to decentralized virtual currencies, which do not allow for the same degree of oversight or regulation that exists in traditional bank-operated systems. Therefore, developing control mechanisms for remittances based on the network's unique properties becomes essential for effective measures.

Our findings suggest that leveraging the network structure—where unethical users cluster in specific communities—holds the key to promoting a healthier remittance network. One concrete approach is to account for the shortest path distance to these communities rife with unethical users when deciding whom to transact with. By prioritizing users located farther from unethical communities, law-abiding users can limit indirect flows of funds into illegal activities. Implementing this strategy requires developing remittance applications that visualize path distances on the network and recommend more ethical transaction routes.

If such a recommendation system were to be widely adopted, it would significantly reduce the risk that well-intentioned users inadvertently finance illegal activities. For instance, when sending funds, an automated evaluation of the recipient's shortest path to unethical communities could trigger alerts if that distance is short, guiding user behavior toward safer options. Over time, as more users adopt this system, inflows to unethical groups would be curtailed, making it increasingly difficult for illicit communities to circulate funds.

By implementing these measures, the overall health of the virtual currency remittance network could be improved, helping to suppress illicit transactions and money laundering. Given the challenges of regulating a decentralized network, it is generally more practical and effective to influence user behavior than to rely solely on blanket policies from a central authority. Moving forward, additional steps such as further enhancing transparency in remittance networks and raising awareness among users should be pursued in parallel to reinforce these efforts.

10.5 Unethical Companies Hidden in Supply Chain Network Paths

10.5.1 *Construction of the supply chain network*

In this section, we construct a supply chain network using inter-company transaction data obtained from the S&P Capital IQ platform. We model the supply chain network by treating each company as a node and each business relationship (customer–supplier) as a directed edge, connecting companies that directly transact with one another in a chain-like fashion. This approach makes it possible to observe not only first-tier suppliers at the upstream side but also second- and third-tier suppliers and nth-tier customers on the downstream side. Using two years of data from 2013 and 2014, the resulting network covers 423,024 companies across 159 industry sectors in 217 countries, forming a massive structure.

One of the key characteristics confirmed in this network is its scale-free property. In other words, a small number of "hub" companies have an exceptionally large number of transaction partners, while most other companies are connected to only a limited number of partners. Because of these hub companies, any two companies in the world can be reached by about six intermediary transactions, forming a highly interconnected network. This also implies that exerting control over a few major hub companies can have a substantial impact on the entire supply chain. As discussed later in this chapter, this point is crucial when considering measures to address unethical companies.

10.5.2 *Identification of unethical companies and analysis of financial impacts*

To identify unethical companies in the network, we used Dow Jones' Adverse Media Entities dataset. This dataset compiles negative news coverage of companies around the world, including their names, dates of media reports, and the categories of reported wrongdoing or scandals (e.g., management fraud, product or service-related issues, and legal violations among a total of 17 categories). By comparing this dataset against 2014 records, we flagged 21,233 companies in the supply chain network that had been reported for past illegal or unethical conduct. These "unethical companies" include firms cited in the news for serious ethical violations such as environmental destruction, labor exploitation, and corruption, and they are considered risk factors within the supply chain.

Next, we grouped each company based on whether its upstream (supply-side) network included any unethical companies and analyzed the impact on their financial data. Specifically, if a company had at least one flagged firm anywhere among its direct suppliers or further up in its supply chain, we labeled it as having "environmental issues in its supply route." Companies with no such flagged firms at all were labeled as having "no environmental issues in their supply route." Comparing their financial indicators, we observed a significant difference in the cost of goods sold (COGS) ratio—the proportion of COGS relative to sales revenue—as shown in Table 10.1. Companies whose supply chain includes unethical companies displayed a lower average COGS ratio, or in other words, a tendency toward a higher gross margin. This suggests that some companies may be reducing costs by procuring from unethical sources, thereby boosting the gross margin of downstream companies in the supply chain.

However, such cost advantages may disincentivize ethical risk investigations within the supply chain. At the same time, companies that enjoy these advantages could face future risks to their reputation (leading to decreased sales) or be subject to penalties, posing challenges for long-term business sustainability. Consequently, increasing transparency in the upstream supply chain and eliminating

Table 10.1. COGS ratio in the presence or absence of environmental issues in the supply route (manufacturing sector).

Category	No Environmental Issues in Supply Route	Environmental Issues in Supply Route
Food	0.81	0.66
Textiles	0.87	0.69
Furniture	0.80	0.65
Chemicals	0.80	0.56
Electronic goods	0.80	0.64

Note: COGS ratio = cost of goods sold/sales revenue.

transactions with unethical companies can also contribute to long-term financial stability.

10.5.3 *Community structure and distribution of unethical companies*

In this section, we analyze how unethical companies are distributed in the supply chain network and point out, as with unethical users in Bitcoin's remittance network, that they concentrate within specific communities. Unlike the Bitcoin remittance network discussed in Section 10.4, the exact transaction amounts in the supply chain are unknown; therefore, we assign uniform weights to all edges. For our analysis, we again employ the Infomap method described in Section 10.4.3 to extract communities.

This study focuses on 3,601 communities, each with at least 21 companies, counting the number of unethical companies within each community. We then conduct a concentration analysis that compares the actual distribution to a random one assumed by a Poisson process. Poisson distribution is a frequency distribution under the assumption of independent, uniform occurrence of events. If unethical companies were randomly scattered across the network, the number of unethical companies in each community would follow a Poisson distribution. Under this assumption, the mean λ of the Poisson distribution is given by multiplying the ratio of unethical companies in the entire network by the size of each community, with the standard deviation $\sigma = \sqrt{\lambda}$. For a community with x unethical companies, we calculate the following z-score:

$$z = \frac{x - \lambda}{\sigma}. \tag{10.2}$$

As shown in Figure 10.1, the actual distribution deviates significantly from the Poisson expectation. Some communities exhibit a z-score exceeding $+20\sigma$ above the mean, whereas roughly 93% of communities have a z-score of zero or below, indicating that they contain virtually no unethical companies.

These results suggest that unethical companies are not randomly scattered but instead are concentrated in particular communities within the supply chain network. Even so, these unethical communities are not entirely isolated from the rest of the network.

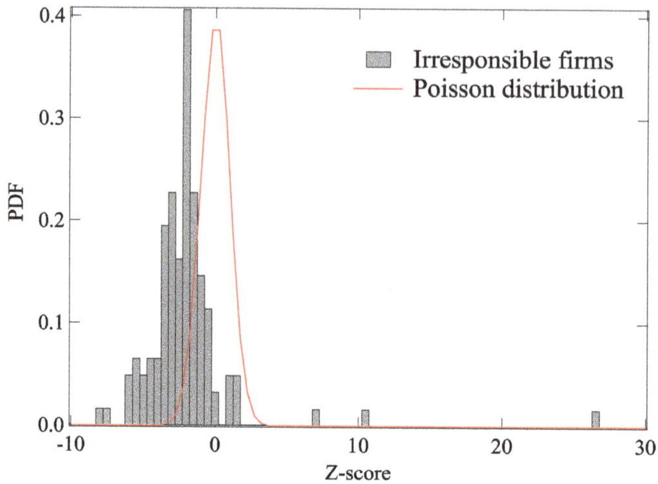

Fig. 10.1. Distribution of unethical companies per community (z-score).

Therefore, stopping the flow of goods from unethical companies or preventing funds from reaching them can be more effectively achieved by targeting the bridging companies that connect these communities to the rest of the network.

10.5.4 *Monitoring unethical communities and the importance of betweenness centrality*

Through network analysis, it is possible to identify the bridging companies that link unethical companies to the rest of the network. Specifically, one can calculate the betweenness centrality of each company based on the shortest paths between all pairs of companies in unethical communities and those in other communities. Focusing on companies with high betweenness centrality highlights those that serve as bridges between unethical company clusters and external, legitimate trading networks.

Although these bridging companies may not themselves engage in unethical practices, they connect "tainted supply sources" to the "clean market." For instance, research by Mizuno *et al.* (2016) shows that in the distribution of conflict minerals from the Democratic Republic of the Congo, companies operating refineries serve as critical nodes, enabling these conflict minerals to flow globally.

Moreover, simulations of conflict mineral diffusion along the network suggest that regulating only a small number of bridging companies can dramatically reduce global damage. Concretely, merely regulating companies that purchase conflict minerals and prompting them to switch suppliers can drastically diminish the worldwide flow of such minerals. This demonstrates that halting problematic flows by controlling the bridging nodes in a supply chain network can indeed be highly effective, supporting the argument for stricter regulation on such key companies.

Hence, while direct regulation or remediation of unethical companies themselves is obviously desirable for improving the overall integrity of the supply chain, many such companies are located abroad or engage in activities that circumvent legal scrutiny, making direct intervention challenging. For this reason, it is crucial to appropriately monitor and manage the bridging companies that link unethical companies to the rest of the supply chain, thereby strengthening the ethical foundations of the entire network.

10.6 Conclusion

This study illustrates the current challenges in managing long and complex supply networks in a volatile global marketplace. In contrast to the urgent demand for resilient and sustainable supply chains across the entire value chain, including both direct and indirect business partners, it remains evident that many companies still lack a comprehensive understanding of their deep-tier suppliers. We addressed this issue by presenting theoretical insights on long-distance supply chains from both micro and macro perspectives. Our investigation underscores the transformation from traditional linear models to multi-tier supply networks and ecosystem-based models, reflecting the contemporary demands for supply chain transparency and control. We highlighted the advances and potential applications of information technologies, such as blockchain, to mitigate supply chain risks.

In addition, recognizing the increased risks associated with long and complex transaction networks, this study proposes a new approach. We present a flow control system designed to detect and mitigate unethical transactions within cryptocurrency and supply networks. This system seeks to preserve the fundamentally decentralized nature of cryptocurrency while addressing the challenges of controlling unethical transactions concentrated in specific communities by recommending routes farther from illicit users. However, the effectiveness of such systems can be limited by the very nature of decentralized technologies, which make it difficult to enforce oversight and accountability. Our control strategy will not work if users don't care about the virtue of the transaction networks; in other words, it requires participants to be aware of being responsible actors in the ecosystem of the cryptocurrency and supply networks.

Supply networks have different levels of granularity that vary across sectors in traceability systems (Ahmed *et al.*, 2023). One potential solution for smart routing in such complex economic networks is to incorporate categorical theory, which provides a formal framework to integrate local interactions into a structured global representation. Mesoscale structures, such as communities, may serve as bridges that mediate micro- and macroscale activities in such systems, making them an important direction for future study.

References

Acemoglu, D. and Tahbaz-Salehi, A. 2024. "The macroeconomics of supply chain disruptions." *The Review of Economic Studies* 91(3): rdae038.

Ahmed, W. A. H., MacCarthy, B. L., and Ahmed, W. A. H. 2023. "Blockchain-enabled supply chain traceability – How wide? How deep?" *International Journal of Production Economics* 263: 108963.

Ahuja, G. 2000. "Collaboration networks, structural holes, and innovation: A longitudinal study." *Administrative Science Quarterly* 45(3): 425–455.

Ambulkar, S., Blackhurst, J., and Grawe, S. 2015. "Firm's resilience to supply chain disruptions: Scale development and empirical examination." *Journal of Operations Management* 33: 111–122.

Barney, J. B. 1986. "Strategic factor markets: Expectations, luck, and business strategy." *Management Science* 32(10): 1231–1241.

Bitcointalk. 2022. "Bitcointalk Forum." https://bitcointalk.org/.

Carpentier-Desjardins, C., Paquet-Clouston, M., Kitzler, S., and Haslhofer, B. 2023. "Mapping the DeFi crime landscape: An evidence-based picture." arXiv:2310.04356.

Carvalho, V. M., Nirei, M., Saito, Y. U., and Tahbaz-Salehi, A. 2021. "Supply chain disruptions: Evidence from the Great East Japan Earthquake." *The Quarterly Journal of Economics* 136(2): 1255–1321.

Chan, A., Ngai, E., and Moon, K. 2017. "The effects of strategic and manufacturing flexibilities and supply chain agility on firm performance in the fashion industry." *European Journal of Operational Research* 259(2): 486–499.

Chesbrough, H. W. 2003. *Open Innovation: The New Imperative for Creating and Profiting from Technology.* Boston, MA: Harvard Business Press.

Chesbrough, H. and Haas, W. A. 2006. "*Open Innovation: A New Paradigm for Understanding Industrial Innovation.*" *Oxford University Press* 400: 0–19.

Choi, T. Y., Dooley, K. J., and Rungtusanatham, M. 2001. "Supply networks and complex adaptive systems: control versus emergence." *Journal of Operations Management* 19(3): 351–366.

Christopher, M. and Peck, H. 2004. "Building the resilient supply chain." *International Journal of Logistics Management* 15(2): 1–13.

Cohen, W. M. and Levinthal, D. A. 1990. "Absorptive capacity: A new perspective on learning and innovation." *Administrative Science Quarterly* 35: 128–152.

Cole, R., Stevenson, M., and Aitken, J. 2019. "Blockchain technology: Implications for operations and supply chain management." *Supply Chain Management: An International Journal* 24(4): 469–483.

Day, G. and Schoemaker, P. 2000. "Avoiding the pitfalls of emerging technologies." *California Management Review* 42(2): 33–38.

Day, G. S. and Schoemaker, P. J. H. 2005. "Scanning the periphery." *Harvard Business Review* 83(11): 135–148.

Dong, L., Qiu, Y., and Xu, F. 2022. "Blockchain-enabled deep-tier supply chain finance." *Manufacturing & Service Operations Management.* https://doi.org/10.1287/msom.2022.1123.

Enkel, E. and Heil, S. 2014. "Preparing for distant collaboration: Antecedents to potential absorptive capacity in cross-industry innovation." *Technovation* 34(4): 242–260.

Erol, O., Sauser, B. J., and Mansouri, M. 2010. "A framework for investigation into extended enterprise resilience." *Enterprise Information Systems* 4(2): 111–136.

European Commission, Directorate-General for Justice and Consumers, Torres-Cortés, F., Salinier, C., Deringer, H., and Bright, C. *et al.* 2020. "Study on due diligence requirements through the supply chain." Publications Office of the European Union.

European Parliament and Council of the European Union. 2024. "Directive on Corporate sustainability due diligence." June 2024. https://eur-lex.europa.eu/eli/dir/2024/1760/oj.

Farrell, H. and Newman, A. L. 2022. "Weak links in finance and supply chains are easily weaponized." *Nature* 605(7909): 219–222.

Gassmann, O., Daiber, M., and Enkel, E. 2011. "The role of intermediaries in cross-industry innovation processes." *R & D Management* 41(5): 457–469.

Giuliani, E. and Bell, M. 2005. "The micro-determinants of meso-level learning and innovation: evidence from a Chilean wine cluster." *Research Policy* 34(1): 47–68.

Grabher, G. 1993. "The weakness of strong ties: The lock-in of regional development in Ruhr area." In *The Embedded Firm. On the Socioeconomics of Industrial Networks*, pp. 255–277.

Gulati, R. 1995. "Social structure and alliance formation patterns: A longitudinal analysis." *Administrative Science Quarterly* 40(4): 619–652.

Gulati, R. 1999. "Network location and learning: The influence of network resources and firm capabilities on alliance formation." *Strategic Management Journal* 20(5): 397–420.

Gulati, R., Nohria, N., and Zaheer, A. 2000. "Strategic networks." *Strategic Management Journal* 21(3): 203–215.

Hohenstein, N.-O., Feisel, E., Hartmann, E., and Giunipero, L. 2015. "Research on the phenomenon of supply chain resilience." *International Journal of Physical Distribution & Logistics Management* 45(1/2): 90–117.

Iansiti, M. and Clark, K. B. 1994. "Integration and dynamic capability: Evidence from product development in automobiles and mainframe computers." *Industrial and Corporate Change* 3(3): 557–605.

Iansiti, M. and Lakhani, K. R. 2017. "The truth about blockchain." *Harvard Business Review*, January 1, 2017. https://hbr.org/2017/01/the-truth-about-blockchain.

Iansiti, M. and Levien, R. 2004. "Strategy as ecology." *Harvard Business Review* 82(3): 68–81.

Jansen, J. J. P., Van Den Bosch, F. A. J., and Volberda, H. W. 2006. "Exploratory innovation, exploitative innovation, and performance: Effects of organizational antecedents and environmental moderators." *Management Science* 52(11): 1661–1674.

Jun, J., Mizuno, T., and Tessone, C. J. 2025. "Socially Responsible Remittance on Bitcoin Networks." Manuscript submitted for publication.

Kalogerakis, K., Lüthje, C., and Herstatt, C. 2010. "Developing innovations based on analogies: Experience from design and engineering consultants." *Journal of Product Innovation Management* 27(3): 418–436.

Lavie, D. 2006. "The competitive advantage of interconnected firms: An extension of the resource-based view." *Academy of Management Review* 31(3): 638–658.

Lohmer, J., Bugert, N., and Lasch, R. 2020. "Analysis of resilience strategies and ripple effect in blockchain-coordinated supply chains: An agent-based simulation study." *International Journal of Production Economics* 228: 107882.

March, J. G. 1991. "Exploration and exploitation in organizational learning." *Organization Science* 2(1): 71–87.

McNerney, J., Savoie, C., Caravelli, F., Carvalho, V. M., and Farmer, J. D. 2022. "How production networks amplify economic growth." *Proceedings of the National Academy of Sciences of the United States of America* 119(1): e2106031118.

Meiklejohn, S., Pomarole, M., Jordan, G., Levchenko, K., McCoy, D., Voelker, G. M., and Savage, S. 2013. "A fistful of bitcoins: characterizing payments among men with no names." In *Proceedings of the 2013 Conference on Internet Measurement Conference*. IMC'13: Internet Measurement Conference, Barcelona, Spain.

Mizuno, T., Ohnishi, T., and Watanabe, T. 2016. "Structure of global buyer-supplier networks and its implications for conflict minerals regulations." *EPJ Data Science* 5: 2.

Moore, J. F. 1993. "Predators and prey: A new ecology of competition." *Harvard Business Review* 71(3): 75–86.

Moore, J. F. 2006. "Business ecosystems and the view from the firm." *The Antitrust Bulletin* 51(1): 31–75.

Nishiguchi, T. 2007. *Global Neighborhoods – Strategy of Successful Organizational Networks*. Tokyo: NTT Publishing.

O'Reilly, C. A. and Tushman, M. L. 2013. "Organizational ambidexterity: Past, present, and future." *The Academy of Management Perspectives* 27(4): 324–338.

OECD. 2021. *OECD SME and Entrepreneurship Outlook 2021*. Paris: OECD Publishing.

Papert, M., Hamper, A., Hoßbach-Zimmermann, N., Schuster, T., Buehler, L., and Pflaum, A. 2024. "Towards the data-driven circular and embedded supply chain: Considerations from an ICT perspective." Working Paper. https://scholar.google.com/citations?view_op=view_citation&hl=en&citation_for_view=7yJ8ir8AAAAJ:B3FOqHPlNUQC.

Peteraf, M. A. 1993. "The cornerstones of competitive advantage: A resource-based view." *Strategic Management Journal* 14(3): 179–191.

Phillips, R. and Wilder, H. 2020. "Tracing cryptocurrency scams: Clustering replicated advance-fee and phishing websites." In *2020 IEEE International Conference on Blockchain and Cryptocurrency (ICBC)*, pp. 1–8.

Pichler, A., Diem, C., Brintrup, A., Lafond, F., Magerman, G., Buiten, G., Choi, T. Y., Carvalho, V. M., Farmer, J. D., and Thurner, S. 2023. "Building an alliance to map global supply networks." *Science* 382(6668): 270–272.

Prahalad, C. K. and Hamel, G. 1990. "The core competence of the corporation." *Harvard Business Review* 68(3): 79–91.

Reid, F. and Harrigan, M. 2013. "An analysis of anonymity in the bitcoin system." In *Security and Privacy in Social Networks*. New York: Springer, pp. 197–223.

Ron, D. and Shamir, A. 2013. "Quantitative analysis of the full bitcoin transaction graph." In *Financial Cryptography and Data Security*. Berlin: Springer, pp. 6–24.

Rosvall, M. and Bergstrom, C. T. 2008. "Maps of random walks on complex networks reveal community structure." *Proceedings of the National Academy of Sciences of the United States of America* 105(4): 1118–1123.

Shao, B. B. M., Shi, Z., Choi, T. Y., and Chae, S. 2018. "A data-analytics approach to identifying hidden critical suppliers in supply networks: Development of nexus supplier index." *Decision Support Systems* 114: 37–48.

Sheffi, Y. and Rice, J. B. 2005. "A supply chain view of the resilient enterprise." *MIT Sloan Management Review* 47(1): 41–48.

Stevens, G. C. and Johnson, M. 2016. "Integrating the Supply Chain ... 25 years on." *International Journal of Physical Distribution & Logistics Management* 46(1): 19–42.

Tiwari, S., Sharma, P., Choi, T.-M., and Lim, A. 2023. "Blockchain and third-party logistics for global supply chain operations: Stakeholders' perspectives and decision roadmap." *Transportation Research Part E: Logistics and Transportation Review* 170: 103012.

Treiblmaier, H. 2018. "Optimal levels of (de)centralization for resilient supply chains." *International Journal of Logistics Management* 29(1): 435–455.

Upadhyay, A., Mukhuty, S., Kumar, V., and Kazancoglu, Y. 2021. "Blockchain technology and the circular economy: Implications for sustainability and social responsibility." *Journal of Cleaner Production* 293: 126130.

Uzzi, B. 1996. "The Sources and Consequences of Embeddedness for the Economic Performance of Organizations: The Network Effect." *American Sociological Review* 61(4): 674–698.

Uzzi, B. 1999. "Embeddedness in the making of financial capital: How social relations and networks benefit firms seeking financing." *American Sociological Review* 64(4): 481–505.

Vanhaverbeke, W., Gilsing, V., Beerkens, B., and Duysters, G. 2009. "The role of alliance network redundancy in the creation of core and non-core technologies." *The Journal of Management Studies* 46(2): 215–244.

Vickery, S. N., Calantone, R., and Dröge, C. 1999. "Supply chain flexibility: An empirical study." *Journal of Supply Chain Management* 35(2): 16–24.

Walletexplorer. 2022. "Wallet explorer." https://www.walletexplorer.com/.

Wang, Y., Han, J. H., and Beynon-Davies, P. 2019. "Understanding blockchain technology for future supply chains: A systematic literature review and research agenda." *Supply Chain Management: An International Journal* 24(1): 62–84.

Wernerfelt, B. 1984. "A resource-based view of the firm." *Strategic Management Journal* 5(2): 171–180.

White House. 2023. "Issue brief: Supply chain resilience." November 30, 2023. https://www.whitehouse.gov/cea/written-materials/2023/11/30/issue-brief-supply-chain-resilience/.

Wronka, C. 2023. "Financial crime in the decentralized finance ecosystem: New challenges for compliance." *Journal of Financial Crime* 30(1): 97–113.

Yamano, H. and Sakata, I. 2022. "Role of brokers and clusters in the inter-firm network dynamics: Evolution map perspective." In *Proceedings of the 2022 Portland International Conference on Management of Engineering and Technology (PICMET)*, pp. 1–10.

Yusuf, Y. Y., Gunasekaran, A., Musa, A., Dauda, M., El-Berishy, N. M., and Cang, S. 2014. "A relational study of supply chain agility, competitiveness and business performance in the oil and gas industry." *International Journal of Production Economics* 147: 531–543.

Zhou, K. and Wu, F. 2010. "Technological capability, strategic flexibility, and product innovation." *Strategic Management Journal* 31(5): 547–561.

Zhou, L., Xiong, X., Ernstberger, J., Chaliasos, S., Wang, Z., Wang, Y., Qin, K., Wattenhofer, R., Song, D., and Gervais, A. 2023. "SoK: Decentralized finance (DeFi) attacks." In *2023 IEEE Symposium on Security and Privacy (SP)*, pp. 2444–2461.

https://doi.org/10.1142/9781800618664_0012

Chapter 11

Monetary Macro Accounting Theory for Blockchain, AI, and Beyond

Renée Menéndez and Viktor Winschel[*,†]
[*]*SRH University of Applied Sciences, Köln, Germany*
[†]*viktor.winschel@srh.de;*
viktor.winschel@gmail.com

Abstract
We develop a monetary macro accounting theory (MoMaT) and its software specification for blockchain, AI, and modernized financial systems. In our money theory, money functions primarily as a medium of payment for obligations and debts, not as a medium of exchange, originating from the temporal misalignment where producers pay suppliers before receiving revenue. MoMaT updates vendor finance strategies (trade credit, inventory financing, and factoring) by applying the legal principles of separation and abstraction to model debt, contracts, property rights, and money. Monetary systems operate at three interconnected levels: micro (division of labor), meso (banking for risk-sharing), and macro (GDP sharing and money issuance). Critical to MoMaT are macro debt relations, and hence the model focuses not on the circulation of money but on debt vortices: the ongoing creation and resolution of financial obligations. The bill of exchange (BoE) acts as a unifying contractual instrument, linking debt processes and monetary issuance across fiat and gold-based systems. A multi-level BoE framework enables liquidity exchange, investments, and endorsements, designed for potential implementation in blockchain smart contracts and AI automation to improve borrowing transparency. Mathematical rigor can be ensured through sheaf theory for invariances between economic levels

and homology theory for monetary policy foundations. Open games can structure macroeconomic analysis with multi-agent models, making MoMaT applicable to blockchain economic theory, monetary policy, and supply chain finance.

Keywords: Supply Chain, Supply Chain Finance, Monetary Theory, Macro Economics.

11.1 Introduction

Economists since Adam Smith in 1776 in *The Wealth of Nations* (Smith, 1776) ask the question: *What is money?* Martin Hellwig, in *The Challenge of Monetary Theory* (Hellwig, 1993), remarks that we have no conceptual foundations for monetary economics and doubts that money is a phenomenon to be discussed within Walrasian market theory.

Since then, new perspectives on the nature of money have been provided. Money emerges in search-theoretic models (Kiyotaki and Wright, 1993) as a medium of exchange. *Money is Memory* (Kocherlakota, 1998) relates to imperfect record-keeping and frictions such as limited enforcement and anonymity. Heterodox approaches like *Modern Money Theory* (Kelton, 2020; Wray, 2012) emphasize the role of states and central banks in defining and managing money beyond a market framework. Walrasian approaches of dynamic stochastic general equilibrium (Gertler and Kiyotaki, 2011) incorporate money as *cash-in-advance* constraints but struggle to account for financial crises. Cryptocurrencies have revived debates on the definition of money, revisiting record-keeping challenges that extend *Money is Memory.* Accordingly, we relate our approach to the concepts in blockchain research. Institutions such as the Bank of England (McLeay *et al.*, 2014) contributed practical insights into money issuance and continue to explore central bank digital currencies (CBDCs) and keep on asking the question, *What is money?* (Starr, 2016).

We develop a monetary macro accounting (MoMa) theory (MoMaT) that functions to facilitate division of labor in decisions on supply chains[1]: *money is needed because production takes time, requiring producers to incur debts to pay suppliers and employees*

[1]See Menéndez (2010) for a precursor of a money theory proposed in this paper.

before receiving payments from customers. Money serves as a *medium of payment* and a *medium of exchange* used in purchase, loan obligation, and disposition contracts involving the transfer of property rights over money or products in economies characterized by division of labor.

MoMaT does not justify relative prices or assign intrinsic value to money. It is based on contractually recorded value judgments made by economic agents. Money functions to record and settle debts arising from contracts but does not itself require having some inherent value for its role in obligation settlements. In order to understand money in debt relations, we look at exchanges involving bookings in two double-entry accounting systems, often termed *quadruple accounting.*[2] We use the term *macro accounting* to distinguish it from traditional *micro or double-entry accounting.* Beyond the micro level of the division of labor and debt networks, we discuss the meso level, where the risk of failing investments is distributed by banks across a portfolio of investments. At the macro level, the GDP is shared, risk is socialized, and money is created, issued, and circulated by central banks. We use the legal principles of *separation* and *abstraction* to clarify conceptual challenges in monetary theory, particularly in situations about debts and payments defining the nature of *money* to be *the physical object* that enables to fullfill the monetary debts of obligation contracts by transferring the property rights on the *object taken to be money.*

MoMaT uses the bill of exchange (BoE) instrument as the principle to understand paper- and gold-based money over the hierarchical levels of economies. A BoE is a formal financial version of the informal *I owe you* contract of a bar beer coaster. We connect to sheaf theory as the mathematics of the transition from local to global structures to model the accounting invariances of assets, equities, and liabilities at the micro level. The meso and macro levels represent invariances in debt and payment relations as sums of receivables and liabilities and payment relations as sums of expenditures and revenues. Open games can implement macro accounting systems, smart contracts, and structural econometric models to analyze macro accounting data. MoMaT applies to monetary policy, supply chain finance, or platform-based demand–supply matching.

---

[2]See United Nations (2010) for a quadruple *System of National Accounts 2008.*

11.2 Microeconomics

Macro accounting records networks of debts in economies characterized by division of labor. To understand them, we use the legal principles of separation and abstraction from the German Civil Code (*Bürgerliches Gesetzbuch*, BGB). They delineate fundamental concepts such as claims, receivables, debts, liabilities, money, and payments.

The *separation principle* asserts that the obligation contract, which establishes a debt relation, and the disposition contract, which governs the transfer of property rights, are associated but distinct legal transactions. Obligation contracts involve two parties, like in purchase, work, or loan contracts, as illustrated in Figure 11.1. In exchanges of goods, money, or loans, the structure consists of, first, the *obligation* contract, which governs the *agreement* to exchange, establish, modify, or extinguish rights, such as ownership of a bicycle and money, and, second, the *disposition* contract, which serves to *fulfill* the obligation, such as the transfer of ownership over the exchanged terms.

Payments are not always executed through the physical handover of money. Instead, another contract on bank deposits enables payments by transferring money ownership to the payee. This involves a crucial distinction: bank deposits are not money but option rights, allowing customers to instruct their bank to withdraw money or to transfer the deposit to others. The role of a bank in the deposit obligation contract is to await customers' instructions before fulfilling the disposal contract by executing a money transfer or withdrawal.

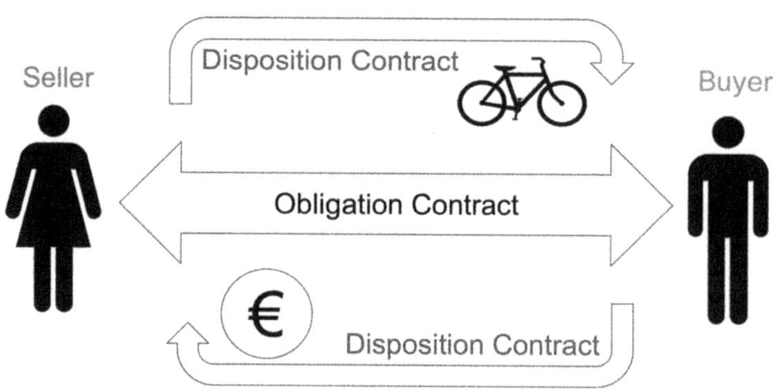

Fig. 11.1. Obligation and disposition contracts.

We denote transfer rights over money in deposits as "money" or commands for money.

The *abstraction principle* states that the *validity of the obligation* contract is *independent of the validity of the disposition* contract. Even if an obligation contract is rendered invalid, ownership transfers executed through disposition contracts remain legally effective. Likewise, if a disposition contract is invalid, the obligation contract remains unaffected. This can create imbalances, where one party acquires ownership without a valid contractual basis. To rectify such situations, Section 812 of the BGB provides a restitution claim, ensuring that the party who benefited without a legal basis must return the asset or compensate the counterparty.

In the principles applied to purchase a product for money (Section 433, BGB), the obligation contract commits the seller to deliver a product and the buyer to provide payment. The disposition contract transfers the ownership (Section 929, BGB) of the product from seller to buyer and money from buyer to seller.

In the principles applied to a loan contract (Section 488, BGB), the obligation contract concerns a loan that obligates the bank to grant access to money and the debtor to repay it. The two disposition contracts are that the bank grants a deposit, enabling the debtor to command central bank money transfers or withdrawals, and that the debtor repays the loan, settling the obligation.

Misconceptions in monetary theory often arise from a failure to apply these principles correctly. An example is the concept of *Kreditgeld* (German for *loan money*). Here, a contradiction emerges: a loan is a two-sided obligation contract, establishing mutual commitments between debtor and creditor. Money, on the other hand, serves as a means to fulfill an obligation, facilitating settlement rather than creating new contractual obligations. By conflating loans and money, such interpretations blur the distinction between the creation of debt and the fulfillment of debt, leading to conceptual inconsistencies in monetary theory.

11.2.1 *Supply chains and pins*

Figure 11.2 shows the need for integrating obligations in supply chains of economies organized by division of labor. Money exists because producers need investments to pay suppliers of resources before being paid by customers. The argumentation line that money

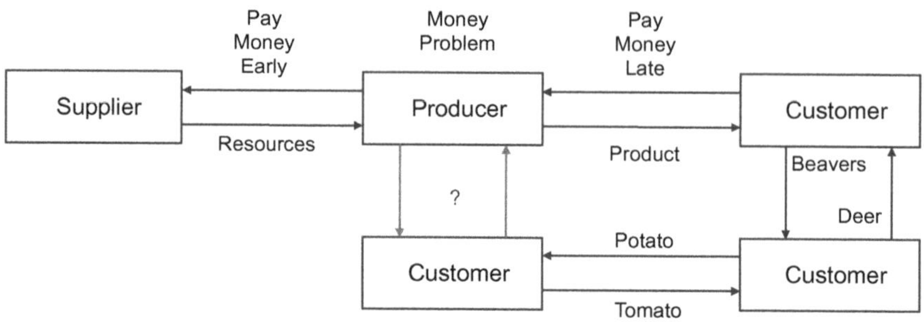

Fig. 11.2. Money demand in supply chains.

solves the problem of the *double coincidence of wants* is only about exchanges within a period of time. It misses the point that the more fundamental problem that monetary systems solve (where money is only one part of the institutional set up) is the intermediation of payments from customers to producers tomorrow versus the need to pay suppliers by producers already today.

A similar pattern arises in the bookings of a BoE (Radke and Thomsen, 2019): *When buying goods, two different interests meet. The supplier of the inputs of production wants to receive his money as early as possible since he has made payments in advance in various ways—having produced, processed, or procured the goods at his own expense. The producer wants to pay as late as possible, as he still has to sell the goods and only receives the money from his customers later* (own translation, *buyer* replaced by *producer*).

The same pattern appears in the first sentence of *The Wealth of Nations* (Smith, 1776), followed by the famous example of the production of pins: *The greatest improvement in the productive powers of labor, and the greater part of the skill, dexterity, and judgment with which it is any where directed, or applied, seem to have been the effects of the division of labor.... One man draws out the wire, another straights it, a third cuts it, a fourth points it, a fifth grinds it at the top for receiving the head ....*

Economies with a division of labor feature sequences of decentralized resource transformations into products spread over production steps, producers, and consumers. A producer is, first, indebted and, second, does not only (if at all) consume his product but also other goods. He sells his product for money, which allows him to buy other goods and to repay debts to investors to pay workers and resource suppliers. Workers are not indebted from the beginning; they use money for consumption or saving.

To emphasize the distinction between production and consumption, we use two terms for products: commodities serve as a means to attract money for producers; goods provide utility through consumption for consumers. Although it may appear that products and money circulate in cycles, their movement is rather like vortices in time, connecting past and future obligations. While money circulates as paper, the paper itself remains the same, facilitating different obligation and disposition contracts. The key focus is on debt contracts and how they originate, are cleared, and eventually conclude. Money flows through different transactions, repaying distinct debts in different contractual contexts.

BoEs have a finite lifespan, ending at maturity, once the BoE is settled, causing the debt relation and the need for money to cease. This contrasts with the concept of money circulation; debt relations continuously emerge and disappear, which form the entities of interest in a money theory.

In Figure 11.2, the question mark denotes that theories of money as a *medium of exchange* overlook the crucial distinction between commodities and goods. The opposing demands for products and money between producers and consumers naturally align with and eliminate the need for a value theory of money in sequential consumer exchanges. A value argument is needed for arguing why to accept worthless money for one's own valuable resources in order to exchange afterwards for another valuable consumption good. The key insight is that producers demand money to repay debts, while consumers acquire goods for money. Since these flows match, monetary theory can be based on MoMa rather than subjective valuations of money.

11.2.2 *Prices, and beavers and deer*

Figure 11.2 also shows another starting point of monetary theories: some products are to be exchanged; here, beavers and deer, as in *The Wealth of Nations* (Smith, 1776), in Chapter 6: *If among a nation of hunters, for example, it usually costs twice the labor to kill a beaver which it does to kill a deer, one beaver should naturally exchange for or be worth two deer. It is natural that what is usually the produce of two day's or two hours labor, should be worth double of what is usually the produce of one day's or one hour's labor.*

Without money, the number of beavers exchanged for the number of deer represents their relative value. The *natural* theory argues that the relative price should depend on the relative amount of labor used to produce the products. The cause of the existence of money is then that money enables exchanges even if owners of deer do not want to exchange them for beavers, tomatoes, or potatoes. This overly restricted requirement is called the *double coincidence of wants.* Money relieves it and enables otherwise impossible exchanges. Money is conceptualized as a numéraire or a neutral commodity for exchange. The value of money is then, for example, given by the welfare increase from enabling exchanges.

In MoMaT, the story can be told through debt relations rather than through money value and relative prices. If owner B of beavers b, measured in units of b, denoted by [b], and the owner D of deer d in [d] want to exchange 1 [b] for 1 [d], they record the difference in value at an agreed-upon price of, say, 2 [b] for 1 [d], i.e., 2/1 [b/d]. This might have been the birth of the marks, measured in [b], on tally sticks, documenting the claim of D to B. If D has trained his son in hunting d at no cost for D, he can be considered a child-abusing entrepreneur who made a profit from a markup over his costs. The next day, D gets one [b] from B, the debt relation ceases to exist, and the tally stick can be thrown away—used as a tooth brush or for burning down the British parliament, as in 1876 (Wikipedia, 2025b), when wooden tally sticks were abandoned after they had been used for 40,000 years as a debt-recording instrument.

In a gold-based system, prices are expressed in gold [kg of gold/b] and converted into money prices [$/b] via money as a numéraire [kg of gold/$]. In fiat systems, prices are directly measured in monetary units [$/b] without requiring a numéraire. The specific currency, such as the dollar or a crypto token, is irrelevant; what matters is that it is a legally defined means of payment, enabling the settlement of debts from obligation contracts through disposal contracts.

Money does not need intrinsic value for producers either. They calculate input and output prices in monetary units, with profits as a markup, where the monetary unit cancels out. Intrinsic value would be counterproductive, obscuring this ratio.

Assigning value to money resembles Russell's paradox (of sets containing themselves), suggesting a need for type theory in monetary theory. A higher-order type theory could model the creation of currencies as the type of a type-generating operation, e.g., where the euro and the ECB are created, rather than the ECB merely issuing euros. A Russell's paradox of central banking is analogous to *who shaves the barber who shaves all those who cannot shave themselves?* as *who provides the means of payments to the bank which provides the means of payments to those banks which cannot provide the means of payments to themselves?*

Rather than a value theory of money, we need money to represent: (A) what is to be paid at the beginning, 100.000 [$], and repaid at the end of an investment, 110.000 [$], with the interest rate being 10.0% = 110/100 − 1.0, (B) a price of a product, 6.59 [$/BigMac], (C) a relative price of two products, 2.45 [BigMac/Cheeseburger] ≈ 6.59 [$/BigMac] / 2.69 [$/Cheeseburger], and (D) a ratio of costs to output prices for calculating profits by markup pricing, like in $\pi = p - c = mc - c$, where $\pi :=$ profit [$/product], $p :=$ price [$/product], $m :=$ markup [$\mathbb{R}, > 1.0$], and $c :=$ costs [$/product].

11.3 Mesoeconomics

At the meso level, banks manage loans, investments, repayments, clearing, and risk allocation. Failed investments are to be booked as consumption expenditures, reducing investors' wealth. Risk absorption involves three layers: producers absorb failures of unproductive use of money; banks distribute risks via interest rates over portfolios of failed and successful investments into producers; and central banks act as unlimited risk absorbers of failed banks.

To properly account for returns and losses from investments, it is crucial to note that banks do not create money but only references to money in deposits. They can instruct the central bank to issue cash but must first incur debt at the central bank to generate loans from it as well. Essentially, banks produce solvency for companies using money as input, with the supply chains being the central bank, bank, and company.

Modern liberal societies, structured around obligation and disposition contracts for property transfers, operate as follows: (1) Central banks issue means of payment to settle monetary obligations. (2) Banks finance investments using central bank money. (3) Companies use loans to pay for resources, labor, and insurance premiums (interest rates) for the possibility of not being able to repay the loans. (4) Consumers or households consume products produced from the resources and companies they own.

11.3.1 *Bill of exchange*

A BoE is a financial instrument used in trade and commerce to provide credit and facilitate payments. It functions as an unconditional disposition contract within an obligation contract, where the *drawer* issues the BoE, ordering the *drawee* to pay a specified amount to the *payee*—often, the drawer—at a future date or on demand at a discount or interest rate. The drawee accepts the order by signing it, becoming the *acceptor* committed to pay.

Figure 11.3(a) illustrates the macro bookings of a BoE-based purchase. The BoE shifts payments into the future, while the product is delivered immediately. The are four micro accountings: Seller, Buyer, Seller Bank, and Buyer Bank and five macro bookings of two micro bookings each: (1): delivery of product: (1a): Seller sells product to Buyer, (1b): Buyer purchases product from Seller. (2): creation of BoE: (2a): Seller issues BoE to Buyer, (2b): Buyer accepts BoE from Seller. (3): "money" exchange for BoE: (3a): Seller sells BoE to Seller Bank, (3b): Seller Bank buys BoE from Seller. (4): transfer of BoE for liabilities: (4a): Seller Bank sells BoE to Buyer Bank, (4b): Buyer Bank buys BoE from Seller Bank. (5): BoE settlement: (5a): Buyer Bank submits BoE to Buyer, (5b): Buyer settles BoE by payment.

The debt flow in the BoE process involves four steps. First, internal receivables and liabilities are created at product delivery. The BoE makes them exchangeable by being a negotiable financial instrument. (A) Debt creation (blue arrow: Buyer to Seller): the Seller delivers the product to the Buyer (1a), creating a receivable for the Seller and a liability for the Buyer (1b); the Buyer formalizes this debt by accepting a BoE issued by the Seller (2a and 2b). (B) BoE monetization (green arrow: Seller to Seller Bank): the Seller converts the BoE into liquidity by selling it to Seller Bank (3a), receiving a credit in return; the Seller Bank now holds the BoE as a receivable (3b). (C) BoE transfer (gray arrow: Seller Bank to Buyer Bank): the Seller Bank transfers the BoE to the Buyer Bank (4a), receiving an equivalent receivable from the Buyer Bank; the Buyer Bank takes on the liability (4b), holding the BoE as an obligation from the Buyer.

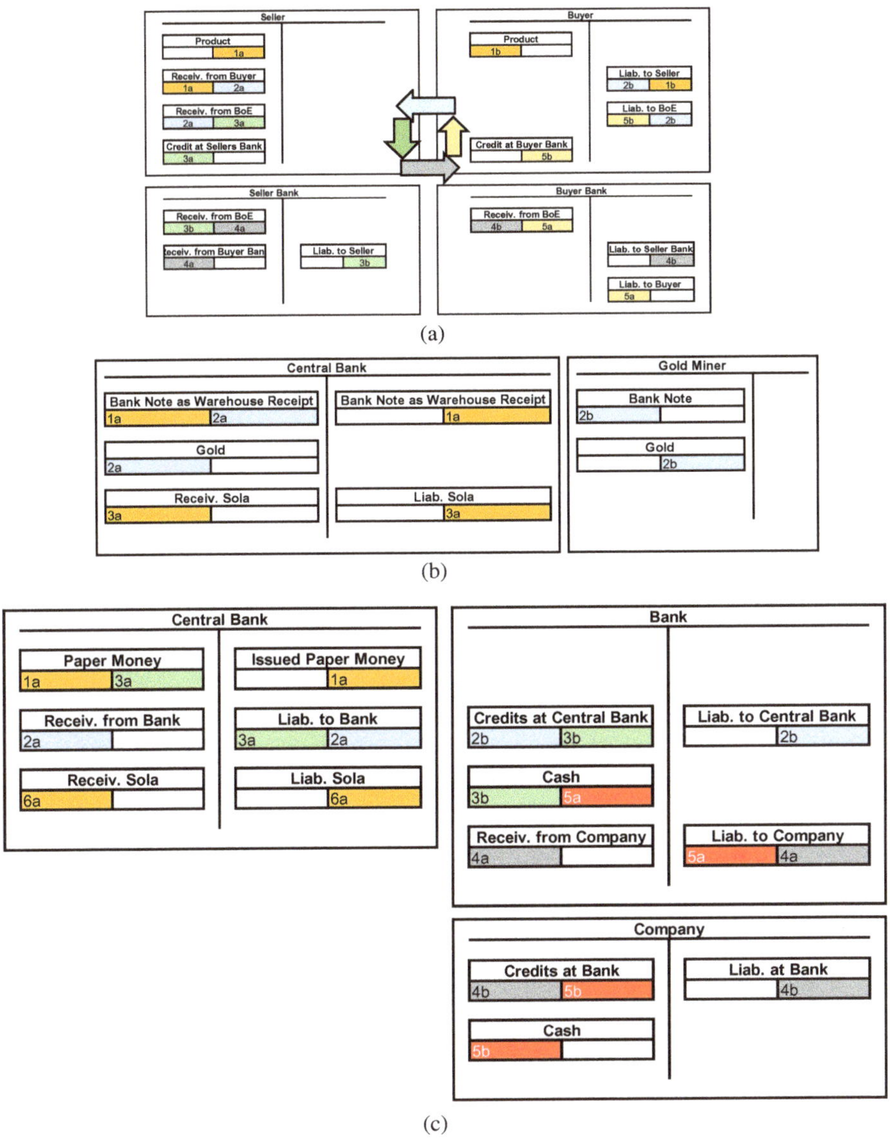

Fig. 11.3. Bill of exchange and money issuance. (a) Bookings of a bill of exchange. (b) Issuing bank notes in gold-based monetary systems. (c) Issuing paper money in fiat monetary systems.

(D) final settlement (yellow arrow: Buyer to Buyer Bank): the Buyer Bank presents the BoE to the Buyer for payment (5a), debiting the Buyer's account; the Buyer settles its debt (5b), completing the cycle.

Each step transforms the debt, moving it through different financial entities. The BoE acts as a transferable financial instrument, facilitating liquidity while maintaining the underlying obligation until final settlement. The process creates a dynamic vortex of obligations, rather than a closed loop over papers of money.

In the BoE booking process, no money is exchanged; only deposits or "money" between the agents are involved. Before money transfers occur, banks usually clear their mutual receivables and liabilities via central bank deposits, possibly followed by settlement in paper money. Figure 11.5 later illustrates that money primarily exists to facilitate debt repayment on the macroeconomic level as well.

A BoE can also act as a substitute for money, as a simplified "Sola" (short of German *Solawechsel*). A BoE is issued by the drawer and sent to the drawee for acceptance before returning to the drawer. A Sola skips this back-and-forth: the drawee creates, signs, and sends it to the payee.

There are two types of Solas (BoEs). The first type is with endorsement: the payee can transfer the Sola to others, e.g., suppliers, by signing on the endorsement list. Each endorser shares the liability: if the BoE is unpaid at maturity, the holder can claim repayment from anyone on the list, with recourse up the chain. Here, the restitution and principle of abstraction come in handy. The second type is without endorsement, which includes acts such as anonymous payment; only the drawee is liable to a payee presenting the BoE at maturity.

The endorsement list is like a *blockchain of the Renaissance* (or, *a blockchain is like an endorsement list*), enhancing credibility as more parties sign on. This financial instrument implemented distributed liabilities while facilitating secure, transferable payments, at least since the Renaissance.

11.3.2 *Schumpeter entrepreneur*

The basic building block of a MoMa system is an investment, defined by Kruschwitz as a time series: an initial payout from investor to producer followed by an expected repayment scheme from producer to investor. The legal principle of separation informs us that, unlike

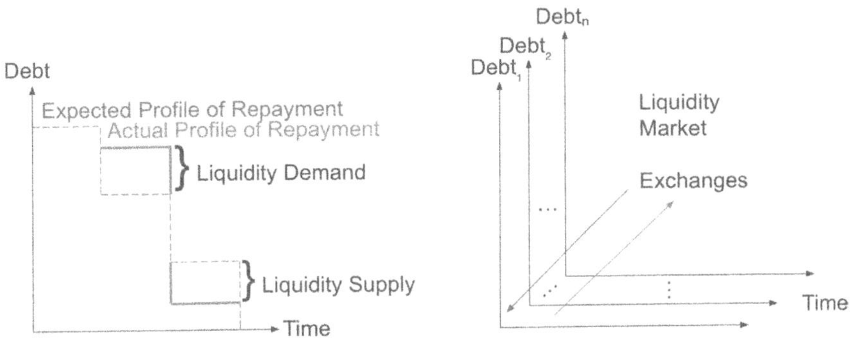

Fig. 11.4. Kruschwitz investment of a Schumpeter entrepreneur.

in “Money is Memory” (Kocherlakota, 1998), memory is given by loan contracts and repayment histories.

Figure 11.4 illustrates the expected repayments as a dotted line. The sales success of producers determines whether actual and expected repayments match. A saying attributed to Schumpeter is, “Entrepreneurs ride on debt to risky success.” Deviations of actual from expected repayments lead to Walrasian liquidity markets matching supply and demand; see Figure 11.4. MoMaT answers Hellwig’s doubt on Walrasian money markets by stating that money is traded but not created at markets, which central banks freely do.

11.3.3 *Banking*

In fiat systems, banks cannot issue the means of payment, just as central banks could not freely create gold in gold-based systems. Since gold discoveries are random or rather unresponsive to monetary policy, alternative claims such as BoEs and bank deposits emerged. We apply *economic archaeology* to derive an applicable monetary theory, in that we study past monetary systems, abstract their functions, and instantiate them in modern technologies for understanding and improving institutional implementations.

The role of banks is illustrated in the bookings of the BoE in Figure 11.3(a), showcasing the simplest form of investment in supply chain finance (SCF). When the Seller Bank purchases a BoE, it invests and bears a risk; if the buyer defaults, the BoE goes to *protest* at a court. The risk persists until the obligation contract is fulfilled, with the Buyer settling the BoE. During this period, the Seller Bank shares joint liability with other endorsers and the drawee. In case of default, restitution claims disentangle the losses among the involved agents. A bank's total portfolio of risky investments must balance returns and losses. If it fails to repay its debts to the central bank, it becomes illiquid, leading to bankruptcy. The interest rate functions as an insurance premium, ensuring that losses are covered before profit is declared.

A fundamental question in monetary theory is whether claims and payments across the hierarchical levels of micro, meso, and macro agents align with macro invariances of debts and payments. The macro invariance of debt relations states that the sum of receivables equals the sum of liabilities. The macro invariance of payments states that the sum of expenditures equals the sum of revenues. These two invariances need to be consistent as well, as debt invariance pertains to state variables, whereas payment invariance concerns flow variables or changes in state variables. These invariances are not empirical or behavioral hypotheses but theoretical necessities for practical, consistent, distributed accounting systems. A bank has to ensure that clearing and settlement possibilities and probabilities between financial BoE or Solas are sufficiently securitized through credibility loans by gold, central bank money, or other forms of assets.

At the micro level, production generates claims and debts or receivables and liabilities, which are exchanged, cleared, and settled using money or other claims. At the meso level, banks create receivables and liabilities, clearing and settling them either through the central bank or money payments. At the macro level, central banks issue money and deposits for bank. They may also refinance or invest in BoEs from companies. Deposits at the central bank serve as commands for money, cleared by banks against each other. Money issuing is recorded in the central bank's micro accounting, but its role as a means of payment for obligation contracts emerges in macro accounting. Central banks alone, by monopolistic authority, define and issue money.

11.3.4 *Supply chain finance*

MoMaT suggests that money functions need to be seen in rather pure form in SCF, as shown in Figure 11.2. A digital BoE-based service, such as dynamic discounting (DD) on an SCF platform,[3] streamlines these processes, making them more efficient and flexible. In DD, GY (a supplier) has a button in its ERP system, next to invoices issued to VW (the buyer). When GY chooses early payment, an accountant presses the button, triggering a transfer of "money" from VW's bank account to GY's. The digital workflow encompasses four steps: (1) GY's request is sent to a digital depository to create a BoE. (2) A bank purchases the BoE, transferring the dynamically discounted amount to VW to pay GY. (3) At maturity, the bank requests full repayment from VW, earning the discount as a return on its loan. (4) The BoE is deleted in the digital depository, as the obligation contract is fulfilled by the "money" transfer of the disposition contract without any further need for money.

The opportunity for services with digital documents, including BoEs, arose in the U.K. in 2023, adopting the Model Law of Electronic Transferable Records (MLETR) of the United Nations Commission on International Trade Law (UNCITRAL) by the Electronic Trade Documents Act (ETDA).[4]

11.4 Macroeconomics

Marx's critique of capitalism collapses in MoMaT: *money is not created from money*. Likewise, the misconception of *interests on interests* fades when interest rates are seen as insurance premiums for cross-investment risk.

The misunderstandings arise from a focus on money circulation rather than on the dynamics of debt (receivables and liabilities) forming vortices, not closed loops. A banknote changing hands may suggest circulation's primacy; however, legally and economically, debt evolution matters, not the movement of money. Money is a means of payment, not the debt itself.

---

[3]This section benefited greatly from discussions with Markus Wohlgeschaffen, product manager at Traxpay, a pioneer in applications of digital BoEs for SCF.

[4]See the Bills of Exchange Act of 1882 (UK Parliament, 1882), the German Wechsel Law of 1933 (Reichsregierung, 1933), and the MLETR of 2017 of UNCITRAL (UNCITRAL, 2017) and its U.K. adaptation ETDA (UK Parliament, 2023).

Geometrically, a vortex spanning time may appear circular when projected along the timeline, much like how money's movement seems cyclical when debt vortices are mapped onto transactions. Just as Copernicus replaced Ptolemy's geocentric model, monetary theory must shift focus: debt vortices, not money flows, define the system. To understand this, we examine money issued under fiat and gold-based systems.

11.4.1 *Central banking*

Before the rise of central banks in the 17th century, banks issued banknotes backed by gold, or other valuable resources, making them debt instruments, a promise by the bank to redeem them for gold. This is modeled as credit (or credibility) loans, i.e., a financial instrument that extends the BoE into a Sola and two more future contracts on gold and products. This construction certifies banks for proper clearing and settlement size and timing.

Founded in 1609, the Wisselbank of Amsterdam (Wikipedia, 2025c) (where *Wissel* is the Dutch word for the German *Wechsel* or BoE) pioneered international payments, crucial for European colonial trade, which required investments in shipping. Long voyages, high risks, and delayed revenues made financing essential. From this model, central banks emerged, including the Bank of England, which managed national currencies such as the pound, backed by sterling silver. Early central banks operated on gold or silver debt, issuing banknotes as documented obligations.

Figure 11.3(b) shows banknote issuance in a gold-based system. The bookings involve two steps. Step 1: issuing a banknote (1a): the central bank prepares to buy gold, effectively expanding the money supply by recording a warehouse receipt. Step 2: gold transaction (2a, 2b): the central bank purchases gold from a gold miner (2a). The gold miner receives a banknote in exchange for gold (2b), serving as a claim on gold. Booking (3a) records the issuance of a Sola, following the same process as issuing a banknote (1a).

Gold was the legal means of payment, but to avoid transferring it in every transaction, banknotes were introduced as claims on gold, redeemable at the central bank. Essentially, a gold miner deposited gold in the central bank, receiving a banknote in return. This note circulated as a transferable payment instrument within a purchase obligation, allowing any holder to exchange it for gold.

In 1971, Nixon ended the gold-based systems, making paper money the basis of contracts under the fiat system. Unlike gold-based banknotes, paper money does not represent central bank debt and lacks inherent claims, meaning *issued paper money* records circulation, not obligations. Without a claim, there is no corresponding liability.

The booking of issuing paper money in the fiat system follows five steps: (1) Money issuance: (1a) the central bank (CB) issues paper money, legally registering it in the *issued paper money* database. (2) Loan to a bank (2a and 2b): the CB grants a loan to a commercial bank. (2a) The CB records an increase in receivables and liabilities. (2b) The bank records an increase in its credit and liabilities. (3) Bank withdraws money from CB (3a and 3b): the bank transforms its option right into a due claim, thereby ordering the CB to hand over the requested amount of paper money. (3a) The CB reduces its liabilities and cash holdings. (3b) The bank decreases its central bank deposit but increases its cash holdings. (4) Bank grants a loan to a company (4a and 4b): the bank extends a loan to a company, creating new "money," i.e., new deposits. (4a) The bank records an increase in receivables and liabilities. (4b) The company records an increase in credits and liabilities. (5) Company withdraws cash (5a and 5b): the company converts part of its bank deposit into "money" for payments (e.g., wages). (5a) The bank reduces its liabilities and cash reserves. (5b) The company decreases its bank deposit but increases its cash holdings.

Issuing a Sola (6a) follows the same principle as creating paper money (1a). Unlike gold-based money, paper money exists by legal decree, allowing unlimited issuance. It enters circulation through loans and withdrawals, enabling transactions without commodity backing. The Sola in 6a illustrates that issuing paper money can be seen as similar to issuing a Sola. However, unlike a traditional Sola or a warehouse receipt, which represents a claim (e.g., gold in gold-based systems), fiat money has no underlying asset to claim. In gold-based systems, central bank liabilities were backed by gold, effectively balancing debt. Gold itself is neither a claim nor a liability like paper money, which carries no inherent claim. Fiat systems require no backing, only legal declaration as a means of payment.

In a fiat system, the central bank starts without debt, just as gold and banknotes balanced out in gold-based systems. Money settles debt but is not debt itself. Since Nixon ended the gold-based system, central banks cannot go bankrupt in their own currency, making fiat systems resistant to bank runs as an accidental feature, not a flaw. No gold or intrinsic value for paper money is needed for the system to function.

Money issuance should align with productive economic activity and investment-driven debt needs. MoMaT identifies SCF variables as being key for monetary policy, now easily tracked via receivables and liabilities in company ERP and accounting systems. Monetary policy and liquidity platforms must consider liquidity demand and supply. Until the 1990s, the Bundesbank used BoE refinancing and the discount rate as policy tools, accompanied by interbank market interest rates and direct interventions at asset markets.

MoMaT defines central bank policy involving three topics: (1) injecting money into the economy through bank loans, creating central bank deposits to create solvency, (2) setting a minimum credibility rating for such loans, and (3) managing the payment system and macro accounting with financial regulations. Following Bagehot's principle, MoMaT advocates unlimited crisis lending at high costs while leaving inflation to government income policies. Unlike conventional monetary economics, MoMaT sees no need for artificial scarcity; money supply should allow for matching the volume of unsettled receivables and liabilities.

In gold-based systems, central banks acted as lenders of last resort, but this failed when they ran out of gold, leading Nixon to abandon the system. In the fiat system, central banks serve as first liquidity providers, able to issue money infinitely. During black swan events and bank failures, central banks can insure losses through bailouts, effectively smoothing investment losses as consumption costs. These bailouts can be distributed at the highest societal level, with the central bank as the ultimate risk-sharing entity.

11.4.2 *Monetary vortex*

In Figure 11.5, we illustrate that vortices of debt, rather than circulating money, are at the core of the dynamics of monetary systems. The macro accounting framework includes the central bank, bank,

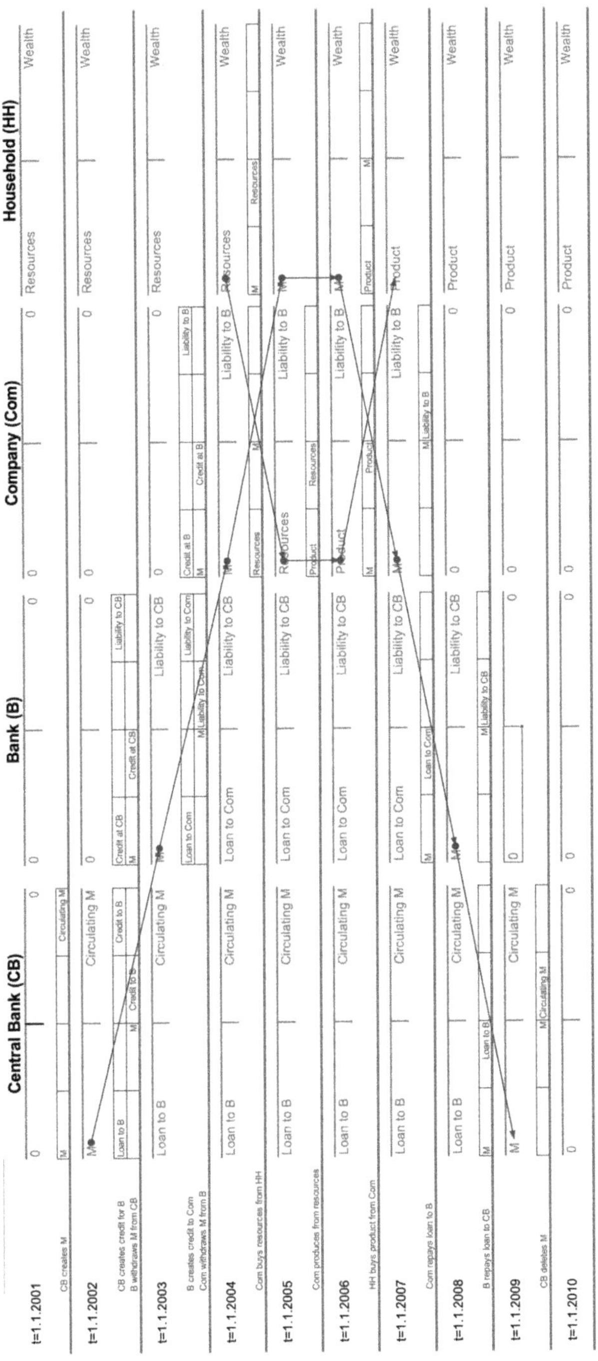

Fig. 11.5. Monetary vortex.

company, and household sectors, where resources, products, liabilities, and money are created, exchanged, and deleted throughout the economy's productive cycles.

At t = 1.1.2001,[5] the household sector holds resources with no liabilities, making assets equal equity (E = A). The central bank issues money as a sovereign act, recorded solely in its own micro accounting system like alchemically creating gold in a gold-based system, but without intrinsic value or backing. It is the only singleton (micro accounting) booking in a macro accounting system. The central bank's balance sheet records cash (M) as an asset and *circulating M* as a liability, marking registered paper money. The central bank then grants loans as credits. t = 2002: The central bank lends to the bank. t = 2003: The bank withdraws cash and lends to a company. t = 2004: The company buys resources or work from households. t = 2005: The company produces goods. t = 2006: The household buys the product, returning cash to the company. t = 2007: The company repays its loan to the bank. t = 2008: The bank repays the central bank. t = 2009: The central bank destroys the money. t = 2010: Balance sheets reset to zero.

This process transforms resources into products or GDP, illustrating an economy characterized by a division of labor, where monetary vortices and debt repayments drive production and exchange over time in MoMa. The monetary vortex in Figure 11.5 charts the flow of money (M) through balance sheets, from issuance to deletion at the central bank. Conversely, the physical vortex traces the conversion of resources into products, moving counter to the flow of money. When viewed along the time axis, top to bottom, the interplay of debts, money, resources, and products creates the illusion of circular flows, much like in Figure 11.2. Money and debt bridge the time gap in production, transforming resources into products and enabling exchange of the GDP. While this may appear as a circular flow, it is in fact a timed vortex of resources and money. Once all debts are repaid (t = 1.1.2010), money can be deleted. Reusing the same money in new debt cycles only creates circulation of money, new and closing

[5]Balance sheets report state variables at a specific time, e.g., at t = 1.1.2001. Bookings in financial statement record flow variables as changes in state variables over a period, e.g., in t = 2001.

parallel debt relations. At $t = 1.1.2010$, wealth and GDP distribution in the household sector reflects how investment risks and failures were absorbed by banks and how resources, labor, and investments were financed from $t = 2002$ to $t = 2009$.

Money functions not only to coordinate labor but also to allocate risk and distribute economic output, the GDP. Modeling risk requires stochastic processes to account for investment failures, treating losses as consumption or costs. Failed investments should not be hidden in *bad banks* or bailed out without a theoretical and political framework. The dynamics of debts, money, resources, and products of the GDP as vortices is akin to our solar system's planets, as shown in Figure 11.6; see the movie at (Youtube, 2025). The planets do not orbit in circles or ellipses around the sun but in vortices, following the sun's trajectory as it travels at approximately 70,000 km/h around the galactic center. This motion appears as a circular orbit only when projected onto a two-dimensional plane through the sun, effectively neglecting the space-time direction in which the sun itself is moving.

Paper money circulation masks debt repayments in anonymous transactions. Vortices can be found as money transactions in the endorsement list of BoEs. Anonymity is like projecting planetary orbits and debt relations on a plane through the sun or on papers of

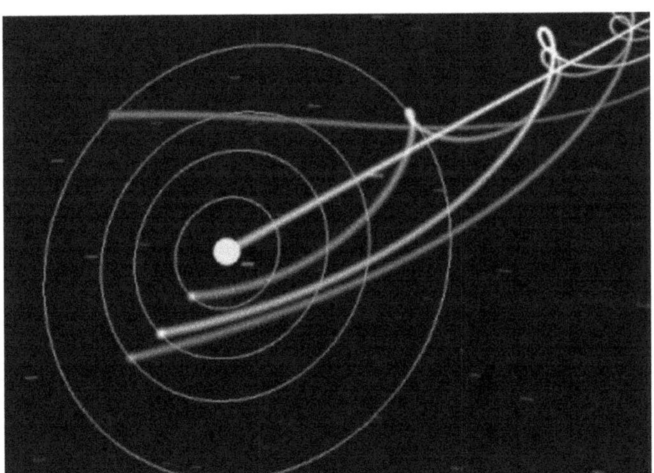

Fig. 11.6. Planetary vortices.

money. To address monetary theory and policy challenges, we must link receivables, liabilities, expenditures, and revenues across economic micro, meso, and macro layers with properly typed financial contracts.

We have seen that endorsement lists of BoEs have a similar functionality as blockchains. These lists represent chains of debt relationships, in which a claim document is passed along. In this sense, they serve as a model for blockchains, i.e., as databases of ownership rights to claims which can be maintained by an authorized depository. In payment processes recorded in endorsement lists or blockchains, we could actually find the monetary vertices discussed above as data ready to be analyzed for liquidity supply and exchange purposes or for analyzing the conduct of a monetary policy.

In this application of an "archaeology of economics," the abstract economic functionality using records of debtors and creditors—actually, even bilateral solvency checks—using the historical technology of pencil and paper is to be transferred and implemented in modern technologies of digital computing and then generalized, for example, to smart contracts and applications of blockchains or other new technologies. The German and international laws of the BoE are treasuries of historical experience and specifications of financial needs—to be potentially used as a pool of ideas for the design of smart contracts in modern times.

11.5 Mathematics

The challenge in monetary theory and policy is to model a MoMa system, as shown in Figure 11.5. MoMa models national accounts as networks of debt contracts across banks, companies, and households using a (reduced-form) Markov model based only on past data. Analyzing this requires MoMaT incorporating structural econometric models with forward-looking agents, as in Winschel and Krätzig (2010) and Heiss and Winschel for econometrics or Kochenderfer *et al.* (2022) for multi-agent AI, both programmable with open games.

An open game (Ghani *et al.*, 2018) is depicted in Figure 11.7 as a string diagram, with a probabilistic extension in Bolt *et al.* (2023). Open games represent time bidirectionally: past to future

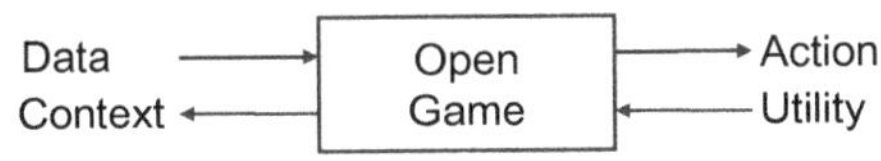

Fig. 11.7. Open game.

(left to right) and future to past (right to left). Decisions form one- or multi-person games, built from smaller n-person games into larger $n+1$-person games via sequential and parallel combinators. In category theory, these correspond to function composition and tensor products, providing a process-oriented approach to mathematics (Dagstuhl Seminar, 2014). Parallel and sequential processes are composed through concatenation and juxtaposition in string diagrams, while hierarchical composition uses equational substitution, enabling both white-box and black-box economic modeling.[6] In a string diagram, the box represents functions (or processes or morphism in category theory) with the open games type

$$G : D \times C^* \to A \times U^*.$$

Open games are compositional because data, action, context, and utility are also open games, and their compositions remain open games. The superscript * denotes contravariance in teleology, goal, utility, belief, or anticipation, where arrows point left, opposite to usual time flow. Open games capture the Aristotelian teleological causality, linking the future to the present (purpose). The other three causes, normative (plan), material (bricks), and effective (work), define physical existence (e.g., of a house), while teleology defines purpose (e.g., living in a house).

String diagrams are not merely representations but formal mathematical objects with semantics for proofs. Open games serve as a visual programming language for forward-looking economic models, making them executable software with provable properties. As both models and runnable programs, they leverage computer science and mathematics to understand and implement economies.

Since open games are similar to the interdisciplinary research on quantum computing programming languages, economic theories

[6] *White boxing* means *making explicit* by showing the content of a *black box*. We can use the *white box* $a = b + c$ to show in $d = a + e$ the *black box* a as $d = a + e = b + c + e$.

formulated in open games are quantum ready.[7] Therefore, transactions of MoMa systems with open games as smart contracts can be about quantum-secured assignments and transfers of property rights comprising non-deletable data with free write and read access on blockchains or distributed ledgers.

Open games represent bidirectional computation, including time flow, relations, double-entry accounting, constraint propagation, or smart contracts. They can model structural econometrics, multi-agent systems, belief formation, or strategic decisions. With built-in back propagation (Fong *et al.*, 2019), they also support parameter estimation and data science algorithms.

Macro invariances can be modeled using sheaf theory over micro accounting automata (Rambaud *et al.*, 2010), embedded in a network of contracts. A compositional semantics for MoMa must derive macro behavior from micro accounting systems interconnected at the meso level. Constraints from micro, meso, and macro invariances should be transparently booked. State transitions follow initial algebras in gold-based systems, while fiat systems can use final co-algebras to model infinite, behavioral structures for booking smart contracts in macro accounting.

Category theory reorganizes mathematics (Dagstuhl Seminar, 2014) as its compositional theory. It can provide semantics to economics in co-algebras (Dagstuhl Seminar, 2015).[8] A compositional theory of MoMa needs to zoom in and out (Willems, 2007) at different behavioral levels of the systems. Systems are to be composed and decomposed while keeping the levels looked at in

---

[7]The papers on co-algebraic games (Abramsky and Winschel, 2015; Pavlovic, 2009) are precursors to open games (Ghani *et al.*, 2018), inspired by the work (Abramsky and Coecke, 2004) on quantum protocols.

[8]The discovery of open-game structures emerged from the search for a mathematical framework addressing Lucas' critique and reflexivity in the social sciences (Wikipedia, 2025a). Reflexive structures in mathematics, such as lambda calculus, higher-order functions, Turing machines, and formal semantics in theoretical computer science (Pavlovic, 2023), provide a foundation. Meta circular interpreters, such as those by Graham (2001) and McCarthy (1960), illustrate this with Lisp implementing itself. Social sciences and economics offer complex epistemological situations where modern semantic tools such as category theory, type theory, or co-algebras can enhance institutional modeling and implementations.

a consistent state. Global and local consistencies and inconsistencies of behaviors interact, and we need to understand how local goals and obstacles can be resolved into a consistently behaving global whole.

Sheaf theory constructs complex models by combining local information into a consistent whole (Robinson, 2016; Schenck, 2023). Like two eyes merging fields of view or an atlas forming a globe, sheaves splice local data into a global structure. In equations, local solutions integrate into a global solution, just as local function approximations combine into a globally defined function. Similarly, Bayesian networks update through local observations, propagating until the entire global model aligns with the data.

A MoMa system integrates economic agents are resource owners, consumers, producers, banks, and central banks, each maintaining local micro accounting of debt and payments. These agents form a network where nodes represent entities and edges track financial flows, ensuring consistency through receivables, liabilities, expenditures, and revenues. Aggregated into macro accounting, this network maintains stability via macro invariances. In sheaf theory, the *global section* represents systemic consistency, which monetary policy must uphold. During crises, its role is to restore the system to this stable state.

The name "sheaf" for these mathematical structures is an analogy to agricultural sheaves, as shown in Figure 11.8. Stalks represent micro accounting data atop the network of local agents, while the macro accounting as a sheaf forms the global structure, bound by consistency conditions, analogous to the thread in the agricultural sheaf. Stability emerges in the sheaf, a property individual stalks alone do not have, much like how money's functionality emerges only at the macro accounting level from booking its issuing in the central bank's micro accounting.

Homology theory identifies obstacles to global consistency and macro invariances, particularly when inconsistencies arise in specific regions or points in time. In MoMaT, these may appear as local liquidity imbalances or bad banks, resolved by issuing BoEs or some monetary policy across micro, meso, and macro levels. This enables a decentralized, automated monetary policy, reducing reliance on discretion. Automated policy is possible, debated as *Taylor functions*,

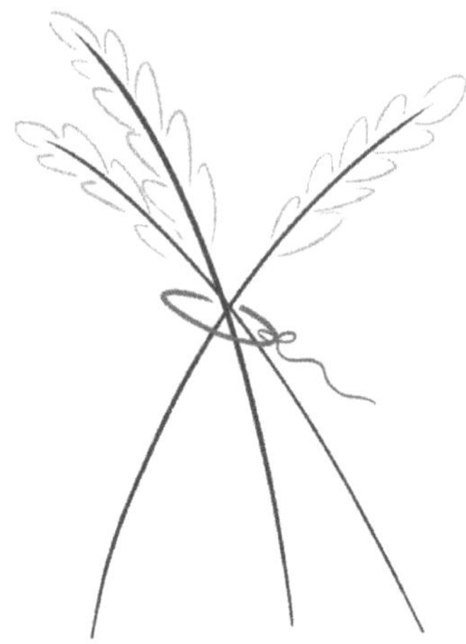

Fig. 11.8. Agricultural sheaf.

which optimally set central banks' interest rates based on inflation or the phase in the business cycles.

11.6 Conclusion

What is money? This question is answered by recognizing that money serves to settle obligations and debt relations, and it fulfills them through the disposition of property rights over money and products. Money as a technology within macro accounting enables division of labor, risk allocation, and GDP distribution across micro, meso, and macro levels of an economy.

At the micro level, money bridges the time gap in production, allowing producers to pay suppliers before receiving payment from customers. To do this, producers take on debt, repaying it with future earnings. Legally, money fulfills obligations in contracts either as payment for goods or repayment of loans without the need for intrinsic value. Monetary units are arbitrary but serve as the legal means to settle debts. At the meso level, banks manage investment risks by pooling loans and balancing returns through interest rates, functioning as insurance premiums. They provide solvency for companies by guaranteeing this solvency at their own risk. At the macro level, central banks issue money and release it to banks for investment. They absorb non-insurable risks as lenders of first liquidity in fiat systems and lenders of last resort in gold-based systems.

Sheaves can structure networks of debts and repayments, ensuring consistency across economic levels through macro accounting invariances. Homology theory can correct local inconsistencies, supporting automated monetary policy. Open games can serve as modeling and computational tools for deductive types in MoMa systems and inductive types in MoMaT for economic forecasts, backpropagation, econometric, and multi-agent AI analysis.

MoMaT defines the functionality of money as a means of payment and the unit of account for the settlement of monetary obligations in two-sided contracts governing obligations and dispositions of property rights. The store of value functionality can be modeled as financial BoEs or Solas in credit (credibility) loans. The means of exchange functionality of money provides a numéraire and a medium of exchange.

Finally, we have provided a link to the blockchain world. The endorsement lists of the BoEs are designed to record exchanges of the claims to the payments at the maturity date. Similarly, blockchains are linked chains of exchanges of claims. We hope that ongoing efforts in blockchain technologies—to provide a permissionless and non-deletable record-keeping system for the transfers of property rights—can take advantage of our monetary theory in advancing a new approach to monetary systems.

References

Abramsky, S. and Coecke, B. 2004. "A categorical semantics of quantum protocols." In *Proceedings of the 19rd Annual ACM/IEEE Symposium on Logic in Computer Science (LICS)*, pp. 415–425.

Abramsky, S. and Winschel, V. 2015. "Coalgebraic analysis of subgame-perfect equilibria in infinite games without discounting." *Mathematical Structures in Computer Science* 2017;27(5):751–761. DOI: 10.1017/S0960129515000365.

Bolt, J., Hedges, J., and Zahn, P. 2023. "Bayesian open games." *Compositionality* 5: 9.

Dagstuhl Seminar. 2014. "Categorical methods at the crossroad." https://www.dagstvuhl.de/en/seminars/seminar-calendar/seminar-details/14182.

Dagstuhl Seminar. 2015. "Coalgebraic semantics of reflexive economics." https://www.dagstuhl.de/en/seminars/seminar-calendar/seminar-details/15042.

Fong, B., Spivak, D. I., and Tuyéras, R. 2019. "Backprop as functor: A compositional perspective on supervised learning." In *Proceedings of the 34rd Annual ACM/IEEE Symposium on Logic in Computer Science (LICS).*

Gertler, M. and Kiyotaki, N. 2011. "Financial intermediation and credit policy in business cycle analysis." *Handbook of Monetary Economics,* Vol. 3, pp. 547–599. DOI: 10.1016/B978-0-444-53238-1.00011-9.

Ghani, N., Hedges, J., Winschel, V., and Zahn, P. 2018. "Compositional game theory." In *Proceedings of the 33rd Annual ACM/IEEE Symposium on Logic in Computer Science (LICS).*

Graham, P. 2001. "The roots of lisp." https://paulgraham.com/rootsoflisp.html.

Heiss, F. and Winschel, V. 2008. "Likelihood approximation by numerical integration on sparse grids." *Journal of Econometrics* 144(1): 62–80.

Hellwig, M. F. 1993. "The challenge of monetary theory." *European Economic Review* 37(2): 215–242.

Kelton, S. 2020. *The Deficit Myth: Modern Monetary Theory and the Birth of the People's Economy.* New York: PublicAffairs.

Kiyotaki, N. and Wright, R. 1993. "A search-theoretic approach to monetary economics." *American Economic Review* 83(1): 63–77.

Kochenderfer, M. J., Wheeler, T. A., and Wray, K. H. 2022. *Algorithms for Decision Making.* MIT Press.

Kocherlakota, N. R. 1998. "Money Is Memory." *Journal of Economic Theory* 81(2): 232–251.

McCarthy, J. 1960. "Recursive functions of symbolic expressions and their computation by machine, part I." *Communications of the ACM* 3(4): 184–195.

McLeay, M., Radia, A., and Thomas, R. 2014. "Money creation in the modern economy." *Bank of England Quarterly Bulletin* 54(1): 14–27.

Menéndez, R. 2010. *Theorie des Kapitalismus als Sozialwissenschaft: Prolegomena Einer Sozialen Zinstheorie.* LIT Verlag: Münster.

Pavlovic, D. 2009. "A semantical approach to equilibria and rationality." In Kurz, A., Lenisa, M., and Tarlecki, A. (eds.), *Algebra and Coalgebra in Computer Science.* Heidelberg: Springer, pp. 317–334.

Pavlovic, D. 2023. *Programs as Diagrams: From Categorical Computability to Computable Categories.* Springer Nature Switzerland 2023.

Radke, H.-D. and Thomsen, I. 2019. *Praxiswissen für Unternehmer: Buchführung.* Freiburg: Haufe.

Rambaud, S. C., Pérez, J. G., Nehmer, R. A., and Robinson, D. J. S. 2010. *Algebraic Models for Accounting Systems*. Singapore: World Scientific. DOI: 10.1142/7445.

Reichsregierung. 1933. "Wechselgesetz." https://www.gesetze-im-internet.de/wg/BJNR003990933.html.

Robinson, M. 2016. "Sheaf and duality methods for analyzing multi-model systems." *arXiv:1604.04647*.

Schenck, H. 2023. *Algebraic Foundations for Applied Topology and Data Analysis*. Springer International Publishing.

Smith, A. 1776. *An Inquiry into the Nature and Causes of the Wealth of Nations*. London: William Strahan and Thomas Cadell.

Starr, R. M. 2016. Responding to Martin Hellwig's Presidential Address: Smith, Knapp, Menger, Hicks, and Tobin Deal with the Hahn Problem. San Diego: University of California. https://econweb.ucsd.edu/~rstarr/HahnProblemJune82016withTable.pdf.

UK Parliament. 1882. "Bill of Exchange Act, 1882." https://www.legislation.gov.uk/ukpga/Vict/45-46/61.

UK Parliament. 2023. "Electronic Trade Documents Act, 2023." https://bills.parliament.uk/bills/3344.

UNCITRAL. 2017. "Model law of electronic trade records." https://uncitral.un.org/en/texts/ecommerce/modellaw/electronic_transferable_records.

United Nations. 2010. System of National Accounts 2008. https://unstats.un.org/unsd/nationalaccount.

Wikipedia. 2025a. "Reflexivity." https://en.wikipedia.org/wiki/Reflexivity_(social_theory).

Wikipedia. 2025b. "Tally stick." https://en.wikipedia.org/wiki/Tally_stick.

Wikipedia. 2025c. "Bank of Amsterdam." https://en.wikipedia.org/wiki/Bank_of_Amsterdam.

Willems, J. C. 2007. "The behavioral approach to open and interconnected systems." *IEEE Control Systems Magazine* 27(6): 46–99.

Winschel, V. and Krätzig, M. 2010. "Solving, estimating, and selecting nonlinear dynamic models without the curse of dimensionality." *Econometrica* 78(2): 803–821.

Wray, L. R. 2012. *Modern Monetary Theory: A Primer on Macroeconomics for Sovereign Monetary Systems*. Springer Nature Switzerland AG.

Youtube. 2025. "The helical model—our solar system is a vortex." https://www.youtube.com/watch?v=0jHsq36_NTU.

https://doi.org/10.1142/9781800618664_bmatter

Index

A

access, 101–105, 107, 110, 112, 114–115, 118
access economy (Rifkin), 114, 118
access for people with disabilities, 110
accountability, 191
accounting, li, 21
accounting invariance, 261
action-oriented, 185
actionable coalition, 12, 53, 59, 63
adaptability, 223–224
adaptable, 196
adaptation, 195–197, 228
adaptive, 183
adaptive decision system, 191
adaptive energy systems, 197
adaptive governance, 191
agency, 137–138
Agentic AI, xxxv
agentic commons, xlv, 24, 190, 196
agentic institutions, xxix, xliv–xlv
agility, 237
AI agents, xxxvii–xxxviii, xliv, 136, 140, 146, 187, 190, 194–196
AI automation, 194
AI autonomy, xxxviii
AI legal rights, xxxviii
AI models, 194
AI property rights, xxxviii
AI rights, xxxviii
AI technologies, 193, 196
AI–blockchain, xxxvi–xxxviii, xlvii, li, 4
AI–blockchain institutions, 191
AI-enhanced, 190
AI-governed blockchain, 193
AI-integrated wallets, xlix
Alexander Hamilton, 78
algebraic geometry, 7, 12
Algorand, xxxvii
algorithmic consensus, 187
algorithmic governance, x
algorithmic stablecoins, 80
AlphaFold, xxxiii
AlphaGo, xxxvii
AlphaProof, xxxvii
anatomy of value generation, 119
anonymity, 242
anti-money laundering (AML), 107, 113
antiseparation property, 65
arbitrage, 20
architecture, 196
Arendt, Hannah, 132
artifacts, 184

artificial intelligence (AI), 130, 147, 149, 182, 196–197, 209, 212, 215–219, 221, 225–226, 229
assemblage of knowledge resources, 183
assemblages, 186
asset management, 101, 106, 108, 111–112
assumptions, 188
auditability, 194
Austrian economics, ix, 214, 216
automata theory, viii
automation and efficiency, 115
autonomous, 111
autonomous agents, x, 190
autonomous solutions, 112
autonomous vehicles, xxxiv

B

Bagehot principle, 276
balance of payments, 91
ban crypto payments, 93
Beer, Stafford, 160–161, 163–166
behavioral approach, 140
behavioral economics, li, 215–216
behavioral recalibration, 191
Betti numbers, 14
betweenness centrality, 250
bidirectional computation, 282
bill of exchange, 261
bill of materials, lii
binary consensus, 62
bitcoin, 14, 74, 79–80, 92–93, 241
bitcoin exchange-traded funds (ETFs), xxxix–xl
Black–Scholes–Merton option pricing model, 19
blockchain algebra, 12–13
blockchain architecture, 117
blockchain query language, 13
blockchain security, xlv, 37, 39, 50
blockchain security; protocol institutions, xlviii
blockchain systems, 102–105, 111, 119
blockchain wallet, 102–103, 107, 109, 113–115, 118
blockchain, critique, xxxi
blockchain–AI commons, vi, xxxv, 191, 195–197
blockchain–AI-powered commons, 196
blockchain-based decentralized autonomous organizations (DAOs), 183, 190
blockchains, xxix–xxxii, xxxvi, xxxix, xli, xlv, 182, 186–188, 190, 193–197, 209, 212, 215–222, 225–226, 229, 240
Bretton Woods, 75
bridging company[ies], 250
Brownian motion, 18–19
BTC, 81
businesses, benefits for, 115

C

capital allocation, xliii
carbon assets, xliii
carbon footprints, 197
CatColab, 8
categorical cryptoeconomics, xlvii, li, 3, 9–10, 15, 27
categorical deep learning, 8
categorical quantum circuits, 8–9
categorical smartnetwork field theory, 3, 26
category theory, xlvii, 3, 7–9, 19, 22, 24, 27, 282
censorship resistance, 81
Central Bank Digital Currencies (CBDCs), xli, xlix, 84, 87–90, 94–95
centralization, 218–220, 222, 225
centralization process of currency issuance, 77
centralized, 197
centralized permissioned custodial stablecoins, 81
CGMY option pricing model, 17, 19
Chainlink, xl
challenges, 190

chaordic economics, l, 209, 212, 220, 221, 224–229
chaos theory, li, 209–210, 212–224, 226
Chern–Simons theory, 20
circle, 85
civic solutions, 102, 108
civil, 195
clean market, 250
climate action, 185, 190
clothing, 184
co-governance, 190
co-produced, 190
cobordism, 25
cohomology, type theory, 11
cold wallets, 106
collaboration, 144, 192, 195–196
collaborative action, xlviii
collaborative structures, 183
collaboratively, 191, 196
collateralized debt position (CDP), 81
collective governance, 190
collective intelligence, 196
commodity-backed and unbacked stablecoins, 80
commodity-backed stablecoins, 94
commons, 186, 190, 193–194
community, 190, 195
community involvement, 146
community structure, 243
community support, 187
community-driven, 194
competing currencies, 79, 84, 89, 95
competing digital currencies, 73–74, 89
competing stablecoins, 85
complementarity, 238
complex, 186, 190, 195
complex interactions, 182
complex systems, 184
complexity, 195, 214, 216, 220, 222, 224
computable economics, viii
computable economy, vii, x–xi
computable institutions, v, vii
computable number, viii
computing platform, xxxi
conflict mineral[s], 250
consensus, xxx, xxxii, xlviii, 10–11
consensus algorithms, 10
context-aware, 183
continuous (value assignment), 65
continuous availability, 117
continuous learning, 195
contributors, 194
control systems engineering, 157–158, 162–166, 169, 172–173
convertible bonds, 19
coordinating action, 190–191
coordination, 135, 192, 195–197
core competencies, 238
correlation coefficient, 245
Cosmos Hub, xlviii, 36, 46–47
creative destruction, vii
credibly neutral network, 94
credit, 21
crowdfunding, 143
crypto assets, 80
crypto Eurodollar market, 75, 77
crypto primitives, xli
crypto trading, 6
crypto-banking panic, 93
crypto-native, xxxix
cryptocurrencies, 6, 74, 84, 103, 108, 113
cryptocurrency, 94, 235, 241, 252
cryptocurrency remittance networks, li
cryptocurrency-backed stablecoins, 80
cryptoeconomic aesthetic theory, 27
cryptoeconomic mechanisms, xxix, xxxv, 5
cryptoeconomic systems, 132
cryptoeconomic theory, v–vi, xi, xlv
cryptoeconomics, xxix–xxx, 54
cryptographic escrows, 14
cryptographic keys, 101–102
cultural norms, 184, 195
currency boards, 95
currency digitization, 75, 78
currency issuance (de)centralization, 79

currency substitution, 93
custodial stablecoins, 86, 105, 110, 115
custody, 105
cybernetics, 157, 163, 165–166, 175, 184, 186, 190, 213, 216

D

DAI, 81
daily practices, 184
DAO funding, 140
DAO governance, 187
darknet markets, 242
data, 190–191
data centers, xxxvi
data framing, 105
data oracles, 194
data sharing, 146
data storage, 146
data streams, 191
data theft, 114–115
debt, li
debt flow, 268
debt relation, 261
debt repayment, 279
decentralization, 77, 81, 101–102, 107, 109, 218–220, 222, 225
decentralization paradigm, 107
decentralized, 182–183, 186, 190, 194, 196
decentralized agents, 190
decentralized AI, 111
decentralized applications (dApps), xxxiii
decentralized approach, 109
decentralized artificial superintelligence, 112
decentralized autonomous organizations (DAOs), xxxviii, 134, 143, 187, 191–195
decentralized banking, 79
decentralized business models, 116
decentralized collaborative action, 57
decentralized control, 224
decentralized finance (DeFi), xxxix–xli, xliii, 5–6, 86, 143–144
decentralized governance, 195
decentralized identifiers (DIDs), 25, 107
decentralized physical infrastructure network (DePIN), xxxix, xlii, 15
decentralized science (DeSci), xliii, xlix, 130–131, 137, 143, 183, 196
Decentralized Science + Artificial Intelligence (DeScAI), xliii, xlix, 133, 136–138, 140–141, 147
decentralized stablecoin issuance mechanism, 82, 86
decision-making processes, 190–191, 195–196
decisions, 194
deep tier supplier[s], 241, 251
DeFAI, xlii
DeFi IP, xli
democratic decision-making, 192
democratic process, 109
democratic redistribution, 187
democratize access, 196
deployments in AI (DeAI), xlii, xliv
derivatives, 6
DeSci economics, 130
detecting patterns, 191
Dexter White, Harry, 75
diagrammatic reasoning, 8
digital assets, xlix, 6, 101, 103, 106, 113
digital blockchain foundation, 191
digital currencies, xlvi, xlviii, 75, 81, 88, 90, 241
digital divide, 104, 110
digital economic infrastructure, xlvi, xlviii
digital economy, v–vii, x
digital identity, 102–103, 107, 113
digital literacy, 115
digital network economies, xxix, xlvi–xlvii
digital resources, 190
digital societies, xlv
digital trust, 5, 26

digital wallets (web2 systems), 102
digitization, 27
directed acyclic graphs (DAGs), 10–11, 14–15
DisCoCat, 8
disposition contract, 265
dissent, 185
distributed, 187, 190–191, 194
distributed ledger technologies (DLTs), 11, 14–15, 74, 90
division of labor, 262, 264
DLT-based financial systems, 90
dollar-backed, 75
dollarization, 93
domain insight, 183
double-entry bookkeeping (DEB), 21–22
Drexler, K. Eric, xxxviii
due diligence, 234
dynamic, 190, 193
dynamic stability, 163–164
dynamical systems, 9
dynamics of debt, 273

E

e-CNY, 88
e-Naira, 88
ease of use, 101–102, 104, 113, 115
economic, 102, 112, 114, 118–119
economic computation, ix
economic design principles, xxx
economic growth, 197
economic models, 186
economic philosophy, 137
economic transitions, vi
economics, 22
ecosystem, 192
ecosystem-based model[s], 251
eIDAS-compliant, 116
eIDAS2.0 regulation, 107
embedded finance applications, 92
embedded wallets, 112
emergence, 211–212, 214, 218, 220, 222–223, 227–228
emerging contribution systems, 190
endogenous collateral, 83
endorsement list, 280
energy, 183–184, 188, 191, 194
energy agents, l
energy systems, 190
energy transitions, 193
energy use, 184
entityhood, xxxviii
environmental markets; energy markets, xliii
environmental objectives, 197
escrow, 11
ETH, 81
Ethereum, 85
ethics, 195
EU digital identity wallet, 113
Euro-pegged stablecoin market, 85
Eurodollar, 76, 91–93, 95
evolutionary, 196
exogenous collateral, 83
exogenous shocks, 239
experience, xxxvii–xxxviii
experiential agents, xxxviii
expertise, 190
external knowledge, 236

F

feedback mechanisms, 190
fiat system, 275
fiat-backed stablecoins, 80
Fibonacci anyons, 22
finance, 16
financial and social inclusion, 114
financial ecosystems, 236
financial primitives, xli
financial stability, 75, 249
financial technology (FinTech), xxxi, xxxix
First Bank of the United States, 78
first liquidity provider, 276
fiscal stability, 75
flexibility, 210, 222, 224, 237
flow control system, 251
flow dynamics, li

fluid dynamics, 15
food, 184
formal verification, xlv, xlvii, 3–4, 16
Foucault, Michel, 136
fraudulent activities, 114
free banking, 78
FTX, 84
funding mechanisms, 143
future of work, xxxiv

G

Galois field theory, 17–18
game theory, viii, 136, 140, 213, 216
gatekeeping, 185
gauge theory, 20
GDP, li
general equilibrium, 260
general systems theory, 184
generalized dynamical systems, 169
geography of transitions, 195
Giddens, Anthony, 137
global financial crisis, 79
global money supply, 77
global participation, 196
global supply chains; supply chains, li
global unit of account, 88
gold-based system, 275
governance innovation, 187, 190, 194, 196–197
governments, benefits for, 115
graph filtration, 14
graph neural networks (GNNs), xxxiv
Grothendieck, 12
Grover's algorithm, 18

H

Hall, J. Storrs, xxxviii
halting problem, viii
hardware wallets, 106
hash time-locked contracts, 14
Hayek, Friedrich, 79, 132, 135
Heads Up Computing, 112
heavy-tailed distributions, 19
Hegel, G. W. F., xliv
heterogeneous capabilities, 238
heterogeneous system, 57
Heyting algebras, 10
hierarchies, 196
higher-order tiers, 235
Hilbert space, 9
homology, li, 12
homology theory, 283
homotopy type theory (HoTT) blockchains, xlv, xlvii, 3, 15–16
hub, 247
humans, 196
hyperobject, 185, 190–191

I

illicit financial flow[s], 242
illicit transactions, 235
illicit users, 252
imagination, 186
immutable, 191
impossible trinity, 83
incentive mechanism, 187, 190
incentive structures, 183
incentive system, 192
incentives, 182, 185–187, 197
incentivization, 146, 195
incentivize, 192
inclusive wallet designs, 118
inclusivity, 138
indirect business partner[s], 251
indirect links, 235
individual citizens, benefits for, 114
industrial activities, 182–183
industrial dynamics, 197
industrial transformations, 192
industrialization, 27
inefficiencies, 191
Infomap, 243
information, 183, 191
information and communication technology (ICT), vi
information economy, vi, 182
information entropy, 212, 216–217, 219, 222, 243
information flow, 222
information processing, 218–219, 222

information society, vi
information technology, xxix–xxx
information theory, li, 212, 216
information-theoretic approach, 141
infrastructure, xliii, xlvii–xlviii
innovation, 193, 195–197
innovation tracking, 195
institutional change, 185
institutional economics, 157–160, 166, 175
institutional ecosystem, 190
institutional engineering, 166, 175
institutional evolution, 197
institutional mechanisms, 190
institutional technology, 182–183, 186, 197
institutional theory, 182
institutions, 157–165, 167–168, 170–172, 174–176, 190, 195–196
insurance premium, 284
integrated AI agents, 191
intellectual diversity, 185
intellectual property management, 139, 196
intellectual property non-fungible tokens (IP-NFTs), 145
Intelligent Learning Organizations, 182–183
inter-community transition[s], 243
interactions, 188, 193
interconnected cybernetic, 187
interconnectivity, 111
interdisciplinary inquiry, 184
intermediaries, 240
international trade payments, 76
internet, 186
Internet of Things application (IoTA), 15
internet of trust, xxxii
interoperability, xxix, xxxi, xlv, xlviii, 3–4, 8, 11, 16, 102, 118
interoperability (Web3), 108
interoperability standards, 118
interoperable agents, 187
interplanetary file system (IPFS), 117
intertwined (antiseparation property), 65
intra-community transition[s], 244
introspection, 188

J

Jefferson, Thomas, 78
job creation, 197
Jones polynomial, 20
judgment, 183

K

Kant, Immanuel, 131
Karhunen–Loève expansion, 18
Keynesianism, 216
Keynes, John Maynard, 75
Khovanov homology, 20
know-your-customer (KYC), 107, 113
knowledge commons, 185–186, 195
knowledge externalities, 239
knowledge firm, 185
knowledge transfer, 194
Kuhn, Thomas, 137
Kuhn–Popper, v

L

LabDAO, xliii
landscape, 192, 194
large language models (LLMs), xxxiv
large-scale, 190
lattice gauge theory, 20
Lawvere–Tierney topologies, 16
layer 2, 90
Lean Theorem Prover, xxxvii
learned insights, 191
learning actors, 185, 191, 193, 195–197
learning commons for sustainability, 196
learning ecosystem, 191
learning experience, 191
learning organization, 182–183, 195–196
learning trajectory, 183
legal scrutiny, 251

legitimacy, 191, 194
lenders of last resort, 276
lenses, 14
liberal societies, 267
Lie algebra, 21
liquidity, 270
Liquity, 82
long-distance supply chains, 239, 251
long-term technological change, 184
loosely coupled network, 237
low-carbon transitions, 184
Lyapunov function, xlvii
Lyapunov stability, 157, 167–168, 171

M

Machine Learning Bills of Materials (ML-BOM), xlvii
macro accounting, 261
macro invariance, 272
macroeconomic, 114
magma, 19
make or buy, 36
Maker DAO, 81
Malthus, Thomas, 133
Markov chain search, 18
martingales, 20
Marx, Karl, 134, 136
massive education, 110
math agents, xxxvii
mathematics, xxxvii
matter, 183
mechanism design, 132, 192–193
medium of exchange, 89, 260
meme tokens, 146
Merkle root, 4
methodologies, 193, 195
microeconomic, 114
Minsky, M., viii
Mirowski, P., viii
MLP framework, 193
mobility, 184
model context protocol (MCP), xxxvii
ModelCollab, 8
modular, 187
monetary macro accounting theory, 260
monetary policy, lii
monetary policy; global monetary policy, xlix
monetary policy; macroeconomics, li
monetary vortex, 278
money circulation, 273
money laundering, li, 246
money, nature of, 260
Move 37, xxxvii
multi-agent AI, 187
multi-level perspective (MLP), 182, 184, 188, 192, 194
multi-stakeholder, 190
multi-system interactions, 193
multi-tier supply network[s], 251
multinational hierarchies, 186

N

Nakamoto, Satoshi, 241
Nash equilibrium, xxxviii, 22–23, 136
negative interest policy, 90
negative lock-in, 237
negative news, 247
neoclassical, 185
neoclassical economics, ix
network as computer, xxxi
network economic models, 116
network persistence, xxxviii, xlv
network resource theory, 236
network science, li
network theory, 213–214, 216
networks, 186, 193
neural networks, actor-critic, 18
niche innovations, 184, 192
niche-level innovations, 192, 194
NIST, xxxvii
non-custodial, 81, 105, 115, 118
non-custodial stablecoin issuance protocol, 87

non-fungible tokens (NFTs), 103, 113
nonlinearity, 223–224
normal-science, 185
North, Douglass, 158–160, 173
numéraire, 266

O

obligation contract, 265
offline capability, 101, 108
offline functionality, 117
on-chain, 92
open, 196
open games, xlvi, 22–23, 281
open science, 141
optics, 14
optimistic rollups, 6
option pricing, 19
options, Bermudan exercise, 19
options, Canary exercise, 19
order, 209–210, 212–224, 226
organizational learning mechanism, 191
organizations, 159–164, 166–176, 193
Ornstein–Uhlenbeck process, 19
Ostrom, Elinor, 132, 137, 158–161, 173
over-collateralized, 90

P

paper money circulation, 279
paper money system, 275
paper wallets, 106
paradigms, 185
paradoxes, 185
Pareto-preferred futures, xxxviii–xlv
participatory, 190
participatory citizenship, 108
path creation, 189
path creator, 188
path dependency, 185
path distance[s], 246
path-dependent systems, 184
peer review, 145, 147
peer-to-peer, 241
performance, 196
permissionless non-custodial stablecoin, 81
permissionless system, 57
personal AI (wallet-borne), 117
philosophy of blockchain, xlix
photonic chip, 18
physical impairment, 110
planetary boundaries, 186
platform, xxxiv, xxxvii, xlvi
poisson distribution, 249
policy, vi, 197
polycentric governance, 182, 187, 194
Popper, Karl, 131
practices, 184, 197
principle of abstraction, 263
principle of separation, 262
Prisoner's Dilemma, 136
private cryptocurrencies, xlix
private currencies, 79
private permissioned blockchain, 90
proactive solutions, 112
proactive wallets, 111
process coordinator, 111
product and permutation algebras (PROPs), 14
product flows, 240
production–consumption chains, 187
progress, xliv, 191
proof-of-personhood, xxxii
proof-of-stake, xxxii
proof-of-work energy demand, xxxii, 187
PROP algebras, 15
property rights, vii
protein language models, xxxiv
  protocol institutions, xxix, xliv–xlvii, l
protocol manifolds, 12
  protocols, xxxvii, 157, 160–162, 164–176, 195–196
  protocol institutions, xxxi, xlix
provenance, xxix
public and private currencies, 78
public currencies, 77
public good, 137, 144
purpose-driven tokens, 183

Q

quadratic funding, 135, 143
quadruple accounting, 261
quantum accounting, 21
quantum approximate optimization algorithm (QAOA), 18
quantum blockchain, 25
quantum computing, xxxvi, 26
quantum cost accounting, 22
quantum field theory (QFT), 20, 25–26
quantum finance, 16
quantum information theory, 22
quantum key distribution (QKD), 18
quantum machine learning, 17
quantum neural networks, 18
quantum random number generator (QRNG), 18
quantum rewinding, 18
quantum states, 9
quantum technologies, xlvii
quantum-safe cryptography, 16, 18

R

random walker, 243
real-time analytics, 183
real-world assets (RWAs), xxix, xxxix–xl, xlvi, xlviii, 80
realigning research, 184
rebound effects, 185, 187
recommendation system, 246
recovery mechanisms, 115
recursive, 196
recursive learning model, 192
redundancy, 237
refugee camps, 109
regeneration, 187
regime, 194
regime shifts, 192
regime-level transitions, 192
regulation, 149
relational dynamics, 184, 192
relative price, 266
relativistic ZKPs, 17
remittance network, 242
renewable energy, 197
reorganization, 186
reproducibility crisis, 130, 145
reputation systems, 134, 140
requisite variety, 163
research activities, 187, 193, 196–197
research commons, 190
research opportunities, 196
research university, 185
reserve currency, 75–76
resilience, 220, 222–234
resilient, 190, 197
resource allocation, 196
resource-based view, 236
resources, 196
responsible actors, 252
responsive, 193
retroactive public goods funding, 135
rhizomatic approach, 189
rhizomatic literature review, 196
risk, li, 19–20
risk absorption, 267
risk factors, 248
robots, xxxiv, xxxviii
RWA-backed stablecoin, 87

S

Sahlis, Marshall, 135
savings and investment imbalances, 90
savings glut, 92
scale, 190
scale-free property, 247
scarcity, 133–134
schumpeter, vii, x
science communication, 187
science-based technologies, 186
scientific self-examination, 188
secure, 197
secure data sharing, 196
security, 101–106, 110–111, 113–114, 118–119
security risks, 105
self-governed, 118

self-organization, 211–212, 216, 223, 228
self-sovereign, 118
self-sovereign identity (SSI), 101, 104, 107–108, 113
self-sovereign individual, 113
semitopological space, 64
semitopology, 12, 64
sensors, 194
set theory, 19
sets, 7
SettleMint, xxxvii
shared computational infrastructure, 190
shared security, 36–40, 43, 45–50
sheaf theory, li, 12, 24, 283
shelter, 184
shortest path, 246
Silver, David, xxxvii
Simon, Herbert, viii
similar entry: blockchain-AI, xxxiii
smart contract risks, 90
smart contracts, x, xxx, 81, 140, 192, 194–195
smart network and categorical smart network field theory, 25
smart networks, xxix, 18
smart-contract-powered protocols, 80
smartnetwork, xlvii
smartnetwork field theory, 25
smartnetwork technologies, 3–4
Smith, Adam, 27, 133
Smith, Vernon, viii
social, 195
social coins, 109
social coordination, 191
social practices, 186
social value, 192
social-practice, 184
societal energy, 197
societal infrastructure, 116
societies, 184
socio-technical configurations, 188
socioeconomic participation, 109
socioeconomic priorities, 197
sociotechnical, 194
sociotechnical systems, 186
sociotechnical transitions, 182
SOFR (formerly LIBOR), xli
software artifacts, xxxvi, xlvii, lii
software wallets, 106
solawechsel, 270
space, semitopological, 64
stabilized regimes, 184
stable currency competition, 79
stablecoins, xl, 74, 80, 84, 88–95
stakeholder integration, 224
stakeholders, 191–192, 196
staking and slashing, xxxii
standards, xlvii
static knowledge, 185
store of value, 89
strategic learning, 196
structural imbalances, 76
supermartingales, xlvii
supply chain, 263
supply chain disruptions, 234
supply chain transparency, 251
supply route, 248
supply uncertainty, 234
supply-chain levels for software artifacts (SLSA), xlvii
surveillance risk, 115, 118
sustainability, vi, l, 188, 195–197, 224
sustainability transitions, 185, 192, 194, 196
sustainable development goals (SDGs), vi
sustainable energy, 190, 193–194, 196–197
sustainable energy futures, 188, 196
sustainable energy innovation, 190
sustainable energy research, 190, 193, 196
sustainable energy systems, l, 193, 197
sustainable energy transition, 184, 188
sustainable-energy research, 183
Sutton, Richard S., xxxvii

SWIFT, 76
symbiotic relationship, 238
symmetric monoidal categories (SMCs), 23
system design, xlviii
systems, 193, 196

T

tainted supply sources, 250
Tambara module, 14
tamper-proof, 183
taxonomy of the stablecoin design mechanisms, 80
technological change, 197
technologies, 197
technology translation, xliii
tensor categories, 25
Terra USD, 83
Tether, 80
theories, 193
theory development, 209
token, 192
token incentives, 134
token lifecycles, 187
token-based incentives, 134, 141
tokenization, xl, xliii, 187
tokenized, 5
tokenized research outputs, 145
tokenized rewards, l
tokenomics, xxx
tokens, 187, 193
topological consensus, 10, 12
topological economics, 24
topological invariants, 20
topological neural networks, xxxiv
topological quantum field theory (TQFT), 20, 22
topology, 7, 12, 23–24, 53
Total Value Locked (TVL), xl
traceability, 240
traditional finance (TradFi), xxxix
transaction cost economics, 214, 216
transaction costs approach, 141, 196
transactional optimization, 109
transactions, 194
transdisciplinary, 185
transformative learning, 185
transitions, 182, 185, 188, 191–192, 193, 195, 197
transitively intertwined (antiseparation property), 65
transparency, 191, 195, 240
transparent, 193–194, 196–197
Triffin, 76
Tron, 85
trust, 108, 110, 112, 115, 117, 191, 194
trust wallet, 105
trust-minimized, 196
Turing complete economy, viii–xi
Turing machine, viii

U

U.S. fiscal debt, 91
un-monetization, 116
uncertainty, 190, 212, 214, 216–217, 219, 222
unethical community[ies], 246
unethical company[ies], 247, 249
unethical transactions, 251
unethical users, 245
unit of account, 85
universal, 118
universal access device, 101, 111
universal state machine, viii
universal wallet, 104, 111
universities, 185
university research systems, 182
unpermissioned system, 57
unpredictability, 190, 210, 212, 218–220
unspent transaction output (UTxO), 13
usability, xlviii, 4, 104, 118
USD-pegged stablecoins, 85
USDC, 82
USDT, 80
user experience, 118
user-centric, 109

V

value assignment, 65
value creation, 101, 103, 114
value functions, 167–168
value plurality, 187
value projection, 114
value-creation, 118
value-transfer technologies, xlvii
values, 183
verifiable computing, xxix, xxxvi, 26
verifiable credentials (VCs), 104, 107–108
virtual asset histories, 13
von Neumann, J., viii
vulnerable groups, 115

W

walled gardens, xxxii
wallet, xlvi, 101, 105–107, 109–114, 116
wallet interface, 104
wallet swarms, 112
wallets (role in Web3), 118
wearable devices, 112
Web2, xxxi, xlix
Web3, xxxi, xlix, 101–102, 105–108, 111, 113, 118
Whitehead, Alfred North, 138
wider landscape, 184
wildcat banking, 78

Y

yield curve, 20–21
Yoneda lemma, 7

Z

zero-knowledge (ZK) rollups, 6
zero-knowledge proofs (ZKPs), xxx, xxxii–xxxiii, xliii, 6, 18
ZX-calculus, 9

www.ingramcontent.com/pod-product-compliance
Lightning Source LLC
LaVergne TN
LVHW070828220926
848486LV00028B/133